LOGIC

An Introduction

LOGIC

An Introduction

LIONEL RUBY

Professor of Philosophy

Roosevelt College

●

J. B. LIPPINCOTT COMPANY

Chicago · Philadelphia · New York

TO MY MOTHER

PREFACE

In that delightful 18th century comedy, *The Bourgeois Gentleman,* Moliere describes Monsieur Jourdain's quest for an education. Jourdain, an unlettered nouveau riche, has employed several tutors to impart culture to him. In the first lesson, the instructor in philosophy endeavors to teach him the difference between prose and verse. Prose, the instructor informs him, is what one normally speaks. Astonished and delighted, our simple friend hurries off to tell his wife that he has had the distinction of speaking prose all his life without being aware of his own powers. In a similar fashion, the average person would probably also be amazed, if not delighted, to learn that he has been reasoning in syllogisms all his life, without being aware of his logical powers.

There are several types of mental activity that are classified under the general head of "thinking," such as daydreaming or reverie, remembering, reaching decisions, and so on, but the science called "logic" is concerned with the type of thinking known as "inference." Inference is a mental activity in which we say, "This is so because that is so," or "This is so; therefore, that is so." Inference, in other words, is present whenever we assert that a given statement is true because another is. Whenever we furnish evidence for our beliefs, whenever we answer the challenging question "Why?" with a "Because" and state our reasons or evidence for believing as we do, we engage in the "logical type" of thinking. We have been logicians all our lives without knowing it.

But though all of us, like M. Jourdain, speak in prose, we may do so well or badly. Similarly, though all of us draw inferences, our evidence may or may not be sufficient to justify our conclusions. It is perhaps unnecessary to call the reader's attention to the fact that he is well acquainted with persons who reason unsoundly. The distinction between sound and unsound inference is a familiar one. And it is this distinction which is the central theme of logic defined as the science of valid inference. Logic is the study of the principles that determine whether inferences are justified or unjustified. This does not mean that the logician is in possession of a secret lore, or that he has a vested interest in certain special principles called "logical," but only that he seeks to clarify what all of us are doing whenever we engage in reasoning.

Some popular criticisms, confusions, and misunderstandings of logic and the use of logical principles call for comment. We find an attitude of hostility toward logic in the following statement by the Chinese writer, Lin Yutang:

Humanized thinking is just reasonable thinking. The logical man is always self-righteous and therefore inhuman and therefore wrong, while the reasonable man suspects that perhaps he is wrong and is therefore always right. (*The Importance of Living,* The John Day Co., 1937.)

Mr. Lin objects to self-righteous individuals who regard themselves as infallible. This is truly an undesirable characteristic and logicians will join with Mr. Lin in deploring this attitude. Few persons, perhaps, are so vividly aware as logicians of the difficulties in attempting to demonstrate that any factual proposition is true. And it is to be hoped that the logical individual will, above other men, never forget that perhaps *he* is wrong and the *other man* right. The reader may also be assured at this point that logicians are only human.

A misunderstanding which we shall call the "fear of logic" is based upon the assumption that logic tends to falsify experience in some mysterious manner. This "logophobia" is expressed in the following remarks from a speech delivered in the House of Commons by Austen Chamberlain, British Foreign Minister in the years following World War I:

I profoundly distrust logic when applied to politics, and all English history justifies me. [Ministerial cheers] . . . Instinct and experience alike teach us that human nature is not logical, that it is un-

wise to treat political institutions as instruments of logic, and that
it is in wisely refraining from pressing conclusions to their logical
end that the path of peaceful development and reform is really
found.*

When Mr. Chamberlain speaks of logic he evidently has in
mind a type of thinking which stupidly applies rigid principles
to situations in which such principles are inapplicable. But such
thinking, far from being "logical," is simply illogical. The logician who seeks to understand the world in which he lives will
not refuse to recognize the "stubborn, irreducible facts" of political realities. Politics is not the same thing as mathematics,
and anyone who treats human beings as if they were nothing
but abstract symbols is following no logical law in doing so.
But it is just as unreasonable to condemn "logic" for such bad
thinking as it would be to condemn the science of arithmetic
because bookkeepers make errors in addition. The question
which the logician asks is: "Have we the evidence which is adequate to prove our conclusions?" It is the logician's task to point
out the principles of proof which are employed in answering
that question.

Comment is also required on Mr. Chamberlain's remark
that "human nature is not logical." If this is so, then perhaps
logic is irrelevant in human affairs. Aristotle, on the other hand,
tells us that man is "the rational animal." Aristotle did not of
course mean that human beings always reason correctly. The
fact that he sharply criticized the writings of his philosophical
predecessors is sufficient proof of this. He meant only that human beings possess the capacity for logical thinking, recognizing at the same time the wide gap between capacity and performance. Though we agree with Aristotle, Mr. Chamberlain's
remark will be acceptable if it is interpreted to mean that we
are emotional as well as reasoning creatures. Human nature is
both logical and non-logical, in different respects. The non-
logical factors call for further discussion.

Strong feelings and emotions, as is well known, make it difficult to think clearly. Prejudice and bias are responsible for
distortions in our perceptions of facts. Wishes beget beliefs, for

* Quoted in L. S. Stebbing, *Thinking to Some Purpose*, Penguin Books, p. 8.

"the wish is father to the thought," often regardless of the evidence. And it is indeed hard to be consistent in applying the same standards to others as to ourselves, as is illustrated by the amusing "inflections" of the adverb "firm," in "I am firm; you are stubborn; he is a pigheaded fool." An English newspaper that asked its readers for other examples of this sort of thing received the following among many others:

"I am righteously indignant; you are annoyed; he is making a fuss about nothing."

"I am sparkling; you are unusually talkative; he is drunk."

"I am beautiful; you have quite good-looking features; she isn't bad-looking, if you like that type."

Modern psychology emphasizes the role of emotion in human behavior. Studies in the psychology of crowds and in mass behavior reveal the ineffectiveness of the appeal to reason in many situations. The studies in "psychodynamics," which use the methods of psychoanalysis in explaining individual and cultural phenomena, reveal the influence of the so-called "unconscious" factors in human behavior. From these and like studies there emerges a picture of the human mind as a kind of dark Dostoevskeian cavern in whose labyrinthine gloom strange and irrational visions brood. We shall acknowledge our debt to the psychologists and social scientists who have revealed the hitherto unsuspected irrationalities in man's nature. Nevertheless, Aristotle was right in saying that man is *capable* of rationality, and insofar as we seek rational consistency in our thoughts, or verifiable knowledge (in the science of psychodynamics as well as in other fields) logic is relevant.

It is perhaps unnecessary to add that logic is not the whole of life. Not only are we sometimes illogical, but large areas of experience are also *non*-logical or *non*-rational. An experience of joy or sorrow is neither logical nor illogical; it is simply an experience. There are areas in which logical analysis may be inappropriate, as in writing lyrical love verses. And certainly logic does not supply the dynamic energies necessary for action. But to the extent that we are interested in acquiring verifiable knowledge, we must concern ourselves with the criteria of proof and the adequacy of evidence, and it is here that logical principles are appropriate.

A word now as to the general plan and contents of this book. There are three parts, each of which discusses an indispensable aspect of the enterprise of rational thinking. The careful thinker will be interested in language, the instrument of thinking; in the soundness of his arguments; and in the truth of his assertions. Part One is concerned with linguistic and semantical problems; in Part Two we shall discuss the principles of valid inference or sound reasoning; and in Part Three we shall examine the methods employed by the sciences of nature and society, seeking to determine the methods whereby these disciplines attempt to furnish us with logically justifiable beliefs. In the classroom approximately 20 per cent of the time might be devoted to Part One, about 50 per cent to Part Two, and 30 per cent to the last part.

In the narrow sense of the term "logic" (defined as the study of valid inference), only Part Two is concerned with logic. But logic is interpreted more broadly throughout, as the study of valid inference *and* its applications in the search for truth. To this end we shall study the nature of language as a preliminary to the study of validity, since we must understand exactly what is being said before we can analyze reasoning, and in Part Three we shall study the problem of applying the rules of inference to the subject matter of the sciences. This third part, which discusses scientific methods is concerned with the field usually called "inductive logic."

Our discussion of valid inference, or deductive logic, is largely based upon the so-called "classical tradition" in logic that began with Aristotle. Though this logic was developed in the Middle Ages, it remained largely unmodified until the 19th century. The prestige of the classical logic was once so great that it was believed that it represented the science of logic in its final form. Modern logic has shown that the older logic was incomplete in that it does not cover all of the logical forms that can be investigated by a more generalized "symbolic" logic. The newer logic has also shown that the whole of logic may be systematized as a rigorous formal science in "mathematical" form. The logical tradition remains unbroken, however, since the older logic has been incorporated into the new. We shall note some of the newer developments insofar as they extend, and require clarification of, the classical doctrine. Our emphasis, however, will be on logic as a part of general education, and on the use of logical principles in the clarification and analysis of everyday discourse.

The author wishes to thank many friends, including colleagues and former students, for their helpful comments and criticisms. In particular he is greatly indebted to Professors A. C. Benjamin of the University of Missouri, Millard S. Everett and Wayne A. R. Leys of Roosevelt College, Douglas N. Morgan of Northwestern University, and Warner A. Wick of the University of Chicago for their very valuable suggestions and criticisms. Special thanks are due also to Mrs. Louise Landes for stylistic criticisms, to Mrs. Elizabeth Bianchi for several useful suggestions, and to Miss Virginia Briska for typing the stencils in the experimental edition. The author's indebtedness to other writers is too great to be detailed, but mention should at least be made of the works by Cohen and Nagel, Frye and Levi, and Castell.

Specific acknowledgment is made in the text to the works from which quotations are drawn. The following authors and publishers gave their kind permission to quote excerpts from their publications: Appleton-Century-Crofts, Inc.; *The Chicago Daily News; The Chicago Sun-Times; The Chicago Tribune;* The Clarendon Press; Coward-McCann, Inc.; Felix Frankfurter; Ginn and Company; Harcourt, Brace and Company, Inc.; Harper and Brothers; Harper's Magazine; Henry Holt and Company, Inc.; Houghton Mifflin Company; Alfred Korzybski and the Non-Aristotelian Library Publishing Co.; Little, Brown and Company; Liveright Publishing Corporation; The Macmillan Company; *New Republic;* Prentice-Hall, Inc.; G. P. Putnam's Sons, American Association for the Advancement of Science, Charles Scribner's Sons; Simon and Schuster, Inc.; Time, Inc.; Whittlesey House; and the Yale University Press.

LIONEL RUBY

CONTENTS

xiii

PART 2   DEDUCTIVE LOGIC

PART 3 THE LOGIC OF TRUTH: SCIENTIFIC METHODOLOGY

Part One

LANGUAGE AND LOGIC

Chapter 1

DISPUTES: VERBAL
AND OTHERWISE

Section I: A Few Examples

1. Scene: A college dormitory at 1:00 A.M. A "bull session" is in full swing.

BILL: But I say that men are not equal. Those who say they are equal are talking through their hats. Just look around you and observe the human race for proof of my statement. Observe the unequal distribution of talents and qualities. Men differ in their mental, moral, and spiritual qualities; they differ in their sizes and shapes and in their strength and skills. Consider the differences in intelligence revealed by intelligence tests. I must conclude that Thomas Jefferson was guilty of preposterous nonsense when he said that all men were created equal. This "truth," far from being self-evident, as Jefferson supposed, is a demonstrable falsehood.

JIM: You don't know what you're talking about, Bill. Men are equal; that is the foundation of our democracy. I don't like to say this, but your point of view reminds me of the fascists, who prated about the "glorious inequality of mankind." All human beings are equal; they are all possessed of a universal manhood by virtue of which every man is entitled to equal opportunities, and no man should suffer discrimination because of his race, color, religion, wealth, or family. Our legal system tells us that all men are equal before the law. Do you deny that? Are you in favor of racial and religious discrimination?

BILL: No, I'm not a fascist and I do not believe in racial and religious discrimination. But I repeat that men are not equal.

Why, most of them don't even have the intelligence to vote properly. Your equality is a myth. It has been said that if all wealth were divided equally, it would soon be back in the hands of the same people again . . .

2. Another night.

TOM: Russia is certainly not a democracy, no matter how long and often they may protest that they are. In Russia there are no opposition parties, and no man dares to oppose the edicts of the ruling class. There are no guarantees against arbitrary arrest, and anyone may be held without trial if he criticizes the government. I believe that it is impossible to have democracy unless you have capitalism and free enterprise, for when the state controls a man's job it has the power of life and death over him, and his freedom has disappeared. His actions and his thoughts must then be subservient to the state.

JACK: And I say that Russia is a democracy. In Russia every man is guaranteed a job and is free from the worst of all fears, namely, economic insecurity. There is no such thing as involuntary unemployment in Russia. And Russia recognizes the principle of equality for all races and religions and for the sexes. Women have equal rights with men in economic, political, and spiritual activities. Russia is a democratic country.

TOM: Russia is not democratic since there is no freedom, not even "economic freedom." There are no free labor unions, since labor unions are not free to strike. If they do, the leaders are immediately liquidated, since striking is considered an act of treason against the state. You can't have democracy when union leaders are stooges of the party and its bosses . . .

The disputes you have just read are examples of a type of discussion which is all too common. Disputes of this type are futile and frustrating. The argument gets nowhere, no one ever convinces anyone else, and the dispute proceeds endlessly if continued in the vein described, until the disputants give up because of mutual exhaustion. They will then part company, each experiencing a sense of profound pity or contempt for the other, and each thinking that "there are none so blind as those who will not see."

Disputes of this type are usually called "verbal disputes," or "verbal disagreements." Such "disputes," as we shall see, may not be actual disagreements, the disagreement being such only in appearance. Before we attempt to analyze them, however, we shall examine an example of a non-verbal dispute, which we shall call a "real" disagreement.

3. A real disagreement.

BEN: If we wish to eliminate strikes and lockouts in the United States, then we ought to require the compulsory arbitration of all labor disputes. The Australians have required such compulsory arbitration for a great many years, and they have reduced strikes to a minimum.

SIDNEY: On the contrary. *The 1939 Year-Book of Labour Statistics,* published by the International Labour Office, shows that for the decade 1929–1939 Australia was the third highest nation in the average number of days lost each year because of strikes and lockouts. In Australia they lost 61 days per 100 employees; in the United States only 36 days were lost.

In Dispute 3 the parties are in actual disagreement. They are in disagreement over whether the compulsory arbitration of labor disputes has or has not been successful in eliminating strikes in Australia, and they are in disagreement over whether or not compulsory arbitration would eliminate strikes in the United States. It is not our concern here to determine whether one of these parties is right, the other wrong. The point is that they are engaged in a genuine dispute.

Let us now return to our examples of verbal disputes. In Dispute 1 Bill and Jim *appear* to be in disagreement over the proposition that all men are equal. Bill says that men are not equal; Jim says that they are. But we soon find that Bill and Jim have used the word "equal" in different senses. By "equal" Bill means similarity in physical and mental attributes; by "equal" Jim means that all men are entitled to justice. Though each has used the same word, each means something quite different from what the other means.

Bill and Jim believe that they are in disagreement over certain facts, but actually they may not be. Each may be right in what he affirms, and wrong only in claiming that he necessarily disagrees with the other. For Bill and Jim defined the word "equal" in different ways, and if we now translate what Bill and Jim *said* into what they *mean,* we shall find that their "dispute" may be summarized in the following manner:

BILL: Human beings are not possessed of the same physical and mental qualities.

JIM: You are wrong, Bill. All men are entitled to justice.

BILL: And I insist that men do not have the same physical and mental qualities.

In other words, the parties are not necessarily in disagreement on any issue whatsoever. They think that they are in such disagreement only because they overlook the fact that the innocent word "equal" has been used in more than one sense. When this is pointed out to the disputants they will probably abandon their original dispute at once. They may then go on to discuss some other related question, but they will abandon a discussion which can have no satisfactory conclusion.

We see, then, that some disagreements are such in appearance only. Dispute 3 was a real or actual disagreement concerning certain facts, but Dispute 1 was a dispute only in appearance. Our discussion indicates that we must distinguish between real and apparent disputes. In a real dispute the parties actually disagree; in an apparent dispute they think they are in disagreement but actually are not, or may not be. A *verbal dispute* is an *apparent* dispute in this sense, for in such disputes the possible actual agreement of the parties is concealed by the fact that *they use a key word in more than one sense.* In such disputes the parties believe that they are in disagreement over the truth of a proposition, but they may be in entire agreement over the facts and differ only in the manner in which they use the key term. When a key term is used in more than one sense the parties may be in agreement, or they may be in disagreement, but the difference in the usage of the key term prevents them from knowing that they are in agreement, or, if in disagreement, from knowing the precise issue over which they differ.

In Dispute 2, the term "democracy" is obviously used in two different senses. Tom is actually saying that there is no freedom in Russia. Jack asserts that there is no economic insecurity in Russia. This is what they really mean in asserting that Russia is or is not a democracy. There is thus no actual disagreement in the propositions asserted by Tom and Jack. But of course to point out these things to disputants will not automatically settle all their differences. When a verbal dispute has been eliminated, the parties become aware of the fact that they had been using the key word in different senses, and there may be nothing further to discuss. But the parties may also not regard this difference in senses as legitimate, and they may go on to discuss how a word should or should not be used. Our point is only that there may be no actual disagreement in their positions as originally stated.

The same type of analysis is often appropriate when *agreements,* rather than disagreements, are verbal rather than actual. An agreement may also be such in appearance only, because of the different senses in which words are used. Such agreements are *verbal agreements.* For example, the United States, Great Britain, and the U. S. S. R. agreed at Yalta and at Potsdam that democratic governments would be established through free elections in Poland and elsewhere. The words "democracy" and "free" were not precisely defined, and it soon became apparent that the parties had entirely different notions as to what the words meant.

Another example: Brown and Grey agree with each other that God exists. But when Brown uses the word "God" he means the personal God of the Jewish-Christian tradition, while Grey accepts John Dewey's definition of God as "the natural forces and conditions—including man and human association— that promote the growth of the ideal and that further its realization." Dewey's God is not a supernatural God, but rather a name for certain natural conditions. The Jewish-Christian conception of God is quite different. Brown and Grey have thus confused an agreement in words with an agreement concerning facts. They were in actual disagreement and in apparent agreement. Their agreement was only in the use of the same word. They were actually talking about different things, almost as it would be were one person to say, "I believe that X is the best candidate," and for the other to answer, "Yes, I agree that Z is the best candidate." Brown might have been horrified if he knew just what it was to which Grey was agreeing. It is, in general, easier to become religious by definition than by conversion.

We may define a verbal agreement as an agreement which is such in appearance only, in which the possible actual disagreement of the parties is veiled by the fact that a key term is used in different senses.

We shall now state a basic principle of all intelligent discourse: In order to agree or disagree with another person both parties must be in agreement with respect to all of the key terms used in their discussion. Paradoxically, it is impossible to disagree with another person without agreeing with him (on the meanings of the terms). Otherwise our discussions move at cross-purposes and there is no meeting of minds.

The basis of all verbal agreements and disagreements lies in the ambiguity of words. An ambiguous word is one which may have more than one meaning, so that it is capable of being understood in more than one sense. These variant meanings give us the equivalents of several different words which happen to be spelled in the same manner. A "spade," meaning a garden implement, has only a remote connection with a "spade," meaning a suit in a deck of cards. These are the equivalents of two different words spelled in the same manner. Now, if we imagine a conversation during a bridge game, during which one of the players (a suburbanite who likes to garden) remarks that he has "three spades" (meaning garden implements) and his partner contradicts him with "You can't have any; the spades have all been played," we would have the basis for a verbal dispute similar to those we have already examined. The two disputants would be talking about altogether different things. (It is perhaps unnecessary to call the reader's attention to the unwritten law among bridge players which makes it a heinous crime to make such remarks during a bridge game.)

One possible misunderstanding must be considered at this point. Note that a verbal dispute is not a "dispute over words." The following example will make this point clear:

PAUL: When most persons mention the word "religion" they refer to membership in some church and to the belief in a personal God.

JOE: I disagree. I believe that most persons use the word "religion" to signify that some person or persons have a whole-hearted devotion to certain social ideals and objectives.

This is a dispute as to the manner in which a word is used. It is a non-verbal, actual, or real dispute, since the parties are in real, and not in merely apparent, disagreement. They differ with respect to language custom or word-usage.

Similarly, though a dispute be over "values" (i.e., over whether something is good or bad), or whether it be over the "correct" meaning of a word (as in "Which sense of religion is the correct sense?"), we shall not call a dispute a verbal one unless key terms are used in such a manner as to conceal a possible real agreement. A verbal dispute is one in which the parties believe that their statements cannot both be correct, whereas actually they may be. Each may be correct in accordance with the sense in which he employs the key term. But in a real dispute the parties cannot both be correct. *Only one* of them can be right, though of course both may be wrong.

Section II: The Analysis of Disputes

In our study of logic we shall learn the principles of correct reasoning, but we shall also learn how to apply these principles to examples. Theory without practice is almost useless in a subject such as this. Practice will make the reader adept at the analysis of disputes in order to determine whether they are purely verbal and so enable him to avoid falling into the traps to which such disputes expose the unwary. And, if it is not too risky an undertaking, the reader may also be able to help others avoid the futile types of disputes.

Every dispute should be examined in terms of the 5-step analysis which we shall now state. The first three steps should be applied to *all* disputes in order to determine whether they are verbal or non-verbal. If the third step is answered in the affirmative, then the dispute is a verbal one, and the remaining steps should then be worked out to reveal the absence of disagreement.

1. What is the point in disagreement, or the issue in dispute?
2. State the sentences expressing the essential positions asserted by the disputants.
3. Do the parties use a key term in different senses so that there is no "meeting of minds?" If so, state the ambiguous term.
4. State the different senses in which each disputant employs the ambiguous term.
5. Restate the essential sentences as asserted by the disputants in Step 2 above, except that you must now replace the ambiguous term in each of these sentences by the variant definitions of this term as found in Step 4. The ambiguous term must not appear in these restated sentences.

We shall illustrate this method of analysis by applying it to Dispute 2, page 4.

The results of the analysis will be as follows:

1. Is Russia a democracy?
2. Tom: Russia is not a democracy.
   Jack: Russia is a democracy.
3. "Democracy" is used in different senses by the disputants.
4. Tom: Democracy means a government which guarantees freedom to all individuals.
   Jack: Democracy means a system in which all men have economic security.
5. Tom: Russia is not a country in which the government guarantees freedom to all men.
   Jack: Russia is a country in which all men have economic security.

The analysis indicates that the parties are not necessarily in genuine disagreement, so far as they have stated their positions. The dispute should therefore be abandoned in its original form. When the parties find that their original "dispute" has vanished, one of several things may happen. They may then find that they are in essential agreement with each other, each granting that democracy may be properly defined in the two senses.

They may say, "We see that the word 'democracy' may be used in different senses, in one of which our question would be answered affirmatively, in the other negatively. Our original question should therefore be answered 'yes' or 'no,' depending upon what one means by 'democracy.'" But the disappearance of the original dispute may also initiate new disputes. Tom may accuse Jack of "misusing" the term democracy, and they may then discuss the question as to whether democracy may properly be defined as Jack defined it. Or Jack may accuse Tom of the same error. In any case, if the parties cannot agree on what they mean by "democracy," it is futile to discuss the question as to whether or not Russia is a "something-we-know-not-what."

Disputes may also arise over statements of fact made by the parties. Is it true that men and women enjoy freedom in the democracies? Is it true that Russia guarantees economic security to all? It is obvious that the possibilities of new verbal disputes also lurk in these questions. What do "freedom" and "economic security" mean? Our analysis of verbal disputes does not dispose of all problems, but it does eliminate a dispute in which the parties themselves do not know what, if anything, is at issue between them.

A warning is necessary at this point. We have emphasized the importance of "defining one's terms." But let us not use this method of analysis for the purpose of quibbling. Let us not be hypercritical where such criticism is unimportant, i.e., where it is reasonable to suppose that the parties use their words in substantially the same ways. When words are sufficiently understood for the purposes of a given discussion, then it is a waste of time to argue over definitions. But an awareness of the linguistic problems of argumentative discourse is always necessary, and most of us err in being too uncritical.

Exercises

A. In the following group, distinguish the real disagreements from those which are merely apparent:

    1. BLACK: The earth has been in existence for only 100 million years.

BLUE: And I contend that the earth is at least 5 billion years old.

2. ROY: When I say it's propaganda, I mean it's a pack of lies, for that is what propaganda means.

RAY: You are mistaken. Propaganda really means any act of influencing or persuading another person to some predetermined end.

3. HARRY: George Washington was the first president.

HENRY (who is slightly deaf): You are mistaken. John Adams was the second president.

4. SAM: Picasso is a great artist because of his profound sense of form, space, and light.

SEYMOUR: In my opinion, his sense of form, space, and light is superficial, rather than profound; so he is not a great artist.

5. SAM: I like Picasso's paintings.

SEYMOUR: You are wrong there. I don't like Picasso's paintings.

6. ED: Monogamy is the ideal form of marriage relationship.

ERNEST: I believe that polygyny is the ideal form.

7. MILDRED: The American people approve of monogamy.

MYRTLE: The Moslems approve of polygyny.

8. GEORGE: The correct spelling is l-a-b-o-r.

GODFREY: And I say that the correct spelling is l-a-b-o-u-r. (Would it make any difference if Godfrey were an Englishman?)

B. In the following exercises, analyze each dispute in terms of the 5-step analysis. Also note whether you think that the parties would abandon their disputes after the analysis is completed or whether they would be likely to disagree over some other question.

1. JOE: A tree which falls in an uninhabited forest does not make a sound when it crashes to the earth. There is no one there to hear any sound, and when no one can hear a sound, the sound does not exist.

AL: There certainly is a sound when the tree crashes in an uninhabited forest. The crash of the tree sets up longitudinal wave motions in a transmitting medium, the air. These longitudinal waves are present in the atmosphere whether or not anyone is present, and so there is sound present.

JOE: But no one's auditory nerve is affected. No sensation is produced through the organs of hearing, and no one can have the mental experience of hearing if no one is in the forest. So you are mistaken in saying that there can be sound in an uninhabited forest.

2. JOHN: I believe that the Western Powers were wholly justified in shooting the Nazi leaders at the close of World War II. But I believe that it was wrong to try them for the violation of international law, for the simple reason that they could not have been guilty of violating something which did not exist. It was wrong to condemn them for violating international law for there is no such thing. Law exists only when a governing body enjoys complete power over the persons within its jurisdiction and issues commands to those persons. Such commands are backed up by "physical sanctions," the power to enforce the commands by physical force. There is no world government, so international law is nonexistent.

PHILIP: And I believe that the Nazis were properly tried for having violated international law. They did violate that law, for they violated the moral, social, and political codes which govern the conduct of nations. International law has existed for a long time. There have been international courts and tribunals; there are treaties which are binding on the nations which sign them. The Nazis violated the moral codes of mankind. They were guilty of deliberate and premeditated murder and so they were properly tried and properly executed.

3. In 1947 the Chicago Art Institute presented a show devoted to abstract and surrealist art. Differences of opinion were rife among the spectators. Jane, for example, said that the paintings were great works of art, for they expressed the mechanical dynamism of our contemporary industrial world and the psychological frustrations which accompany living at high speed. John, on the other hand, said that this "modernistic stuff" was not art at all, since none of the paintings looked like anything real. Jane insisted that the art was great; John was equally firm in asserting that she was wrong.

4. STACE: The Nazis were violators of the principles of morality, which require that we be just to our fellow men, that we act to increase their happiness, and that we respect the dignity of our fellow human creatures.

SUMNER: On the contrary, the Nazis acted quite morally in terms of the prevailing standards in Germany. The mores can make anything right, and since their community or group approved what they did, they acted morally. Of course, *we* don't approve of their conduct; *we* don't choose to behave that way, and people who acted like the Nazis would act immorally in the United States. But they were quite moral in Germany.

5. During the 1930's, estimating the number of persons unemployed in the United States became a popular pastime for statisticians. These estimates often varied widely. On one occasion the National Association of Manufacturers asserted that there were only 3 million unemployed; the CIO claimed that there were 7 million unemployed. Assuming that the disputants made their estimates on the basis of statistics gathered by competent sources of information, how do you account for this difference in figures? Explain why this dispute may have been a purely verbal one, and analyze accordingly.

Chapter 2

THE MEANING OF "MEANING"

Section I: Semantics and Logic

In the first chapter we noted the importance of the linguistic aspects of reasoning. Verbal disputes reveal an unawareness of the pitfalls into which language difficulties may lead us. When we engage in such disputes we confuse disagreements over the meaning of words with disagreements over the manner in which such words are applied to a particular situation, but we do not know that this is what we are doing.

Our analysis of disputes raised a number of problems and questions concerning language usage. Some of these questions, and others which may have occurred to the reader, are the following:

1. Does each word have a correct meaning? Does a word *really* mean one thing, and not some other thing, so that some senses in which a word is used are legitimate, others illegitimate?

2. If we answer the above questions in the affirmative, how are the correct meanings determined? Does the etymology of a word give us its correct meaning?

3. May an individual define a word to suit himself?

4. What is the meaning of ambiguity and how does it arise?

5. What is a good definition?

The answers to these questions all involve the problem of *meaning,* the basic problem in the relationship between language and reasoning. This problem will occupy our attention in the remainder of Part One. We shall be concerned with the influence of language on thinking and reasoning in order that we may know what we are doing when we use words in discourse. A knowledge of the principles of meaning will enable us to eliminate some of the obstacles which stand in the way of clear thinking because of the improper use of language, and help us to avoid falling prey to various kinds of linguistic confusions.

The relationship of language to thinking is much closer than is commonly suspected, and linguistic investigations may yield surprising results. For example, the children in an underprivileged neighborhood did very poorly in an intelligence test which contained questions such as, "A hand is to an arm as a foot is to a ———." It was later discovered that "is to" was an unfamiliar concept to these children. When "goes with" was substituted for "is to," their I.Q.'s immediately increased. Similarly, a public opinion poll phrases its questions in a specific manner. Phrased in a different way, the "public opinion" sought for might reveal quite different results.

The general study of meaning, in particular, the study of the meanings of words in their relationship to the things for which they stand, is today called "semantics." The term "semantics," derived from the Greek word *sema,* which means "sign," was introduced into modern usage by the French linguist Michel Bréal, in his *Essai de Semantique,* published in 1897. "Semantics," however, is but a new name for a type of linguistic investigation which is almost as old as philosophy itself, though only in recent years has this subject emerged as a full-fledged discipline. Today it refers to a vast and complex field of investigation, into which our present discussion will offer only a few glimpses. It is also important to note that the interests of writers on semantics are very diverse. Thus we find that some writers are primarily interested in the anthropological aspects of language and in the origin of language (Malinowski, Koffka, Köhler). A number of logicians are interested in the analysis of systems of signs (Carnap, Morris). A third group is interested in the psychological analysis of meaning (Ogden, Richards, Walpole). Finally, we note a group of writers who call themselves "General Semanticists" (Korzybski, Hayakawa, Stuart Chase). These writers believe that semantics may be usefully employed as a therapeutic agent for the elimination of social maladjustments and personal neuroses. But all writers on semantics have in common a concern with the problem of meaning. We turn now to the nature of this problem.

Section II: Signs and Symbols

To say that words have meaning is to say that they refer to something other than themselves. To "refer to something other than itself" is to function as a *sign*. Thus all words are signs, and all meaning-situations are sign-situations.

A sign-situation involves three aspects: The sign, such as a word, which in itself is simply a noise or a mark on paper; the thing signified, or referred to, which we shall call "the referent"; and persons or interpreters who refer to or who are referred to the referent. Thus a sign is something which refers to something for someone.* This three-fold aspect of sign-situations may be shown in a "triangle of reference," viz:

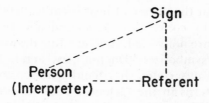

* The expression "refers to something" requires a qualification and a cautionary remark. Some signs are exceptions to the rule, for some words have no referents. Examples are such words as "and," "or," "not," "all," "some," etc., which serve certain logical functions, and ejaculations such as "ouch," "wow," and "yippee," which merely express feelings without designating referents. But the rule will hold for all other types of words, and we shall ignore this qualification in the following discussion.

Though we shall speak of referents as "things," for simplicity's sake, the reader should note that referents are not necessarily physical objects in the external world, i.e., things which can be seen and touched. They may be events, activities, relations, conditions, and so on. We must therefore reject such views as those of Stuart Chase, as expressed in his *Tyranny of Words,* that words have meaning only when they refer to "something real enough to be kicked." Referents may be abstractions, such as "energy"; or feelings, such as those of pleasure and pain; or creatures of man's imagination, such as dragons and other mythical monsters. The words "centaur" and "mermaid" have referents, though none such exist in the physical world of space and time. We do not confuse the referents of the world of the imagination with the referents of the real world when we know what we are doing.

Signs may be divided into two major types, natural and conventional. A natural sign is an event in our experience which refers to some other event because our experience has taught us that the two events are associated or connected in some fashion. Thus, a Kansan sees a dark cloud on the horizon, and he interprets what he sees as the sign of an approaching tornado. The cloud is a natural sign of the tornado. A conventional sign, which we shall call a "symbol," is an artificial construct made by human beings for the purpose of referring to something. A symbol is a sign which is deliberately employed in order to convey a meaning. Symbols become part of a language when human beings agree that they shall "stand for" given referents. Symbols are signs, but not all signs are symbols.

One or two details may be noted before we leave these definitions. Some objects may combine the functions of natural and conventional signs. Thus, a thermometer which indicates that the temperature is 100° F. on a July afternoon combines both types. The movement of the mercury is a natural sign of heat, but the fact that the degree of heat is called "100° Fahrenheit" is established by convention. It should also be obvious that many symbols are nonverbal. A yellow line drawn in the middle of a highway symbolizes "Do not pass here." Road-markers, numbers, diagrams, codes, shorthand systems, gestures, or even the use of lanterns in the "Ride of Paul Revere" ("one if by land and two if by sea") are all symbols. We should also note that though symbols refer to things other than themselves, they may also be interesting for their own sakes. A theme song on a radio program is a symbol of a certain type of entertainment, but the theme music may also be enjoyed for its own sake. Word-symbols may of course also possess such aesthetic qualities, as in poetic expressions.

Section III: Communication

Successful communication occurs only when a speaker and hearer make the same connections between symbols and the things which they are intended to signify. The hearer must be referred to the referent to which the speaker wishes to direct his attention. The typical form of the process of successful communication may be illustrated by the following diagram, which combines the triangles of reference for both the speaker and the hearer:

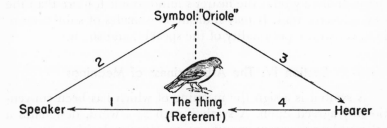

Symbol:"Oriole"

2   3

Speaker ← 1 → The thing ← 4 → Hearer
(Referent)

Arrow 1 represents the situation in which the speaker thinks of something before he has found the word he wishes to use. (The word and the referent may also come to the speaker's mind simultaneously.)

Arrow 2 represents the finding of the word to stand for the thing. (The connection between the word and the thing is indicated by the broken line.)

Arrow 3 indicates the word coming to the attention of the hearer.

Arrow 4 indicates that the hearer's mind is referred to the referent.

The diagram indicates that the hearer has correctly interpreted the symbols used by the speaker. Communicator and communicatee have the same terms in mind. But this happy consummation is not always attained, as we have already noted in our discussion of verbal disputes. Failures in communication occur when the symbol refers to different referents for the speaker and hearer. Let us symbolize these different referents by R_1 and R_2. The triangles of reference will then appear as follows:

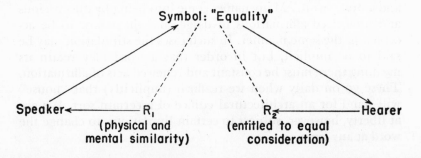

Symbol: "Equality"

Speaker ← R_1 R_2 → Hearer
(physical and mental similarity)   (entitled to equal consideration)

Successful communication occurs only when the reference is the same for both the speaker and the hearer. But note that the symbol may refer the hearer's mind to much more than the ostensible referent. It may indicate fine shades of subtle meanings, reveal the personality of the speaker, and so on.

Section IV: The Arbitrariness of Meanings

A symbol is a sign the meaning of which has been conventionally agreed upon. A symbol, such as a word, designates a referent by agreement or convention. Human decisions are thus required in order to establish the meaning of symbols, and such decisions are arbitrary ones, since "arbitrary" means "resting on a judgment which is not fixed by rule or law." This means that any object may be given any name which we choose to confer upon it. Names arise as a result of human agreements, or stipulations. This is illustrated in its purest form by the procedure whereby new words are coined today, as when chemists invent a new name for a new element. The procedure is wholly conventional and proceeds in something like the following manner: "Let us call this new element 'argon'." This is a stipulation entered into by mutual consent. This naming activity is arbitrary in the sense that any other name might have been given to this element, such as "aeron," a name earlier suggested.

No generation ever makes up its living vocabulary as a whole in this manner, since we inherit most of our words from our linguistic tradition, and certainly language did not originate by such conscious stipulations. "We can hardly suppose," as Bertrand Russell said in *The Analysis of Mind,* "that a parliament of speechless elders met together and agreed to call a cow a cow and a wolf a wolf." Many names come into being by unconscious and unnoticed affirmations in usage, and they come to be accepted in the same manner. In such cases the stipulation may be said to be implicit, but in order that a word may retain its meaning there must be constant and renewed acts of affirmation. These go on daily when we reaffirm (implicitly) that "house" will stand for an architectural edifice of a certain sort. We are at liberty, however, subject to certain limitations, to change the word at any time.

Though all symbols result from human decisions, note that a few symbols resemble their referents, so that their relationship to their referents is not a *merely* arbitrary one. We refer to *onomatopoetic* words, which sound like their referents, i.e., words such as "bow-wow," "buzz," "boom," "crack"; and to *iconic* signs, which look like their referents. Examples of the latter are diagrams, maps, and sketches. Nevertheless these signs are also symbolic by convention and agreement.

The conventional or arbitrary nature of symbols has not always been recognized. At one time it was believed that words have a "natural" relation to their referents, i.e., that the relationship was grounded "in the nature of things." We shall call this view the "natural theory." In Plato's dialogue, *Cratylus,* Socrates asserts that there is a natural connection between words and things. He believed that the gods call things by names which are naturally correct, but that human beings often erroneously call things by wrong names. The Garden of Eden incident, in which God asked Adam to name all things, is a variant of the natural theory, for Adam, as God's agent, would presumably give things their "right" names. Hebrew would then be regarded as the natural language. The natural consequence of such a view is that all other languages are incorrect, and this indeed is the assumption which underlies the story of the Tower of Babel, concerning the supposed origin of the multitude of languages. The babelization of tongues is described as a punishment for man's presumption in seeking to reach too high. Inventions of new international languages such as Esperanto and Basic English may be regarded as efforts to remove these consequences of sin.

The natural theory was aptly criticized by the English philosopher John Locke, in his *Essay on the Human Understanding,* with the remark that if names were natural, all human beings should speak the same language. The natural theory was also rejected by Aristotle. "By a noun," said Aristotle, "we mean a sound significant by convention . . . nothing is by nature a noun or name—it is only so when it becomes a symbol." *(De Interpretatione.)* This is the view which we accept.

Names are thus neither right nor wrong in a logical sense— they simply are what they are. Words may be appropriate or inappropriate according to aesthetic standards; they may be in accordance with customary usage or not, but the criteria of truth and falsity are not applicable to the names we use for referents. This is not to deny the great importance of aesthetic and customary standards, especially the latter. There *is* a significant sense in which words may be said to be "right" or "wrong." A student of botany is expected to be able to identify flowers by name, and if he is unable to identify members of the Polemoniaceae family correctly he may fail to receive credit in the course. Communication requires that we use words in their customary senses. Failure to know the "right name" in this sense is usually due to ignorance. We must learn the conventionally-agreed-upon names of things.

Nevertheless, words *are* the results of stipulations, and it follows that writers or speakers may present their own individual stipulations for the meanings of any words. When Mr. Hugh Walpole, in his *Semantics,* tells us that whenever he uses the word "interpret," he will mean "to be affected by," he has violated no rule of language or logic. But writers should exercise some restraints in exercising their freedom to stipulate their own meanings if they desire successful communication with an audience. Mr. Walpole's stipulation is an unusual one, for it requires, as he says, that we speak of a window "interpreting" a stone when the stone breaks the window. The novelty of this usage may result in a blockage of communication for many readers. But the "freedom to stipulate" sometimes enriches the language when novel usages win general acceptance.

The courts also place certain restraints upon individual stipulations. It would be no defence in a suit for libel to plead that when you called Jones a "swindler," you had previously stipulated that whenever you used the word "swindler" you should be understood to mean "native-born citizen." Custom also places limitations on our complete freedom to stipulate meanings. A young man who informed his girl friend that he would mean "Darling" whenever he called her "Snake" might have difficulty in achieving the desired results. We may also note that many writers conceal their novel stipulations and thus mislead their hearers or readers. When the Japanese conquered half of Asia, they stated that they were setting up a "Greater East Asia Co-prosperity Sphere." "Co-prosperity" was used in a highly novel sense, without notice as to what the Japanese had in mind. In contemporary political discussions, words like "democracy" and "freedom" are also used in novel senses by many writers.

In this section we have noted the arbitrary and conventional character of all symbols. Symbols are the results of stipulations, conventions, and agreements. Names are not "natural." Thus, several types of answers are possible to the question "Why is a certain thing called by its name?" We may answer that we call it by that name because it is customary to do so, or because we choose to, or because that name appears appropriate to us. The procedure of conferring proper or personal names on children is typical of the naming procedure.

A boy is called "John." This is an arbitrary act in the sense that we might have called him by any other name. The parents' reasons for calling him "John" rather than some other name are wholly external to the naming activity as such. His parents may have wished to give him his father's name or to honor a biblical hero, but these are "external" reasons. The fact that a new-found planet is called Pluto rather than Mickey Mouse, because it is customary to name planets after Greek divinities, is simply an aesthetic reason of appropriateness. The naming process is an arbitrary matter.

The reader may now raise the question of the relationship of etymologies to the meanings of words on the assumption that the root-form of a word determines its meaning in some non-conventional sense. But the fact that the English language obtained many of its words from Romance, Germanic, and Greek roots does not argue against the theory that the relationship between a symbol and referent is an arbitrary one. "House," for example, is derived from Germanic roots, i.e., *Haus;* and *Haus* in turn was derived from an earlier language; but somewhere in the past the begetting of these words was the result of the arbitrary naming activity. When we call a self-moving vehicle an automobile, from the Greek root *autos* (self) and the Latin *mobilis* (movable), it may appear that the choice is not a wholly arbitrary one. But the ancients (or their predecessors) had no such reasons of appropriateness when they used *autos* and *mobilis* for these referents. Etymologies do not affect the arbitrary nature of the naming process.

Section V: Etymologies

The subject of etymologies, briefly touched on at the end of
the last section, deserves further attention. Etymology is a
branch of philology which deals with the derivation of words
and traces them back to their immediate or remote sources, thus
giving us the history of individual words. Etymologies often
throw important light on the meanings of words and sometimes
reveal significant meanings not before clearly noted or understood. But though it is always interesting and generally useful
and instructive to know the roots and origins of the words in
our intellectual currency, the source of a word does not determine its present meaning. Linguistic changes and customs control in these matters, so that etymologies are logically irrelevant
with respect to the present meanings of words. If human beings
agree to use a certain word to symbolize a given referent, the in-
consistency of the present usage with the original meaning is
irrelevant. Thus the word "democracy," in its original sense,
meant government directly by the people. Today the word has
been extended in its meaning, and has a customary application
to representative forms of government. If this is the referent of
the term today, then the narrow etymological meaning is no
longer the only meaning. The former meaning has not necessarily been superseded by the new meaning; a new meaning has
been added to the former one.

We shall now note some of the applications of etymological
knowledge. Most etymologies are genuinely enlightening in
clarifying the meanings of words, and the study of the roots of
words is always fascinating. To cite some examples, the word
"philanthropist" is derived from two Greek roots: *philein,* to
love, and *anthropos,* man. A philanthropist is a "lover of mankind." Similarly we have "philosopher," which combines *philein*
and *sophia* (wisdom). Sophia is the root of sophisticated and
sophistry, words in which knowledge, rather than wisdom is
emphasized. Sophomore combines *sophos* (wise) and *moros,* a
Greek word meaning fool. This derivation reveals a penetrating
insight.

Some etymologies are merely interesting without being useful. It is interesting to know that the beverage "gin" got its name

from its origin in Geneva, Switzerland, but that the "gin" in Whitney's "cotton gin" was an abbreviation of "engine." Other interesting derivations are found in the words "gringo" and "grog." The Mexicans sometimes call Americans "gringos" because American soldiers sang a song during the war with Mexico, the first lines of which ran, "Green grow the rashes, O." Grog, the beverage containing rum and water, served to British sailors, and the term "groggy," used for drunkenness and for the general state of stupefaction, have an interesting history. An eighteenth century English admiral named Vernon was nicknamed "Old Grog" by his men because of the cloak of grogram (after the French words, *gros grain,* meaning coarse cloth) which he habitually wore. Vernon instituted the custom of serving a mixture of rum and water to the sailors, and the drink was called "grog."

But etymologies may also be misleading. Many words have meanings today which bear no significant relationship to their root words. Examples are "knave," from the German *Knabe,* or boy; "spinster," which originally meant "one who spins"; "assassin," an eater of hashish; and "orchestra," which originally meant the dancing place in a Greek theater. Or, consider the use of the word "barbarian." Its most important sense today refers to cruel and savage people. The word comes from the Greek, where all foreigners were called barbarians, without exception. The word originated among the Greeks to designate the languages of foreigners, which were unintelligible to them and sounded like "bar-bar-bar." The word carried the connotation of contempt also, since the Greeks considered themselves to be a superior people. But our use of "barbarian" today comes from the fact that the word came to be applied to the "foreigners" who overran the Roman Empire, committing many acts of vandalism and horror in the process. The point of this illustration is that the "real" meaning of barbarian is not "foreigner," though this is the word from which it is derived.

The last examples point to a very important truth, namely, that etymologies do not give us the "real" meanings of words. Words mean what we agree that they shall mean, since all symbols are established by "conventions" or agreements. Barbarian does not really mean foreigner, though that is the word from which it is derived. The present meaning of the word "etymology" itself is a case in point. The derivation of the word is found in two Greek words: *etymos,* true, and *logos,* which means "word" or "law." The earlier etymologists accepted the natural theory, and held that the true meanings of words could be traced through their shapes. But modern linguists mean by etymology the history of words, in which we simply retrace words back to their roots, or at least as far back as possible.

Our conclusion is that etymologies are interesting, useful, instructive and enlightening, but that they are logically irrelevant in the sense that they do not determine what the meaning of any word is today. Etymology could give us the "true" meanings of words only if there were an original "natural" language from which all other languages had been derived. But we have rejected the notion of such a natural language. At best, then, etymologies can take us back to the original words, but if these original words have no etymologies of their own, then they came into being by actual or implied acts of stipulation. Words mean what we decide that they shall mean, or what custom decides. As Humpty-Dumpty sagely remarked in *Through the Looking Glass,* "The question is, Which is to be master . . . ?" We or the words?

Section VI: Growth and Change in Language

We have been discussing some of the formal aspects of semantics, and we have learned that meanings are the results of affirmations. We shall presently discuss some of the linguistic errors which result from a failure to recognize the correct principles of symbolism, but first we shall examine some of the historical aspects of language growth and change so that the reader may be able to place the theoretical aspects of the subject within the perspective of living language.

Languages, are not "made"—they grow. They are not manufactured as complete wholes except in artificial languages such as Esperanto, and even this international language is based upon Latin roots which were already familiar. The origin of language is a subject shrouded in mystery, a subject of which nothing certain is known. There have of course been many theories as to how languages originated, but these are merely speculations.

As examples of such theories, some of which have received amusing nicknames, we may cite the following: The "Bow-wow," or "Ding-dong" theory holds that the first words were onomatopoetic, or imitations of the sounds of nature. The "Pooh-pooh" theory (for the expression indicating contemptuous indifference) holds that the first words were expressions of strong emotion. The "Yo-he-ho" theory, that words originated in work activities for the purpose of expediting such work, is illustrated by the singing of the Volga boatmen as they pull on their ropes. But as noted, these theories must be regarded as nothing more than suggestive guesswork.

The researches of anthropologists into the languages of primitive peoples have uncovered linguistic elements which may have been *stages* in the growth of language. One such element is a type of verbal usage called the "holophrase," in which a single word stands for a complete sentence or thought. A single word may stand for "There are fish in the stream," but the language in which this word appears may contain no word for "fish" as such. This suggests that language may have begun with words for complete activities or experiences rather than with words for individual objects. Thus the whole appeared before the parts; sentences before the parts of speech. A single word combined the functions of both subject and predicate.

A later stage in the development of language may thus involve a breaking down of the holophrastic sentence into its parts. Specific names will be given to things, to their qualities, to activities, and to relations. Further development then goes on in two directions, towards the process of analysis, or breaking a thing down into its parts, and towards synthesis, which involves the process of building up a whole from its parts. Classes are broken down into subclasses (analysis), and individual things are joined together into classes of things (synthesis).

Language and thought are of course indissolubly united in these developments. Language develops with thought, and thought develops with language. Whether thinking is possible without language is a question we need not discuss here, but it is certain that thought would be extremely limited without language. And it is thinking which finds distinctions among things which were formerly thought to be alike, and which finds resemblances among things which were formerly thought to be different. Language reflects these developments in thinking by adding new words to the vocabulary as new distinctions and generalizations appear, and words, in turn, help thought in making further distinctions and classifications.

Different languages reveal different stages in the developments toward analysis and synthesis. When we find a word which covers a very large group of things, and find no words for important distinctions within the group, this may indicate that the process of analysis has not been carried through, or it may mean that the distinctions were not considered important enough to warrant new names. Thus, among the Hopi Indians, the same word stands for "He is running" and "He was running." The modern Slavic languages have the single word "finger" to signify both fingers and toes as these words are used in the English language. We have carried the process of analysis into the general class of digits of the hands and feet. The failure to distinguish these digits by different words may indicate that the distinction was not considered of sufficient importance to require separate names. On the other hand, the failure to carry the process of synthesis far enough is found in some primitive languages, such as the Tasmanian, which have words that designate the species within a genus without having words for the genus itself. Thus the Tasmanian has names for different types of trees, but no name for "tree" as such. In such cases further synthesis is required. These primitives may not have generalized sufficiently to see the similarity among all classes of trees. A contrary fault is found in persons who look at all trees, as if they were simply "trees," without being able to distinguish one variety from another.

Languages which make fine discriminations may reveal lack of generalizing power, and languages which have general words may lack discriminating ones. The most developed languages are those which are richest in words designating both discrimination and generalization. These words, however, are invented only after thought has done its job of noting distinctions and similarities.

Human interest is responsible for these developments in language. Frequently, interest in certain generalizations or distinctions disappears, and words then fall into disuse. This frequently happens in cases where the discriminating process has been carried too far for general interest. An English journal, *Tid-Bits,* once noted the fine distinctions made by previous generations with respect to the dismemberment of flesh and fowl at the dining table. Where we use the single word "carve," they "allayed" a pheasant, "disfigured" a peacock, "spoiled" a hen, "tranched" a sturgeon, and so on. Words designating different types of collections of living things, depending upon the type of creature involved, also seem to be losing out in general speech. Thus we have such words as "herd" of cattle, "flock" of sheep, "pack" of wolves, a "shoal" of fish, "covey" of partridges, "bevy" of larks, etc. These distinctions may become of lesser importance to city-dwellers, but this would mean a loss of richness in the language.

Thus far we have noted some of the general factors in the growth and change of language. We shall now note some more specific types of change, change being omnipresent in language, which is a living, dynamic thing. Old words take on new meanings, and new words are invented for familiar referents. Custom is king in these matters, but custom supersedes custom. Thus the meanings of words are narrowed, extended, or completely changed through use. "Paper" once referred only to papyrus, but now refers to many other substances. Its meaning has been extended. "Surgeon," on the other hand, has had its meaning limited in sense, since it once referred to anyone who worked with his hands. Words may also change their forms without change of meaning, as in changes in spelling.

We also find new languages growing out of old ones. Thus the "Romance" group of languages (French, Italian, Spanish, Portuguese, Roumanian) developed out of Latin in western Europe, and similarly all of the European languages, as well as the Hindu Sanskrit, probably developed out of a common mother tongue. Similarities such as those found in the English "mother," Greek *meter,* Latin *mater,* Russian *mat,* and the Sanskrit *mata;* or among the English "two," the Greek and Latin *duo,* the Russian *dva,* and the Sanskrit *dvau* make a common origin probable. Their common "progenitor" language is assumed to be the "Indo-European" root language, though no

historical evidences of this language have been found. This
Indo-European language is a hypothetical construct. It is worthy
of mention here that the so-called "Aryan race" is the supposed
race of people who spoke this hypothetical root language. Nothing whatsoever is known concerning the characteristics of this
race, if indeed there was such a race, though many pages have
been written concerning the glorious "blood-qualities" of this
people.

Why do languages change in these ways? Linguists have
noted such reasons as mishearing, misunderstanding, defective
memory, imperfect speech organs, laziness, the desire to be
distinctive in one's utterance, the need to express new ideas,
and the desires for clarity, euphony, and economy. We may also
note the influence of foreign languages on each other. Gradual
and unnoticed changes develop in time into very large modifications of the original language.

Change is not all, of course, for language customs do endure
—sometimes over very long periods of time. There are also
various ways in which we attempt to stop the flow of change in
usage. The dictionary, for example, attempts to fix the definitions of words, but even such "fixed" definitions give way to new
usages, and many dictionary definitions become obsolete in
time. Dictionary definitions are written by scholars who are
specialists in their respective fields, and these scholars tell us
how words are used in terms of the prevailing customary usage.
The writer of a dictionary definition is a historian rather than
a law-giver, a judge rather than a legislator. Dictionaries do not
lay down laws of usage which command us to use words in certain ways. The usefulness of the dictionary lies in its giving us
information as to the commonly accepted senses of words in
order to facilitate successful communication.

A word is also required here as to the authoritativeness of
dictionary definitions. We must always remember that a few
very important words have no universally accepted meanings,
and there is thus no genuine custom which we can follow. The
word "propaganda" is a case in point. There are almost as many
definitions of propaganda as there are individuals who define
the word. Words like "truth," "morality," and "beauty" are
words which have been defined and redefined for the past 2000

years and the search for adequate definitions of these terms is not yet concluded. Obviously the dictionary cannot solve these problems, for no one has as yet solved them. In a discussion concerning the meaning of "beauty" the dictionary can do no more than help to initiate discussion; it cannot settle the matter.

It is because of the changing meanings of words in daily use that scientific and professional terminologies are invented. Ordinary words become ambiguous by acquiring new meanings, and science requires precise and unambiguous terms so that misunderstanding of referents will be reduced to a minimum. Technical vocabularies are accordingly invented, as in the biological sciences, where Latin names for diseases, plants, and animals are used. Latin terminology is also a great convenience for international communication. Since these words are not in daily usage, custom cannot modify them. Considerations of this sort led Professor Spearman, the English psychologist, to propose abandoning the word "intelligence" in psychology and to employ as a substitute the symbol "G-factor" for the referent which many psychologists have in mind when they employ the term. Instead of speaking of an individual's "intelligence quotient," one would speak of his "G-factor quotient." The ambiguity of the term as presently used would thus be eliminated.

The practice of inventing new vocabularies, however, also has some disadvantages, particularly in the social sciences, where unique terminologies make scientific writings unintelligible to the uninitiated. There is also the danger that the invention of a professional vocabulary for items of common experience may result in a pretentiousness of diction that may conceal a barrenness of thought, as in the professional report that "clinical observations and statistical correlations reveal that pre-adolescents exhibit multiform tendencies and predispositions toward variant and differential patterns of behavior." What is meant here is that it has been observed that small children do not all act in the same manner. A different type of professionally obscure language is found in the writings of some philosophers, such as in those of Heidegger, the contemporary German existentialist philosopher. It is said that his German readers must have his German writings translated into German before they can understand him.

We have emphasized the element of change in language, but again, we must remember that the great body of words is relatively permanent and unchanging. Language is like a tree; its leaves change with the seasons, but its roots are relatively stable. Shakespeare used many words which have become obsolete, but the great body of his vocabulary has the same meaning today as it had in the sixteenth century.

Section VII: Some Errors of Symbolism

In this section we shall note some of the important errors which result from the failure to understand and apply the principles of symbolism studied in this chapter. Our list is not exhaustive, of course, and we shall also have occasion to note other types of errors of symbolism in later chapters. The discussion of the four errors noted in this section will also help to clarify the correct principles of symbolic usage studied in this chapter.

1. The magical power of words.

This error results from the failure to note that words are mere "noises" which acquire meaning through their association with referents. It is a primitive superstition that the "name" has a mysterious power or magical potency. Primitives believe that words have a causal or magical influence over events. This superstition lies behind the "abracadabra" of the medicine man, the "Open Sesame" which caused the cave door to open for Ali Baba, and the practice of tribesmen who change their names after being cursed, so that they may escape the evil which has become attached to their names, and thus to themselves. It is common practice for primitives to burn the name of their enemy even after his body has been destroyed. J. G. Frazer, in *The Golden Bough,* reports that the Malagasy soldier refuses to eat kidneys, for the word for kidney in his language is the same as the word for "shot"; thus he believes that he will be shot if he eats kidneys.

Another form of verbal magic is found in the belief that some words are so holy and sacred that they must never be uttered by man. Among the ancient Hebrews the name of God, "Yahweh" or "Jehovah" was "unnamable," and its actual utterance was forbidden in both speech and prayer. God could be spoken of only by the use of the substitute word or surrogate "Adonai." The pre-war Japanese considered the name "Hirohito" sacred. A peasant who unwittingly conferred this name on his son committed hara-kiri upon discovering his error.

Words have no causal influence on events; they can bring neither luck nor disaster through the airwaves set up when they are spoken. But from primitive times until today superstitious beliefs abound. We "knock on wood" after noting our good fortune; the dice player pleads with the dice and uses such endearing expressions as "Little Joe" and "Big Dick" to influence the bounce; the bettor on horses believes in the magical potency of the name. All these exemplify the belief in the magical power of words to influence events.

We may note, finally, the use of *euphemisms*, i.e., the use of an agreeable expression for a disagreeable event. We avoid mentioning the word "death," and say "passed on," "went to his reward," "departed," "sleeping," and so on. These circumlocutions are used to transform evil into good. It is as if our refusal to mention the awesome word would somehow obviate the disaster itself. Euphemisms, however, may also be used in nonmagical ways, as noted below.

2. Words as guarantees of facts.

We often overlook the fact that the referent of a word may be a creation of our own imagination. This error has two aspects. We may assume that the existence of a word guarantees the existence of a corresponding thing in space and time. But proof must be offered for the existence of facts; the mere utterance of the word is insufficient. The existence of the word "Devil" does not guarantee the existence of an actual Lucifer or Beelzebub waiting for those who fail to take out the appropriate fire insurance. When we speak of the "State" or "consciousness" as *things* separate and apart from the "entities-in-relation" to which these terms refer, we commit the same error in the form known as *hypostatization* or *reification*.

A second aspect of this error is found in the assumption that "good" words guarantee the existence of good things, and "bad" words bad things. The proverb says that "we give a dog a bad name and then hang him." Men stand condemned in the public eye merely because they have been called "Reds," "communists," "reactionaries," or "fascists." Similarly, organizations confer "good" names upon themselves in order to mislead the public. Thus, a fascist organization called itself the "Christian Front." A fascist magazine called *The Galilean* was published by "The Fellowship Press." A Communist organization seeking to prevent American aid to England in 1940 called itself "The People's Committee." The use of a "good" name does not guarantee the existence of a good thing.

The manner in which propaganda organizations and advertisers use the emotional associations attached to "value" words in order to manipulate their audiences requires little comment. Orators and demagogues use attractive or unattractive names in order to mislead us. Thus, most Americans abhor a totalitarian form of government, usually called "fascism." We abhor "fascism." But Huey Long, who led a fascist type of political movement during the depression of the early thirties, predicted that the United States would soon have a fascist government. He added: "But when it comes it won't be called fascism." We should remember that fascism is fascism whatever it is called, in the sense that the kind of referent to which fascism refers, is what it is, regardless of what we call it.

Euphemisms may also illustrate the use of words as guarantees of facts, as in the use of "Tourist" for "Third Class" on ocean liners, or on Russian trains, where "Third Class" has been changed to "Third Category," since the Russians have abolished all class distinctions. The use of euphemisms, however, is not necessarily an error of symbolism. Social conventions may dictate the use of certain agreeable expressions. (False modesty carries this tendency to an exaggerated degree.) Euphemisms may even give us a more realistic description than "brutal" terms, as when a "Home for Incurables" changed its name to "Institution for Chronic Diseases." The new name gave the patients a more hopeful attitude, and science may find cures for diseases now considered incurable.

But in no case, of course, does the name offer a guarantee concerning either the existence or the value characteristics, good or bad, of the referent to which it refers. A rose, as Juliet remarked, would smell as sweet though called by any other name.

3. The use of words without referents.

Human beings sometimes use words without thinking of the referents to which they refer. This type of evil is sometimes encouraged by educational systems in which students repeat words and formulas without understanding their meaning. Justice O. W. Holmes had this type of error in mind when he admonished us to "think things, not words." In general, it is good educational practice for students (or readers generally) to translate what they read into their own words in order to be sure that they are avoiding this evil, for "one's own words" usually have clear referents.

George Orwell, the English critic, in *Modern English Writing* described this vice as involving the use of "meaningless words." "In art criticism," he writes, "words like romantic, plastic, values, human, dead, sentimental, natural, vitality" are "strictly meaningless, in the sense that they not only do not point to any discoverable object but are hardly expected to do so by the reader." Mr. Orwell exaggerates, but his remarks call attention to a serious fault in the type of writing to which he refers. One may also question the use of the expression "meaningless words," on the ground that a word without meaning (such as "higher-gloob") is, strictly speaking, not a word at all. Mr. Orwell means that words are often used without thinking of any definite referents.

What we refer to by this error, then, is not the use of meaningless expressions, such as are found in the following amusing example of "double-talk" (from the work of the master in this field, David Ross):

We have a lot of fun, and do you know, the entrain does not findle the boller, either. After all, who am I to shrake the leavings? I am a mere bildring. My life is neither frenner or planrate. The pen is the outgrabe of the mome, the hordling always does the gets.

No words are meaningless in themselves, but words are often used without meaning when the writer or speaker uses them without having referents in mind. But the reader should be cautioned against making this charge against a writer, for the unintelligibility of a piece of discourse may be due to his own inadequate vocabulary. "No cenobites are troglodytes" contains words unfamiliar to many persons who speak the English language, but it is unexceptionable as a meaningful sentence.

Confusions also abound with respect to the use of "abstract" words, i.e., words of wide generality such as the words cited by Mr. Orwell. Stuart Chase, for example, often speaks of abstractions as if they were necessarily meaningless because their referents are not "real enough to be kicked." As examples, he cites such words as "capitalism," "fascism," "communism," and "democracy." But these words have meaning, however they may be used by careless writers and however ambiguous they may be. One should take the trouble to find out exactly what a writer means when he uses these words, though it is undoubtedly true that many persons use them without having any specific referents in mind. When Max Weber writes in his *Sociology of Religion,* "We shall examine the influence of religious ideas on the development of an economic spirit or the ethos (ethics) of an economic system," his language is highly abstract, but he means something by these words. Such highly abstract language may be undesirable in terms of "good style," but that is another matter.

Our point is that we should be sure that we have referents in mind when we use words. The reader may ask himself, for example, just what he has in mind when he uses expressions such as "God is Love" or "Love your enemies." And what specific referents are referred to when it is said that "Capitalism exploits the working class"? The hearer of this statement may suspect that the speaker has no referents in his mind. It then becomes appropriate to ask that the words be translated into concrete language in order to make the ideas clear. The ultimate test of meaning lies in the "cash value" of the words used, i.e., in the actual existences to which they refer.

4. The "real" connection between words and things.

All meanings are arbitrary. Failure to note the arbitrary relationship between symbol and referent has already been discussed in connection with etymologies. The fourth error is based upon the failure to remember the arbitrariness of symbols. Many persons think of words as "really belonging" to certain referents, as if there were some indissoluble or "real connection" between them. The error occurs in certain typical forms.

A "young lady" now famous among writers on semantics approached an astronomer shortly after the planet Pluto was discovered, and asked him how it was that the astronomers knew that the newly discovered planet was *really* Pluto and not some other planet. The error lies in the assumption that names "belong" to certain things and to no others. This type of error is also the source of much humor. Thus Gracie Allen asks a male acquaintance whom she has just met to call her "Gracie." To his remonstrance that he hardly knows her, she responds, "Why, just as soon as I was born my mother called me Gracie, and she didn't know me at all."

The belief that some words "really mean" some referents, or that certain things "must" be called by certain names, assumes that the thing could not be called by any other name. To say "Pigs are so-called because they are such dirty animals" illustrates this point. But names seem to belong to things only because they have become associated with things of a certain type; the connection is always an arbitrary one. These associations, of course, will influence our subsequent use of the names. Names remind us of pleasant or unpleasant associations. This also applies to the personal names of men and women. But the relationship of the name to the individual is arbitrary.

A variant of this error is found in the belief that communism *really* means one of its definitions. Or that the form of government in the United States is *really* that of a republic, so that it is *wrong* to call the United States a democracy. But all names are arbitrary designations for their referents, and if the Ameri-

can people wish to emphasize certain aspects of their government which are called democratic, there is no linguistic law
which forbids them from doing so. Custom is supreme in determining the usage of words. No thing can once and for all
pre-empt the use of any name for itself.

As previously pointed out, the expression "Things should
be called by their right names" does have a legitimate meaning,
if we do not interpret "right" names as "real" names. For success in communication, words should be used in their customary
meanings. If most people think of a "free" society when the
word "democracy" is used, then it is improper for a speaker to
call a totalitarian state a democracy merely because he chooses
to do so or because he has a peculiar and private undisclosed
definition of the term in his mind. The use of words in this
manner is dishonest if there is a deliberate intent to mislead
people into thinking that the speaker has their referent in mind
when he actually has another. This subject will be discussed
more thoroughly in the chapter on "definition."

Exercises

The following exercises should be analyzed and discussed in
terms of the material covered in the relevant sections of the chapter.
Since these exercises are designed to test the student's comprehension of the text, the relevant principles should be mentioned in connection with the student's analyses.

A. *Signs and Symbols.*

Classify the following signs as natural or conventional:
   a. A chemist dips litmus paper into his test tube. He inter-
      prets the sign, red, or the sign, blue, as meaning acid or
      base.
   b. During the invasion of France in 1940 the Nazis put
      weird wailing sirens on their Stuka bombers in order to
      terrify the Allied soldiers.
   c. A work of abstract art which we do not "understand."

B. *The Arbitrariness of Meanings.*

   1. Humpty-Dumpty said: "There's glory for you." "I don't
      know what you mean by 'glory,' " Alice said. Humpty-

Dumpty smiled contemptuously. "Of course you don't—till I tell you. I meant, There's a nice knock-down argument for you." "But 'glory' doesn't mean 'a nice knock-down argument,'" Alice objected. "When I use a word," Humpty-Dumpty said in a rather scornful tone, "it means just what I choose it to mean, neither more nor less." (Lewis Carroll, *Through the Looking Glass*, Ch. VI.)

2. The Book of Genesis (II, 19–20): "And out of the ground the Lord God formed every beast of the field, and every fowl of the air. And brought them unto Adam to see what he would call them, and whatsoever Adam called every living creature, that was the name thereof. And Adam gave names to all cattle and to the fowl of the air, and to every beast of the field." Mark Twain wrote that one of these animals gave Adam great difficulty and he appealed to Eve for help: "What name shall I give to this animal?" "Call it a horse," answered Eve. "But why a horse?" "Well," said Eve, "it looks like a horse doesn't it?"

3. Parson Thwackum, in Henry Fielding's *Tom Jones*: "Religion is not manifold because there are various sects and heresies in the world. When I mention religion, I mean the Christian religion; and not only the Christian religion, but the Protestant religion, and not only the Protestant religion, but the Church of England."

4. Our own conclusion is that, if by autocracy is meant government without prior discussion and debate, either by public opinion or in private session, the government of the USSR is, in that sense, actually less of an autocracy than many a parliamentary cabinet. (Beatrice and Sidney Webb, *Soviet Communism: A New Civilization?* Scribner's, 1936, p. 479.)

5. "I believe in democracy, but in a democracy which is made up of 100 per cent white, Protestant, and native-born American citizens."

C. *Etymologies.*

1. Look up the etymologies of the following words and state whether you consider their etymologies useful or misleading:

a. propaganda	e. gentile	h. liberal
b. neurasthenia	f. bolshevik	i. radical
c. polite	g. pagan	j. conservative
d. boor		

2. Comment on Jespersen's remark that "we get no further at

all towards understanding what a tragedy is when we are informed that the word must once have meant 'goat song.'"
3. "Electronics" is an incorrect word, for "electron" comes from "amber," i.e., electricity. But radio waves are not electrical, since they are waves set up in the ether by electrical disturbances. They are like waves in water set up by the motion of a stick. The waves, not the stick, are spread. We should use the term "radiovision," since television means "distant sight." (Commander McDonald of the Zenith Corp.)

D. *Growth and Change in Language.*

George Orwell translates the following passage from *Ecclesiastes* into what he calls "Modern English of the worst sort": Ecclesiastes: "I returned, and saw under the sun, that the race is not to the swift, nor the battle to the strong, neither yet bread to the wise, nor yet riches to men of understanding, nor yet favor to men of skill; but time and chance happeneth to them all."
Modern English: "Objective consideration of contemporary phenomena compels the conclusion that success or failure in competitive activities exhibits no tendency to be commensurate with innate capacity, but that a considerable amount of the unpredictable must invariably be taken into account." ("Politics and the English Language," *New Republic,* June 17, 1946.)

E. *The Errors of Symbolism.*

Check the following for possible errors of symbolism. Note whether the error involves the Magical Use of Language, Words as Guarantees of Facts, the Use of Words without Referents, or the "Real Connection between Words and Things." Explain your answers.
1. The French call it *"pain,"* the English call it "bread," but its real name is *"Brod."*
2. An Arab was being cursed by a compatriot. He threw himself on the ground in order that the curse-words might fly harmlessly over his head.
3. The following answers are given by children:
"Could the moon have been called 'sun' and the sun 'moon'?"—*No.*—"Why not?"—*Because the sun makes it warm, and the moon gives light.*
Roc (6½) admits that God might have changed the names: "Would they have been right or wrong?"—*Wrong.*—

"Why?"—*Because the moon must be the moon and not the sun, and the sun must be the sun.*

"But if everyone had called the sun 'moon' and the moon 'sun,' would we have known it was wrong?"—*Yes, because the sun is always bigger, it always stays like it is and so does the moon.*

"Why is the sun called what it is?"—*Because it behaves as if it was the sun.* (Jean Piaget, *The Child's Conception of the World,* Harcourt, Brace, 1929, pp. 81–4.)

4. State Senator John McNaboe of New York bitterly opposed a bill for the control of syphilis in May, 1937 because "the innocence of children might be corrupted by a wide-spread use of the term . . . This particular word creates a shudder in every decent woman and decent man." (Stuart Chase, *The Tyranny of Words,* Harcourt, Brace, 1938, p. 63.)

5. Wherefore, be it resolved: To resolve every universally considerate wish evoking critical-concept into a reasonably efficacious resistance-eliminating inanimate-device of time-saving-calculability and contiguous-service time-synchronization, that may be factorable from "possibility" to "probability," thus intent to streamline man's competitive-volition, unknown to him, into a scientifically designed direction-of-least-resistance, upon the occasion of his each and every initial-dislodgment from habit-inertia. (R. Buckminster Fuller, *Nine Chains to the Moon,* J. B. Lippincott Co., 1938.)

6. The United States is not a "great democracy," for our forefathers established a great republic. A democracy is a country where the people rule directly, not through their elected representatives.

7. It is improper to call the "American Revolution" a *revolution,* because the word really means a fundamental change in the basic social, economic, and political institutions of a country. There have really been few real revolutions in the history of mankind, such as were the French Revolution of 1789 and the Russian Revolution of 1917.

8. In the fourth inning of a baseball game between the Chicago Cubs and the Cincinnati Reds, the first Cincinnati player made a hit. The narrator, Bert Wilson, announced, "Fans, that was the Reds' first hit, but you will note that I did not mention the fact that the Reds had made no hits in the first three innings. If I had, and the next man had

made a hit, hundreds of fans would have written protesting letters to me telling me to keep my big mouth shut."

9. A gelding is a horse which has ceased to be entire.

10. Wilfrid Lay, an English writer, was pleading for greater frankness in sex discussion in families. He advocated that parents should not stress concealment of the body in the home; in fact, he urged, "parents should sometimes appear before their children in *puribus naturalibus.*"

11. A bill before the Illinois legislature proposed that no liquor could be called "whiskey" if it contained more than 50 per cent neutral spirits. A spokesman for the liquor industry stated that stocks of whiskey in Illinois were already low, and that if the bill were passed stocks of whiskey would immediately decrease by 75 per cent.

12. The Divine is properly so-called.

13. Speak of the Devil and he's sure to appear.

14. "Mother, when I was born, how did you know that I was Charlie and not some other little boy?"

15. The Russians never execute enemies of the state—they are liquidated.

16. Abraham Lincoln once asked an audience, "If I call the tail of a horse a leg, how many legs will the horse then have?" "Five," they responded. "No," answered Lincoln, "calling a horse's tail a leg doesn't make it one."

17. From Lewis Carroll's "Jabberwocky":
    'Twas brillig, and the slithy toves
    Did gyre and gimble in the wabe:
    All mimsy were the borogroves,
    And the mome raths outgrabe.

18. "For Portsymasser and Purtsymessus and Pertsymiss and Partsymasters, like a prance of findigos, with a shillto shallto slipny stripny." (James Joyce, *Finnegans Wake.*)

19. The word "God" has meaning, therefore it refers to something. But the word as we use it refers to nothing else than a supernatural being; therefore, the supernatural being, God, exists.

20. Stuart Chase reports that he collected a hundred responses from various persons as to their reaction to the word "fascism." He asked those questioned to tell him what kind of picture came into their heads when they heard the term. A few of the answers mentioned by Chase were:

> Schoolteacher: A dictator suppressing all opposition.
> Governess: Obtaining one's desires by sacrifice of human lives.
> Lawyer: A state where the individual has no rights, hope, or future.
> College student: Hitler and Mussolini.
> Schoolboy: War. Concentration camps. Bad treatment of workers. Something that's got to be licked.
> Author: I can only answer in cuss words.
> Elevator starter: I never heard of it.

Chase then quotes the following definition of fascism by Harold Laski:

"I suggest the conclusion that Fascism is nothing but monopoly capitalism imposing its will on the masses which it has deliberately transformed into slaves. The ownership of the instruments of production remains in private hands."

Chase states that the "student of semantics" will react to this definition as follows:

Meaning in the form of a row of abstractions does not satisfy him. He finds three high-order terms equated and an inference applied to one or all of them: private property = capitalism = fascism. He is immediately suspicious of the identification of three timeless, spaceless, descriptionless entities. He never saw an "ism" imposing its will. He asks what are the referents for "private ownership," "monopoly capitalism" and "fascism." He wonders what is meant by "capitalism imposing its will on the masses," remembering that this is a stock phrase in socialist propaganda . . . "Ownership of the instruments of production" troubles him as another stock phrase. He recalls how Berle and Means in their *Modern Corporation and Private Property* show that many legal "owners" of large corporations have nothing to say about their property . . . "Private hands" worries him more. He knows that whatever titles private persons may hold to property in Germany or Italy, the Government jolly well tells them when, where, and how much to let go of.

He is not disposed to argue with Mr. Laski, because the

apparent meaning has faded into a series of semantic blanks. Laski is not necessarily wrong; he is saying nothing worth listening to.

But should one not be afraid of fascism and fight against it? The student of semantics is not afraid of evil spirits and takes no steps to fight them . . . If the armies of Mussolini or Hitler invade his country, he is prepared to fight. But he refuses to shiver and shake at a word. (Stuart Chase, *The Tyranny of Words,* Harcourt, Brace, 1938, pp. 188–93.)

Discuss the following:
a. Of which error of symbolism is Laski guilty, according to Chase?
b. What is Chase's attitude toward abstractions, such as "fascism?"

Chapter 3

AMBIGUITY

Section I: The Meaning of Ambiguity

There are many obstacles in the path of successful communication, but ambiguity is undoubtedly the worst offender. By ambiguity is meant the fact that symbols are capable of being understood in more senses than one. Thus a symbol may be interpreted differently by speaker and hearer; communicators and communicatees are at cross-purposes and there is no meeting of minds.

Most of the words in any language have more than one referent. This is in many ways a boon rather than an evil, for the range of possible meanings in any limited number of words is greatly increased. Our vocabularies are enlarged when one word has different meanings in different contexts; the single word then becomes the equivalent of many different words. In many cases the differences in referents may be on a "large" scale, as when the word "secretary" refers in turn to "a person who attends to correspondence," "an executive officer in the government," "a writing desk," and "a South African bird with long legs." There are many other words in which the differences in the referents are of a more subtle nature, the shifts in meaning being less obvious, as in the different ways in which the word "man" is used in the following contexts:

All *men* are mortal.
The child is father to the *man*.
Those were the days when *men* were *men*.
What a piece of work is *man*! How infinite in capacity!
The football team is under*manned*.

Successful communication occurs only when the reader correctly interprets the symbols used by the writer. In our discussion of the "triangle of reference" we showed how this occurs. When the communication is successful then the communicator and the communicatee have their minds referred to the same referents; they have the same *terms* in mind. They have "come to terms." But ambiguous words are obstacles to such happy consummations; communication is frustrated. We have already noted examples of such frustration in our discussion of the manner in which ambiguous words like "democracy," "equality," and "law" may lead to verbal disagreements. When such failures of communication occur, the speaker and the hearer have different referents in mind.

But note that ambiguity is an evil only when it results in these frustrations of communication. In scientific discourse, where the aim is to achieve clear and precise reference, ambiguity is an unmitigated evil. But there are other fields of thought in which ambiguity may have certain desirable effects. This is the case in poetry, where ambiguity may sometimes contribute to the poetic effect by suggesting a rich aura of implied meanings: "Life is a tale told by an idiot, full of sound and fury, signifying nothing"; "Faith is the substance of things hoped for; the evidence of things not seen." In this manner poetry approximates the effects produced by music, which, among all of the arts, is certainly the most expressively ambiguous. One of the great charms of music lies in the ambiguity with which it expresses moods, so that each hearer may interpret the musical score in his own way. Ambiguity also has more mundane uses. Diplomatic language has developed the art of saying things ambiguously so that failure to agree will be masked by "face-saving" language. Finally, the ambiguous aspects of words are exploited as a rich source of humor. Gagsters and punsters thrive on the double-meanings of words. Our primary interest, of course, is to learn how to avoid ambiguity in scientific discourse.

Ambiguity is the direct opposite of synonymity (the use of synonymous words). An ambiguous word refers to several referents; in synonymity a single referent is referred to by several different words. "Spade" refers to at least two referents: a playing card and a garden implement. Fool, lout, simpleton, oaf, dunderhead, ninny, nincompoop, and Mortimer Snerd all refer to the same referent, or to substantially the same referent, since few synonymous words are absolutely identical in meaning. The difference between ambiguity and synonymity may be revealed schematically:

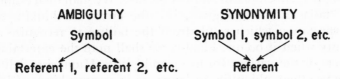

Symbol

Referent 1, referent 2, etc.

Symbol 1, symbol 2, etc.

Referent

Section II: The Analysis of Ambiguity

Though many words have more than one meaning, the context of surrounding circumstances will usually clarify the sense in which the word is used. The initial ambiguity is often completely eliminated by the context. We shall be primarily concerned with cases in which the ambiguity is not eliminated by the context, cases in which we find a blockage of communication. In the verbal disagreements studied in Chapter 1 we saw examples of ambiguity that were not clarified by the context, at least not for the persons participating in the discussions. In this chapter we shall examine the different ways in which ambiguity may result in the failure of communication.

When two or more interpretations of an author's language are possible, the reader does not know what is in the author's mind. We should be clear as to the task of the logician in analyzing this situation. The logician cannot eliminate ambiguity; his primary task is to call attention to the fact that ambiguity occurs and to show the different ways in which it occurs. The logician can also help to make the reader sensitive to ambiguities in places where ambiguity might be unsuspected. The logician can also advise the reader to find out what was in the author's mind before the reader interprets ambiguous language. The reader's task here may be likened to that of a judge whose task it is to decide what the legislature meant by the ambiguous language in a law. The court will investigate the circumstances in which the law was passed, the remarks of legislators concerning the intent of the law, and so on. In other words, the context will be studied for light on the probable meaning of the words.

We shall examine the manner in which ambiguity occurs in the use of words, phrases, and sentences. We shall also note ambiguities in emphasis and significance. We shall then examine the "fallacies" of ambiguity, i.e., the errors in thinking and interpretation which result from the failure to recognize ambiguity when it occurs. Finally, we shall note the entertaining aspects of the various forms of ambiguity. Humorists deliberately use the ambiguities of language in various kinds of jokes and "gags." Such uses are of course not "fallacies," since the ambiguity is recognized by both humorist and reader.

Section III: The Types of Ambiguity

1. Simple ambiguity.

By simple ambiguity we shall mean the fact that single words or phrases may refer to more than one referent, even after we have examined their contexts. Verbal disagreements are based upon this type of ambiguity. Any statement containing a word which is ambiguous in its context exemplifies this vice. "The early Christians were communists." Since the word "communist" has more than one referent in this context, ambiguity exists. Before the reader denies the truth of this sentence he should find out what the writer means. Questions may also involve simple ambiguity, as in "Do you believe in God?" "God" means different things to different persons, and a yes-or-no answer is inappropriate until we learn what referent the questioner has in mind. Spinoza, for example, defined God as "everything which exists." Spinoza was a deeply religious man whose pantheistic philosophy was permeated with devotion to God. The Catholic Church, however, has condemned his pantheism as equivalent to atheism.

Simple ambiguity is closely related to "vagueness," but should be distinguished from it. An ambiguous word has several distinct referents; a vague word lacks precision and definiteness in its reference. Thus, the question, "Has there been any progress during the past 2000 years?" involves the use of the vague word "progress." The reader spontaneously responds to such a question with his own questions: "Progress in what sense? In spiritual growth? In the advancement of the common man? In a material sense?" The word "progress" is vague rather than ambiguous, for in each case it means "advancement toward a definite goal," but the question does not specify the goal involved.

Vagueness, rather than ambiguity, will also be found in the following incident. In the summer of 1947 General Eisenhower was reported to have said that "the United States Army is a 'poor second' to that of Russia." Congressman Short asked, "In what sense?" In quantity? In quality? The United States Army has never been equal to the Russian army in size either in war or peace. Here too, "poor second" is not ambiguous, since it means "far behind the first," but its meaning is not precise.

Questions containing vague words cannot be answered without further clarification of their meaning. It is interesting to note how careful thinking may result in the discovery that "clear" words are actually vague. Thus, the question "Is this building moving?" may appear to be clear. But we must ask: "In relation to which frame of reference?" In relation to the sun, this building is moving at a speed of 18 miles per second. In relation to the earth, however, it is stationary.

Simple ambiguity has two forms, written and oral. The phonetic sound "teers" may stand for two different words: "tiers," and "tears." An amusing example of oral ambiguity based on this sound is found in the following:

> A reporter was describing a scene at the House of Commons to another reporter. "There, on the floor of the house, stood the Prime Minister speaking," he said, "back of him were the members of the Cabinet, in front of him sat the members of the Opposition, and in tiers around him sat the other members of the House."
>
> The second reporter was very young and very earnest. "Not really *tears*," he exclaimed. "Poor chaps!" (Albert Levi and Albert Frye, *Rational Belief,* Harcourt, Brace, 1941, p. 108.)

Simple ambiguity lies at the basis of much humor, especially in puns. Jokes which are called *"double-entendres"* by the French simply refer to the fact that ambiguity means "double-meaning."

A somewhat crude example will be found in the following:
A man invited a friend as guest for dinner. At the table the
man's wife and children were seated and the host then pro-
ceeded to violate all of the rules laid down by Emily Post.
Somewhat shocked, the guest asked, "Do you always do this before your children?" "No," replied the host, "sometimes they
do it first." Another example is found in Wordsworth's remark,
"If I had a mind to, I could write like Shakespeare."

2. Amphiboly.

Amphiboly refers to the fact that the meaning of sentences
may be ambiguous, not because any of its words are ambiguous
but because the grammatical construction of the sentence permits several interpretations as to its meaning. The amphibolous
sentence is capable of being understood in more than one sense.
This may result in a failure in communication. A sentence combines words in order to express a thought. The referents have a
certain relationship in the mind of the speaker. The grammatical construction of the sentence may fail to direct the hearer's mind to the relationship referred to by the speaker. The
logician calls the reader's attention to these factors. The grammarian seeks to teach writers how to make themselves clear.

Vivid examples of amphiboly are found in humorous ex-
aggerations of this fault. Thus, the following account was re-
portedly given by a newspaper reporter, with reference to the
departure of the famous pre-war dirigible from the Lakehurst
airport: "The Graf Zeppelin was leaving the Lakehurst airport.
Among the last to enter was Mrs. Smith, lone woman passenger.
Slowly her huge nose was turned into the wind. Then, like some
huge beast, she crawled along the grass . . ."

Grammarians have noted a type of error similar to amphiboly in the error called "the dangling participle," as in
"Zooming along under her own power, Jane was fascinated by
the spectacle of the glider before her." The participle "zooming" seems to refer to Jane. The words are unambiguous, but
ambiguity results from the manner in which they are put together.

A famous historical source of amphiboly is found in the Delphic oracle, in ancient Greece. The oracle was certainly the most astute diplomat who ever lived and also the Nostradamus of its time, except that, unlike Nostradamus, the oracular pronouncements were right 100 per cent of the time. This success was due to the use of amphiboly. The oracle was consulted on the eve of great undertakings, for knowledge as to success or failure. The oracle always retained its reputation for infallibility because of the manner in which it made its pronouncements: "Apollo says that the Greeks the Persians shall subdue." Cyrus, the Persian King, sent messengers to the oracle for a prophecy concerning a projected war. The messengers were informed that "the King yet lives that Cyrus shall depose." The variant interpretations of these statements are obvious.

Amphibolous sentences of the type just noted may be called *completely* amphibolous in that the reader does not know how to interpret them correctly. In most cases, though two or more interpretations are possible, it will generally appear that one interpretation is more reasonable than the others, either from the context or the customs of speech. Thus, when a law court is presented with an amphibolous document, the "reasonable" interpretation will be applied. For example, a licensing agreement between the holder of a patent and the manufacturer provided that the manufacturer would pay the patentee "50¢ a unit for producing 5000 units or less, and 30¢ a unit for all units of an output of over 5000 units." The manufacturer claimed that when the output exceeded 5000 units he was obligated to pay 30¢ per unit for *all* units produced. The court ruled that the agreement meant "50¢ for the first 5000 units and 30¢ for all units in excess of 5000." Otherwise the patentee would receive less royalties for a production of 6000 units than he would receive for 4000.

It is impossible to state whether a sentence is true or false until we understand its meaning. An amphibolous sentence must be given a definite interpretation before we can judge it as true or false. For example, a man says, "All women are not fickle." By this he may mean either that "some women are not fickle" or that "no women are fickle." If the speaker is available we should question him to determine what he meant. If he is not available, how shall we interpret the statement?

Note that the sentence takes the "All . . . are not . . ." formation. The logician adopts a rule of interpretation here, stating that all such statements shall be read as if they meant *"Not all* women are fickle" or "Some women are not fickle," unless he has clear evidence from the context or elsewhere that the speaker meant "No women are fickle." In the sentence "All human beings are not perfect" the speaker probably means "No human beings are perfect," but in "All Germans are not Nazis" he probably means "Some Germans are not Nazis."

Other types of amphiboly that require interpretation are such sentences as "All agree with me who are not ignorant of the facts." This may mean either "All persons who agree with me are persons who are not ignorant of the facts" or it may mean "All persons who are not ignorant of the facts are persons who agree with me." The speaker may mean either one, but in the absence of further evidence, the grammarian will adopt the latter interpretation as the more likely one.

3. Ambiguity in emphasis.

By this type we mean that a unit of discourse may make different kinds of sense depending upon which of its parts we accent or emphasize. We should always seek to give writings the emphasis which the author intended them to have, but when the writing is ambiguous in this respect, the reader may be unable to determine where the proper emphasis lies. The full and complete meaning of a sentence may even require that we hear it spoken. Thus the invitation "I hope that you will come to dinner" may accent "I," "you," or "dinner" when it is spoken. When you leave, you say, "The dinner was very good." You may accent "dinner." It is for this reason that classroom instruction is superior to mere reading for most students, since the instructor gives oral emphasis to the most important words.

Ambiguity of emphasis occurs when a reader does not know which parts of a writing deserve chief emphasis. Troublesome cases of this sort occur when a writer presents somewhat conflicting points of view, as in Book V of Plato's *Republic*, concerning the nature and status of women in his ideal state. The reader will find "equalitarian" remarks such as, "The only difference between men and women consists in the fact that women bear and that men beget children," and "Women do not differ from men in the kind of education they should receive, and there is nothing peculiar about women which would affect them so far as being executives of the state is involved." But elsewhere Plato says that "women are inferior to men in all pursuits followed by each." Again, that "men and women possess the same qualities and differ only in their comparative strength and weakness." Does Plato believe that women are essentially the same as men, or does he hold that the weaker sex is the inferior sex?

When summaries are made of writings, ambiguity of emphasis may create similar difficulties. The summarizer should emphasize the most important elements. When excerpts and quotes are given they should be truly representative of the author's meaning. Summaries, however, open the door to many errors of carelessness or deliberate misinterpretation, to be discussed further under the "fallacies of ambiguity." Book reviewers are often accused of "not having read the whole book" when the author thinks that his position has been misinterpreted. The reviewer's misinterpretation, however, may be due in whole or in part to the author's failure to make his points clear. Or the author may state somewhat conflicting positions, as in the selections from Plato's *Republic*.

A different type of problem concerning emphasis or "accent" occurs in problems of punctuation. Literary scholars seek to interpret Shakespeare's meanings accurately, but there are variant readings of many of the plays. The Folio and the Second Quarto editions, the oldest sources, differ in many important respects. Consider the different possible readings of Hamlet's speech to Guildenstern (II, 2, 315). The Neilson and Hill version of the speech, based upon the Quarto version, is stated as follows:

What a piece of work is a man! How noble in reason! How infinite in faculty! in form and moving! How express and admirable in action! How like an angel in apprehension! How like a god!

The Everyman's edition, following the Folio version, prints the lines as follows:

What a piece of work is a man! How noble in reason! how infinite in faculty! In form and moving how express and admirable!
in action how like an angel! in apprehension how like a god!

4. The ambiguity of significance.

The ambiguity of significance is not a genuinely semantical
problem, but it is convenient to deal with it at this point. By
this type we refer to statements whose semantical meaning may
be clear, but whose factual significance is not. As an illustration,
consider the statement that there were 141 deaths due to traffic
accidents in the United States during the Thanksgiving holiday
weekend in 1947. The significance of such a statement is ambiguous in many respects. An isolated fact means something, of
course. We all deplore the large number of deaths reported. But
its full significance would require knowing whether the number
was higher or lower than the number killed during the previous
year's holiday weekend, and whether the figures for a non-holi-
day weekend are higher or lower.

Many other examples of such ambiguous isolated statements
come to mind. "There are three million unemployed in the
United States." Up or down since last month? In comparison
with last year? What is the normal number of unemployed even
in periods of "full employment?" Many statements are ambiguous to the uninitiated though not to the well-informed.
"You have five billion germs in your mouth." What is the significance of that fact to a non-physiologist? In all the examples
cited we find statements whose referential meaning is unambiguous, but whose significance is subject to varying interpretations.

The significance of many statements is ambiguous until we
answer the questions: "Who said it?" and "under what circumstances?" In the fall of 1947 a United States congressman said,
"We will be at war with Russia in one month." Who was the
speaker? A responsible or an irresponsible talker? A criticism
of the policies of the federal administration should be judged
on its own merits, but in the absence of further evidence the
significance of the statement will depend upon whether or not
the speaker is generally considered to be a partisan for the op-

position. If the speaker is thought to be impartial, greater weight will be given to such criticism. In a law court great weight is given to statements which are called "admissions against one's own interest."

Another important distinction concerns the question as to whether a statement is being made in jest or in earnest. "Smile when you call me that" is a type of comment which emphasizes the ambiguity of significance. Persons whose humor is "dry" often make ironical or sarcastic statements that should not be interpreted literally.

An amusing example of the ambiguity of significance occurred when the late Heywood Broun, a wit among drama critics, once wrote that a certain actor, *J*, was "the world's worst 'actor.'" Broun was sued for libel and acquitted. Sometime later, *J* appeared in another play, and Broun, reporting the performance, wrote: "Mr. *J* was not up to his usual standard last night."

Section IV: The Fallacies of Ambiguity

Thus far we have noted four different types of ambiguity in words and sentences. Ambiguities arise for the following reasons: (a) Single words have more than one meaning; (b) the grammatical construction of a sentence permits more than one interpretation of its meaning; (c) we do not know how to accent or emphasize the words in a sentence or the important parts of a unit of discourse; and (d) we do not know the significance of a statement. When ambiguity exists, the careful reader should be aware of this fact. He should seek further information and ask the appropriate questions in order to interpret the statements correctly.

By "fallacies" of ambiguity, we refer to cases where the speaker or reader fails to recognize the existence of ambiguity, and draws unwarranted conclusions because of this neglect. These errors occur either in use or interpretation. The speaker may use ambiguous words in an illegitimate manner; the hearer may incorrectly interpret a speaker because of failure to note the existence of ambiguity. We shall now consider the errors arising from the various types of ambiguity.

1. Equivocation.

This is an error involving the use of ambiguous words. Equivocation means the use of an ambiguous word (or root, or phrase) in more than one sense in a given unit of discourse. Equivocation often results in errors of reasoning, leading to unjustified inferences, and it must be carefully guarded against. (This error will be considered again under the title "four-term fallacy" in our analysis of the syllogism.)

Some examples: If we were to argue that Miss Jones is a long-legged bird because all secretaries are long-legged birds and she is a secretary, we would commit the fallacy of equivocation. "Secretary" is used in two different senses. The same error may occur in a less obvious manner. Thus, a preacher argued that the existence of laws of nature proves that there is a God, for all laws imply the existence of a law-giver. The word "law" is used equivocally here. In "laws of nature" law means "a description of the uniform behavior of natural events." In the second sense it refers to "commands issued by a governing body." A law-giver is necessary in order to have civil laws, which are prescriptive or commanding. But scientists use the term "law of nature" in a purely descriptive sense having no relation to commands. This use of the term "law" in two senses in a single unit of discourse is called an equivocal usage. When an ambiguous word is used only once, the fallacy is simple ambiguity.

Equivocation may of course be used deliberately for the purposes of wit and humor. "Your argument is sound, nothing but sound." Thus Benjamin Franklin's pun, "If we don't hang together, we'll hang separately." Or the absurd syllogism, "Some dogs have shaggy ears. My dog has shaggy ears. Therefore, my dog is *some* dog."

Equivocation must be avoided in serious argument. We must use our words with the same meaning in all cases. If we do not use our words consistently there can be no communication or reasoning.

2. Accent.

"Accent" is an error which results from giving an obviously improper accent or emphasis to the words in a sentence or to the ideas in a unit of discourse. It usually occurs when units of discourse are ambiguous, for variant interpretations are then likely. Misinterpretations of ambiguous remarks may of course occur honestly, as through carelessness, or they may be deliberate, with the intent of distorting the meaning of a writing. We shall note three typical ways in which the fallacy occurs:

a. The incorrect emphasis of the words in a sentence.

The commandment says, "Thou shalt not bear false witness against thy neighbor."

If one were to stress the word "neighbor," implying that it is permissible to bear false witness against those who are not our neighbors, this would be an obvious misinterpretation.

b. The incorrect interpretation of amphibolous sentences.

If one were to interpret the example given earlier as meaning that *Jane* was zooming along under her own power, the amphibolous sentence would be misinterpreted.

c. Incorrect summaries.

When a summary is made of an author's statements, it should stress the most important elements. When a unit of discourse is improperly summarized, the fault may lie with the author, whose meaning was not clear. On the other hand, the summarizer may distort the author's meaning either carelessly or with the intent to deceive. We shall now examine some of the forms in which this type of accent occurs.

The first form to be noted here is what we shall call "excerpt-lifting." Dishonest examples of excerpt-lifting abound. A dramatic critic writes that he "liked all of the play except the lines, the acting, and the scenery." He is quoted as having said that "he liked all of it." Ironical remarks are always open to this kind of misinterpretation. A schoolteacher tells her civics class that "communism is the best type of government if you care nothing for your liberty or your material welfare." She is quoted as having said that "communism is the best type of government." Unwitting errors of the same sort occur when a student fails to distinguish between a lecturer's own views and those which he quotes, or even between a speaker's own views and those which he attacks.

The careful thinker will always be on his guard against quotations taken out of their context and he will ask, "Let's have the whole of that quotation." This does not mean that quotations are improper, but only that quotations should be fair and accurate representations of the meaning of the author.

Newspaper headlines purportedly summarize the news, but may distort the meaning by improper emphasis. The "headline reader" is thereby misled. "Let me write the headlines," an editor once said, "and I care not who writes the news." Advertisements may achieve similar results by the use of large case type in bold letters. The "come-on" elements will be presented in large letters, and the less attractive ones will be minimized by the use of small type. A famous example is one that was used by Barnum to advertise the first Canadian concert of the Belgian violinist Ysaye. It read,

THEIR EXCELLENCIES,
THE PRINCE AND PRINCESS OF BELGIUM
have been asked whether they
WILL ATTEND THE CONCERT OF YSAYE,
WORLD'S GREATEST VIOLINIST

A form of summary called "special pleading" or "stacking the cards" is perhaps of greatest importance in this connection. Speakers emphasize only those elements in a report which suit their purposes and omit the rest. This may be permissible practice for debaters and lawyers who seek to win a case, but it is not in the spirit of the seeker after truth. Thus a speaker on a town-hall radio program reported that the conservatives in the British Parliament "stood up and cheered" when they were informed that the British army in India had killed 500 Indians. The hearer's reaction would normally be that these conservatives were ghouls. Another speaker on the same program then read the full report of the incident, taken from the Parliamentary reports. It then appeared that there had been deaths on both sides during rioting, that 500 Indians had been killed, that the government intended to preserve law and order at all costs. (Cheers from conservative benches.)

Accent, of course, is sometimes a fruitful source of humor

when the incorrect interpretation of accent or emphasis is deliberate. Thus, Humpty-Dumpty says to Alice: "They gave it
me—for an unbirthday present." "I beg your pardon?" Alice
said with a puzzled air. "I'm not offended," said Humpty-
Dumpty.

Another: "Would you—be good enough"—Alice panted
out, after running a little farther, "to stop a minute—just to get
—one's breath again?" "I'm *good* enough," the King said, "only
I'm not strong enough. You see, a minute goes by so fearfully
quick. You might as well try to catch a bandersnatch!"

Exercises

A. *Simple Ambiguity.*

 1. Find seven different senses of the words "right," "good," and
    "fast."
 2. Find the important ambiguous words in the following sen-
    tences. State two different senses in which the word might be
    understood. Also show how each question might be answered
    "Yes" and "No."
    a. Were the early Christians communists?
    b. The OPA was inconsistent with the American way of do-
       ing things.
    c. Will Hitler be regarded as a great historical figure by
       future historians?
    d. Is the inside of a ripe watermelon red before it is opened?
    e. Thomas Jefferson said that he hoped we would have a
       revolution every 20 years.
    f. Which Americans are "un-American"?
    g. A cub reporter was assigned to report a social gathering.
       "Among the most beautiful young ladies present," he
       wrote, "was our genial mayor, J. S. Zipf." When asked to
       explain, he insisted, "Well, that's where he was."
    h.
       "Beauty is truth, truth beauty,—that is all
       Ye know on earth, and all ye need to know." (Keats.)
 3. Which type of simple ambiguity is found in the following?

    Here the Red Queen began again. "Can you answer useful
    questions?" she said. "How is bread made?"
    "I know that!" Alice cried eagerly. "You take some flour—."
    "Where do you pick the flower?" the White Queen asked.
    "In a garden or in the hedges?"

"Well, it isn't picked at all," Alice explained, "it's ground—."
"How many acres of ground?" asked the White Queen. "You
mustn't leave out so many things." (Lewis Carroll, *Through
the Looking Glass,* Ch. IX.)

4. Discuss the following items involving simple ambiguity:
   a. The cartoonist Mauldin pictured two senators in con-
      versation. One asked the other, "Senator, when you speak
      of the American way do you mean *your* American way or
      mine?"
   b. A speaker at a meeting of philosophers stated that he had
      found that every philosopher who uses the words God and
      Religion means something different from what other phi-
      losophers mean. But, he argued, this was quite proper,
      since every person who uses these words actually does
      mean something different from what other people mean.

B. *Amphiboly.*

Point out the different senses in which the following examples
may be interpreted. Which interpretation appears most reasonable?

1. All men are not evil.
2. "Where never is heard a discouraging word, and the skies
   are not cloudy all day."
3. "Hercules the dragon will slay."
4. Wanted: Young girls to sew lace trimmings on the eleventh
   floor.
5. After the general watched the lion perform, he was taken to
   the city hall and fed 25 pounds of meat before a large
   crowd.
6. While we were eating a young man the son of the proprietor came in.
7. "I shall lose no time in reading your manuscript."
8. Serve the meat when thoroughly stewed.
9. Newspaper headlines:

U. S. MISSIONARY	HALT WORK ON
HELD BY JAPS IN	FILM TO HONOR
HONG KONG SAFE	U. S. WAR HEROES

10. All are prejudiced who know only one side of the facts.
11. A *Chicago Daily News* sportswriter wrote that Jim Jeffries,
    in Hollywood to make a movie, was asked, "I say, Jeff, do
    you think you could whip Joe Louis?" "Son," answered Jim
    slowly, "I've whipped better men than Joe Louis." "And
    right here," said the writer, "came the argument. Did the
    old boilermaker mean that he had whipped better men
    than Joe Louis IS or than he HAS whipped?"

12. How much is 3 times 2 plus 4?
13. An insurance policy read, "This policy shall be incontest-
    able on no grounds other than non-payment of premiums."
14. "I haven't got none."
15. In a lease given by White to Smith, Robinson guaranteed
    that Smith would fulfill his obligations, in the following
    document: "I hereby bind myself to White for the true and
    faithful performance of the agreement on the part of Smith
    in case Smith should die within three years I agree to pay
    up to that time and deliver the property to White as above
    stated."
16. From Kant's *Fundamental Principles of the Metaphysic of
    Morals*:

    In this manner, then, results a harmony like that which a
    certain satirical poem depicts as existing between a married
    couple bent on going to ruin, "O, marvellous harmony,
    what he wishes, she wishes also"; or like . . . the pledge
    of Francis I to the Emperor Charles V, "What my brother
    Charles wishes, that I wish also (viz. Milan)."

C. *Ambiguity in Emphasis.*

Note the manner in which the following items may take on different meanings when we accent different words, by punctuation or
otherwise:

1. Woman without her man is a beast.
2. From the collegiate magazine, *Ohio State Sundial* (quoted in
   Time, Nov. 11, 1946.):
   HE: I suppose you dance?
   SHE: Oh, yes, I love to.
   HE: Great! That's better than dancing.
3. In an English class, the teacher was explaining the use of the
   past perfect tense in "had had." An exercise was given to
   John and Jim involving the use of "had" and "had had."
   The result: "John where Jim had had had had had had had
   had had had had the teacher's approval." Interpret the sentence by supplying the proper punctuation marks in order to
   give it sense.
4. Nothing is too good for you.
5. The Elizabethan translators of the Bible always italicized
   words which the translators added to the text in order to
   make the text clear. In I Kings, 13:27 we find the following:
   "And he spake unto his sons, saying, Saddle me the ass. And
   they saddled *him*."

D. *The Ambiguity of Significance.*

    1. John L. Lewis ordered all mines closed in 1947 because of unsafe conditions. He later sent the following telegram to all of the union's district presidents: "I confirm policy of immediate resumption of production at each mine as fast as it is certified by federal mine inspectors as being in conformity with the federal mine safety code." What is the significance of the word "immediate?"

    2. You will find that British statesmen always put the interests of England first.

    3. Department store sales in dollars are ten per cent higher than last year for the same month.

    4. Congressman X said, "The Marshall Plan will not work."

    5. The colonel was not drunk today.

E. *Equivocation.*

In the following examples, find the ambiguous word which is used twice in two different senses, and state the two senses in which that word (or root) is used:

    1. Those were the days when men were men.

    2. Business is business.

    3. The maintenance of a nuisance is, of course, a crime. Now, Junior is a little "nuisance." Therefore his maintenance is a small crime.

    4. It is not right for a poor man to expect help from his rich brother, since he has no right to compel his brother to give him such help.

    5. Since tall carpenters are tall men, it follows that good carpenters are good men.

    6. A crust of bread is better than nothing. Do you also agree that nothing is better than true love? Then you must agree that a crust of bread is better than true love.

    7. No news is good news. Strikes and lockouts are no news. Therefore, strikes and lockouts are good news.

    8. The civil law is often distinguished from the common law, and civil law is often distinguished from criminal law.

    9. "You are inconsistent," protested a member of a jury to the foreman. "Yesterday you told me that there was a presumption of this man's guilt, but now, when I say that we may presume that he is guilty, you contradict me." (A. Castell, *A College Logic.* Copyright 1935 by A. Castell. Used with the permission of The Macmillan Company.)

    10. "In the United States we have political freedom; in Russia

they have economic freedom. The United States should
move toward Russia's economic freedom and Russia should
move toward our political freedom." (Henry A. Wallace)

F. *The Fallacy of Accent.*

1. A whiskey is widely advertised under the name BONNIE
   ANGUS, A BLEND. The law requires that the label state an
   analysis of the contents. This reads: "ALL THE WHISKIES
   IN THIS BOTTLE ARE AT LEAST 5 YEARS OLD. 38%
   whisky, 72% neutral spirits."
2. Plato said that women are always inferior to men.
3. In an article entitled "The Ethical Teachings of Jesus,"
   which appeared in the *Outlook,* in 1910, Dr. Lyman Abbott,
   pastor and publicist, argued as follows to prove that Christianity is not hostile to the rich man:

   My radical friend declares that the teachings of Jesus are not
   practicable, that we cannot carry them out in life, and that
   we do not pretend to do so. Jesus, he reminds us, said, "Lay
   not up for yourselves treasures upon earth;" and Christians
   do universally lay up for themselves treasures upon earth;
   every man that owns a house and lot, or a share of stock in
   a corporation, or a life insurance policy, or money in a savings bank, has laid up for himself treasures upon earth. But
   Jesus did not say, "Lay not up for yourselves treasures upon
   earth." He said, "Lay not up for yourselves treasures upon
   earth *where moth and rust doth corrupt and where thieves
   break through and steal."* And no sensible American does.
   Moth and rust do not get at Mr. Rockefeller's oil wells, nor
   at the Sugar Trust's sugar, and thieves do not often break
   through and steal a railway or an insurance company or a
   savings bank. What Jesus condemned was hoarding wealth.
   (Reported by Upton Sinclair in *The Profits of Religion.)*

4. A newspaper headline:

   ### ATOMIC WAR
   unlikely says senator

5. Lawyer, to witness on the stand: "Oh, so you *say* you were
   not there, do you?"
6. In the following example, indicate how the fallacy of accent
   might be committed in a professor's remark to a student:
   "Your thesis is both good and original. Unfortunately, the
   original things in it are no good, and the good things are not
   original."

Chapter 4

THE USES OF LANGUAGE

Section I: Neutral, Emotive, and Directive Words

In Chapter 2 we examined the manner in which words act as symbols for referents. The types of referents symbolized by words are things, ideas, states of mind, emotions, relations, attributes of things, and activities. Whenever referents are referred to, symbols are used in a "cognitive" or "referential" manner, i.e., the mind is "directed" to a referent. Words are used in this manner whenever we wish to communicate information to others. But the communication of information is not the only purpose for which human beings use language. Language is also used to evoke emotional attitudes and feelings and to direct the activities of others.

With rare exceptions all words symbolize referents in the "cognitive" manner. But in addition to such references the speaker may wish to express his own emotional attitudes, to arouse the emotional attitudes of others and to get others to act in a certain way. We shall therefore speak of the three uses or purposes of language: the informational use, the expressive use, and the directive (or practical) use. (The expressive use has two aspects, the expression of the feelings of the speaker and the evocation of feelings in the hearer.)

Words thus have three functions. They are symbols which point to referents. But they may do more than that. "To close" refers to an activity. But when the verb is used in its imperative sense, as in "Close the window," it calls forth activity on the part of others and becomes a "directive" word as well as a referential one. Similarly, some words may stir emotional attitudes in the hearer. The word "kiss," for example. This word is a symbol for an activity, the act of osculation, whereby two persons salute each other mutually by the touching of the lips. But in addition to its referential function, the word may stir an emotional attitude in the reader. When words have the purely (or almost purely) cognitive or intellectual function, we shall call them neutral symbols. When they stir emotional attitudes we shall call them emotive symbols. Directives form a third group.

Whether a word has a neutral or emotive significance to a hearer (or speaker) depends upon the past experiences of the individual. The word "moon" has a neutral meaning to an astronomer, an emotive meaning to a lover. "Sex" has a neutral meaning to a biologist, an emotive meaning to an adolescent. The distinction is a relative one, depending upon the particular experiences of the individual. A word may be neutral to an individual in one context, emotive in another; neutral at one time and emotive at a later time. "Bread" was a neutral word for Frenchmen before 1940; an emotive word in 1945. These individual associations with words are the basis for the "word-association" tests used by criminologists in crime detection. Words associated with the crime will arouse emotional responses in the guilty person, whereas they will be neutral to the innocent.

Thus words are "neutral" or "emotive" depending upon the effects which they have on us, not because of characteristics inherent in the words themselves. Nevertheless, since there are large areas of experience shared by most human beings within a group, we can reasonably presuppose that *some* words will tend to arouse emotional responses in the hearers. "Pencil" and "paper" are neutral words to most persons, but words such as "God," "atheist," "love," "Red," and "Fascist" will be emotive. These emotive words arouse attitudes of "for" and "against," approval or disapproval.

The importance of context should also be emphasized. When a political scientist writes that "Caesar aspired to be dictator" or "Mussolini was the dictator of Italy," the word "dictator" has a primarily neutral significance, though emotional overtones may not be altogether absent. But when a well-known Chicago newspaper constantly referred to Franklin Delano Roosevelt as a "dictator," the word had a primarily emotive significance.

The newspaper sought to arouse the feelings of fear and hatred in the reader. In order to know whether a word has a neutral or an emotive significance for a speaker, we must know something about his background, intention, and purposes.

Section II: The Three Purposes of Discourse

The major uses of language are the informational, expressive, and directive. We speak in order to inform others ("The diameter of Betelgeuse, the largest star, is 300 times that of the sun." "Jane left for Florida yesterday.") We speak to express our feelings ("Great!" "Bravo!" "The dirty dog!") or to affect the feelings of others, as in tales of horror, or in poetic lines such as "Comes the blind Fury with the abhorrèd shears, and slits the thin-spun life." Finally, we speak in order to influence the actions of others. ("Do unto others as you would have others do unto you." "Man the guns!") All of these uses are indispensable in communication. Man is a rational animal, but a large part of his speech and thought is concerned with nonrational matters. In our social relations we greet people with conventional expressions, we tell anecdotes to amuse our friends, and we state our feelings of approval and disapproval for a host of things and activities.

It is doubtful whether any person uses language in a manner which exemplifies only one of the purposes noted. Our purposes usually are mixed. Consider the sentence, "Capitalism is a horrible conspiracy to exploit the workers and to grind the faces of the poor." Assuming that the speaker sincerely means what he says, we shall find all of the uses of language in this unit of discourse. The speaker wishes to inform his hearers that capitalism has certain effects on the lives of human beings. (His language is, of course, ill-adapted to its informative purpose.) The sentence is also expressive. We detect that the speaker is emotionally moved by the "crimes" of capitalism; his sentence is a kind of agonized cry. The words are also intended to affect the feelings of the hearer so that he will sympathize with the victims. Finally, the speaker has a directive purpose in mind. He wishes to move the hearer emotionally so that the hearer will do something about the plight of the workers and the poor.

With this reminder that all the uses of language may be found in a single unit of discourse, we turn to a detailed examination of the purposes of discourse. Though language is mixed, the mixture is made up of distinguishable elements.

1. The informative purpose of discourse.

The desire to inform others concerning facts, i.e., that something is or is not the case, is obviously a major purpose of communication. Little comment will be required, except to note the types of words which best fulfill this function of discourse. If it is one's purpose to inform others concerning facts, neutral words * will be most appropriate, since emotive words * may arouse the reader's emotions and interfere with his understanding of the facts. Emotion tends to distort the judgment; it is also a highly individual factor and emotive words may affect different hearers in different ways. In the ideal type of scientific discourse, then, emotive words will be eliminated insofar as this is possible. It would be impossible, however, to dispense with all words having emotional significance for readers of books on contemporary political issues, for many key words will inevitably arouse emotions in some readers. Vague emotive terms such as "reactionary" should be avoided, and words like "communism" should of course be used with great caution. But since some persons *are* communists, it is merely a matter of pure information to call them such, even though the word is also an emotive one for many readers.

The speaker who desires to inform will also avoid "question-begging" epithets, by which we mean words which prejudge facts, or take disputed conclusions for granted. An example of this occurs when we refer to an accused person as "that criminal" before he has been proved guilty. Good informative language will be made up of statements which are readily verifiable. This point is constantly applied in courts of law. If a witness states that an injured man "has not walked normally since the accident," an objection will be raised to the use of the word "normal." The witness should describe the facts, the exact manner in which the injured man walks. "Not normal" pre-

* That is, words that would be typically considered as such.

judges the issue; testimony should describe facts on which the jury may base its own judgments.

2. The expressive purpose of language.

Language may be used to express one's own feelings or to affect the feelings of others, or both. The presence of neutral or emotive words, however, is not a reliable indicator of the purpose of the speaker. The fact that a speaker uses such emotive words does not prove that he is expressing his own feelings or that he desires to affect the feelings of others; contrariwise, he may use neutral words that are likely to stir emotion. We are presently concerned with the *purpose* we call expressive, and not with emotive words as such.

a. The desire to express one's own feelings.

We use language in spontaneous expressions of feeling, as in "Ouch!" "Damn!" or the groan of the patient in the dentist's chair. Profanity furnishes many examples of this use of language, from its mild damns to its roaring expletives. Astonishment is spontaneously expressed in words like "Bro-ther!" Frequently the use of language in this manner appears to be without the intent to communicate anything to others. But when we say "How terrible!" or "How perfectly divine!" we not only express our own feelings, but we also indicate that the referent has a certain valuable or disvaluable quality. We thus communicate some information, even though very little.

We may also note a type of expression which appears to be "talk for talk's sake," a kind of perpetual motion of the larynx. Some people may talk just to "let off steam" or "to get a load off their chests." Such expression of feelings has a practical value in acting as a safety valve for pent-up emotions. The Catholic confessional and the session in the office of the psychiatrist may make use of this type of expression for therapeutic purposes.

The presence of the self-expressive purpose of language is not always obvious. A good deal of poetry is written for self-expression, and so also are many sentences written by critics of poetry, as in the rhapsody,

Each poet, from Homer to our own day, has been to some extent and at some point, the voice of the movement and energy of poetry; in him poetry has for the moment become visible, audible, incarnate, and his extant poems are the record left of that partial and transitory incarnation. (Mackail, *Lectures on Poetry*.)

The writer is expressing his feelings in these remarks, in addition to whatever other purpose we may find. Frequently, too, we find writers who fall in love with words and use them because of the emotional satisfaction derived from their use. Goethe, in discussing free will, said, "The word 'freedom' sounds so beautiful, that we cannot do without it, even though it should designate an error."

b. The desire to affect the feelings of others.

Various motives are included within this aspect of expressiveness. We may seek sympathy from the hearer or to have him share in our gladness. We may seek to stir his emotions as a means to a practical end, with an ultimate directive purpose in mind. This very important use of expressive language will be more fully dealt with under the "directive" purpose. Another very important use of this aspect of expressive language is the "poetic use," which we shall use in a broad sense as referring to the creation of literary works for artistic purposes. The poet's primary purpose is to convey an experience to the reader which will be enjoyed for its own sake. It is not the poet's primary aim to instruct us through the communication of information or to move us emotionally so that we will act, but to affect our feelings, attitudes, intelligence, and imagination in such a manner that we will live through an enriching experience.

We must remember that the purposes of discourse are never pure and rarely simple. The poet may also communicate information and he may also arouse our desire to correct social maladjustments, as in Steinbeck's *Grapes of Wrath*. But unless he succeeds in what we have called the poetic function of language, his work will be a tract, and not a poem.

We must repeat again that though some words are most appropriate for a particular purpose of language, this is not a "one-to-one" relationship; that is, types of words and the purposes of discourse are not correlated as a button is correlated with a buttonhole. The poet does not necessarily use a "poetic" language. In the past, of course, academicians sometimes promulgated rules concerning the kinds of words they considered admissible in poetry. To cite one example, in France, during the 1820's, only "noble" words were considered appropriate in poetry. Lytton Strachey (*Landmarks in French Literature*) states that the use of the common word *mouchoir* (handkerchief) actually produced a riot in Paris during a performance of *Othello*. But the idea is still prevalent that poetry uses only emotive words. Since the poet seeks to evoke feelings and attitudes, he will usually make liberal use of emotive words, and such use is appropriate. Consider, for example, the following experiment by Thouless (*How to Think Straight,* Simon & Schuster, 1939). Thouless took the lines from Keats' "Eve of St. Agnes,"

> Full on this casement shone the wintry moon,
> And threw warm gules on Madeline's fair breast,

and rewrote them, substituting neutral words for the emotive ones, to read,

> Full on this window shone the wintry moon,
> Making red marks on Jane's uncolored chest.

Thouless triumphantly noted that the poetic effect disappeared. But his lines are a parody. It is simply not true that poetry *must* use "poetic" words. Robert Frost writes poems containing an unusual amount of neutral words, as in the first lines of "The Death of the Hired Man" (*Complete Poems of Robert Frost,* Henry Holt and Company, 1949):

> Mary sat musing on the lamp flame at the table
> Waiting for Warren. When she heard his step,
> She ran on tiptoe down the darkened passage
> To meet him in the doorway with the news
> And put him on his guard. "Silas is back."

The poet aims at an effect in the mind of the reader. If he achieves his aim he has created a poem.

3. The directive purpose of language.

The directive purpose refers to a speaker's desire to arouse others to action. To this end he may use the type of words we have called "directives," such as verbs in the imperative mode. Thus: "Vote for Zipf!" "Live dangerously!" "Workers of the world, unite!" But the directive purpose may be present without the use of such directives, or "motivators." Frequently, the speaker who wishes to get others to act will choose to accomplish his purpose in a more subtle manner, for fear that a direct appeal may cause suspicion or resentment. Every parent has used the method of suggestion rather than direct appeal to get action from a small child: "Now, you wouldn't want . . . would you?" But the readiest manner in which speakers get individuals to act without the use of motivators is through an appeal to the emotions. Psychologically, a very close connection is found between our emotions and our tendencies to act, since all emotions tend to seek fulfillment in action. Love and hate make us want to do something. Our resentment against injustice or what we conceive to be injustice stimulates us to take up arms against it. The speaker who wishes action will thus seek to stir emotions as an indirect means of achieving his purpose.

A classical example of the manner in which emotive language is used to stir action is found in Mark Antony's funeral oration in Shakespeare's *Julius Caesar*. A short selection from the oration will suffice:

> If you have tears, prepare to shed them now.
> You all do know this mantle: I remember
> The first time ever Caesar put it on;
> 'Twas on a summer's evening, in his tent,
> That day he overcame the Nervii:
> Look, in this place ran Cassius' dagger through:
> See what a rent the envious Casca made:
> Through this the well-beloved Brutus stabb'd;
> And as he pluck'd his cursed steel away,
> Mark how the blood of Caesar follow'd it,
> As rushing out of doors, to be resolved
> If Brutus so unkindly knock'd, or no;
> For Brutus, as you know, was Caesar's angel:
> Judge, O you Gods, how dearly Caesar loved him!
> This was the most unkindest cut of all.

The Roman mob finally leaves Antony, resolved to wreak their vengeance on the traitors who stabbed their beloved Caesar, whom they had previously suspected of the desire to become a dictator over them.

Emotive words and the expressive use of language are thus well adapted to stirring emotion which results in action. But neutral words and the informative use of language may also stir emotional attitudes which lead to action. A prospectus which states that "thousands of your fellow-Americans are making thousands of dollars each year raising minks" will stir the emotion of cupidity and lead to investment of one's savings. "The X nation is mobilizing its troops" is informative, but will stir action. The lack of correlation between the language used and the purposes of the speaker may be illustrated by examining the sentence: "Here comes a lion." A circus attendant might use the words to convey information; uttered by a child, the words might express delighted rapture; but if the lion had just escaped from its cage, the words would direct us to take cover.

The importance of emotion-stirring words in directing action is revealed very interestingly in *The Fine Art of Propaganda* (Harcourt, Brace & Co., 1937), by The Institute for Propaganda Analysis. The writers attempted to classify the devices and techniques of the propagandist, who seeks to influence the actions of others. Among the emotion-stirring devices listed were the following:

Name calling: the use of "bad names" attached to individuals or groups, such as "Red," "Fascist," "radical," and "reactionary." These words usually stir emotions of dislike and hatred and result in action against those so referred to.

Glittering generalities: the use of "virtue words" or phrases such as "the American Way," "our Christian civilization," "the family is the bulwark of the nation," and "Uncle Sam." When these honorific slogans are attached to individuals and groups, we tend to act favorably toward them.

Testimonials: the fact that "important people" approve of a program will stir the attitude of reverence and imitation. Contrariwise, the fact that "bad people" are for or against a program will stir feelings of aversion and result in action contrary to theirs.

Plain folks: the speaker talks to us as if he were one of us common people, "just an ordinary Joe," even as you and I. We trust him; he has aroused the sentiment of brotherhood within us. We act as he suggests.

Band wagon: "Everybody else is with us, why not you?" Man is a gregarious animal and hates to be apart from the crowd. We hop on the band wagon.

Ceremonial language is another form of directive language. Greetings such as "Nice day," "Foul weather, isn't it?" or "Pleased to meet you" are not necessarily spoken to convey information. Social intercourse requires the use of language rituals, and we utter ceremonial phrases in order to establish a friendly attitude in the person spoken to. Feelings of communion are stirred, leading to the type of action desired.

We may note finally that directive language may be used in order to *prevent* action. Just as emotive words may arouse an emotional attitude toward "neutral" events, so "neutral" language may create an attitude of indifference toward events which would normally stir strong feelings within us. Apologists for foul deeds customarily use this type of language. They tell us not to believe in "atrocity" stories, which, they claim, are "nothing but propaganda." But the atrocities may really exist, and the reader may thus fall a victim to "propaganda against propaganda."

Section III: Appropriate and Inappropriate Language

We have distinguished the uses of language and have noted that most discourse is mixed. Each type of usage is a legitimate one—in its proper place. Poetry, eloquence, ringing calls to action, and eulogies have their honored and legitimate places in discourse, and no sensible person will wish to disparage the use of emotive words in these fields. As logicians, however, it is important that we should know what we are doing and even more important that we should know what others are doing when they speak to us. We shall now examine some "misuses" of language, by which we mean the use of inappropriate language within the specific context. When we are interested in receiving information, we want facts and not an emotional harangue. To use emotive language in a scientific discourse is a misuse of language, as would be a technical explanation of chlorophyll in a poem about daffodils.

When a biologist reads a report of an experiment, he wishes the unvarnished truth, facts without emotional coloration. When the same biologist attends a rally of his political party he is willing that his emotions should be stirred with respect to social programs and ideals. Action requires emotional motivation, for purely thinking beings would probably make no distinctions between good and evil. When the biologist opens his morning newspaper, and reads about a recent strike, about conditions in Europe, or a discussion of election issues, does he desire information or emotional stimulation? Obviously, in order to act intelligently, he must know what the facts are. A newspaper editor may quite legitimately express his own opinions about national policies, but he should give his readers the facts in neutral language so that the reader will be adequately informed. The same considerations hold when we listen to a political speech. The political speaker is quite naturally a partisan for a point of view. But if he is worth listening to, if he expects to convince men of good will who want to make intelligent decisions, he should present facts on which to base such decisions. But the actual state of affairs is well described in the following:

Overstatement, understatement, half-truths, distorted logic, innuendo, and sheer intellectual dishonesty characterize the utterances of far too many of our public men. They bandy opprobrious terms about, in describing each other. This juvenile penchant of many American public men serves, upon analysis, to demonstrate the contempt in which they hold the electorate. It is not sufficient, for their purposes, that the electorate be informed fully and correctly, and then permitted to draw its own conclusions . . . They seek to inflame rather than to inform. They seek to excite passion rather than reason. They appeal to fear instead of intelligence. And, in so doing, they evidence a contempt for the body politic and its ability to understand the issues of the day. (Milburn P. Akers, the *Chicago Sun-Times*.)

As samples of inappropriate language let us examine the two following news items:

Renewing Republican demands for a congressional investigation of our occupation program, Senator C today accused the administration of inflicting a "deliberate policy of mass starvation" upon Germany, without distinction as to age, guilt or innocence. The policies we have pursued, the senator asserted, have "degenerated into the callous and inhuman practices of the Nazis themselves" . . . Senator C attributed the starvation policy to a "conspiratorial clique" of "vengeful fanatics" in the administration who formulated the Morgenthau plan to impose a Carthaginian peace upon Germany.

The Virginia vigilantes tried to lynch labor in the House again last week. For one bad moment it seemed that they might get away with it. They didn't. But in the effort they identified some of the men and forces willing to join their mob. The *New York Times,* for instance, was right out in front holding the rope . . . indeed, the daily press was almost all there. So was Southern democracy . . . Representative Howard W. Smith, Virginia banker and axe man for the Byrd machine, was, as usual, the instigator.

The reader's reaction to these passages will of course be influenced by whether or not he considers the statements *true.* Though it is easier to detect faults when we disagree with the speaker, the candid reader will recognize, nevertheless, that both of these selections use very intemperate language. Note the question-begging epithets which do not furnish the facts on which the conclusions are based, such as "starvation policy," "tried to lynch labor." Note the emotionally toned words: "degenerated," "vengeful fanatics," "lynch," "mob," and "axeman." These words are calculated to arouse fear and hatred in the reader. There is very little information; the reader has only a vague idea as to what events are taking place. An intelligent citizen demands facts on which to base his decisions and attitudes. Even though one's sympathies are with labor, he should object to such items as the second sample, for only knowledge of the facts will enable one to successfully meet unfair criticisms of labor's position. These examples are flagrant misuses of emotive language in situations in which statements of fact are required.

An opposite type of inappropriateness that we touched on earlier consists in writing in a detached, cool, objective, "scientific" manner to gloss over unpleasant facts. George Orwell has noted some typical words in such writings:

Defenseless villages are bombarded from the air, the inhabitants driven out into the countryside, the cattle machine-gunned, the huts set on fire with incendiary bullets: this is called *pacification*. Millions of peasants are robbed of their farms and sent trudging along the roads with no more than they can carry: this is called *transfer of population* or *rectification of frontiers*. People are imprisoned for years without trial, or shot in the back of the neck or sent to die of scurvy in Arctic lumber camps: this is called *elimination of unreliable elements*. ("Politics and the English Language," *New Republic*, June 24, 1946.)

Section IV: The Logical and the Non-Logical Uses of Language

1. The truth values of sentences.

The logician is interested in language with respect to its "truth-values," i.e., he is interested in statements insofar as they are true or false. A statement is true or false in the logical sense when it is capable of being verified or disproved by evidence. Not all statements are true or false in this sense, nor do speakers always seek to make "truth-value" statements. Poetic utterances are obvious examples of statements to which the criteria of truth and falsity in a logical sense may be irrelevant. The poet may use metaphorical language which has "poetic truth" (i.e., adequacy in terms of feelings and attitudes), but not literal truth. To examine poetic utterances as if they were intended to be literally true is a gross misinterpretation of the poet's purpose. This error is a common reason for the inability of many persons to appreciate and enjoy poetry. Thus, when Wordsworth writes, "The river glideth of its own sweet will," his statement is not false; scientific truth is irrelevant. When Shelley writes of the skylark,

> Hail to thee, blithe spirit,
> Bird thou never wert,

"he did not really mean to deny that the lark belongs to the class Aves," as it has been well remarked. When Macbeth said "Life is a tale told by an idiot, full of sound and fury, signifying nothing," his statement must not be interpreted literally, though it does contain a profound judgment concerning life and is, in a sense, verifiable. One should therefore not read poetry for a collection of informative sentences. One may find true statements in poetry, but the reader who picks up Wordsworth's "I Wandered Lonely as a Cloud" for botanical knowledge concerning daffodils would be sadly mistaking the poet's purpose. A poem is not a proposition, but an experience.

The logician is interested in language insofar as it states propositions, i.e., statements which are either true or false. The grammarian tells us that there are four types of sentences, declarative, interrogative, imperative, and exclamatory. Obviously, ordinary questions are neither true nor false, nor are imperatives, or commands. Thus, neither "Is the window open?" nor "Close the window" make statements which are true or false. Declarative and exclamatory sentences, on the other hand, *may* be propositions. Poetic utterances of the types noted above are declarative sentences which are not propositions. A declarative sentence is a proposition when it states that something is or is not the case, in a manner verifiable by factual evidence. Exclamatory sentences such as "The Cubs won!" and "How rapidly he played that difficult passage!" are obviously sentences which make statements concerning facts, in addition to expressing the satisfaction and amazement of the speaker.

Though questions and commands are not propositions, further analysis is required. What are usually called "rhetorical questions" are not questions at all, but concealed statements. For example, when a speaker says, "What's the world coming to, anyway?" he is not requesting information, but saying, "The world is in really bad shape." Questions may also carry *concealed assumptions* that certain facts actually exist, and these questions thus imply the truth of certain propositions. Such questions are called "complex questions." For example, during a trial the prosecuting attorney snapped, "Tell me sir, have you stopped beating your wife? Answer yes or no!" The question assumes that the witness has been beating his wife, and a yes-or-no answer would acknowledge the truth of this assumption. If the witness had never beaten his wife, then the question is illegitimate. Complex questions assume that certain facts exist; they may be called "legitimate" when either the assumptions made by the questioner are true, or when both the speaker and hearer would be willing to accept them as true. But the use of such questions is generally an exceedingly important type of trap for the unwary witness or citizen. When we are asked, "Why is it that labor leaders are so much less concerned with the general welfare than are the leaders of business?" the reader's tendency is to say, "You know, that never occurred to me. I wonder why it is so." He immediately puts his mind to work helping the questioner. But before we seek explanations of a fact, we should be sure that the fact exists. We should critically examine the truth or falsity of the assumptions concealed in questions.

Similarly, commands may contain concealed assumptions. In "Be careful" we assume that a dangerous situation exists. The apprentice who was asked to bring the journeyman a left-handed monkey wrench was victimized by an illegitimate command.

2. Ought Sentences and Evaluations.

Difficult problems of interpretation arise when we seek to classify "ought" sentences and "evaluations" in terms of our distinction between the logical and the non-logical uses of language. Let us note the nature of these problems.

Ought sentences:

Consider the sentence, "One ought never to tell a lie." Is this sentence one which gives information? Does it express the feelings of the speaker and affect those of the hearer? Is it a directive statement? Is it perhaps all three combined? The word "ought" requires close examination.

The word "ought" is used in at least three different senses, logical, conditional, and unconditional. Thus, in "If you worked out the addition correctly, you ought to have gotten the sum of 625," the word ought is used in a purely logical sense. In "If you want to keep in good physical shape, then you ought to keep regular hours," the word is used in a conditional manner, i.e., you are advised to keep regular hours on the condition that you want to keep in good physical shape. The third use is unconditional or categorical: One ought never to tell a lie. No condition is stated; the ought is stated without any ifs, ands, or buts.

The logical use of "ought" states a sentence which clearly involves a proposition: The sum of these numbers is 625. The sentence is informative. The conditional example is easily translatable into a proposition: Keeping regular hours is a means towards keeping in good physical shape. This sentence is a proposition which is used for a directive purpose. It is the third use which arouses difficulties. What exactly does it mean?

It appears to be a command, or directive, but a pure directive, as we have seen, is neither true nor false, as "Close the window." "One ought never to tell a lie," however, also appears to be true in some sense. We may mean that the "ought" should be interpreted conditionally, though we did not state the condition explicitly. Such an interpretation would give us: "One ought never to tell a lie if he wishes to have a good reputation." Finally, the sentence may simply express the fact that the speaker hates lying and liars and that he uses this form of expression to indicate his feelings.

If an unconditional or categorical "ought statement" is interpreted as a command, then it is neither true nor false. If it is merely an expression of emotion, then it simply tells us something about the speaker. If it is interpreted as a concealed type of conditional "ought statement," then it can be translated into a proposition in the same manner as we translated the other conditional "ought statement." Finally, we should note that some ethical theorists would accept none of these translations, but would hold that unconditional "oughts" are unique in meaning. An adequate discussion of this problem, however, would take us beyond the scope of semantical analysis.

Sentences containing evaluations:

By "evaluations" we mean statements which assert that something does or does not possess a specific kind of value. Our discussion will be limited, however, to moral and aesthetic values. We shall consider sentences which declare that persons are morally good or evil or that things are beautiful or ugly. Consider the sentence: "Picasso's paintings are great works of art." How shall we classify this sentence—as informative, expressive, or directive? Does the statement tell us something about Picasso's paintings or about the speaker? When Churchill, in one of his eloquent speeches, referred to Hitler and Mussolini as "those wicked men," was he giving us information about Hitler and Mussolini or about himself? Or about both?

The problem, simply stated, is this: If evaluations give us information concerning the thing evaluated, then they are statements of fact, and, like all statements of fact, will be true or false. On the other hand, if they are mere expressions of the feelings or emotions of the speaker, then they are simply forms of expressive language, and neither true nor false concerning the thing evaluated. Under the latter interpretation, the evaluations quoted above would be equivalent to the following sentences: "I like Picasso's paintings;" "I hate Hitler and Mussolini." We must also consider the possibility that evaluations contain concealed "oughts." Perhaps they mean "This is the way I feel about Picasso and Hitler, and you ought to feel as I do."

Evaluations, of course, often purport to be statements of fact. Most persons would regard the following as an example of a *false* evaluation: "The homes in the slums of Chicago are architecturally more beautiful than the homes of the movie stars in Beverly Hills." But if this is false, it is a statement of fact and not a mere expression of the feelings of the speaker. Our present interest in these sentences, however, lies in calling attention to the semantical problems involved in evaluations. The solution of these problems, if there is a solution, must be found in the sciences of ethics and aesthetics. Further discussion of these questions will also be found in Chapter 19.

Exercises

1. Explain the following diagrammatic summary of the types and purposes of language:

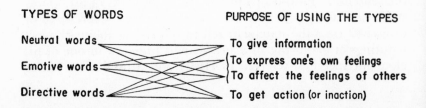

TYPES OF WORDS   PURPOSE OF USING THE TYPES

Neutral words — To give information

Emotive words — To express one's own feelings / To affect the feelings of others

Directive words — To get action (or inaction)

2. Are the words in the following lists necessarily emotive in nature? Are they usually emotive? Explain?
    a. "Our opponents are petty bourgeoisie, capitalists, fascists, hyenas, hangmen, cannibals, lackeys, flunkeys, mad dogs, white guards, and renegades."
    b. "O'Donnell always uses the words 'world-saver,' 'do-gooder,' 'internationalist,' 'global-thinker,' and 'post-war planner' contemptuously, usually accompanied by the adjectives 'dreamy,' 'starry-eyed,' 'breast-beating,' 'sweaty' or 'slobbering,' and alongside the phrase 'pay-roll patriot.' 'Dumbarton Hoax,' 'San Fiasco,' and the 'crime conference on the Crimea' are O'Donnellisms." (*PM*, Sept. 23, 1943, quoted in Black, *Critical Thinking*.)
    c. Realm, throne, chariot, sword, shield, banner, clarion, scepter, royal.
3. State the purpose or purposes which are probably fulfilled by the following:
    a. A thing of beauty is a joy forever.
    b. How do you do?
    c. Blessed are the meek.
    d. Hatred and happiness are not compatible.
    e. A man's best friend is his dog.
    f. "I think there must be something in the place," said Mrs. Nickleby, "for, soon after I was married, I went to Stratford with my poor dear Nickleby, in a post-chaise from Birmingham—was it a post-chaise though!" said Mrs. Nickleby considering; "Yes, it must have been a post-chaise, because I recollect remarking at the time that the driver had a green shade over his left eye . . ."
4. The following items are from James Harvey Robinson's *An Introduction to the History of Western Europe* (Ginn and Company, 1931). Show how each item illustrates a different function of discourse:
    a. We must learn, above all, to study sympathetically institutions and beliefs that we are tempted at first to declare absurd and unreasonable. The aim of the historian is not to prove that a particular way of doing a thing is right or wrong as, for instance, entrusting the whole government to a king, or forbidding clergymen to marry. His object is to show how a certain system came to be introduced, what was thought of it, how it worked and how another plan gradually supplanted it.
    b. Louis XIV exhibited as woeful a want of statesmanship in the treatment of his protestant subjects, as in the prosecution of disastrous wars.

    c. New Zealand, during the closing decade of the nineteenth century, became famous for its experiments in social reform.

5. In the following items what is the chief purpose of the discourse? If there is more than one purpose, is one subordinate to the others? Which type of words are most important in each selection? Do you consider the language used in each case appropriate for the speaker's purpose? Is there any sense in which you consider the language inappropriate?

    a. We will answer their demand for a gold standard by saying to them: You shall not press down upon the brow of labor this crown of thorns, you shall not crucify mankind upon a cross of gold. (W. J. Bryan)

    b. I warn John L. Lewis and his communistic cohorts that no second carpetbag expedition into the Southland, under the red banner of Soviet Russia and concealed under the slogans of the CIO will be tolerated. If the minions of the CIO attempt to carry through the South their lawless plan of organization, if they attempt to demoralize our industry, to corrupt our colored citizens, to incite race hatred and race warfare, I warn him here and now that they will be met by the flower of Southern manhood, and they will reap the bitter fruits of their folly. (Speech in the U. S. House of Representatives, June, 1937.)

    c. All the "best people" from the gentleman's clubs, and all the frantic fascist captains, united in common hatred of socialism and bestial horror of the rising tide of the mass revolutionary movement have turned to acts of provocation, to foul incendiarism, to mediaeval legends of poisoned wells, to legalize their own destruction of proletarian organizations, and arouse the agitated petty bourgeoisie to chauvinistic terror on behalf of the fight against the revolutionary way out of the crisis. (Communist pamphlet.)

    d. The things which will change "the world" are the great discoveries and inventions, the new reactions inside the social organism, and the changes in the earth itself on account of changes in the cosmical forces. These causes will make of it just what, in fidelity to them, it ought to be. The men will be carried along with it and be made by it. The utmost they can do with their cleverness will be to note and record their course as they are carried along, which is what we do now and is that which leads us to the vain fancy that we can make or guide the movement. That is why it is the greatest folly of which a man can be capable, to sit down with a slate and a pencil to plan out a new social world. (William Graham

Sumner, "The Absurd Effort to Make the World Over," from the *Essays of William Graham Sumner,* Yale University Press.)

6. The following "definitions" appeared under the title "Primer for New Voters," in Sidney J. Harris's column, *Strictly Personal.* Does the reader share Mr. Harris's indignation?

"Public servants"—officeholders who belong to your party.

"Bureaucrats"—officeholders who belong to the other party.

"Communist"—any liberal New Dealer.

"Fascist"—any conservative Republican.

"Necessary expenditures for public welfare"—a padded payroll when your party is in office.

"Look at the record"—the partisan presentation of a mass of falsified statistics, half-truths, glittering generalities, and empty platitudes.

"Great statesmanship"—when your party has a strong leader.

"Political dictatorship"—when the other party has a strong leader.

"The Constitution"—a noble document that every politician is for, hardly any politician has read, and virtually no politician understands.

"Liberty and Justice"—what a candidate begins talking about when he is afraid to discuss his record.

"Will of the people"—the result of an election in which not more than 40 per cent of the voters go to the polls to elect a candidate they had no voice in choosing, after a campaign of insults and outright lies. (From *The Chicago Daily News,* Oct. 1, 1946.)

7. Which of the following items are propositions?
   a. Render unto Caesar the things which are Caesar's.
   b. What immortal hand or eye could frame thy fearful symmetry?
   c. No women are fickle.
   d. My darling!
   e. Much have I traveled in the realms of gold.
   f. We hold this truth to be self-evident: that all men are created equal.

8. Identify the complex questions (or commands) in the following group. Where assumptions concerning facts are present, do you consider such assumptions legitimate or illegitimate?
   a. "Why did God become Man?" (This was the title of a book by the philosopher Anselm during the Middle Ages: *Cur Deus Homo?*)

   b. Is God omnipotent?

   c. Does God exist?

   d. Why did the United States declare war on Germany immediately after Pearl Harbor?

   e. Have you given up your evil habits?

   f. How do you account for the great popular support for restrictions on unions?

   g. Explain why democracy has been successful in the United States.

   h. Explain why comic books are responsible for juvenile delinquency.

   i. How do you explain the fact of mental telepathy?

9. Do the following statements exemplify the logical or the non-logical use of language? Justify your answers.

   a. Woman's place is in the home.

   b. Many Americans think that it is sinful for cousins to marry.

   c. Cannibalism is morally wrong.

   d. Unemployment is the most important problem facing capitalism today.

   e. Dante is a greater poet than Edgar Guest.

   f. When the great spirit of Abraham Lincoln looks through the long corridor of time upon the party he founded, he sees that from the day of his passing on the torch until the last day of the Republican party in office, it held aloft the light of inalienable liberties of men. (Herbert Hoover.)

   g. Your car ought to run OK now.

   h. You ought to sleep more if you want to gain weight.

   i. I ought not to do unto others what I would not want them to do unto me.

10. Comment on the following items, concerning the interpretation of evaluations.

   a. Such fundamental errors as that of mistaking a dynamic use of language for an informative (that is, regarding the statement, "Amlie is a communist," as a statement about Amlie instead of as clinical evidence of the state of mind of the speaker) are not difficult to deal with—merely telling most people that such errors can be made goes a long way. (S. I. Hayakawa, *New Republic,* Nov. 15, 1939.)

   b. In his *Philosophy and Logical Syntax* R. Carnap says that to say "Killing is evil" is the same as to say "Do not kill," i.e., it is a command in misleading grammatical form, the expression of a wish, and therefore neither true nor false.

Chapter 5

THE DEFINITION OF "DEFINITION"

Section I: The Importance of Definition

In Oscar Wilde's play, *Lady Windermere's Fan,* the Duchess says: "Do, as a concession to my poor wits, Lord Darlington, just explain to me what you really mean."

"I think I had better not, Duchess," answers the Lord. "Nowadays to be intelligible is to be found out."

Lord Darlington has stated a reason why some persons refuse to define their terms, for when we define our terms we explain "what we really mean," with all the risks attendant thereto. But if we desire to avoid obfuscation and discussions which move at cross-purposes, we must give definite and precise meanings to our terms. A definition sets a term within its proper boundaries, and the injunction "Define your terms!" is of first importance.

Throughout the discussions in the previous chapters we have frequently noted the importance of definition. Our discussion of ambiguity in verbal disagreements revealed the importance of defining one's terms. Whether or not all men are equal depends upon what we mean by "equal." The answer is Yes or No, depending upon the senses in which the term is understood. To say that words have different senses is to say that they may be defined in different ways. Similarly, diplomatic questions concerning whether or not a certain nation has fulfilled its international obligation under treaty to institute "free" and "democratic" governments in areas within its control will depend upon the definitions of these terms.

The most important question in many discussions is "What do you mean by ———?" For example, *Euglena,* a water organism, behaves like a plant under some conditions and like an animal in others. Is *Euglena* a plant or an animal? Neither?

Both? Our answers will depend upon our definitions of plant and animal. Is *Forever Amber* an obscene novel? Exactly what do we mean by "obscene"? We can now appreciate the importance of Voltaire's famous remark, "Before I will discuss anything with you, you must define your terms."

The subject of definition is of very wide scope. We shall examine many of its aspects in the discussion which follows. But before we do so we must note two important distinctions among the ways in which words refer to their referents, i.e., in "extension" and "intension," and as "abstract" and "concrete." These distinctions are indispensable to an understanding of the nature or definition of definition, and we now turn to these distinctions.

Section II: Two Basic Distinctions

1. The extension and the intension of terms.

The first distinction is that between the extension and intension of terms. We shall also employ synonyms for these terms: extension is synonymous with denotation; intension with connotation.

By the extension of a term we refer to the set of objects to which the term is applicable; we refer to each and every being to which the term may be applied. The extension of "man" refers to all of those creatures who are men: FDR, Wayne Morse, Joe Kelly, Hi Ginsburg, Julius Caesar, and so on. The extension of the term "football player" covers such individuals as Eckersall, Red Grange, Berwanger, Sid Luckman, Sammy Baugh, John Lujack, and so on. The extension of "President of the United States" covers such individuals as Washington, Jefferson, and Lincoln. The extension of a term is the set of individuals or things to which the term applies.

Consider the following terms: physical being, living being, animal, mammal, dog, spaniel. The extension of each term covers the set of objects to which the term is applied, assuming, of course, that we use these words unambiguously. Now note the order in which the terms are arranged, from left to right. The left-hand class is larger than the one on its right; the classes are ordered in accordance with the relative size of the classes to which each term refers. The extension of the left-hand class covers the extension of the one on its right, but not vice versa. The extension *decreases* as we move from left to right in our list. The set of objects to which "living beings" applies is smaller than the set of objects called "physical beings." "Animals" is a smaller class than "living beings," and so on. The smallest possible extension is one which refers to a single individual, which may be thought of as a class having only one member. The name "Trixie," for example, denotes a single individual. This is a characteristic of all proper names.

Let us now examine the meaning of "intension." We have said that Julius Caesar is included in the extension of "man." Why? Because he has the characteristics of a man, such as animality, rationality, etc. Whenever we answer the question, Why is X included under the extension of a term? we think of the *characteristics* which an object must possess in order to be included within a certain class. The statement of these characteristics is the term's *intension*. The intension of the term "President of the United States" is "chief executive officer." The intension of "football player" is "athlete who plays in a game in which a large inflated ball is carried, thrown and kicked, etc." The intension of a term is what is usually called its definition. The extension, on the other hand, simply refers us to the set of objects to which the definition applies.

Extension and intension are thus intimately related, but they refer to objects in different ways—extension to a listing of the individuals who fall within its quantitative scope, intension to the qualities or characteristics of the individuals. When we are asked, Which is the larger class—dogs or cats? we think of the extension of each. When we are asked, Which is the friendlier animal? we think of the intensional aspect of the terms.

We must now draw a distinction between two types of intension, subjective and conventional. By *subjective* intension we refer to the characteristics which a *given individual* may think of when he thinks of "dogs." The subjective intension refers to the individual associations attached to a term in any given individual's mind. These associations will not be exactly the same for any two persons. "Dog" arouses connotations in my mind which differ from those in yours, for our experiences with dogs have been different and may change in the future. To one man the dog is a friendly animal; to another he is dangerous. The *conventional* intension, on the other hand, refers to those characteristics which are necessary and sufficient for regarding an object as belonging within the extension of a term. A *definition* usually states the conventional intension of the term. The conventional intension states the elements which all dogs have in common, and this type of intension is the same for all persons. Thus, Peter may regard Rover with affection; John may regard him with aversion. Peter thinks of a friendly animal when he thinks of dogs; John of an unfriendly animal. Their subjective intensions differ. But both agree that Rover is a dog, since the conventional intension of "dog" is the same for both. They do not disagree with respect to the essential characteristics which distinguish a dog from other animals. In other words, the *context* of our experiences with dogs influences our subjective intensions, which we may call the "marginal" associations aroused in our minds by a term, but it does not affect the conventional intension.

Another related distinction is that between logical and physical identity. When a bookkeeper adds up a balance, the word "dollar" means exactly the same thing every time it is used, for one dollar is logically identical with any other dollar. The conventional intension of "dollar" is *exactly* the same on each occasion of its use. Physically, however, no two objects in the world are identical. No two paper dollars are exactly the same physically. No two leaves are exactly alike, and it is only the grossness of our vision which makes two grains of sand appear to be alike. No two fingerprints are alike physically. But when we say that the FBI took A's fingerprints, and that they also took B's fingerprints, the use of the term "fingerprint" is logically identical on each occasion.

2. The abstract and the concrete.

We think about things in different ways. We may think of

dogs "in general," i.e., of the conventional intension of "dog."
When we think of "triangularity," we think of those characteristics possessed by all triangles, whether they be large or small,
colored blue or red, whether they be equilateral, isoceles, or
scalene. We may think of "man" as a "rational animal." In all
these cases we are thinking abstractly. On the other hand, we
may be thinking of Rover, or of John, or of this triangle, △;
these are examples of the concrete.

Words are not abstract or concrete because of something in
the words themselves. "Humanity," "triangularity," "beauty,"
and "justice" are called abstract words because they refer to
referents "abstractively," that is, we use them to refer to the
general qualities possessed by a group of things. Words are abstract because of the way in which we use them; it is the word's
designation which makes it abstract or concrete. The important
distinction is between two ways of thinking. When we think of
an individual object or situation in all of its fullness of individuality, we are thinking concretely. When I think of Abraham
Lincoln, the fine day we had yesterday, or the fact that the roller
on my typewriter is loose, I am thinking concretely. But when
I think of the mortality of all men, or of the principle that the
volume of a gas is related functionally to its temperature, I am
thinking abstractly. The expression "concrete language" refers
to things which can be perceived by the senses; "abstract language" to those qualities or attributes which are possessed by the
concrete objects within a certain class.

The concrete and the abstract are correlative terms, by
which we mean words which mutually involve each other.
When we speak of the *abstractions* triangularity or humanity
we refer to that which all *concrete* triangles or men have in
common. Humanity or triangularity do not "exist" apart from
individual men and triangles, but this does not mean that abstractions are "unreal." The abstractions refer to characteristics
that are actually possessed by the concrete things. We call an
object a "man" because he possesses the qualities to which the
abstraction refers. We can think of those qualities, or attributes,
or relations, apart from the specific individuals in whom they
are "embodied," even though the qualities cannot "exist" apart
from the concrete.

Exercises

1. Which items should be included within the extension of "ath-
   letes"? Which are part of the conventional intension of the term?
   of your subjective intension?

   <table>
   <tr><td>a. Bob Hope</td><td>g. sound in wind and limb</td></tr>
   <tr><td>b. football players</td><td>h. having great physical strength</td></tr>
   <tr><td>c. Joe Louis</td><td>i. chess players</td></tr>
   <tr><td>d. bridge experts</td><td>j. having sportsmanlike attitude</td></tr>
   <tr><td>e. being a good runner</td><td>k. barflies</td></tr>
   <tr><td>f. having competitive spirit</td><td>l. ping-pong players</td></tr>
   </table>

2. Arrange the following terms in the order of extension, so that the
   term having the largest extension will be at the top of the list; the
   one with the smallest extension at the bottom:
   a. quadrilateral
   b. square
   c. figure
   d. rectangle
   e. parallelogram
   f. plane figure
   Now arrange them with the term having the maximum intension
   at the top of the list, decreasing the intension as you go down.
3. Explain the rule, "The extension and intension of terms vary inversely." Use the terms in Exercise 2 as an illustration of the rule.
4. Compare the extensions of "crow" and "crows not over five feet
   tall." Does this comparison indicate that the rule in Exercise 3
   should be modified?
5. Proper names may become common nouns, as "a Nero," "a Wa-
   terloo," "a Quisling." But do proper names as such possess connotation? Does "John F. Smith" connote anything?
6. Comment on the following items from Korzybski's *Science and
   Sanity* (The International Non-Aristotelian Library Publishing
   Co., 1948) in terms of the distinction between logical and physical
   identity:
   a. Now, returning to the analysis of the object which we called
      "pencil," we observe that, in spite of all "similarities," this
      object is unique, is different from everything else, and has a
      unique relationship to the rest of the world. Hence, we
      should give the object a *unique name*. Fortunately, we have
      already become acquainted with the way mathematicians
      manufacture an endless array of individual names without

unduly expanding the vocabulary. If we call the given object "pencil$_1$" we could call another similar object "pencil$_2$," etc. In this way, we produce individual names, and so cover the *differences*. By keeping the main root word "pencil," we keep the implications of daily like and also of *similarities*. (p. 381.)

b. And so individualizing (indexes) and temporal devices (dates) etc., should be used *conjointly*. Thus, obviously chair$_1$ ^{1600} is not the "same" as chair$_1$ ^{1940}, nor is Smith$_1$ ^{Monday} the "same" as Smith$_1$ ^{Tuesday}. (p. xxxvi.)

7. S. I. Hayakawa, writes that "one of the premises upon which modern linguistic thought is based" is the premise that "no word ever has exactly the same meaning twice." Hayakawa continues, "The extent to which this premise fits the facts can be demonstrated in a number of ways. First, if we accept the proposition that the contexts of an utterance determine its meaning, it becomes apparent that since no two contexts are ever *exactly* the same, no two meanings can ever be exactly the same. How can we 'fix the meaning' even for as common an expression as 'to believe in' when it can be used in such sentences as the following?

'I *believe in* you.' (I have confidence in you.)
'I *believe in* democracy' (I accept the principles implied by the term democracy.)
'I *believe in* Santa Claus.' (It is my opinion that Santa Claus exists.)

"Secondly, we can take for example a word of 'simple' meaning like 'kettle.' But when John says 'kettle,' its intensional meanings to him are the common characteristics of all the kettles John remembers. When Peter says 'kettle,' however, its intensional meanings to him are the common characteristics of all the kettles he remembers. *No matter how small or how negligible the differences may be between John's 'kettle' and Peter's 'kettle,' there is some difference.*

"Finally, . . . if John says 'my typewriter' today, and again 'my typewriter' tomorrow, the extensional meaning is different in the two cases, because the typewriter is not *exactly* the same from one day to the next (nor from one minute to the next); slow processes of wear, change, and decay are going on constantly. Although we can say, then, that the differences in the meanings of a word on one occasion, on another occasion a minute later, and on still another occasion another minute later are *negligible* we cannot say that the meanings are exactly the same." (S. I. Hayakawa, *Language in Action,* Harcourt, Brace, and Co., 1941, pp. 49–50.)

Discuss the following:
   a. Does the ambiguity of "believe in" prove that this phrase
      never has the same meaning in different contexts? Compare
      "I believe in you" and "Jim believes in Joe."
   b. Comment on the "kettle" argument in terms of the distinc-
      tion between subjective and conventional intension.
   c. Comment on the "typewriter" argument in terms of the dis-
      tinction between logical and physical identity.

Section III: The Types of Definitions

There are several types of definitions, each appropriate for
different needs and purposes, though all definitions seek to enlighten the hearer by clarifying the range of the application of
a word. We shall consider three types of definitions: (1) word
substitution, (2) explicating the extension or denotation of a
word, and (3) explicating the intension or connotation of a
word. We shall call the latter type "analytical," since it analyzes
an abstract concept. Each of these types gives us the range of
application of the word, but in different ways, and each type is
appropriate for certain purposes and inappropriate for others.

1. Definition by word-substitution.

A person who is attempting to work out a crossword puzzle
is usually interested in this type of definition, i.e., one which
provides him with synonymous terms. "Alar" means "wing-
shaped." A reader confronted with the sentence "No cenobites
are troglodytes" would probably turn to the dictionary. He
will learn that a cenobite is a member of a religious community,
such as a monastery or convent. "Troglodyte" has the synonym
"hermit." He is informed that two different words designate
the same referent and that we may substitute one of these words
for the other.

A synonymous definition has value in that it substitutes a
familiar word for an unfamiliar one. The same result may be
obtained by the use of a familiar antonym, or word of opposite
meaning. Thus, the meaning of "atypical" is clarified when we
learn that it means the opposite of "typical." Correlatives, or
related terms which presuppose each other, such as husband
and wife, may be used in a similar manner.

2. Extensive or denotative definition.

This type of definition states the extension of a word by citing examples which are familiar to the hearer. Example: Fascism means the type of government which prevailed in Italy, Germany, and Japan in recent years, and which still prevails in Spain (1950). Extensive definition presents a *list* of the things to which the term is applied and defines by example. This type of definition is useful for many purposes, as in a definition of "lively arts" (vaudeville, the circus, comic strips, swing music, etc.). But an extensive definition does not analyze the nature of the thing being defined. The extensive definition of fascism does not tell us anything about the *nature* of the governments which existed in Italy and Germany. We also note that an extensional definition presupposes an understanding of the intensional meaning of the term, since we could not identify Germany as an example of fascism unless we had some notion as to what fascism meant in its intensional sense.

Extensive definitions may also cite single examples, as in the following definitions: "A 'pun' refers to the manner in which the word 'hang' was used in Benjamin Franklin's remark"; "The color 'violet' is the color which you will find at the extreme right end of the spectrum."

When an extensive definition is accompanied by a demonstrative gesture which specifies the referent by actually pointing to it, we have what is called definition "by demonstration," or "ostensive" definition. Examples: *"This* is an ocarina," *"That* is an aileron." We point to a specimen of the class of things denoted by the term and call it by its name. The demonstrative gesture may also occur in a figurative sense, as in "The sound which you will hear in a moment will be the tone of a bassoon." The demonstrative method of defining is probably the most important pedagogical element in the educative process, for it is the method whereby a child learns most of the words in his early vocabulary. A ball is given to an infant. The giving of the ball is accompanied by a demonstrative gesture and the words "This is a ball." Helen Keller has vividly described the manner in which she first learned that the word "water" meant that which was flowing over her hands from a fountain. Another great educative value of this method is that it eliminates the dangers of mere bookish knowledge, or the vice of "thinking words, not things," and thus prevents us from losing ourselves in abstractions. John Dewey, America's most important philosopher of education, has constantly emphasized the value of personal experience, in this direct sense or in an imaginative sense, in understanding new concepts.

The use of extensive definition will help us to clarify an important philosophical problem concerning the definability of such terms as "beauty" or "good." The English philosopher, G. E. Moore, in his *Principia Ethica,* urged that "good" is an indefinable term, comparable in its indefinability to such a term as "yellow." If the reader is not aware of the difficulties presented by the attempt to define a color quality in its sensuous sense, let him consider how he would define "yellow" to a person who had been blind from birth. But discussions concerning whether or not a given term is indefinable may easily degenerate into verbal disputes unless we recognize the ambiguity of the word "indefinable" and draw a distinction between different kinds of definition. When it is said that "yellow" is indefinable, what is usually meant is that it is impossible to give this term an analytical definition, for yellow is a simple quality, and only complex entities (which have "parts") may be analyzed. But certainly "yellow" can be defined by demonstration to a person with normal vision by pointing to an example, and an extensive type of definition may be given for words such as "good" and "beauty," whatever our conclusion may be with respect to the possibility of analyzing these terms.

3. Intensional, connotative, or analytical definition.

Example: Democracy is a system of government in which the people periodically elect their governing officials in free elections and which guarantees the ideals of freedom and equality. Note how this definition differs from those previously discussed. Here we are not given a synonymous term, nor a demonstrative gesture, nor a mere list of democratic governments. We are given the intensional or connotative meaning of the term, i.e., an analysis of the referent which we have in mind when we speak of "democracy." Henceforth we shall use the term "analytical" for this type of definition. (We are not concerned as yet with the adequacy of any particular example of this sort.)

When we speak of "definition" we usually refer to this type of definition. For example, in a discussion concerning the existence of God, one of the speakers asks for a definition of the term. An analytical definition would normally be expected, since it would be quite inadequate to define by a synonym, such as "Deity." Similarly, it is definition in the analytical sense which is required when such vague or ambiguous terms as democracy, communism, art, or religion are used. What is desired is a clarification of the nature of the referent. It is only when the referent of a synonym is clearly understood that we are satisfied with a synonym for an unknown word. This was the case in our substitution of "hermit" for "troglodyte," where an analytical definition was not called for. But if the reader had been unfamiliar with the referent of the word "hermit," then this term might have required analysis.

In the next section we shall examine some of the criteria which must be fulfilled by an adequate analytical definition. But before turning to the criteria we shall examine the structure which such definitions exhibit. And henceforth we shall employ two new technical terms, *definiendum* and *definiens*, to designate the two formal parts of every definition. The *definiendum* is the word being defined; the *definiens* is the defining part of the definition. In a definition such as "Man is a rational animal," "man" is the *definiendum;* "rational animal," *definiens.*

With respect to structure, the *definiens* of an analytical definition has two parts, which are usually called the *genus* and the *differentia.* Genus is used in a special sense, as meaning the *general class* of things to which the definiendum is assigned, and *differentia* refers to the *special characteristics* possessed by the definiendum. Thus, in our previous definition, we may say that "animal" is the *genus,* or general class to which man belongs, and that rationality is his *differentia* within the class of animals. If "dog" were defined as "an animal," the definition would be incomplete, since no *differentia* is stated.

We should also note that the distinction between genus and differentia is not an absolute one. For example, a whale is a marine mammal of fish-like form. But we might also define a whale as a marine, or fish-like creature which is a mammal.

Which term is called genus will depend upon the aspect which we wish to emphasize as appropriate to the need for the definition. But all analytical definitions tell us that something belongs to a general class of things, and that it is distinguished from other members of its class by certain characteristics.

The manner in which the differentia distinguishes the definiendum from other things within the general class may take varied forms. Here again the purpose of the definition will be the controlling factor. In scientific definitions we find an emphasis on the manner in which things are produced, or the manner in which they produce certain results. Thus, a metal may be defined by a layman in terms of its qualities of hardness, heaviness, malleability, etc. But a chemist defines it as "any chemical element which combines with oxygen so as to form a base." (A base is a compound which combines with an acid so as to form a salt.) In contemporary physics concepts are defined in terms of operations. But we will find genus and differentia in all analytical definitions.

Exercises

A. Which types of definition are found in the following?
1. Labor unions are organizations such as the United Steelworkers, the Auto Workers, the Brotherhoods of Machinists, Teamsters, etc.
2. Capitalism is a system in which there are large accumulations of capital.
3. Erne means a sea-eagle.
4. The symbol $\angle$ means "included in the class of."
5. Exercise 1 was an example of a denotative definition.
6. A sexagenarian is a person who is in his sixties.
7. A company is a unit in an infantry regiment.
8. Left means the opposite of right.
9. A parent is a person who brings children into this world.
10. A mule is an animal which is half horse and half donkey.
11. An explorer is a bum with an excuse.
B. Distinguish the definiendum from the definiens and the genus from the differentia in the following definitions:
1. A lady is a woman of good breeding.
2. The soul is a psychic substance.

3. A good citizen is one who pays his debts and obeys the laws.
4. A lemur is a small mammal related to the monkeys. They are mostly nocturnal, with fox-like faces and soft fur, and are of about the size of a cat.
5. "The concept of length involves as much as, and nothing more than, the set of operations by which length is determined [e.g., laying a measuring-rod along a straight line]." (P. W. Bridgman, *The Logic of Modern Physics*.)

Section IV: The Criteria of an Adequate Analytical Definition

We shall now discuss the criteria, or "rules," to which an adequate *analytical* definition must conform. Five criteria will be considered.

1. The definiens should be equivalent to the definiendum: it should be neither too broad nor too narrow.

The definiens in an analytical definition may be regarded as a description of the items referred to by the definiendum. "Rational animal" describes the beings referred to by the word "man." In an "equivalent" definition, the description in the definiens will apply to exactly the same class of things as the definiendum, and not to a larger or a smaller class. The definition "Man is a living being capable of feeling the sensations of pleasure and pain" is too broad, for the definiens applies to *all animals,* and not merely to men. The definition of man as a "rational, carnivorous mammal" would not apply to all men, since some of them are vegetarians. This definition covers too little ground, and is too narrow. But "Man is a rational animal" is an equivalent definition. Such definitions are also "reversible," for we can turn them around and say: "All rational animals are men."

If we sought a definition of "Christianity" (in the religious sense), we would want a definition that applied to *all* Christians, and *only* to Christians. The definition should cover both Protestants and Catholics, and should exclude Mohammedans, etc. The description in the definiens should apply to the class of beings referred to by the definiendum, to *all* of them and *only* to them. Consider the diagram on the next page:

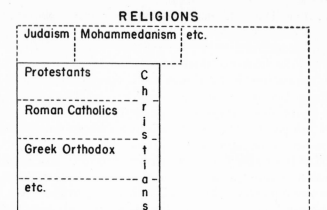

The definiendum "Christians" refers to the persons who are included within the rectangle with the solid lines. The description given in the definiens must apply to all of these individuals and to no others. The definition "A Christian is a person who believes in the reality of ideals" would apply to all religions, not only to the Christian. On the other hand, to define a Christian as "a person who accepts the doctrines of Jesus, as stated exclusively in the New Testament, and without reliance on tradition" would exclude Catholics from the class of Christians. The first definition is too broad, the second too narrow. The definiens should apply to all cases properly included within the extension of the definiendum, and should exclude all cases not properly included. It must cover exactly the right amount of territory, and state the exact boundaries of the term, neither more nor less. Every definition must be tested in order to determine whether it is too broad or too narrow. The following tests should be applied:

a. *Does the definiens cover* sufficient *ground, i.e., does it cover all cases to which it is applicable?* The answer to this question should be affirmative. "A triangle is a plane figure." We ask: Are all triangles plane figures? The answer is Yes, so the definiens covers sufficient ground, and satisfies the first test.

b. *Does it cover* too much *ground, i.e., does it cover cases to which it is* not *applicable?* The answer to this question should be *negative*. Does "plane figure" cover things other than triangles? Once again the answer is Yes, so the definition fails to pass the second test.

When the answer to the first question is negative, the definition is too narrow; if the answer to the second is affirmative, it is too broad. Let us try a second example: "A triangle is a 3-sided plane figure all of whose sides are equal." We ask, Are all triangles 3-sided plane figures all of whose sides are equal? The answer is No, so the definition is too narrow.

"Man is a rational animal" passes both tests, and is thus an equivalent definition. Some definitions, on the other hand, may fail to pass both tests: "Man is an animal over five feet tall." Not all men are over five feet tall, and many animals over five feet tall are not men.

The principle involved in these tests is that the definiens must apply to *all* of the items denoted by the definiendum, and *only* to these. (1) The first test requires that it should be proper to prefix the quantifier "All" before the definiendum. When we do this in the case of "A man is a rational animal" we get "All men are rational animals." The prefix "All" is proper in this case, and the definition has passed the first test. If a definition fails to pass, it is too narrow; if it passes we know only that it is not too narrow. (2) The second test determines whether the definiens applies *only* to the items denoted by the definiendum. It requires that it should be proper to *reverse* the order of the definiendum and the definiens, and to prefix "All" before the restated definition. Since we can successfully reverse "A man is a rational animal" to "All rational animals are men," the definition has passed the second test. If the reversed statement is true, the definition is not too broad; if false then it is. When we reverse the definition "A dog is an animal" into "All animals are dogs," we have a false proposition, so the definition is too broad. When a definition passes both tests, it is neither too broad nor too narrow, and it is thus an equivalent definition.

The rule of equivalence is the most important of the criteria of an adequate definition, and the vices of being too broad or too narrow are the Scylla and Charybdis on which most definitions founder. But equivalent definitions are not easily constructed, except, of course, in mathematics, where the notion of equivalence symbolized by $\equiv$ is a familiar one. "A triangle is a plane figure bounded by three sides." * *All* triangles and *only* triangles are three-sided plane figures, and all three-sided plane figures are triangles. But when we deal with key words such as religion, beauty, art, and propaganda, we find that the quest for adequate definitions is never-ending. As an example of the difficulties we encounter in these fields, consider the problem of defining "religion." It appears inadequate to define religion without some reference to belief in a God, but Confucianism and Buddhism do not involve such beliefs. It would be presumptuous indeed to say that creeds which hold the allegiance of almost a third of the human race are not religions. John Dewey, in *A Common Faith,* has argued that it is utterly impossible to find an adequate equivalent definition of religion. If this is so, then we must be satisfied with something less than perfection, and must seek to clarify the range of the term as adequately as may be possible.

It should be obvious that an adequate definition cannot be constructed on the basis of rules, nor can a definition be checked for adequacy on the basis of rules alone. Familiarity with the subject matter is indispensable in order to apply the tests. One must know the facts concerning religion or political institutions in order to check definitions in those fields. The rules merely tell us how to use our knowledge.

2. The definiens should state the essential characteristics of the definiendum.

By "essential characteristics" we refer to characteristics which are important in terms of the purposes for which the definition is required. "Essential" is thus used in a relativistic manner, since what may be essential for one purpose is not so for another. If we were interested in a definition of "man" in order to contrast men with the lower animals, it would not be satisfactory for most purposes to define man as "the animal who can fly a jet plane at supersonic speed," nor as "the animal capable of laughter," which is an equivalent definition, as the

---

* We assume that the lines are straight.

former is not. An unessential characteristic is usually referred to as an "accident."

In a political discussion concerning conservatism and radicalism, a definition of "conservative" may be requested. To define a conservative as "a man with good sense" may or may not be true of conservatives, but the definition would not state an essential characteristic for the purpose of the given discussion.

3. The definiens should clarify the nature of the definiendum.

A definition should clarify the nature of the thing defined. It should inform and enlighten the person addressed. Typically, neutral or informative language, rather than "poetic," "literary," or expressive language, will be appropriate, and figurative terms will be avoided. "Sickness is Nature's protest against the misdirection of her forces" is a "poetic" type of definition. A good definition will also avoid the vice of obscurity, i.e., the dark and non-transparent. (Is this a figurative definition?)

The admonition against obscurity requires care in its application. That which is obscure to one person may not be so to another. To the uninformed all things are obscure. The type of audience addressed should be taken into account. Material that is obscure to the general public may be quite clear to the average college student. The test should be: Would a reasonably well-informed person in the audience being addressed find the definition obscure? If one cannot confidently answer this question in the affirmative, then he should not criticize the definition on this ground.

4. An analytic definition should avoid word-substitution.

Word-substitution is a legitimate form of definition for many purposes, but not when we desire an analysis of the nature of the referent. The present rule has several aspects. The definiens should not repeat the definiendum, nor should it state synonyms, antonyms, or correlatives, of the definiendum. To commit these faults is to be guilty of "circularity."

   a. Do not repeat the word being defined. Polonius informs
the King and Queen of Hamlet's strange condition:

> Your noble son is mad;
> Mad call I it; for, to define true madness,
> What is't but to be nothing else but mad?

The same error is found in a definition of literature as "writing
which has a literary quality," or of democracy as "a system of
government which uses democratic procedures." These require
no comment. But note that the rule does not forbid the following type of definition: "A good citizen is a citizen who seeks to
promote the common welfare." The repetition of "citizen" in
the definiens is unexceptionable, since only the meaning of
"good" in "good citizen" is in question. Note also that the purpose of the definition is always a controlling consideration. A
definition of a Communist for legal purposes as "A person who
holds a membership card in the Communist party" clarifies the
nature of the referent for a given purpose.

   b. Do not use synonyms or antonyms or correlatives. "A
good man is one who is virtuous" substitutes the synonym "virtuous" for "good," but this would usually be wholly unsatisfactory, since this definition would immediately raise the question
"But what is virtue?" "Right conduct means conduct which is
not wrongful" gives us an unhelpful antonym. "A cause means
that which has an effect" involves the correlative terms "cause"
and "effect," since a cause is that which has an effect and an effect is that which has a cause. But what is the analytical meaning of these terms? This question is not answered.

5. A definition should be positive rather than negative.

   An analytical definition, which seeks to analyze the nature
of the referent, should tell us what the thing is, rather than what
it is not. "A man is not a creature who breathes through gills" is
true, but of little help. Obviously, a negative definition which
aims at completeness would have to describe everything in the
universe which was not the thing being defined. This absurdity

is avoided by most negative definitions in that the thing being defined will usually be contrasted with some closely related things, as in the following: "A Protestant is a Christian who is not a Catholic." But this definition is both a violation of the present rule and also too broad. Negative definitions of this type may be improved by making the list of negations exhaustive within a narrow "universe of discourse."

Negative definitions sometimes serve a useful purpose in high-lighting the nature of the thing being defined by contrasting it with closely related things, just as a color is heightened by contrast. This rule should therefore be taken simply as a warning that we should in general "accentuate the positive." Indeed, there are many occasions when a negative definition will be quite satisfactory, as in the definition of a bachelor as "an unmarried man," or "adult male who is not married." Parallel lines may be defined as "lines which do not intersect, no matter how far extended." The controlling consideration is: Does the definiens give us an adequate analysis of the subject matter?

Exercises

A. Check the following definitions for equivalence. Some familiarity with the subject matter is required. Apply the two tests and state whether the definition is equivalent, too broad, too narrow, or both too broad and too narrow.

1. Amnesia is a form of mental disease.
2. A dog is a domesticated animal having four legs.
3. A co-ed is a woman attending a school of higher learning, such as a college or university.
4. A circle is a figure whose radii are equal.
5. Poetry is a form of literature written in metrical language.
6. An alcoholic is a person who drinks large quantities of alcoholic beverages.
7. A phonograph is a device for the recording and reproducing of sounds.
8. A man is a featherless biped. (An ancient Greek once plucked a chicken in order to criticize this definition. Why?)
9. A chair is a piece of furniture used as a seat for one person and having a back and four legs.

10. A man is a primate with erect posture, a highly developed brain, and the capacity of speech.

11. A beautiful object is one which possesses formal design and is pleasing to the eye.

12. Fascism means a totalitarian government in which a dictator rules.

13. Capitalism is a system of industrial organization which develops large scale production.

14. Propaganda means any attempt to influence the opinions of others.

15. A cause means the invariable antecedent of any event.

16. Following are popular definitions of "beauty," or "a beautiful object":

   a. That which causes pleasure to the eye or ear.

   b. A work of art which reveals the individuality of its creator.

   c. A work of art which achieves the purpose of its author.

   d. A work which expresses an intuition of the artist. (Croce.)

   e. That which has unity in variety.

   f. A work which causes a mental state in the spectator such that thought and emotion achieve a harmonious equilibrium.

   g. Pleasure regarded as the quality of a thing. (Santayana.)

B. Check the following definitions for violations of Rules 2–5. Find the most striking violation in each case. Try each rule before you make your decision. Also note that more than one rule may be violated by a given example. Also note whether you think the definition a satisfactory one despite the fact that a rule is violated.

1. A lady is a woman in whose presence a man behaves like a gentleman.

2. Peace means the absence of war.

3. A good man is one who always does the right thing.

4. A Siamese is a person who comes from Siam.

5. Independent means the state of not being dependent.

6. Time is the moving image of eternity. (Plato.)

7. A Communist means a person who is dissatisfied with everything.

8. Faith is the substance of things hoped for; the evidence of things not seen. (St. Paul.)

9. Life is that which distinguishes living from non-living things.

10. A cynic is one who knows the price of everything and the value of nothing. (Oscar Wilde.)
11. A human being is an animal who knows how to use chopsticks.
12. An automobile is a vehicle which is not horse-drawn and which does not run on tracks.
13. A star is a stellar body seen in the heavens at night.
14. A moral man is one who does not lie, steal, or live intemperately.
15. The du Pont Company recently adopted the following definition of nylon: "A generic term for any long-chain synthetic polymeric amide which has recurring amide groups as an integral part of the main polymer chain, and which is capable of being formed into a filament in which the structural elements are oriented in the direction of the axis."
16. A fanatic is a man who redoubles his efforts after he has forgotten his aim. (Santayana.)
17. Social dancing is a stilted form of perambulation slightly impeded by a semico-operative member of the opposite sex.
18. A politician is a man who sits on a fence with his ear on the ground.
19. Herbert Spencer's definition of evolution: "A continuous change from indefinite, incoherent homogeneity to definite coherent heterogeneity of structure and function, through successive differentiations and integrations."
20. Spencer's definition was parodied by Kirkman, as follows: "Evolution: A change from a nohowish, untalkaboutable, all-alikeness to a somehowish, and in general talkaboutable not-all-alikeness by continuous somethingelseifications and stick-togetherations."
21. Tickling has been defined as "an intensely vivid complex of unsteady, ill-localized and ill-analyzed sensations, with attention distributed over the immediate sensory contents and the concomitant sensations reflexly aroused."
22. A crossword puzzle has been defined "an intensively rectangular and essentially heterogeneous concatenation of dissimilar verbal synonyms, i.e., similitudes, replete with internal inhibitions, yet promulgating extensive ratiocination and meticulously designed to promote fulminating vituperation, dispel hebetudinosity and develop speculative, contemplative, introspective, deliberative, and cogitative faculties."

Section V: Plato and the Rules of Definition

The criteria of an adequate definition were known to Plato (427–347 B.C.), and his dialogues are a rich mine of material in definition analysis. The following passages present a highly condensed version of his *Euthyphro,* in which the definition of piety is discussed. The selections are from a translation published by the Macmillan Company.

A word as to the background of the conversation. Euthyphro is on his way to swear out a warrant against his father for murder. It appears that Euthyphro's father had become incensed against a drunken overseer who had killed a slave. The overseer was bound up hand and foot and died of exposure while awaiting a decision concerning his punishment. Euthyphro believes that his father is guilty of murder and that moral duty, or "piety," requires that he have his father prosecuted. In reading these passages, note the irony so characteristic of Socrates in his conversations with the self-opinionated. After reading this selection answer the questions at the end.

SOCRATES: Good heavens, Euthyphro! Surely the multitude are ignorant of what makes right. I take it that not everyone could rightly do what you are doing; only a man who was already well advanced in wisdom.

EUTHYPHRO: That is quite true, Socrates.

SOCRATES: Was the man whom your father killed a relative of yours? Nay, of course he was: You would never have prosecuted your father for the murder of a stranger?

EUTHYPHRO: You amuse me, Socrates. What difference does it make whether the murdered man was a relative or a stranger? The only question that you have to ask is, did the slayer slay justly or not? But my relatives are furious with me; so little do they know the divine law of piety and impiety.

SOCRATES: Tell me, then: what is piety and what is impiety?

EUTHYPHRO: Piety means prosecuting the wrongdoer who has committed murder or sacrilege or any other such crime.

SOCRATES: But many other actions are pious, are they not, Euthyphro?

EUTHYPHRO: Certainly.

SOCRATES: I did not ask you to tell me one or two of all the many pious actions that there are; I want to know what is the essential form of piety which makes all pious actions pious. [1]

EUTHYPHRO: Well, then, what is pleasing to the gods is pious, and what is not pleasing is impious.

SOCRATES: Beautiful, Euthyphro. Now you have given me the sort of answer that I wanted. Whether what you say is true, I do not know yet. But of course you will go on to prove the truth of it. . . . Now, the same action is pleasing to some gods, and displeasing to others; dear to Zeus, but hateful to Cronos. So the same action will be pious and impious at the same time? [2]

EUTHYPHRO: Well, I should say that piety is what all the gods love and that impiety is what they all hate. I think that the definition is right this time.

SOCRATES: We shall know that better in a little while, my good friend. Now consider this question. Do the gods love piety because it is pious, or is it pious because they love it? [3]

EUTHYPHRO: They love it because it is pious; it is not pious because they love it.

SOCRATES: Then piety is not what is pleasing to the gods. Piety, and what is pleasing to the gods, are different things. My question, Euthyphro, was, What is piety? But it turns out that you have not explained to me the essence of piety; you have been content to mention an attribute which belongs to it, namely, that all the gods love it. [3]

EUTHYPHRO: But, Socrates, I really don't know how to explain to you what is in my mind. Whatever we put forward always somehow moves around in a circle, and will not stay where we place it. [4]

SOCRATES: I would rather that our definitions had remained firm and immovable than have all the wisdom of Daedalus and all the riches of Tantalus to boot. But I will do my best to help you to explain to me what piety is: for I think that you are indolent. Don't give in yet. Tell me; do you not think that all piety is just? [5]

EUTHYPHRO: I do.

SOCRATES: Well, then, is all justice pious too? Or while all piety is just, is a part only of justice pious, and the rest of it something else?

EUTHYPHRO: I do not follow you, Socrates.

SOCRATES: Yet you have the advantage over me in your youth no less than in your wisdom. But, as I say, the wealth of your wisdom makes you indolent. Exert yourself, my good friend: I am not asking you a difficult question. What I mean may be explained by this illustration: odd numbers are part of numbers, so that where you have the odd you must also have number, though where you have number, you do not necessarily have the odd. Now I think you follow me?

EUTHYPHRO: I do.

SOCRATES: Well, then, this is what I meant by the question which I asked you: is there always piety where there is justice? or, though there is always justice where there is piety, yet there is not always piety where there is justice, because piety is only part of justice? Shall we say this, or do you differ? [6]

EUTHYPHRO: No; I agree. I think that you are right.

SOCRATES: Now observe the next point. If piety is a part of justice, we must find out, I suppose, what part of justice it is. Now, if you had asked me, just now, for instance, what part of number is the odd, and what number is an odd number, I should have said that whatever number is not evenly divisible by two, is an odd number. Is it not so?

EUTHYPHRO: Yes.

SOCRATES: Then you see if you can explain to me what part of justice is piety.

EUTHYPHRO: Well, then, Socrates, I should say that piety is that part of justice which has to do with the attention which is due to the gods, and that what has to do with the attention which is due to man, is the remaining part of justice. [7]

SOCRATES: But what result is accomplished by our attention or service to the gods?

EUTHYPHRO: I think that nothing is dearer to them.

SOCRATES: Then piety means that which is dear to the gods? [8]

EUTHYPHRO: Most certainly.

SOCRATES: Do you not see that our definition has come around to where it was before? Surely you remember that we have already seen that piety, and what is pleasing to the gods, are quite different things. . . . Then we must begin again and inquire what is piety? Do not deem me unworthy; give your whole mind to the question, and this time tell me the truth. For if anyone knows it, it is you; it cannot be that you would ever have undertaken to prosecute your father for the murder of the overseer unless you had known exactly what piety is. You would have feared to risk the anger of the gods, in case you should be doing wrong. So tell me, my excellent Euthyphro, and do not conceal from me what you hold it to be.

EUTHYPHRO: Another time, then, Socrates. I am in a hurry now, and it is time for me to be off.

Exercises

The questions refer to the material immediately preceding the numbers in brackets.

1. Which type of definition did Euthyphro offer? Why is Socrates dissatisfied with his answer?
2. State the second definition and Socrates' criticism of it.
3. Does the third definition deal with essence or accident? Explain.
4. What is Euthyphro beginning to discover?
5. Note Socrates' new and more constructive approach. We must state the genus. Under which general class does he place piety?
6. Are piety and justice equivalent to each other? If not, which is the larger class?
7. Which part of the analytical definition is Euthyphro now supplying?
8. Why is Euthyphro guilty of "reasoning in a circle"?

Section VI: Truth and Falsity in Definitions

In our discussion of the criterion of equivalence in definitions, we made an assumption which was not explicitly stated; namely, that a definition could be true or false. Thus, in testing the definition "Man is a rational animal" we asked, "Is it true that all men are rational animals?" and, "Is it true that all rational animals are men?" Our interpretation, based upon the assumption that definitions may be true or false, is usually referred to as the "realistic" interpretation of definitions.

We must now consider a quite different attitude toward definitions, one which holds that definitions are neither true nor false. This point of view is called "nominalistic." The nominalist draws a sharp distinction between definitions and factual propositions. "Germany invaded Russia on June 22, 1941" is a factual proposition, and is of course either true or false. But a definition, according to the nominalist, merely tells us what a word means and is thus nothing but a stipulation or declaration as to how a word will be used by the speaker. If definitions are nothing but such stipulations, then they can be neither true nor false. This view is expressed by Whitehead and Russell, in their *Principia Mathematica* (Cambridge University Press, 1910, p. 11).

A definition is a declaration that a certain newly-introduced symbol or combination of symbols is to mean the same as a certain other combination of symbols of which the meaning is already known . . . A definition is concerned wholly with symbols, not with what they symbolize. Moreover it is not true or false, being the expression of a volition, not of a proposition . . . Definitions are merely typographical conveniences.

The nominalistic point of view is also expressed by Frye and Levi, in their *Rational Belief*. These authors assert that definitions are neither true nor false. They also present a test to determine whether a given sentence is a factual proposition or a definition. Their test is: Can you substitute the word "means" for the word "is" in the sentence? If you can, they say, then the sentence is a definition, and neither true nor false. Examine the sentence, "The Eiffel Tower is taller than the Washington Monument." Since "means" cannot here be substituted for "is," the sentence is a factual proposition. But "Man is a rational animal" permits the substitution into "Man means a rational animal" and is thus neither true nor false.

If we accept the nominalistic interpretation, then it would not be *untrue* to define "man" as "any book with a blue cover, weighing more than two pounds." We could say only that this is not the customary meaning of the word "man" in the English language, or that such a definition would serve no useful purpose. Definitions, in other words, would be classified as customary or uncustomary, useful or useless, but not as true or false. Definitions are regarded as nothing but stipulations as to how we shall use a given word, so that the definition "Man is a rational animal" may be translated into "Let the word 'man' stand for 'rational animal.'" An act of stipulating is like a command, or a directive, or other imperative types of statements, neither true nor false.

The controversy between the realists and the nominalists over the truth values of definition often overlooks the fact that we may stipulate a definition of "definition" itself. In other words, not even the word "definition" has a "real" meaning. But, this point aside, when we examine the manner in which definitions are customarily presented we shall find that some definitions are merely nominal stipulations as to how a term will be used, whereas other definitions are presented as *true* descriptions of the definiendum. A descriptive definition differs from ordinary descriptions in that it presents a description which is, or which purports to be, *equivalent* to the class of objects described. Following this distinction, the problem of truth or falsity of definitions may be clarified by the following considerations:

(1) A mere stipulation is neither true nor false. In an earlier chapter we learned that words are affixed to referents by acts of affirmation, which are logically arbitrary. There are no "real" names of things. When we say, "Let us call this color 'burnt sienna,' " we have given a name to a referent. This is the "naming-activity," and activities are neither true nor false.

(2) A definition may sometimes serve the purpose of mere typographical convenience, to save space and time. "Let < mean the same as 'included in the class of.' " ("Dogs < animals" will then read "Dogs are included in the class of animals.") "Let 'definiens' mean the same as "the defining part of the definition.' " Such definitions are merely "nominal" and neither true nor false, since they represent mere stipulations, or agreements.

(3) When we consider the context or setting in which analytical definitions are usually requested, we shall find that definitions are something more than mere stipulations as to how a term shall be used. In a discussion of poetry, someone may request a definition. A speaker says: "Let us use 'poetry' to mean 'verse with rhyming couplets.' " This definition would be rejected as wholly inadequate by most persons. Why? Because it is uncustomary or useless? Yes, but why is it uncustomary or useless? The reason is that when we speak of poetry we have in mind such writings as are commonly found in the productions of Homer, Dante, Shakespeare, Shelley, Keats, and others. When we ask for a definition of poetry we want a description of those characteristics which are common and peculiar to these works; we wish to know the qualities which all poems have in common, and which other writings do not have. In other words, we want an equivalent definition. If we should say "Poetry is writing which always has verse with rhyming couplets," our definition would now be false. It would not describe its subject matter correctly.

(4) It is important to note, however, that even a realistic or descriptive definition involves a stipulation. Thus, an equivalent definition involves two aspects, stipulation and analysis. On the one hand, there must be the stipulation, explicit or implicit, that the word "poetry" will be the name for the works of Shakespeare, et al. The use of the word "poetry" for these works is of course a mere arbitrary stipulation, and thus neither true nor false. The second aspect, analysis, requires that the definiens contain a description of the common and peculiar characteristics of these writings. Similarly, the definition of man as "a rational animal" has these two aspects: (a) We stipulate that the name "man" will be used to designate beings such as those who go to ball-games, movies, dances, polling booths, and so on. We stipulate that the definiendum shall designate such referents as these. This stipulation is an arbitrary one. (b) We then analyze the nature of these referents who are arbitrarily called "men." The two aspects, which correspond to the extensional and intensional aspects of meaning, may be illustrated by a diagram:

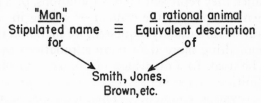

We might have called the referents Smith, Jones, and Brown, "palookas." Such "calling" would not be false, though it would be uncustomary. If we adopted this new name, then it would again be true to define "palookas" as "rational animals."

Definitions of words such as propaganda, love, religion, law, usually require realistic descriptions of the common and peculiar characteristics of the referents. When we use such words as these we have a vaguely apprehended notion as to the characteristics of the referents, and desire to refine our crude notions by careful analysis. Conflicts over the meanings of these words are not mere conflicts as to the customary usage of these terms, since custom differs from custom, and many writers misunderstand the nature of the referents involved. A good definition thus contributes to knowledge.

Exercises

1. Comment on the following, from Frye and Levi, *op. cit.,* p. 24:

> Note that of a definition we may ask, Is it meaningful? and Is it useful? but we cannot ask, Is it true? It is impossible to question the truth of a definition. *Definitions are neither true nor false,* simply because the test of truth or falsity is not applicable to them. A definition is merely the explicit resolution to use words in a certain manner. When Euclid says, "A scalene triangle is one having three unequal sides," he is to be understood as saying, "Henceforth I shall use the words scalene triangle *to mean* triangle with three unequal sides." There is no issue of truth or falsity here. *A definition is a linguistic convention.* It is *a stipulation,* to all intents and purposes a command, and is indeed to be treated as logically analogous to an imperative statement. "Shut the door!" True or false? Neither, certainly. "Let the words scalene triangle have the meaning triangle with three unequal sides." True or false? The same.

2. Are the following definitions real or nominal?
   a. A triangle is a plane figure having three sides.
   b. "Let us use the term 'triangle' for 'any plane figure having three sides.' "
   c. " 'Interpret' shall be understood to mean 'to be affected by.' "
   d. A man, understood as denoting Smith, Jones, etc., is a marine animal having the appearance of a fish.

3. What stipulation is required to make the following a true definition? "A man is a creature that lives in water and breathes air through its gills."

4. Discuss the following problems in definition with reference to the nominalist-realist controversy. Do the definitions aim at stipulation or true description?
   a. Dr. Zilboorg says that present day psychiatry does not possess any satisfactory definition of mental illness or neurosis. To illustrate, he told a story: A psychiatrist was recently asked for a definition of a "well-adjusted person" (not even slightly peculiar). The definition: "A person who feels in harmony with himself and who is not in conflict with his environment." It sounded fine, but up popped a heckler. "Would you then consider an anti-Nazi working in the underground against Hitler a maladjusted person?" "Well," the psychiatrist hemmed, "I withdraw the latter part of my definition."

Dr. Zilboorg withdrew the first half for him. Many persons in perfect harmony with themselves, he pointed out, are in "distinctly pathological states." (*Time,* Nov. 24, 1946.)

b. Definition is of crucial importance in tariff problems. The Canadian tariff was higher on vegetables than on fruit. How should a shipment of rhubarb be taxed? The botanist defines a fruit as the matured seed-vessel of a flowering plant. Thus tomatoes are fruit, rather than vegetables. But most people would call a tomato a vegetable. The test adopted by the customs court was: Is it served with meat as a vegetable, or is it eaten as a dessert?

c. Slander is defined in law as defamation of reputation by speech; libel as defamation in permanent form, capable of wide circulation, such as writings or drawings. How should a court rule on the question as to whether defamatory remarks made by a radio commentator are slander or libel?

d. Joseph A. Padway, counsel for the U.M.W. stated that the Norris-La Guardia Anti-injunction Act specifically outlawed use of injunctions in a labor dispute. Wasn't this case a labor dispute? "Calling it a labor dispute does not make it one," said the judge (Goldsborough). Gradually the arguments came down to: Was the case actually a labor dispute? Padway, attempting to prove it a labor dispute, pointed out that terms and conditions of employment were involved, etc. (*Time,* Dec. 9, 1946.)

5. The term "spiritual integration" is used in the following selection. Criticize its use in this context: "Dali produced these paintings during one of the most destructive periods in history and, conscious of his responsibility to become more constructive than ever before, reaffirmed in these canvasses his ideal of spiritual integration as opposed to the worldwide physical disintegration . . . Included in the show (is): 'Napoleon's Nose transformed into a pregnant woman, strolling his shadow with melancholia amongst original ruins.' " (From an art gallery's press release.)

Section VII: The Construction of Definitions

We have been concerned with the analysis and criticism of definitions. We shall now discuss the problem of *constructing* adequate analytical definitions. This is sometimes a very difficult task, particularly when there is controversy over the "proper" meaning of a word.

Let us assume that we require a definition of "art." We should first stipulate that the word will denote certain referents: "Let the word 'art' stand for productions in the fields of painting, sculpture, architecture, literature, and music." This stipulation clarifies the extension of the term, and eliminates certain ambiguous usages of the word "art" as in "Medicine is an art rather than a science" or in Plato's references to the arts of cobbling and the training of horses. Our next task is to analyze the nature of the referents for which the word stands. We must seek for the characteristics which are common and peculiar to paintings, poems, etc., so that our definition will have the virtue of equivalence. We shall leave to the reader and the art critic the task of finding the common and peculiar characteristics of works of art, and also the more difficult problem of defining "greatness" in works of art.

Let us now examine a more complicated type of problem, that of defining the word "propaganda." If the reader will examine the definitions of this term in several dictionaries and in a dozen books dealing with public affairs, it is a safe guess that he will find as many definitions as there are writers. This is, of course, a highly unsatisfactory situation, for when a speaker uses the word we cannot know what the speaker is referring to, and communication breaks down. The multiplicity of definitions of this word is such a scandal that a public-spirited citizen in New York is reported to have offered a prize of $1000 to anyone whose definition of the word would win general acceptance. It has also been seriously suggested that the use of the word be discontinued because of the extraordinary variety of its meanings.

When we examine the many definitions of "propaganda," however, we find that the word is used in two fundamentally different senses. In popular usage the word carries a derogatory connotation and refers to dishonest types of persuasion that seek to mislead the public. This meaning is rather widely accepted, for to call a speaker a "propagandist" is to tar him with the brush of opprobrium. On the other hand, we find a "neutral" definition of propaganda popular among some social scientists: "Propaganda is the expression of opinions or actions by individuals and groups deliberately designed to influence opinions or actions of other individuals or groups with reference to predetermined ends." (From *Propaganda Analysis*, by Clyde R. Miller.) Those who accept a variant of this latter definition tend to speak of *all* speakers as propagandists. They also recommend that we draw a distinction between bad and good propaganda, depending upon the aims of the propagandist. But neither of these definitions has won universal acceptance.

At this point the reader may ask, "But can we not arbitrarily stipulate *any* meaning for propaganda, and let the matter go at that?" We must certainly agree that where there is confusion over meanings it is highly desirable that speakers should inform their audiences of the sense in which they will use the word, but, as we have already noted, stipulation is not a merely arbitrary matter if we wish to define a word so that our definition will be "equivalent" to the referents denoted by it. Thus, some stipulations will be found satisfactory; others not. A stipulation that propaganda shall be understood to refer to "love poetry" will be wholly useless. When we think of "propaganda" we refer to certain kinds of activities that we apprehend only vaguely, and the search for a definition is the search for a description of these activities. Thus we reject some stipulations as inadequate, and distinguish between definitions which describe our referents correctly and those which do not.

The attempt to construct an adequate definition of propaganda might proceed along the following lines: We begin with a stipulation that the word shall denote certain kinds of activities, such as wartime broadcasts by government agencies that seek to create a defeatist spirit in the enemy, to defame him, or to bolster the morale of one's own people. The government's posters used for the sale of war bonds during the last war are also good examples of the denotation of the term. These posters showed pictures of soldiers lying on foreign beachheads and asked the question, "Do you want our boys to die for the lack of guns?" followed by "Buy bonds!" The "Freedom Train," which sought to popularize knowledge of our civil liberties, in order to create affection for the democratic form of government is another example.

If these examples are typical of the items properly included in the extension of the term "propaganda," then we must reject the two types of definitions noted above. Propaganda is not necessarily a dishonest type of persuasion which seeks to mislead the public. The "Freedom Train" did not mislead, and its purpose was a laudable one. The derogatory definition is thus too narrow. The neutral definition, on the other hand, is far too broad, for it covers *all* persuasive discourse, including the explanation of a formula in a class in mathematics, and even such expressions as "Please pass the salt" at the dinner table. It is worthy of note here that the Institute for Propaganda Analysis, which adopted the neutral definition cited above, also developed the classification of the tricks and devices of propaganda noted in Chapter 4. But it is surely inconsistent to define propaganda as equivalent to all persuasive discourse, and then to speak of the special tricks and devices of the propagandist. Unless propaganda is in some sense evil, why should we be warned against its diabolical devices?

Let us now seek to analyze the referents denoted by our term. We begin by seeking for an adequate genus. Let us suggest the following: "A form of directive language used by groups desiring the public's support and action for the group's objectives." (These objectives may be political, economic, religious, and so on.) Our genus states that the propagandist desires action from his hearers. In this respect he differs from the educator, who is interested in communicating knowledge or truth in order to enlighten his audience.

We must now attempt to find the proper differentia. Here, too, the distinction we have drawn between the educator and the propagandist is the crucial one. The educator will seek to teach the truth, and will not conceal relevant portions of the truth in order to influence his hearers in a given direction, but will present all of the relevant facts and permit his hearers to make up their own minds. He assumes that his hearers are rational beings who can think intelligently and who will act wisely when they know the evidence. The propagandist, on the other hand, seeks action, not truth. He wishes to mold his hearers' minds in a certain direction, regardless of the evidence. If the truth will serve his purpose, then he will tell the truth, but he has no real devotion to truth rather than to falsehood. And since action may be hindered by an appeal to thought, the propagandist will seek to inflame his hearers' emotions as the most effective prelude to action.

These considerations lead to the following definition:

"Propaganda is directive language which seeks to get action for a group's objectives by the means best calculated to achieve action, usually by appealing to the emotions rather than to the intelligence of its audience and which disregards the truth when it appears convenient to do so."

This definition should be examined critically to determine whether it adequately states the characteristics which are both common and peculiar to propaganda. The reader should note that our definition appears to make all propaganda "bad," since it appears to be an intrinsically undesirable form of persuasion. This point must be clarified. A propagandist may of course have our good in mind, as was the case in the sale of war bonds during the war. The sale of these bonds was required in order to avoid inflationary tendencies which would have disrupted the economy and interfered with the effective prosecution of the war. But the government did not explain these facts to the people. The posters implied that the failure to buy bonds would mean that the soldiers would have no ammunition. The picture of a dead soldier was an emotional appeal which brought more action than would a reasoned argument against inflation. Since a rational appeal would presumably have brought no action, this propaganda may have been necessary and few persons will object to its use. But when we give people propaganda instead of truth we treat them as children rather than as adults, unable to decide issues by a complete and truthful presentation of the relevant facts. Propaganda, then, is an intrinsically undesirable means of persuasion, but will be required so long as people lack the wisdom to choose wisely on the basis of rational considerations. In any case, those who have the wisdom to do so will always distinguish between the propagandist's appeals and his real purposes.

Before we leave the subject of definition, a warning is necessary. Stanley Baldwin, onetime Prime Minister of Great Britain, expressed an attitude of hostility toward the process of definition when he remarked, "Don't let us be too keen on definition . . . If we try to define the Constitution too much, we may split the Empire into fragments, and it will never come together again. Politically, if ever a saying was true, it is this: 'The letter killeth, and the spirit giveth life.' "

Susan Stebbing, in *Thinking to Some Purpose* (Penguin Books, p. 13), commented on this remark. She wrote,

He supposes that the logician must demand a definition, and that the definition must set forth precisely determinable characteristics. But whosoever demands such a definition of that which lacks precisely determinable characteristics is being illogical. The mistake consists in demanding that a sharp line be drawn concerning characteristics which are not in fact sharply distinguishable.

Logicians, in other words, will not commit the error against which Miss Stebbing warns. We must, of course, use a word in a determinative sense, for otherwise we would be guilty of using "words without referents," but we must not be too rigid in applying a term whose boundaries are not precisely delimited. We must take a similar attitude toward our definition of propaganda.

Exercises

1. Criticize the definitions of propaganda found in the following: Joe and Jim are listening to a famous radio commentator who is pontificating in his usual pontifical style. Jim says, "Oh, turn that guy off; that's just propaganda." Joe retorts brilliantly, "Whaddaymean, propaganda?" Jim answers, "Just a pack of lies." Joe: "My dear fellow, you have a sadly antiquated notion as to what propaganda is. Propaganda means any speech or action which has the purpose of influencing the actions of others. It follows that every public speaker is a propagandist. The only possible distinction we can make is whether or not we like the particular type of propaganda which is being dished out. If you like it, it is good propaganda so far as you are concerned; if you don't like it, it is bad."

2. Construct an adequate analytical definition of a "big" word, such as "religion," "democracy," "socialism," "communism," or "fascism."

3. The only difference between "propaganda" and "education" really is in the point of view. The advocacy of what we believe in is education. The advocacy of what we don't believe in is propaganda. (Edward L. Bernays, *Crystallizing Public Opinion*, Liveright, 1923, p. 210.)

Part Two

DEDUCTIVE LOGIC

Chapter 6

LOGIC AND ARGUMENT

Section I: Argument and Assertion

In Part Two we shall study the principles of valid reasoning, i.e., the principles which determine whether an argument is sound or unsound. Since the argument is the fundamental unit of reasoning, our first task is to understand the nature of argument.

In popular speech an "argument" often refers to a dispute, wrangle, or battle of ideas. The logician uses the term to denote a unit of discourse in which reasons are presented to support our beliefs. An argument thus has two parts: a statement of a belief, and the mention of the reasons for this belief. The *belief* may also be called the "thesis" or "conclusion"; the *reasons* may be called "proof" or "evidence," but the argument always contains both. An example is Montaigne's argument, "A wise man will not fear the loss of his life, for it is foolish to fear the loss of something the loss of which one will never regret." The conclusion is stated before the comma; what follows is the reason or proof for the conclusion. The argument is the whole.

An argument must be distinguished from a mere assertion, which simply states beliefs without furnishing the reasons or evidence on which they are based. To illustrate the difference between argument and assertion, let us examine three excerpts from a speech delivered by Mr. George Marshall, the former Secretary of State, in Chicago, Illinois, on November 18, 1947:

(1) It seems evident that as regards European recovery, the enlightened self-interest of the United States coincides with the best interests of Europe itself and of all those who desire to see conflicts of whatever nature resolved, so that the world can devote its full attention and energy to the progressive improvement of the well-

being of mankind. The place to begin that process is in Europe.

(2) Without a revival of Germany economy there can be no re-vival of Europe's economy. But we must be very careful to see that a revived Germany could not again threaten the European com-munity.

(3) We recognize that our people will be called upon to share their goods still in short supply and will have to forego filling a por-tion of their own requirements until the greater needs of Europe have been met. This is a direct contradiction of the allegation that we are seeking to dump surplus goods in Europe in order to avoid the depressing effects of oversupply.

The first two items represent mere assertions and do not state arguments. Marshall simply states his beliefs or opinions in these items and does not give us the evidence on which they are based. He feels that it is unnecessary to do so, probably because they appear so evident to him. But the third item states an argu-ment. The fact that we are sending goods to Europe at a time when they are in short supply, Marshall says, is proof that we are not dumping goods in Europe. This item contains both a belief and a statement of the evidence for that belief.

We are not at the moment concerned with whether we agree or disagree with Mr. Marshall. We are concerned only with the distinction between an argument and a mere assertion of a belief. An argument is a whole in which we say, "This is so be-cause of that," or "This is so; therefore, that is so." Before we proceed it will be well to acquire some facility in the ability to analyze an argument into its parts and to distinguish an argu-ment from a mere assertion.

An argument has two parts, evidence and conclusion. Note that the order of these parts is immaterial. The conclusion may be stated first, last, or it may be sandwiched between the evi-dence. The three possibilities follow:

1. Evidence stated first . . . *therefore* . . . conclusion.
2. Conclusion stated first . . . *because* . . . evidence.
3. Part of evidence . . . *therefore* conclusion . . . *because* remainder of evidence.

The following arguments are respective examples:

1. All men are mortal, and Socrates is a man; *therefore,* Socrates is mortal.
2. Socrates is mortal *because* all men are mortal and Socrates is a man.
3. All men are mortal; *therefore,* Socrates is mortal *because* he is a man.

These forms state exactly the same argument, despite the difference in the arrangement of its parts. We should also note that arguments may substitute other words for "therefore" and "because," or they may omit such words entirely. These words are the transitional words in the argument, indicating the parts which constitute the evidence and the parts which constitute the conclusion. Words which substitute for "therefore" are "so," "hence," "consequently," etc. These words always immediately precede the conclusion. Substitute words for "because," are "for," "since," etc. These words always immediately precede the evidence. There are other words which the student will note, but careful reading should always disclose just what the author of the argument is trying to prove, or "put across," even though some of the transitional words may be omitted.

Exercises

Read the units of discourse stated below, and distinguish collections of mere assertions from arguments. Are beliefs alone stated, or are reasons given for the beliefs? If the unit is an argument, analyze it into two parts, evidence and conclusion, and restate it with the conclusion first (Form 2 above).

1. All men are mortal and fallible, so some mortal beings are fallible.
2. All men are mortal, and all men are fallible, and all men are sinners.
3. Since only citizens can vote, John must be able to vote, for he is a citizen.
4. If a man is able to vote, then I know that he must be a citizen. John must be a citizen, for I know that he can vote.

5. Good sense is of all things the most equally distributed among men; for everybody thinks himself so abundantly provided with it that even those most difficult to please in all other matters do not commonly desire more of it than they already possess. (Descartes)

6. There is no race in the whole world that consists of families of uniform character. Every race embraces many diverse family lines. It is incorrect to assume that all the members of a racial group possess uniform characteristics because they are similar in some respects. All people who are blond and who have blue eyes have not the same characteristics and there is no reason to give inordinate weight to this single feature. (From "remarks" by Franz Boas in a pamphlet, 1934.)

7. There are thousands of persons on the federal payroll who don't earn their pay but who are kept on until they can retire. The commission studying this matter may recommend that these workers be let off with adequate severance pay.

8. Nicholas Remigius, a prosecutor of witches, is reported to have stated his technique of crime detection in the following words: "Tie the hands of the accused women, and throw them into a tank of water. If they sink and drown then we may presume that they are innocent. On the other hand, if they float, then they are certainly guilty and should be burned."

9. The first condition of free government is government not by the arbitrary determination of the ruler, but by fixed rules of law, to which the ruler himself is subject. We draw the important inference that there is no essential antithesis between liberty and law. On the contrary, law is essential to liberty. (L. T. Hobhouse, *Liberalism*, Henry Holt.)

10. Can the reader find any arguments in Section I of this chapter?

Section II: The Law of Rationality and Evasions Thereof

We have distinguished arguments from mere assertions. An argument is discourse containing inference, in which we say, "This is so because of that." But the inference may be sound or unsound. In Part Two we will be concerned with the principles of sound reasoning. Before proceeding to the principles, however, let us consider the aim of logical thinking and the manner in which this aim may be frustrated.

Every person who is interested in logical thinking accepts

what we shall call the "law of rationality," which may be stated as follows: *We ought to justify our conclusions by adequate evidence.* The meaning of adequacy will be explained in detail as we proceed. Let it suffice here to say that we mean evidence which is good and sufficient in terms of the kind of proof which is required. There are occasions when we require conclusive proof, as in mathematics, and there are occasions when it is sufficient to establish the probability of a given conclusion, as in weather prediction. But in all cases the evidence must be adequate to its purpose.

Adequate evidence is evidence which is relevant to the conclusion to which it is directed. We need not define "evidence" or "relevant," since we may assume that these words will be generally understood by most persons. Unless the meaning of these words were understood by the reader of a book on logic prior to his reading the book, he would not be able to follow the author's reasoning. The reader must be warned, however, that "relevance" is not always easily determined. When we say that one fact is relevant to another, we mean that there is a connection of some kind between them. This connection is not always apparent. For example, a historian investigating the causes of the decline and fall of the Roman Empire must consider only matters relevant to his study. Should he study the history of the building of the Great Wall in China, and the practice of human sacrifice among the Aztecs? Both facts may appear irrelevant, but we find to our surprise that the first fact is relevant. For the Great Wall was built to keep the Huns out of China, and they turned west instead. In their travels for pillage and loot they finally came to the Roman Empire and had an important role in its destruction. But all of us understand what relevance means. When one fact is irrelevant with respect to another, then that fact, like "the flowers that bloom in the Spring," has "nothing to do with the case."

Though few, if any, will have the temerity or the foolishness to challenge the law of rationality, it is often evaded. Evasion usually occurs through carelessness, but it may also occur through design. In this section we shall note some of the typical ways in which the obligation to support beliefs by adequate evidence is evaded.

In every argument we find the assertion of a belief, which we shall call "P." Someone says that P is true. When we ask the speaker, "Why?" or "What reasons do you have for believing that P is true?" we ask for evidence. We then expect adequate evidence to support his belief. This adequate evidence should be relevant to the question at issue, and it should be good and sufficient evidence. In the rest of this chapter we shall be concerned with the *evasion* of the requirement that evidence be furnished. The proverb says that we asked for bread and were given stones. Paraphrased, we shall find that we asked for evidence and received the Argumentum ad Misericordiam, or the Argumentum ad Hominem, or the Argumentum ad Verecundiam. We turn now to these evasions, seven of which will be considered.

1. The Appeal to Authority.

This evasion has the following structure: Jones says that P is true. When asked, Why? he answers, "Because X says so." Now, P (the *probabundum,* or proposition to be proved) should be proved by adequate evidence, but the fact that X says it is true is not *evidence* for its truth. The citing of authority is an evasion of the law of rationality.

There is no doubt that sensible people must rely on authorities for many of their important decisions. When a physician tells us that we need an operation we rely on his authority. We accept the authority of the weatherman that rain is probable. We have neither the time nor sufficient knowledge to investigate the evidence for all of our beliefs. The point, however, is this: No belief is true merely because someone says so. It is true because of the evidence in its behalf. When we trust an authority, we merely place credence in the fact that *he* has evidence. And if we wish to *know,* rather than merely to believe, we should inquire into the evidence on which his conclusions are based. For example, the reader believes that the earth is in motion. On what evidence?

In general, three questions should be kept in mind when considering the statements of an authority: Is the cited authority an authority in the specific field in which he has made his pronouncements? Does the authority have evidence to prove his statements? Do all qualified investigators agree on the general soundness of the type of proof offered? A great physicist may be an authority in the field of nuclear physics, but that does not qualify him to be dogmatic in the field of religion. A man may be very critical in one field and very uncritical in another. A theologian may be an authority in the field of theology, but he is not necessarily an authority on the question of the existence of God, since not all qualified investigators are agreed on the soundness of his methods of proof. On the other hand, we accept the statements of astronomers that the mean distance of the sun from the earth is close to 93 million miles, because they are authorities with respect to such matters, their evidence is available to all, and all qualified investigators agree on the soundness of their methods. We accept our physician's statement that we should take medicine for our ailments for similar reasons (or at least we believe them to hold). But even the acceptance of competent authority is never a substitute for *proof*.

When the authorities are in conflict, i.e., when "the doctors disagree," two courses of action are open to us. If the problem is a purely theoretical one, and we are not required to take immediate action, we should suspend judgment. If action is required, we should accept the authority who appears to be most competent and trustworthy.

The appeal to authority is often called the "Argumentum ad Verecundiam," a learned-sounding Latin phrase which means the "appeal to reverence." A revered authority or tradition is often regarded as infallible, so that anyone who disagrees is in some sense disloyal to that which ought to be revered. This type of appeal is sometimes employed with respect to the theory of evolution. We may be told that evolution cannot be true because it is contrary to the story in the Book of Genesis. But this question must be decided by those who have examined the available evidence, and the writers of that ancient book did not possess our present knowledge. Reverence is not a substitute for evidential proof. Reverence was also exhibited by the mediaeval professor who looked through Galileo's telescope, but who continued to teach the ancient astronomical ideas because he pre-

ferred to distrust the evidence of his senses rather than doubt
the authority of Aristotle.

The fact that "everybody knows that this is so" is no proof.
The masses of men have frequently been mistaken. They once
thought that the earth was flat. They still believe that the speed
of a falling object depends on its weight. The voice of the people
is not necessarily the voice of God on all questions.

2. The Appeal to Emotion.

The structure of this evasion: "The proposition 'P' is true."
Why? "Because I (or you) have strong feelings concerning it."
But strong feelings do not constitute evidence for the truth of a
proposition. The fact that people feel absolutely certain about
the truth of their religions, for example, does not guarantee
such truth. Christians, Jews, Mohammedans, and Buddhists all
feel certain concerning the truth of their religions, but only
evidence can determine which, if any, of these religions are
"true."

The appeal to emotion takes two forms, one subjective or
personal, and the other objective or social. In its *personal* form
the appeal is to one's own emotions. A person is convinced of
the truth of a proposition because he "cannot bear to think it
untrue." If I feel so strongly about it, his argument goes, then
it surely must be true. But wishes are fathers to thoughts, and
this is an evasion of the law of rationality. The argument is
usually not stated in this bald manner, but it is often found in a
concealed form.

In the *objective* form the appeal is to the emotions of other
persons, when a speaker substitutes emotional appeals for evidence. In traditional logic this is called the "Argumentum ad
Populum," the appeal to the people, or, in less flattering terms,
to the mob. The masses of men are often moved by emotion
rather than by reason. Speakers inflame crowds of people with
emotionally loaded language, rabble-rousing and prejudiced
appeals, by spell-binding, pulling the heart strings, and appeals
to popular sentiment. But the truth is not always one with our
emotions. Mark Antony's speech, part of which was quoted in
Chapter 4, is an excellent example of the use of this evasion. It

is Mark Antony's task to convince the mob that Caesar was not a dictator. His argument, reduced to its structure, goes as follows: If Caesar's wounds are pitiful to behold, then Caesar could not have aspired to be a dictator. If Caesar remembered you in his will, then he did not aspire, etc. Emotion overcomes reason, but again, no evidence.

Mark Antony's speech is also a good example of a special variety of the appeal to emotion called the "Argumentum ad Misericordiam," or the "appeal to pity." This appeal is used by attorneys for the defence who tell the jury that the prisoner at the bar has a wife and four small children. It was this type of argument which Socrates disdained to use in his speech defending himself to the Athenian jury, as reported in Plato's *Apology*. Finally, we note the "appeal to laughter." This means that we meet an opponent's arguments, not by evidence, but by a joke, which arouses laughter at the expense of the other person, to divert the attention of the hearers from the issue. But laughter, like loud talking, is never a substitute for evidence.

3. The Argumentum ad Hominem.

The Latin title means an argument addressed "to the man." We shall use this title to designate an attack which purports to be an attack against the truth of a proposition, but which directs its force against the man who asserts its truth rather than against the proposition itself. Proof that a proposition is false requires evidence of its falsity, and not an attack against the speaker. Its structure: The proposition "P" is false because the speaker is a certain sort of person.

To illustrate. A woman reads Schopenhauer's *Essay on Women,* aptly described by G. K. Chesterton as "that hideous essay." Schopenhauer writes:

It is only the man whose intellect is clouded by his sexual impulses that could give the name of the fair sex to that undersized, narrow-shouldered, broad-hipped, and short-legged race: for the whole beauty of the sex is bound up with this impulse. Instead of calling them beautiful, there would be more warrant for describing women as the unaesthetic sex. Neither for music, nor for poetry, nor for fine art, have they really and truly any sense or susceptibility; it is a mere mockery if they make a pretense of it in order to assist their endeavor to please. Hence, as a result of this, they are incapable of taking a purely objective interest in anything.

And more of the same. He says that women are interested only in acquiring husbands, in dress, jewelry, and cosmetics. Now, practically all women and most men would disagree with Schopenhauer. But how does the typical woman reader meet Schopenhauer's argument? By pointing out that his statements are untrue, or highly misleading in their selectivity? No. She attacks Schopenhauer himself, stating that he must have been a disappointed lover or must have had a very unhappy childhood to write such tripe. But this attack does not meet his argument. "Attacking the man" is an evasion of the law of rationality, and it is not a proper substitute for presenting evidence to refute his argument.

In general, the "ad hominem" takes the form of directing one's attack toward the speaker rather than to what he has said. The implied assumption is that his being a certain kind of person, or having a certain personal history, tends to make his statements false. Thus we answer an opponent by noting that he is a millionaire or a poor man, as the case may be, young or old, an employer or a member of a labor union. The popularity of the "psychoanalytic" method in recent years has made this method of approach a common one. Instead of meeting an opponent's arguments with evidence we seek to psychoanalyze him. If he says that a strong government is desirable, then we find that he is seeking a substitute for a "father-image." If he thinks a weak government is desirable, then he is in revolt against his father-image. We usually seek such explanations for views with which we disagree, since we seldom seek a psychological explanation of ideas with which we agree. It is as if the speaker were to say, "Your ideas are so patently false that it is difficult to see how an intelligent man could assert such things. So there must be a psychological explanation." But if we believe that ideas are false, then we are duty-bound to present the evidence. A pejorative psychological analysis of the supposed psychological causes of a belief is no substitute for logical analysis. Indulging in "personalities" is irrelevant with respect to the logical force of ideas. Euclid's geometry stands or falls on its own merits, whether or not Euclid was a kind husband and father.

We should not confuse the ad hominem with an attack against a man's character. If we say that X is a liar, or dishonest, or a spy, we have made allegations which are either true or false, but the ad hominem does not occur unless we contend that what X *says* is *false* because he is a certain kind of person. This distinction should be borne in mind when considering a special variety of the ad hominem called "Poisoning the Wells." This figure of speech means that whatever some people say should be suspected or ignored, just as we should regard all of the water drawn from a poisoned well as poisoned. In practice, this takes the form of an attack which seeks to discredit a witness, by alleging that he is a dishonest witness. This is sometimes a legitimate procedure, provided that we do not confuse this attack with a disproof of what the speaker says. This important distinction requires careful analysis.

In a law court a witness testifies that he observed the defendant in the act of committing the crime. The attorney for the defence then presents "character witnesses" who testify that the witness is a notorious liar who has been previously convicted of perjury. This evidence proves that the witness is untrustworthy, and that his testimony is of little worth with respect to its credibility. The jury would be unlikely to accept his statements at face value and would be well advised to disregard his evidence. But liars sometimes tell the truth, and we have not proved that what the witness says is false. We also discredit a speaker when we find that he has been paid to give his testimony, that he is an apologist for special interests or groups, that he is notoriously biased or prejudiced, or that he is insincere, and so on. If we know that a person is a communist, and as such would never find any fault with Russia, his statement that Russia is right in a particular international dispute would carry little weight. In the same manner we discount a Republican's attacks against a Democratic administration, and vice versa, because we feel that such criticisms are apt to be prejudiced. But in none of these examples have we proved that the speaker's statements are false.

We also discredit a speaker when we accuse him of being in-consistent, but this is not to prove his last statement false. For example, ex-Governor Arnall of Georgia stated that he thought it inadvisable to outlaw the Communist Party. An opponent retorted, "But Governor, a year ago you favored outlawing this party." The Governor answered that he had reconsidered, and now believed it would be a mistake to suppress ideas with which he disagreed. The fact that the Governor was inconsistent did not prove that he was now wrong (or right). But when we find a person consistently inconsistent, then we lose respect for his mental quality and integrity, and in such cases he becomes a discredited witness. Though we may admire people who have sufficiently flexible minds to change their opinions with new evidence, we do not admire those whose opinions change, like weather vanes, with every shift in the winds of doctrine. But though an attack against a man's authority may be legitimate, we must never confuse this with an attack against the ideas he has expressed.

A similar distinction must be made when we read a history of ideas. When a historian gives us a sociological or a socio-political-economic interpretation of ideas, he "explains" how a particular thinker came to develop his sytem of thought. For example, Thomas Hobbes (1588–1679) advocated the principles of absolute monarchy in his *Leviathan*. It is highly enlightening to know that Hobbes was personally a rather timid man. Per-haps he desired the security which a strong king would give him. We may also learn that he wrote in a time of troubles, when the social situation was disorganized and chaotic and when men longed to escape the horrors of civil war. The historian may ex-plain how the principle of absolute monarchy reflected the social needs of the time. But insofar as Hobbes presented a reasoned defence of his principle for *any* society, then his argument must be met with logical criticism as well as sociological interpreta-tion.

The same considerations apply to John Locke's (1632–1704) defence of constitutional monarchy. Locke was an apologist for the reign of William and Mary, the constitutional monarchs who ascended the throne in 1689 at the invitation of the Eng-lish Parliament. But Locke's argument for the advantages of representative government can also stand on its own feet. Edmund Burke (1729–1797) was a liberal in his early career. The French Revolution aroused a horror of revolution in him and he became an extreme conservative, arguing that social reform was certain to cause more harm than good. But once again, our knowledge of the conditions which led him to this position do not in themselves invalidate the argument. It may be that Burke's psychological experiences gave him an insight which he had not previously had.

The value of the historical explanation of ideas is that it may call into question our unthinking acceptance of assumptions which appear to be eternally valid. The critical mind welcomes a questioning of first principles. "Truth" is a very complex matter in the field of political philosophy, and history reveals that most political ideas play a very practical role in organizing society under certain historical conditions. Nevertheless, political programs are also techniques for achieving certain goals, and as such their validity transcends their immediate historical setting.

Before we leave this topic we shall note a popular type of defence against the ad hominem attack. We may meet an ad hominem by another ad hominem, directed against its proponent. This type of defence is called the "tu quoque," which means "You're another." An illustration: X, a forty-year-old professor argued in favor of a military draft in 1941. He stated that it was necessary for the defence of the nation. A student interposed, "You favor the draft because you are in the higher age bracket and are not in danger of being drafted." The professor responded with the tu quoque, "By the same token, you are against the draft merely because you are afraid that you will be drafted. The question is, Is the draft necessary for the welfare of the country?" The tu quoque settles nothing, but is a useful rhetorical device to expose the evasion called the ad hominem. Similarly, if we are told that we believe in the truth of P merely because we have been "conditioned" in a certain way, the proper retort is that our opponent considers P false merely because *he* has been conditioned in a different way. We shall usually find that those who use the ad hominem seldom realize that it may be applied to themselves. Thus, a

Marxian sees the doctrines of classical economics as false, "since they are merely products of a special historical situation," but the Marxian economics is regarded as infallibly true and not as the mere product of a historical situation. But the critic may be hoisted with his own petard.

4. Argumentum ad Ignorantiam.

This means the "appeal to ignorance." It has the structure: "P is true." Why? "Because you can't disprove it." This type of evasion often occurs in discussions which involve religious faith. Thus a man may argue that the Book of Genesis gives a literal account of the creation of the world. A skeptic may state that this account appears improbable to him, though he may also admit that he cannot disprove it. The religious protagonist then asserts, "You must now admit that it is true, for you cannot disprove it." This is the appeal to ignorance or inability to disprove. But inability to disprove is not equivalent to proof. Only evidence give us proof. If we accepted this evasion we should be required to believe that the Angel Gabriel visited the prophet Mohammed and informed him that God had decided that the Mohammedan religion was to supersede the Jewish and Christian religions. For how would you go about disproving this claim? We are not required to accept the improbable merely because we do not know how to disprove it. As cautious thinkers, we will withhold belief until we have positive evidence in favor of a proposition.

5. Begging the Question.

This evasion, known in traditional logic as "Petitio Principii," has the following logical structure: "P is true." Why? "Because P is true." The "evidence" here merely restates the conclusion. There is thus no independent relevant evidence whatsoever; we have merely assumed the truth of that which we are supposed to prove. The conclusion is used to establish itself.

This evasion is seldom stated in this bald form. The fact that we use the conclusion to establish itself is usually concealed in various ways. X argues that it is wrong for women to sit at bars.

When asked, Why? he answers, "Because I know that it isn't right." The expression "wrong" and "not right" are equivalent to each other. "Arguing by definition" usually involves begging the question. Thus, X asserts that all Christians are virtuous men. Y then points to the example of Thwackum, who is a Christian, but no exemplar of virtue. "Ah," answers X, "Thwackum may attend his church regularly, but he is no Christian, since if he were, then he would be a model of virtue." This is begging the question by definition, since X has *defined* a Christian as a virtuous man. Thus his statement "All Christians are virtuous men" was a mere statement of the tautologous remark that "All virtuous men are virtuous men." This is certainly true, but it is no proof that "Christians," in the sense of "being a member of a Christian church," are all virtuous men. The original proposition appeared to be a significant statement only because the implied tautology was concealed.

Complex questions (Have you stopped beating you wife?) are also examples of begging the question, though in a different form. For such questions begin by assuming that which should be proved. Note that we are not saying that we can dispense with all assumptions. We must always begin with the knowledge which we already have, with the beliefs we consider true. We should be critical of our beliefs, but beliefs are unavoidable. Few of us are as careful concerning assumptions as was the man who was famous for never saying anything he was not sure of. While driving through the country with a friend they passed some sheep. "Those sheep seem to have been sheared recently," said his friend. "Yes," answered the careful man, "at least on one side."

Charles Lamb, the English essayist, was also a careful man. He is reported to have refused to admit that 2 plus 2 is 4 until he knew what use would be made of his admission. But assumptions are forms of begging the question only when they assume that which *should* be proved. When we refer to a man on trial as "that criminal," we assume what should be proved. The great tragedy of lynching is not merely the fact that men are executed in a lawless manner, but that they are lynched on mere accusation, without trial to determine whether or not they actually are guilty.

One of the most interesting and complicated forms of this evasion is called "reasoning in a circle." The conclusion is used to establish itself, but it is smuggled into a chain of reasons, rather than into only one. It often occurs in the schematic form shown by the following:

Assertion that P is true: Proof: Because Q is true. (Question: How do we know Q is true?)

Proof that Q is true: Because R is true. (Question: How do we know R is true?)

Proof that R is true: Because P is true. (But this is what we started out to prove!)

An example is found in the chain of reasoning reported to have been developed by Joseph Smith, founder of the so-called Mormon Church. Smith said that he could be trusted when he asserted that he was God's true prophet on this earth (P). What proof? Because the Book of the Mormon says that Smith is a true prophet (Q). What proof that we can rely on the Book of the Mormon? Because it is the word of God (R). How do we know that it is the word of God? Because Smith assures us that it is, and whatever he tells us can be believed (P). Whether Smith actually argued in this way or not, this is a good example of reasoning in a circle.

6. Diverting the Issue.

The law of rationality requires that we furnish evidence for or against the proposition in issue and not for some other proposition. The evasion we call "diverting the issue" takes the following structures: P is true (or false) because I can prove R (where the truth of R is irrelevant to the truth of P). This evasion is seldom found in this bald form, for usually R bears some superficial resemblance to P, and it may appear that we have proved P when we have proved R.

An example: In 1940, Mr. Robert M. Hutchins, Chancellor of the University of Chicago, argued against the proposal that the United States should send military aid to England during the early stage in the World War. He sought to prove his point by the rhetorical questions, "Do you think that a victory for the

British Empire will result in the disappearance of all of the ills which afflict us here at home?" and "Are we to help the British Empire every time it goes to war?" His argument boils down to the following: We should not help England (P) because I can prove that such action will not result in a Utopia (R), or We should not help England (P) because I can disprove the thesis that we should help England whenever England goes to war (R). But what the chancellor should have proved was that it was not in the interest of the United States to help England in 1940. His evidence should have shown (if such evidence were available) that we would have been better off by not helping her then. The wise man will always choose the better when he cannot get the best.

Another example: A group of law students were discussing the abilities of the various members of the freshman class. One of them insisted that Littleton, a student whose class recitations contained frequent references to Schopenhauer, Nietzsche, and other philosophers, was a true genius. His friends turned upon him with withering scorn and the challenge, "A genius! What possible basis is there for calling him a genius?" "Well," came the immediate response, "he's no damn fool!"

In debates this type of diversion is of frequent occurrence. One of the debaters may seek to divert the issue to one which his opponent will find more difficult to prove or to one which he can more easily prove. X asserts that "all corporation executives are opposed to labor unions," and then adduces evidence to prove that it would be absurd to believe that "all corporation executives are friendly to labor unions." But the proof of the falsity of the second proposition does not prove the truth of the first. Certainly it is not the case that *all* executives are friendly, for some are and some are not. But this is quite different from saying that none of them are friendly.

Similarly, if X asserts that "some executives are friendly," Y may then seek to prove that it is false to assert that "all are friendly." But Y is not disproving the falsity of X's statement; he is disproving a different one. This type of diversion is called an "extension," since it extends the opponent's statement beyond what was actually asserted.

7. Special Pleading.

We ought to furnish adequate evidence for our beliefs, and this means that we ought to state the evidence as fairly and completely as it is possible to do so. To deliberately select evidence which is favorable to our thesis and to conceal unfavorable evidence is to violate this law. Few human beings are capable of perfection in this matter. Charles Darwin was an outstanding example of a thinker who conscientiously sought to find all the possible evidence which might upset his theory and who candidly admitted the gaps in his account of the evolution of life. At the opposite pole we find the fabled geologist who worked out a highly original theory concerning the rock formations in a certain valley. The examined evidence confirmed his theory, and he was in a state of exultation over the sensation which his paper would make in scientific circles. He walked up a hill to enjoy "his" valley, when his eye fell on a large boulder, a type of rock which should not have been there if his theory were true. He thereupon put his shoulder to the boulder and pushed it down the other side of the hill!

"Special pleading" is the evasion committed by speakers or writers who carelessly overlook "negative" facts. The following is an example: "The New Deal of the early thirties was a disaster. It unbalanced the budget, increased the national debt, passed unconstitutional legislation, etc, etc." This argument tells us that the New Deal was a disaster "because of the following list of facts . . ." But this listing of evidence, whether true or not, is very one-sided. No mention is made of facts on the other side. Its structure: "P is true." Why? "Because of the following list of facts: Q, R, and S." But facts A, B, and C, which might tend to disprove P, are ignored, either carelessly or deliberately.

The term "special pleader," however, should not be used for those who merely fail to state the evidence completely, for complete evidence is often an unattainable ideal. Outstanding examples of the evasion are found in political debates where each side claims all the credit and finds nothing but ill in its opponent's records. Lawyers are also notorious special pleaders, since their chief purpose is to win the case rather than to find the truth. Witnesses in a law court who swear under oath are required to testify to the truth, the whole truth, and nothing but the truth. This is obviously a precaution against special pleading. Each part of the affirmation is necessary. Otherwise the witness might tell the truth part of the time and lie the rest of the time. He could then say that he had told "the truth," but not "nothing but." Or he might tell only the truth but leave out a good part of it. Thus the requirement that he tell the "whole truth."

Exercises

A. The following group contains examples of each of the evasions of the law of rationality. The correct answers are found at the end of this set, but the student should attempt to identify each of the fallacies before looking up the answers. The seven evasions are the following:

(1) The appeal to authority (Argumentum ad Verecundiam).

(2) The appeal to emotion.
   (a) The appeal to one's own emotions.
   (b) The appeal to the emotions of others (Argumentum ad Populum, ad Misericordiam, Appeal to Laughter).

(3) The Argumentum ad Hominem (Poisoning the Wells).

(4) Argumentum ad Ignoratiam.

(5) Begging the Question (Reasoning in a Circle).

(6) Diverting the Issue (Diversion, Extension).

(7) Special Pleading.

In each case find the proposition (P) in issue. Then show the structure of the evasion in the following way: "P is true (or false) because . . ." State the nature of the evasion.

1. Your argument that the Taft-Hartley Law has contributed to labor unrest is without merit, since you are an International Representative of the CIO and would therefore be against the act no matter how good it was.

2. A wholesaler sued a retailer for $200, claiming that he had shipped that amount in goods to the defendant and had not been paid. The retailer claimed that he had paid the bill. The wholesaler plaintiff stated that he had no record of the payment. The retailer defendant then said that the court should dismiss the case, since the plaintiff could not disprove his claim that he had paid the bill.

3. It has been argued that the Inquisition must have been a beneficial institution, since whole peoples invoked and defended it, men of the loftiest souls founded it, and even its adversaries applied it to their own purposes, answering pyre with pyre.

4. Henry, a necessitarian, believes that human beings have no free will. He argues that in all choices between two courses of action, the strongest impulse will prevail, i.e., that the strength of the impulse decides the issue, not the "will." How do we know that the strongest impulse always prevails? By the very fact that it prevailed.

5. We should not prepare for war, for from so wicked a thing as war there can come only disaster and doom immeasurable.

6. Jones says that he is in favor of an army draft at the present time. Smith: "But why? We are not at war." Jones: "This is a period of crisis." Smith: "Well, so far as I am concerned, I favor the time-honored constitutional way of doing things." Jones: "But in time of national crisis we must disregard the constitution."

7. Under the capitalistic system there are many poor people, there is waste of men and materials, cut-throat competition, the glorification of the acquisitive instinct, depressions on the one hand and inflation on the other. This proves that the system is thoroughly bad and should be discarded.

The above arguments may be analyzed as follows:

1. "The proposition: 'The Taft-Hartley Law has contributed to labor unrest (P)' is a false proposition because you are a certain kind of person." Ad hominem.

2. "I paid the $200.00 (P). This is true, since you cannot disprove it." Ad ignorantiam.

3. "The Inquisition was a good institution (P) because many people approved of it." But whole peoples can be wrong about such things. Ad verecundiam, or appeal to authority.

4. P: "The strongest impulse always prevails (hence no free-will)." How do we know that it does? "Because it does." This is begging the question.

5. This is a highly "loaded" statement. "All wars are evil (P) because we feel strongly about war." Appeal to emotion. (What are the consequences which come from a refusal to to fight?)

6. This is an example of a diversion. The question is whether it is right that "we should have an army draft at the present time (P)." Smith diverts the issue to "the constitutional way of doing things," and Jones falls into the trap. (The draft is constitutional.)

7. Highly selected and one-sided facts to prove that "capitalism is bad (P)." Special pleading.

B. Analyze this group as before. Each type is represented by one example.

1. The attorney for the defence handed his brief to the barrister with the written notation, "We have a very poor case. Abuse the plaintiff's lawyer."

2. "Educated people do not believe in the devil."
"But I know some college graduates who do."
"I said *educated* people; the college graduates you refer to aren't really educated, because if they were, then they wouldn't believe in the devil."

3. How do we know that this man is guilty of having committed this horrible crime? I have encountered many examples of crime in my experience, but never one so horrible as this one. Consider this crime carefully and I am sure that you will agree with me.

4. Since it is impossible to prove that immortality is false, there being absolutely no positive evidence against it, we may rest assured in the confident belief that our souls are immortal.

5. Religion brought intolerance into the world, denied freedom of thought, retarded scientific progress, and was a divisive influence in that it separated group from group, each creed believing that it alone was good and all others bad. Therefore religion has done more harm than good.

6. Every slip of the tongue is significant in that it reveals some unconscious and suppressed desire. There can be no question about the truth of this statement, since it was put forward by Sigmund Freud, the founder of psychoanalysis.

7. Senator McKellar argued that Mr. David Lilienthal was not to be trusted as the head of the Atomic Energy Commission. He charged that Mr. Lilienthal's parents were born in Hungary, a country which has recently come under the domination of *communists*.

C. In the next group the evasions should be located and identified. What is the probandum in each case?

1. Dromedary cigarettes are without question easiest on the throat and most healthful. Our private statistical researches prove beyond doubt that more doctors smoke Dromedary than any other brand.

2. Modern art is greater than traditional art because all the best critics say so. Who are the best critics? You can identify them by the fact that they prefer modern art to traditional art.

3. Free enterprise is not as good a system as socialism. I need only point out that free enterprise does not work perfectly. Letting every one decide things for himself will not result in Utopia.

4. Will the farmer benefit by the increased wages which labor will receive if we raise our tariffs? There is no question that he will, since labor will buy more of the products of the farm.

5. But Doctor, surely your advice that I should stop smoking cigars cannot be sound advice since you smoke cigars yourself.

6. The American people are against war. Do you think that, if put to a vote, the mothers of the United States of America should like to see their sons sent across the seas and slaughtered in the European dogfight?

7. Why do I think the Demlican party is the best? Because that is the way my father voted.

8. "Gibbon is a literary historian." Why? "Because he has a literary style."

9. Those who are opposed to the elective system in colleges sometimes present as evidence the fact that the students who scatter most in their choice of studies accomplish least. This fact, they argue, proves that the elective system ought to be abolished.

10. *Open the Door, Richard* must be the greatest song ever written. No other song ever became so popular in so short a time, and since music is written for the public, what the public approves of must be the best.

11. ELMER: I oppose all forms of imperialism, both the Russian type and the type represented by the Marshall Plan.
    PHIL: But the Marshall Plan is not imperialism in the usual sense of that term.

ELMER: Oh, so you think that the Marshall Plan represents a policy of pure benevolence on the part of the United States?

12. We'll give this here hoss thief a fair trial, but send to town for a good strong rope.

13. Strikes should be abolished by law, for strikes are costly things for management, the workers, and the public.

14. The House of David sect in Benton Harbor, Michigan, was reported to believe that every member of the sect was immortal. When it was pointed out that the members showed the same mortality rates as other groups, the answer was that those who died were not true believers, since if they were they would not have died.

15. Bishop Wilberforce scored a telling hit in his famous debate with Thomas Huxley on the subject of evolution. He simply inquired casually whether Huxley was descended from the monkeys on his mother's side or his father's side of the family. (Clarke.)

16. We now know that there are no significant differences between men and women with respect to mental capacity. All arguments against coeducation therefore fall to the ground.

17. I feel that if we don't prevent the establishment of life tenure for the Chief Executive, the republic eventually will be undermined and destroyed. The New Deal is the height of totalitarian nationalism. Our Republican tradition is based upon uncompromising independence and the interests of the republic. (Alfred M. Landon, 1941.)

18. In 1941, in a radio debate, Frederick J. Libby argued that it was against the best interests of the United States to help England or otherwise meddle in the "European" war. Thomas Y. Elliott remarked that Mr. Libby's objections were without merit, since he was head of a "Christian Pacifist" organization, which was opposed to all wars, whether they were aggressive or defensive, and for whatever reason they might be fought. Mr. Libby accused Mr. Elliott of the argumentum ad hominem. Was his objection justified?

19. Russia has real freedom, and capitalism allows no freedom. What proof do I have? Because, by definition, capitalism enslaves the workers.

20. This witness is not telling the truth, for he was convicted of perjury some years ago.

21. I shall prove that the corrupt Democratic party does not deserve your support and that the reliable Republican party does.

22. Reuben Maury, editorial writer, wrote isolationist editorials for the *New York Daily News,* and interventionist articles for *Collier's* in 1940. Would this information have been relevant to the truth of what he said in either publication?

23. Salesman to undecided customer: "Shall I wrap it up, or do you wish to have it delivered?"

24. The Taft-Hartley Law is bad because Congress acted out of motives of pure expediency.

25. A pacifist argued that all wars are morally evil. When a friend asked if he meant that we should not fight even if the enemy invaded us, he answered, "But no one will invade us."

26. Psychological hedonism is the theory that every human action is always motivated by the individual's desire to benefit himself alone in what he does. If the opponent of this theory presents the case of a Marine who threw himself on a grenade, giving up his own life in order to save his buddies from certain death, the psychological hedonist is not impressed. He argues that it must have been done for selfish reasons, as proved by the very fact that it was done.

27. "In what grave and important discussion," a Van Buren editor asked, "are the Whig journals engaged? How are they enlightening the public mind and supplying material for that deep and solemn reflection which befits a great people about to choose a ruler? We speak of the divorce of the bank and the state; and the Whigs reply with a dissertation on the merits of hard cider. We defend the policy of the administration; and the Whig answers 'log cabin,' 'big canoes,' 'Go it, Tip, come it, Ty.' We urge the re-election of Van Buren because of his honesty, sagacity, statesmanship, and show the weakness and unfitness of his opponent; and the Whig answers that Harrison is a poor man and lives in a log cabin. We show that he is not a poor man, that he does not drink hard cider except from choice, that his home is not a log cabin but a fine house; . . . the Whigs reply, 'No matter, the prairies are on fire.'" (J. B. McMaster, *A History of the People of the United States;* vol. 6, p. 565, D. Appleton-Century Company, 1906.)

28. You say that the United States has the highest living standards of any nation in the world? I can disprove that statement by pointing to the sharecroppers in the South. Is that what you mean by a high living standard?

29. Aristotle stated that "the good" meant that which the good man approves. *(Nichomachean Ethics.)*

30. A railroad spokesman said, "The Union's spokesman accuses us of speaking the language of the railroads. We wouldn't dream of suggesting that he speaks the language of the unions."

31. That man should not be hired to work in the State Department. He talks exactly like a communist would.

32. Nietzsche: "Those who disagree with me when I say that mankind is corrupted prove that they are already corrupted."

33. Karl Marx and F. Engels, in the *Communist Manifesto*: "But don't wrangle with us so long as you apply, to our intended abolition of bourgeois property, the standard of your bourgeois notions of freedom, culture, law, etc. Your very ideas are but the outgrowth of your bourgeois production and bourgeois property, just as your jurisprudence is but the will of your class made into a law for all, a will whose essential character and direction are determined by the economic conditions of existence of your class."

34. "Treason can never prosper. What's the reason?
    That when it prospers none will call it treason."

35. When we buy from a foreign country, we get the goods, but they get the money. When we sell to a foreign country, we get the money, but they get the goods. How much better, then, to buy and sell in our own country, for in that case we retain both the goods and the money.

36. The ideas of "progress" and "individualism" are products of eighteenth century philosophers, and they reflect the special conditions of that age. So these ideas are out of date today and not valid for our society with its different social and economic conditions.

37. I pay no attention to writers who criticize communism, for they are all prejudiced. The fact that they criticize communism is in itself proof that they are prejudiced.

38. Communism is not, in any real sense of the word, a faith, for its philosophy is materialistic, and thus opposed to faith.

39. If every person over sixty were given a pension of $200 per month, then they would buy more goods; this would increase the need for workers, whose wages would rise, and they in turn would raise their standard of living. Business would be kept at a high level, and everyone would benefit.

40. A Chicago newspaper commented as follows on President Truman's statement that "we won that war for freedom": "Whose? The Poles? The Lithuanians? The Hungarians? The Yugoslavs? They were all freer before the war for freedom. They are all, and many others besides, enslaved now."

Chapter 7

SYLLOGISMS, PROPOSITIONS, AND TERMS

Section I: Introduction to the Syllogism

In the previous chapter we noted the significance of the law of rationality, which requires that the evidence or reasons should be sufficient to prove our beliefs or conclusions. We also noted the distinction between conclusive proof and evidence which is merely sufficient to establish probabilities. The remainder of Part Two will be devoted to the principles of conclusive proof, or *validity*.

The argument is the fundamental unit of reasoning. We shall study various types of arguments, but our chief emphasis will be devoted to the *syllogism,* one of the basic forms of deductive reasoning. The syllogism will be defined, in a very broad sense, as an argument in which two premises lead to a conclusion. The importance of this form of reasoning has been recognized by logicians since the time of Aristotle (384–322 B.C.), though Aristotle, it may be noted here, treated it in a limited manner, and analyzed only one of its types. Much misunderstanding, however, is still prevalent concerning the nature of the syllogism. It has been called "artificial," and "outmoded." We shall endeavor to show that such criticisms rest on misunderstandings, and to justify, at least in part, the following statement by the American philosopher, W. P. Montague.

Far from being artificial or outmoded, the Aristotelian syllogisms are the blood and flesh, or at least the connective tissue, of all human discourse; and indifference to the logical laws which they exemplify is intellectual triviality, for it means indifference to the laws of any possible universe that the intellect can comprehend. (*The Ways of Things,* Prentice-Hall, 1940, p. 35.)

We shall begin our discussion of the syllogism with the simplest kinds of examples, and develop the complexity of the subject by gradual stages. In order to facilitate our understanding of the logical form of such arguments we shall state them in the schematic form shown below. This form of presentation, which misleads many persons into thinking that syllogisms are "artificial," is adopted because it clearly indicates the structure of the argument. Thus:

> All men are mortal
> Socrates is a man
> Therefore,   Socrates is mortal

The form of this syllogism is "artificial" in the sense that people do not argue in this schematic form. In ordinary discourse, as Montague has put it, the same argument might go like this: "Socrates, yes, even the divine Socrates, must be mortal, because we know that he is a man, and, alas we have to remember that whoever is man is also mortal." We shall deal with arguments in ordinary discourse in due course, but we will use the schematic form whenever we wish to clarify the logical structure of a syllogism.

Let us now consider the essential nature of syllogistic reasoning. Consider the following set of circles:

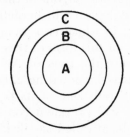

There are three circles, marked A, B, and C. A is inside B, and B is inside C. We shall now construct a syllogistic argument concerning these circles: If a circle A is inside a circle B, and B is inside circle C, then A must be inside C.

Stated schematically, we find:

> A is inside B
> B is inside C
> Therefore,   A is inside C

If the premises of this syllogism are granted, then we must accept the conclusion. In this simple example we find the essential meaning of "validity": *An argument is valid when the premises necessitate the conclusion.* If it is impossible, granted the truth of the premises, that the conclusion should be false, then the argument is valid. If the reader grasps this simple example of valid reasoning, then he will be able to understand the more complicated examples, for all rest on principles of the same order.

In a valid argument, the truth of the premises guarantees the truth of the conclusion. Why is this so? We shall not attempt to answer this question, if indeed an answer is possible, but we will assume that we live in the kind of world in which such things are so, and that the "light" of reason guides us correctly in such matters. If we know that a letter is inside an envelope and that the envelope is locked in a trunk, then it follows that the letter is inside the trunk. In any event, we shall assume that such reasoning is logically correct.

If we now return to the Socrates syllogism, we shall find that its validity rests upon the same principles. Its form or structure is exactly the same as the circles illustration. As logicians interested in validity, we are concerned with form or structure, rather than with content. The form is the framework or mold; the material or content is that which is poured into the mold. The use of symbols will help us to exhibit forms, and we shall therefore use symbols frequently. Let us then substitute the letters A for Socrates, B for men, and C for mortal. If we now draw circles for each of these letters, we will have exactly the same circles illustration we used above:

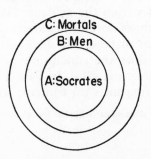

Diagrams enable us to "see" the structure of arguments with the eye of the senses as well as with the eye of the mind, and we shall resort frequently to diagrammatic illustrations. The use of these diagrams in logic is similar to their use in geometry. They are not indispensable, but they are very helpful aids in reasoning. We shall usually use circles but other types of diagrams might also be used, such as maps. For example, examine the following syllogism:

The residents of the 15th ward are residents of the North Shore

The residents of the Gold Coast are residents of the 15th ward

Therefore,   The residents of the Gold Coast are residents of the North Shore

This syllogism might be illustrated by the following map:

| NORTH
14th Ward | SHORE
15th Ward |
| | Gold
Coast |

This map shows that the syllogism is valid, just as the circles do. The circles, however, are easier to draw, and are generally preferred.

An introductory word concerning the relationship of "validity" to "truth" may be considered at this point.* A valid argument is one in which the premises "necessitate" the conclusion. The sole problem, in discussing validity, is whether the conclusion logically follows from the evidence. We shall not be concerned, in our study of formal deductive logic, with whether the premises are true or false. We shall ask: *Assuming* that the premises are true, does the conclusion logically follow? If it does, then the argument is valid. In Part Two we shall be concerned with structure, not with content; with the *form* of the

* A more thorough discussion will be found in Chapter 16, Section II, page 311.

argument rather than with the *truth* of what is stated. Thus (1) an invalid argument may be composed of true statements, and (2) a valid argument may be composed of false statements. Examples of each of these possibilities are as follows:

(1) All Muscovites are human beings
All Russians are human beings
Therefore, All Muscovites are Russians

(2) All Holy Rollers are chain-smokers
All Moslems are Holy Rollers
Therefore, All Moslems are chain-smokers

The first of these syllogisms is invalid, even though each statement is true. It is invalid because the premises do not logically justify the conclusion. (The reasons for its invalidity will be discussed later). The second syllogism is valid, even though each of its constituent statements is false. Its form is exactly the same as our circles illustration, as you will find if you substitute *A* for Moslems, *B* for Holy Rollers, and *C* for chain-smokers. A valid argument is one in which, assuming that the premises are true, the conclusion logically follows. A wholly satisfactory argument, of course, is one in which the premises are true, and the reasoning valid; but our only concern at present is with the meaning of validity.

Section II: The Categorical Proposition and Its Parts

In the last section we became acquainted with some simple examples of syllogistic reasoning. We saw how the validity of an argument could be exhibited through the use of circles or other types of diagrams. In the course of our study we shall find that not all syllogisms are so simple as those we have examined, and we shall also learn that syllogisms are not all of the same type. We have begun with examples of the "categorical syllogism," and shall deal with such syllogisms exclusively in the first few chapters of Part Two. Later we shall study hypothetical, alternative, and disjunctive syllogisms. Syllogisms are classified on the basis of the types of propositions which enter into their construction. We shall, accordingly, study different types of propositions.* The same thought, moreover, may be expressed by different types of propositions. As examples of different types of propositions which may express the same thought, consider the following: (1) "Good readers are persons who find logic an easy subject," and (2) "If a person is a good reader then he finds logic an easy subject." The first of these is categorical, which means "unconditional"; the second is hypothetical, or "conditional." The first simply states a fact without conditions. The second, that something will be the case on the condition that something else will hold. But for the time being, we shall confine our attention to categorical propositions.

Our first task is to analyze categorical propositions which contain subjects and predicates. These terms are defined as follows:

Subject: The thing or entity of which we assert something.

Predicate: That which is asserted of the subject.

Examples: The desk is brown. "Desk" is the subject; that of which we make an assertion. "Brown" is that which we assert of the subject. Or: Dogs are animals. "Dogs" is the subject, and "animals" the predicate. When we speak of "subject" in logic, we always mean the *complete* subject. In "The desk which was bought five years ago and which was moved out of this room yesterday by two men wearing blue jeans is an antique" all the words preceding the verb "is" constitute the subject.

A categorical proposition (of the subject-predicate type) is made up of various elements: (1) The subject and predicate are called *terms*. Thus there are two *terms; a subject term,* and a *predicate term*. (2) There is the *copula* (a word meaning "that which joins"), which joins the subject term to the predicate term. The copula will always take a form of the verb "to be." ("Men *are* mortal." "This section *is* hard to understand." "I *am* a student of logic.") Note, however, that "is" and "are" are copulas only when they link the subject to the predicate. In

---

* A proposition, as we learned earlier, is a sentence which is either true or false. Not all sentences are either true or false; for example, directive sentences or interrogative sentences. A proposition, in other words, states that something *is* or *is not* the case. We need not know whether a sentence is true or false in order to call it a proposition, as in "There is oil beneath this building." We do not know whether this statement is true or false, but it is surely one or the other.

"Students who are conscientious are bound to succeed" only the second "are" is the copula. The first is simply part of the subject term. And finally, (3) there are the "quantifiers," words such as "all," "some," "no," or "none," which indicate the extent to which we refer to the members of the subject term, as in "All men are mortal" or "Some women are fickle." Note that the quantifiers are not part of the subject term.

In graphic form, the proposition consists of the following elements:

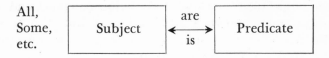

Exercises

Identify the subject term, predicate term, copula, and quantifiers (if any):

1. Some movie stars are happily married.
2. All birds are members of a class of vertebrata called "aves."
3. Socrates is mortal.
4. Dogs are friendly animals.
5. Birds which are in the hand are things equivalent to two in the bush.
6. The ships which sailed last night are sloops which are very fast.

Section III: The Class-Analysis of Subject-Predicate Propositions

We shall interpret all subject-predicate propositions as asserting that two classes have certain relations to each other. This means that we shall think of the subject term as referring to a class of individuals or things, and similarly with the predicate. Let us carefully define the meaning of "class." A class means a group of things, or a collection of things having some characteristic in common. This characteristic may be a "natural" one, as in the group of things called "mammals." The common characteristic may also result from an arbitrary act of selection, as in "The people you saw on the street today." These people constitute a group having in common the fact that they were seen by you today. The class may consist of individuals who do not take more than two lumps of sugar in their coffee. Thus there are no limitations on grouping any entities into a class. We may even find a common characteristic between "a very heavy elephant" and "the thought of the square root of minus one in an angel's mind." They belong to the class of things which were used as illustrations in this paragraph.

Every entity may be said to belong to an infinite number of classes. Thus "tiger" belongs to the following classes and to an infinite number of others: existing things, physical things, living things, things found in jungles, in zoos, things which inspired the poems of William Blake, and so on.

A class, then, is any collection of things having some common characteristic. The members of a class need not be actually existing things. We may speak of "sprinters who can run one hundred yards in less than nine seconds" or "human beings who are without sin," though neither class has any members. A class having no members is called a "null" class.

The importance of thinking of subjects and predicates as classes of things should be obvious, since it is our purpose to test the validity of syllogisms by the use of diagrams. When we think of "Orioles are birds" as representing two classes of things, the manner in which the circles should be drawn is immediately apparent. Similarly with "Birds are living organisms." These propositions may be diagrammed separately or they be combined, as in the following:

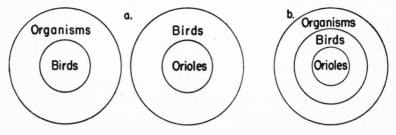

These relationships may also be exhibited by a "map" that emphasizes the fact that the classes are always collections of individuals. In the following "map" diagram each small circle stands for an individual member of the class to which it belongs:

LIVING ORGANISMS

An important qualification of the above remarks must now be noted. Some sentences have single individuals as their subjects, as in "Ferdinand is a non-belligerent bull" or "This book is a logic text." In such cases the subject term is stated to be a *member* of the predicate class, and is not *included* within it. In other words, *class-inclusion* refers to the relationships of two classes to each other; *class-membership* to the relationship when the subject term is an individual. But though we shall have occasion to note situations in which this distinction is an important one, we shall nevertheless usually treat an individual subject in the same way as we treat a class. We shall use a circle to diagram the individual subject. We shall treat the individual, for most purposes, as a class having only one member and *include* it within another class.

The form in which many sentences are stated may not clearly indicate that the subject and predicate terms refer to classes of things. When we encounter such sentences we must translate them into the proper form so that the relations of two circles to each other will be clearly indicated. A fuller discussion of this subject must be reserved for a later chapter, but we shall now note a very simple form of completion which some sentences require. Thus, "The desk is brown" is an incomplete sentence for class-analysis, since "brown" is not the name for a collection of things. A class is made up of individual things, each of which could be pointed to, and it would be impossible to point to a "brown." When either subject or predicate is stated as an adjective, we must always add the "completing complement," or noun, in order to refer to a collection of individual things. Completed, the above sentence would read, "The desk is a brown thing." The sentence "All men are mortal" requires the addition of "beings," or we could simply add an "s" to "mortal," for "mortals" is a noun that refers to a class.

We shall now introduce the symbol $<$, using it to mean "class-inclusion" (or class membership). When this symbol stands between two classes, for example, A $<$ B, we shall interpret it as meaning "A is (are) included in the class of B." The symbol is actually a substitute for the copula, and it emphasizes the relationship of the inclusion of one class in another. The grammatical copula represents the more traditional type of usage; the symbol of inclusion, the more modern usage. We shall use both. Frequently, however, we shall find that the symbol expresses our meaning more accurately, especially when the subject is an individual. Thus, "Franco is a dictator" really means "Franco $<$ dictators," i.e., "Franco is in the class of dictators." The symbol emphasizes the fact that the predicate class is a plural noun. Note carefully the exact words for which the symbol $<$ stands: *It means "are included in the class of" or "is a member of the class of."*

Exercises

Restate the following sentences, substituting the symbol of class-inclusion ($<$) for the copula, and supply the completing complement where necessary. The predicate should be stated in the plural form in all cases. Read each proposition orally, using the words for which $<$ stands.

1. Some movie stars are happily married.
2. Americans are peace-loving.
3. All philosophers are reflective.
4. Ferdinand is gentle.
5. Liberals are idealistic.
6. Liberals are idealists.
7. Her eyes are blue.
8. This book is a logic text.

Section IV: Affirmative and Negative Propositions

The propositions we have thus far examined have all been affirmative in quality. Each sentence asserted that a certain predicate may be affirmed of a subject. All have been of the form "S *is* P," using "S" for the subject of a categorical proposition and "P" for its predicate. But a categorical proposition may also assert that a certain predicate *cannot* be affirmed of a subject, or that the predicate class is *excluded* in whole or in part from the subject class. The presence of words like "no" or "not" usually indicate that a proposition is negative, as in "No S is P," or "Some S's are not P's," or "S is not P." Examples of such negative propositions in words are: "No men are angels," "Some men are not egoists," "Jane Russell is not an actress." The distinction between affirmative and negative propositions is referred to by logicians as one of "quality."

Note carefully the following sentences: "Nurses are non-combatants," "Nurses are not combatants." These sentences have the same meaning, but the first is stated affirmatively; the second, negatively. The difference between them centers in the copula. Does the copula indicate that the subject *is* something-or-other, or that it *is not?* There are many adjectives and nouns which are prefixed by "non," but the use of such terms does not make the propositions negative. The question is whether the negation belongs to the copula. "S is P" and "S is non-P" are both affirmative, but "S is not P" is negative. "No men are angels" asserts that angelic qualities cannot be affirmed of men; hence it is negative.

Exercises

Distinguish the following as affirmative or negative.
1. He is unwise.
2. He is not unwise.
3. He is not disinclined.
4. No metals are non-conductors.
5. Some women are not intuitive.
6. No S is P.

7. S is not non-P.
8. All non-S are non-P.
9. No non-fools are persons who do such things.
10. Teetotalers are persons who do not drink hard liquor.

Section V: Universal and Particular Propositions

In the last section we distinguished between affirmative and negative categorical propositions. We shall now classify propositions as "universal" or "particular." This distinction is based upon the extent to which we make reference to the members of the class of things named by the subject term. When we refer to all of the members of the subject class, as in "All nations are preparing for war," the proposition is universal. When reference is made only to some of the members of the subject class, as in "Some nations are preparing for war," the proposition is called particular. The distinction between universal and particular proposition is one of "quantity."

Propositions which have an individual person or thing as subject are classified as universal. Thus, "H. G. Wells was a second-rate novelist" or "This pen has a ballpoint" are universals, though their subjects consist of single persons or things. The justification for this usage is that when the subject is an individual we refer to all of the subject, not to part of it. It is easy to distinguish any universal proposition from a particular proposition if we remember that a particular uses the quantifier "some" or other word indicating that only part of the subject class is being referred to.

When the subject class has no quantifier, as in "Women are fickle," we are uncertain as to whether the writer is referring to all women or only to some. We shall adopt the convention of interpreting such indefinite statements as referring to all, unless the context makes it clear that "some" is intended. When the context does not indicate which quantifier is intended, assume that the proposition is universal.

To sum up, there are two types of universal propositions, general and singular. A universal-general proposition refers to *all* of the members of the subject class; a universal-singular has as its subject a *single* individual person or thing. A particular proposition is one which speaks of *some* of the members of the subject class. In tabular form:

Universal: (General—uses quantifer All)
(Singular—has a single thing or person as subject)
Particular: (Some)

(The reader should note that all of the illustrations in this section have been affirmative in quality. The same principles apply to negative propositions, as we shall see in the next section.)

Exercises

Classify the following affirmative propositions as universal-general, universal-singular or particular:
1. All fish live in water.
2. Some dogs are homeless.
3. This book is heavy.
4. That theory is discredited.
5. You are wrong.
6. Lazy students are failures.
7. T. S. Eliot is a British subject.
8. Those apples look edible.
9. Some apples are not tangy.
10. That group of men should be watched.
11. Human beings are never satisfied.

Section VI: The Four Types of Categorical Propositions

We have classified propositions in terms of quantity and quality: as universal or particular, and as affirmative or negative. Combining the four elements in the two classifications we derive four different combinations, which we shall label as A, E, I, and O in accordance with the custom of logicians:

Universal-Affirmative	A form
Universal-Negative	E form
Particular-Affirmative	I form
Particular-Negative	O form

Henceforth, we shall use the letters A, E, I, and O to signify the combinations for which they stand. These letters were originally used by mediaeval logicians, who derived them from the first two vowels in the two Latin words, *affirmo* (I affirm) and *nego* (I deny). Thus the affirmative forms are A and I; the negative forms are E and O. We shall now study these forms in detail and we shall diagram them in four different combinations of circles, a method of diagramming invented by the Swiss mathematician and physicist Euler (1707–1783).

1. The A-form

Examples: "All Arabs are Moslems" and "Ali-Baba is a Moslem."

The A-form (universal-affirmative) has two types, the general and the singular. Using the symbols "S" for subject and "P" for predicate. "All S is P" represents the general form and "S is a P" represents the singular. We are already acquainted with the universal and affirmative nature of these types.

In class terminology, we write "All S < P" or "S(an individual) < P."

The same circle diagram will be used for both:

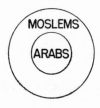

2. The E-form.

Examples: "No Arabs are Hindus," and "Ali-Baba is not a Hindu."

The E-form (universal-negative) also has two types, general and singular. These forms have not yet been explained. We recall that a universal proposition refers to *all* of the subject. The assertion that "No Arabs are Hindus" refers to *all* Arabs, for it states that each and every one of them is excluded from the class of Hindus. Similarly in "No logic texts are easy to read," we assert that all logic texts are outside the class of books which are easy to read. The E-form is thus universal, for it refers to *all* of the subject-class.

The E-form is negative for it denies that a certain predicate can be affirmed of the subject. It asserts that the subject does not belong to the predicate class; the relation of inclusion is denied *in toto*. This is the same as to say that the subject class is *completely excluded* from the predicate class.

The singular E-form, "Ali-Baba is not a Hindu," should be analyzed in the same manner. Here we say that the predicate cannot be affirmed of an individual, or that this individual is *excluded* from the predicate class. Individual subjects, as we saw earlier, are treated as universals.

In circles, we use the same form for the general and singular universal-negative. "No S is P," and "S (an individual) is not a P," are exhibited by two circles which have no point of contact, viz.:

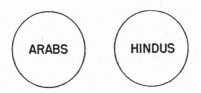

When we write an E-form in class symbolism we require a new symbol, ⊄, called the symbol of exclusion, and standing for the words "are excluded from the class of." The E-form in class terminology will take the following forms: "All Arabs ⊄ Hindus," "Ali-Baba ⊄ Hindus." These are read, "All Arabs are excluded from the class of Hindus," etc. Note carefully the sharp difference between the traditional statement of the E-form and its class statement: "No S is P" and "All S ⊄ P." The latter clearly emphasizes the fact that the members in one circle are *outside* the members in the other.

3. The I-form.

Example: "Some Arabs are Moslems."

The I-form (particular-affirmative) asserts that part of the subject class is included within the predicate class. "Some S is P." In diagrammatic form, we find that the S and P circles intersect:

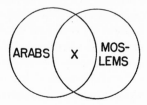

The area marked X indicates that there are individuals who are members of both classes.

In class symbolism: Some S < P.

4. The O-form.

Example: "Some Arabs are not Moslems."

The O-form (particular-negative) asserts that some of the members of the subject class are excluded from, or "outside of" the predicate class. This form is particular, since the quantifier is "some," and negative since it asserts that part of the subject *is not* in the predicate class. In the traditional manner we say, "Some S is not P." In class symbolism we use the symbol of exclusion once more and write, "Some S ⊄ P," which should be read, "Some S is excluded from the class of P."

In circles:

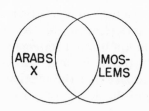

Note the position of the "X" in this diagram. It is in the subject circle outside of the predicate circle, and indicates that there are members of the subject class who are outside the predicate class. In the I-form, the position of the X indicated that there were some entities which were members of both classes.

The four types of categorical propositions reveal all of the possibilities in the relations of one class to another. There are four possibilities, covered by the forms we have designated under the letters A, E, I, and O. One class is wholly or partially included within another, or it is wholly or partially excluded from another. These forms alone can be diagrammed in circles; a proposition which can be diagrammed in circles must be in one of these four forms. Some further refinements in the relations of these circles will be discussed in the next chapter.

The four forms may be presented schematically, as in the following table:

TYPES OF PROPOSITIONS		TRADITIONAL FORM	CLASS-TERMINOLOGY
A Universal-Affirmative	General	All S is P	All S $<$ P
	Singular	X (an individual) is P	X $<$ P
E Universal-Negative	General	No S is P	All S $\not<$ P
	Singular	X (an individual) is not P	X $\not<$ P
I Particular-Affirmative		Some S is P	Some S $<$ P
O Particular-Negative		Some S is not P	Some S $\not<$ P

The reader should carefully note the two forms of expression in which each type of proposition may be stated. The "traditional" form of expression states each type in ordinary language, and the "class-terminology" form expresses the same type in the symbols of class inclusion and exclusion. These different forms of expression are exactly equivalent to each other, and the reader should familiarize himself with these equivalences. Note in particular the two different ways in which the E-form is expressed.

Exercises

Classify the following propositions as, A, E, I, or O, and define each in terms of quality and quantity, (universal-affirmative, universal-negative, etc.)

1. No saints are sinners.
2. All politicians are interested in votes.
3. Some statesmen are politicians.
4. Some politicians are not statesmen.
5. Lewis is not a timid man.
6. Shakespeare is a great poet.
7. Some explanations are non-luminous.
8. Some types of non-compliance are worthy of chastisement.
9. All saints are excluded from the class of sinners.
10. Some citizens are excluded from the class of voters.
11. Those exercises are quite difficult.

Section VII: The Distribution of Terms

A new technical term, "distribution," must now be added to our logical vocabulary, and we will have completed our analysis of categorical propositions. This term is used in a precise and technical sense by logicians, and its customary meaning should be ignored. The understanding of this term is of great importance, since distribution is the fundamental idea in the analysis of the syllogism.

We shall speak of the "distribution" of terms. To say that a term is distributed means that we have referred to *all* of the members of the class designated by that term. Thus, when we say "All dogs are animals," the term "dogs" is distributed because we have referred to *all*. We have referred to each and every member of the class "dogs." In "Some books are texts" we have referred to only part of the class of "books," and the term "books" is undistributed.

We shall now examine the manner in which the A-E-I-O forms distribute their terms. Since it is quite easy to understand the notion of distribution when applied to the *subjects* of propositions, we shall dispose of this aspect of the problem very briefly, and then give a more extended discussion to the distribution of the predicate terms in each of the four forms. The *subjects* in the four forms are distributed as follows: A and E, the universals, distribute their subjects, for a universal proposition always refers to *all* of the members of the subject class. I and O, the particulars, which are prefixed by the quantifier "some" do not distribute the subjects, since "distributed" means that *all* have been referred to. The subject of a universal proposition is always distributed; the subject of a particular proposition is always undistributed. We turn now to the distribution of the *predicate terms* in each of the four forms.

1. The A-form: "All dogs are mammals."

"Mammals," the predicate term, is undistributed. The proposition does not inform us concerning all mammals; no reference is made to each and every member of the class of mammals. It does not say that all mammals are dogs. We are informed that some mammals are dogs, but that is all. We may now generalize our finding in this case: The predicate term is undistributed in all A-form propositions.

In the typical A-form proposition the predicate class is larger than the subject class. But the two classes may be co-extensive, as in "All triangles are 3-sided figures." In this case we know (from our knowledge of mathematics) that reference is also made to all members of the predicate class. But *as such,* an A-form proposition of the form "All S is P" tells us that its subject is distributed but it does *not* tell us that the predicate is. We shall therefore follow the rule that an A-form leaves its predicate undistributed. If we follow this rule we will never go beyond the information actually given to us.

We shall use the symbols "d" and "u" for distributed and undistributed. We may thus write our A-form as follows: All dogs (d) are mammals (u). Using S and P once more, and using the symbol of class inclusion, we have $S(d) < P(u)$. Note that the quantifier "all" is unnecessary in this symbolic form, since "d" means "all." Note also that the singular A-forms are treated in the same manner as the general.

2. The E-form: "No crows are green birds."

The predicate term "green birds" is distributed here. The proposition states that "All crows are excluded from the class of green birds." This obviously means that *all green birds* are outside the class of crows, so an E-form distributes both its subject and predicate. We are given information concerning each and every member of both classes.

Using the symbols of distribution, our proposition may be written as "No crows (d) are green birds (d)." The student should become adept at translating all E-forms into class terminology, viz.: "All crows (d) are excluded from the class of green birds (d)," or "All crows (d) $\nless$ green birds(d)." In completely symbolic form, this would read: $S(d) \nless P(d)$. The singular E-form is treated in the same manner.

3. The I-form: "Some Germans are militarists."

The predicate term is undistributed. We are informed that the two classes, Germans and militarists, overlap, i.e., that some Germans are militarists and conversely, that some militarists are Germans. We have received no information concerning *all* militarists. We have not been told that *all* militarists are Germans, but only that some are. Thus the predicate "militarists" is undistributed. In class-symbols: $S(u) < P(u)$.

4. The O-form: "Some Arabs are not Moslems."

The predicate of an O-form is distributed. The proposition asserts that all Moslems are completely outside the class designated by the subject term. This will become clear if we remember that the Arabs of Lebanon are Christians. These Arabs are "some Arabs," and none of them are Moslems, so all Moslems are completely outside of the Lebanese Arabs. All O-forms will be interpreted in the same manner: their predicates are always distributed. In symbols: $S(u) \nless P(d)$.

Our discussion of the distribution of terms in the A-E-I-O forms may be summed up in the following table, omitting the brackets from the signs of distribution:

		Subject	Pred- icate	Traditional form	Class ter- minology
Universals { Aff.	A	d	u	All Sd is Pu	Sd < Pu
Universals { Neg.	E	d	d	No Sd is Pd	Sd ≮ Pd
Particulars { Aff.	I	u	u	Some Su is Pu	Su < Pu
Particulars { Neg.	O	u	d	Some Su is not Pd	Su ≮ Pd

Note that the signs of distribution for A and E will apply to both the general and singular types of these forms. It will also be helpful to remember the pairings among these propositions with respect to distribution. Thus, both universals distribute the subject terms; the particulars do not. Both negative propositions distribute the predicate terms; the affirmative propositions do not.

Exercises

Classify the following propositions as affirmative-negative, as universal-particular, as general-singular (where relevant), as A, E, I, or O, and indicate the distribution of the subjects and predicates of each:

1. All composers are geniuses. A   A
2. Johann Sebastian Bach is a genius.
3. No composers are geniuses. E
4. Philip Emanuel Bach is not a genius. E
5. Some composers are geniuses. I
6. Some composers are not geniuses. O

Chapter 8

THE ANALYSIS OF CATEGORICAL SYLLOGISMS

Section I: The Definition of the Syllogism

A syllogism, in the broad sense of the word, is an argument made up of two premises and a conclusion. There are, as we noted in the previous chapter, different types of syllogisms, but we are at present concerned only with the categorical type, sometimes called the "Aristotelian" syllogism, since it was the only type recognized by Aristotle. A categorical syllogism is an argument made up of three categorical propositions, which contain between them three and only three terms.

Later on, we shall study non-categorical types of syllogisms. The fundamental distinction between the categorical and the non-categorical types lies in the types of the propositions of which the syllogism is composed. Categorical syllogisms are composed of categorical propositions, which are made up of terms. Such propositions are called "simple," as distinguished from propositions whose constituent elements are sub-propositions. The latter are called "compound." The following is an example of one type of compound proposition: "If all men are rational beings, then all men are entitled to justice." This proposition has two sub-propositions as its constituent elements: "All men are rational beings" and "All men are entitled to justice." Non-categorical syllogisms are based upon compound propositions. But we shall come to these later. For the time being we shall be concerned exclusively with categorical propositions and categorical syllogisms.

A categorical syllogism may be more precisely defined as an argument composed of two categorical premises and a categorical conclusion, containing three and only three terms, in which the three terms are combined in such a way that a term in one premise will be the same as the term in another premise, and the other two terms will be the same as the terms which appear in the conclusion. The reader need not bother to memorize this definition, since its meaning will become quite clear in a moment. The definition indicates that a relation between two classes of things is established by virtue of their relation to a third class. For example, let us suppose that we are concerned with the question as to whether hay fever is in the class of infectious diseases. The solution of this problem requires that we relate these two classes to a third class. We must seek for a third term which will connect the two terms with which we begin. We may connect them by the class of "allergy diseases." Since we know that "all allergy diseases are non-infectious" and that "hay fever is an allergy disease," we draw the conclusion that "hay fever is not infectious." This is an example of a categorical syllogism.

In this chapter we shall be concerned with the analysis of categorical syllogisms, with the primary aim of learning the rules of validity in such arguments. We shall also learn how to test the rules of validity by drawing diagrams. For clarity in presentation we shall begin by stating all syllogisms in a schematic or "artificial" form, dealing with syllogisms as they appear in living discourse in a later chapter. The difficulties encountered in analyzing complicated syllogisms, as we shall see, are chiefly problems of language and not of form.

Section II: Basic Words in the Analysis of Categorical Syllogisms

The categorical syllogism is an argument containing two premises and a conclusion.

$$\left. \begin{array}{l} \text{All actors are egoists} \\ \text{All movie stars are actors} \end{array} \right\} Premises$$

Therefore, All movie stars are egoists $\}$ *Conclusion*

There are three propositions, each with a subject and predicate term. There are three different terms in the syllogism, each of which is used twice. The three terms (or classes of things) in our example are "actors," "egoists," and "movie stars." Each term is used twice, making three pairs of terms. Henceforth, when we speak of a "term" we must remember that it is used twice.

The terms are called "middle term," "major term," and "minor term." These words are defined as follows:

Middle term: The term which appears in *both premises*. Since each term is used twice, and twice only, the middle term does not appear in the conclusion. "Actors" is the middle term.

Major term: The predicate of the conclusion is called the "major" term. "Egoists" is the predicate of the conclusion. The major term is also found in the first premise, "All actors are egoists." It appears twice.

Minor term: The subject of the conclusion is called the "minor" term: "Movie stars." It also appears in the premise, "All movie stars are actors."

The *major premise* is the premise which contains the major term. The *minor premise* contains the minor term. Each of the premises also contains the middle term. The appropriateness of the term "major" lies in the fact that the predicate of the conclusion is usually the largest class mentioned in a syllogism. By definition however, "major term" means "predicate of the conclusion." The major term appears in one of the premises, and that premise is called the major premise.

In analyzing syllogisms we shall use symbols for our three terms. The choice of symbols is an arbitrary matter. Thus, in analyzing the syllogism above, we might use A for actors, E for egoists, and M for movie stars. Our syllogism symbolized would then appear as

All A are E
All M are A
Therefore, All M are E

But other forms of symbolization may be used. Traditionally, logicians used M for the middle term of the syllogism, S for the minor term, and P for the major term. Using these symbols, we shall use M for actors, S for movie stars, and P for egoists, and we would have

All M are P
All S   are M
Therefore, All S   are P

The student should note carefully that S and P in this symbolization stand for the minor and major terms respectively, and not for subject and predicate, except that they stand for the subject and predicate of the *conclusion*.

Finally, we note a simple method of symbolization which uses A, B, and C for the three terms of any syllogism, following the order in which the terms appear. Thus we might use A for actors, B for egoists, and C for movie stars.

> All A are B
> All C are A
> Therefore, All C are B

Exercises

Identify the middle term, major term and minor term in the syllogisms below. Note that each type of term appears twice. Also identify the premises as major and minor.

1. All men are mortal
   Socrates is a man
   ∴ Socrates is mortal
2. All politicians are opportunists
   No statesmen are opportunists
   ∴ No politicians are statesmen
3. All S are M
   No P are M
   ∴ No S are P
4. All A are B
   No C are B
   ∴ No C are A
5. Some K are M
   No N are M
   ∴ Some K are not N

Section III: Preliminary Analysis of Categorical Syllogisms

The analysis of a syllogism requires the application of certain techniques. We shall illustrate these techniques by applying them to the first syllogism in the previous exercises. (Since we have not yet examined the rules of validity, our analysis at this stage must be of a preliminary nature.)

The first step requires that we identify the three propositions in terms of the A-E-I-O classification.

> All men are mortal (this proposition is in A-form)
> Socrates is a man (this proposition is in A-form)
> ∴ Socrates is mortal (this proposition is in A-form)

The next step in our preliminary analysis is to symbolize
each term with a letter. Use A for men, B for mortals, and C for
Socrates. After this has been done we must insert the signs of
distribution for each term in each premise. In order to do this
we need simply to follow the standard rules of distribution for
the A-E-I-O forms, as summarized on page 169. Since our syllogism has three A-forms, each proposition will have the same
signs of distribution: subject (d) and predicate (u). We shall
thus write our syllogism as follows:

> *A-form*:   All men (Ad) are mortals (Bu)
> *A-form*:   Socrates (Cd) is a man (Au)
> *A-form*: ∴ Socrates (Cd) is a mortal (Bu)

As a final step at this stage, "gather" the symbols, stating
them in the class analysis form:

> *A-form*:   Ad < Bu
> *A-form*:   Cd < Au
> *A-form*: ∴ Cd < Bu

Note that the quantifiers need not be stated when we use the
symbols, since the signs of distribution indicate whether the
propositions are A-E-I-O forms.

Exercise

Analyze syllogisms 2–5 in the previous exercises in the same manner.
Where symbols alone are given, only part of the analysis will be
required.

Section IV: The Rules of the Categorical Syllogism

We shall now consider the nature of a *valid* categorical syllogism. The categorical syllogism has five rules of validity. These
rules resemble the axioms of mathematics. A syllogism which

violates no one of these rules is valid; if any one of the rules is violated, then the argument is invalid. We shall not attempt to "prove" these rules, though when we draw diagrams to illustrate the manner in which they are applied, we shall "see" that they must hold. As we noted earlier, if all of B is in C, and A is in B, then A must be in C. The principle involved in this reasoning may be generalized: If one class is wholly included within another then any part of the first class is part of the second. Why is this so? Some thinkers hold that this is simply a characteristic of the language which we speak, others that logical relations are grounded in the nature of things, so that we simply "see" that these principles characterize the world in which we live. The latter view would appear to be nearer the truth. In any case, however, we must recognize that not all logical principles can be proved, since every proof requires the use of principles which are themselves not proved.

The five rules or axioms of the syllogism may be divided into two groups, as follows:

A. Rules concerning the proper distribution of terms (rules of quantity):

> Rule 1. The middle term must be distributed at least once.
>
> Rule 2. A term which is distributed in neither premise must not be distributed in the conclusion.

B. Rules concerning negative propositions (rules of quality):

> Rule 3. No conclusion is necessitated by two negative premises.
>
> Rule 4. If either premise is negative, then the conclusion must be negative.
>
> Rule 5. A negative conclusion cannot be drawn from two affirmative premises.

We shall now study these rules in detail. But before we analyze a syllogistic argument in terms of the rules, we should inspect it in order to determine whether it meets the definition of a categorical syllogism. It must have three and only three terms, each of which is used twice, with a middle term appearing in each of the premises.

Rule 1. The middle term must be distributed at least once.

The following syllogism violates this rule.
        All dogs are animals
        All cats are animals
∴ All cats are dogs

Let us analyze this syllogism, using the symbol A for dogs, B for animals, and C for cats. We then note that each proposition is in the A-form, which means that the subject of each is distributed and the predicate undistributed. Setting up our symbols in the proper form we find:

        A-form: Ad < Bu
        A-form: Cd < Bu
        A-form: ∴. Cd < Au

The middle term is B. We note that it is u in both of the premises. The rule requires that it be d at least once. When the present rule is violated we are guilty of the fallacy of "undistributed middle term."

Let us now examine the rationale of this rule. In the example just analyzed, the conclusion states a connection between dogs and cats which goes beyond the evidence in the premises. In order to establish a connection between the two terms in the conclusion, they must be connected by a middle term, and this middle term must be involved in its whole extent at least once. The circle diagrams will illustrate the reason why this argument is invalid. Thus, the following circles satisfy the information given by the premises, but without showing the conclusion drawn above:

The diagram indicates that dogs belong in the class of animals, and that cats are in the same class. It does not prove that dogs are cats.

A word now as to the meaning of validity and the manner in which the circle diagrams should be used to check the "correctness" of the rules. A valid argument is one in which the premises necessitate the conclusion. Granted the premises, the conclusion must follow. The conclusion of a valid argument could not possibly be false if the premises were true. This was illustrated by our early examples, as in "A is in B, and B is in C, etc." But in an invalid argument, the premises might be true and the conclusion false. Now, when we draw the circles, we should ask ourselves, Can we draw circles which correctly depict the information stated in the premises, and not get the conclusion stated in the argument? In our example, this is precisely what we were able to do. The conclusion "All cats are dogs" requires that the circle for cats be drawn inside the circle for dogs. But in the illustration, the two circles were drawn outside of each other, showing that no dogs are cats. Since we were able to draw the circles in a way which shows that the conclusion might be false, despite the truth of the premises, the argument is invalid.

Note that it is irrelevant that the conclusion of an invalid argument happens to be true, as in the following:

All Texans are human beings (A-form: Td < Hu)
All Americans are human be- (A-form: Ad < Hu)
    ings
∴ All Texans are Americans (A-form: Td < Au)

Here again we find the middle term undistributed. Now, this argument *might* be diagrammed as follows, consistent with the premises:

But the question we must ask is: Can we draw the circles in such a way that the conclusion will *not* be realized? We can.

First draw the diagram for the first premise, as follows:

The second premise states that "All A is H." Where shall we draw the circle for A? Consistent with the premise that "All A is H" we might draw the second circle in the following different ways:

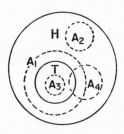

This diagram shows that the circle for A may be drawn at four different places. Where shall it be drawn? At this point we should look at the conclusion and ask ourselves whether the A circle can be drawn in a way which will make the conclusion false. The conclusion is that all T are A. Circles A_2, A_3, and A_4 all make the conclusion false, so the argument is invalid. In a valid argument, on the other hand, it is impossible to draw the circles for the premises in a way which fails to necessitate the conclusion drawn by the argument.

Let us now examine a different type of illustration of the "undistributed middle":

>Some football players are college graduates. (Au < Bu)
>Some college graduates are philosophers. (Bu < Cu)
>∴ Some football players are philosophers. (Au < Cu)

We diagram the minor premise first:

Our next question is whether we can diagram the second premise in a way which will show that the conclusion might not follow even though the circles are consistent with the premises. This can be done in the following way, which indicates the possible falsity of the conclusion that some members of A are

members of C: (A (x) B (x) C)

Rule 2. A term which is distributed in neither premise must not be distributed in the conclusion.

This rule obviously applies only to the major and minor terms, since the middle term never appears in the conclusion. The violation of this rule is called "illicit process," or "illicit distribution." When the major term is improperly distributed in the conclusion, the fallacy is that of "illicit major"; when the minor term is improperly distributed, we have "illicit minor."

The following syllogism shows a violation of this rule:

All Moslems are vegetarians   M d < V u
No Hoosiers are Moslems   H d ≮ M d
∴. No Hoosiers are vegetarians   H d ≮ V d

Note that V was "u" in the premise and "d" in the conclusion. Thus the fallacy is that of "illicit major term." A term undistributed in the premise must not be distributed in the conclusion. The major premise gives us information concerning some vegetarians; the conclusion makes a statement concerning all. This is to "out-talk" our information.

When we diagram this argument, we draw circles for the major premise first. The minor premise requires that we draw the circle for Hoosiers, "H," outside the Moslems circle. The minor premise might thus be drawn in the four ways shown below:

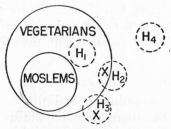

Since the "H₁" and "H₂" circles both definitely indicate the possible falsity of the conclusion, the argument is invalid. (Circles H₃ and H₄ do not indicate such falsity. The reason why H₃ does not do so will be explained in Section VI.)

Rule 3. No conclusion is necessitated by two negative premises.

The following premises represent a violation of this rule:
          No Marines are cowards Md ⊄ Cd
          No cowards are aviators Cd ⊄ Ad
No valid conclusion can be drawn from these premises. Why not? Let us draw the circles for the first premise:

The second premise tells us that A must be drawn outside of C. The conclusion must then assert a necessary connection between M and A. But we cannot establish an absolutely certain connection between M and A on the basis of the information contained in the premises. When we draw A outside of C, A may be wholly or partially included within M, or wholly or partially excluded from M. Since no single one of these possibilities is necessary, whichever we choose, another will be possible.

Rule 4. If either premise is negative, then the conclusion must be negative.

Rule 5. A negative conclusion cannot be drawn from two affirmative premises.

The last two rules are of lesser importance, since violations are rarely encountered, but these rules are required to cover possibilities which may occur. A syllogism might violate one of these rules and yet be consistent with the others, as in the following examples:

        Violation of Rule 4:
        All Communists are Stalinists
        Some Brazilians are not Stalinists
     ∴ Some Brazilians are Communists

Violation of Rule 5:
All men are rational animals
All rational animals are moral agents
∴ Some moral agents are not men

The student will have little difficulty in showing that the conclusion in Rule 4 is not necessitated. The fact that some Brazilians exist outside the Stalinist circle does not prove that they exist within the communist circle. Drawing a proper diagram for Rule 5 presents difficulties which will be discussed in Section VI.

We may now note that the three rules concerning negative propositions may be summed up in one formula: If *negative* propositions are used in a syllogism, then one and only one premise must be negative and the conclusion must be negative. Rule 3 emphasizes "one and only one negative premise"; Rule 4 that the conclusion must be negative when the conclusion is negative; and Rule 5 that a premise must be negative when a premise is negative. But the separate rules clarify each aspect and show the three ways in which the formula may be violated.

Section V: The Analysis of Categorical Syllogisms

We are now ready to analyze syllogisms in terms of the rules of validity. The rules must not be violated; if any one of them is violated, then the syllogism is an invalid argument, i.e., the conclusion is not justified in terms of the evidence. In this section we shall analyze two simple syllogisms for your instruction. Our analysis should proceed through the following steps:

1. Assuming that the following syllogism has been given to you for analysis, write it out on your notepaper. It is convenient to separate the premises from the conclusion by a line:

All Hoosiers are Americans
All Texans are Americans
∴ All Hoosiers are Texans

2. We must now repeat the steps we learned in our "preliminary analysis," in Section III. We shall use A, B, and C for the three terms, each of these symbols being used twice; we shall letter the terms accordingly, and underline each term as we do

so. The syllogism will then look like this:

$$\frac{\text{All } \underline{\text{Hoosiers}} \text{ are } \underline{\text{Americans}}}{\text{A} \qquad\qquad\qquad \text{B}}$$

$$\frac{\text{All } \underline{\text{Texans}} \text{ are } \underline{\text{Americans}}}{\text{C} \qquad\qquad\qquad \text{B}}$$

$$\therefore \frac{\text{All } \underline{\text{Hoosiers}} \text{ are } \underline{\text{Texans}}}{\text{A} \qquad\qquad\qquad \text{C}}$$

3. We now identify each proposition in terms of the A-E-I-O classification. In our example all three are A-forms. We now insert the distribution signs for each proposition, each proposition being considered as a separate unit. Thus:

A-form: $\dfrac{\text{All } \underline{\text{Hoosiers}} \text{ are } \underline{\text{Americans}}}{\text{Ad} \qquad\qquad\qquad \text{Bu}}$

A-form: $\dfrac{\text{All } \underline{\text{Texans}} \text{ are } \underline{\text{Americans}}}{\text{Cd} \qquad\qquad\qquad \text{Bu}}$

A-form: $\therefore$ $\dfrac{\text{All } \underline{\text{Hoosiers}} \text{ are } \underline{\text{Texans}}}{\text{Ad} \qquad\qquad\qquad \text{Cu}}$

4. We now gather the symbols together, in class-analysis form:

$$Ad < Bu$$
$$Cd < Bu$$
$$\therefore \overline{Ad < Cu}$$

5. The syllogism should now be examined for possible violations of the rules. If any rule is violated, then the syllogism is invalid. Rule 1 tells us that the middle term must be distributed at least once. B is the middle term. We find that it is u, or undistributed, in both premises. It was not d, or distributed *at least once*. Rule 1 has been violated, and the syllogism is invalid.

6. The manner in which the circle diagrams will show the invalidity of this example was explained in our discussion of the rules.

We shall now analyze a second example. Steps 1–2–3 would give us the following statement of a second syllogism:

A-form: $\dfrac{\text{All } \underline{\text{Hoosiers}} \text{ are } \underline{\text{Americans}}}{\text{Ad} \qquad\qquad\qquad \text{Bu}}$

E-form: $\dfrac{\text{No } \underline{\text{Texans}} \text{ are } \underline{\text{Hoosiers}}}{\text{Cd} \qquad\qquad\qquad \text{Ad}}$

E-form: $\therefore \dfrac{\text{No } \underline{\text{Texans}} \text{ are } \underline{\text{Americans}}}{\text{Cd} \qquad\qquad\qquad \text{Bd}}$

Step 4 requires the gathering of the symbols: $\quad$ Ad $<$ Bu

$$\underline{\text{Cd} \not< \text{Ad}}$$
$$\therefore \text{Cd} \not< \text{Bd}$$

In Step 5 we test for violations of the rules. The middle term, A, is distributed twice. This satisfies Rule 1, which requires that it be distributed *at least* once. Rule 2 tells us that a term which is undistributed in the premises should not be distributed in the conclusion. Examine the conclusion. Both C and B are distributed since the conclusion is in the E-form. But B was "u" in the major premise, and Rule 2 has thus been violated. The syllogism is invalid.

Exercises

Analyze the following syllogisms in accordance with the method shown in Steps 3–5. If a rule is violated, then the syllogism is invalid. If no rules are violated, then the syllogism is valid. For convenience in class-room discussion it is desirable that all students should use the same symbolization for the terms. The use of "A," "B," and "C" is recommended for these exercises. Draw the circle diagrams for the first five syllogisms. Remember that the circles should indicate that the conclusion of an invalid argument need not be true, even though the premises are true.

1. All bankers are golfers
   All middle-aged men are golfers
   ∴ All bankers are middle-aged men

2. All Republicans are free-enterprisers
   No Democrats are Republicans
   ∴ No Democrats are free-enterprisers

3. Some Hindus are vegetarians
   All Brahmins are Hindus
   ∴ Some Brahmins are vegetarians

4. All Communists are opponents of the Marshall Plan
   Vishinsky is an opponent of the Marshall Plan
   ∴ Vishinsky is a Communist

5. All ministers of the gospel are shepherds of men
   Some teachers of philosophy are not ministers of the gospel
   ∴ Some teachers of philosophy are not shepherds of men

6. Some believers in democracy are advocates of a planned society
   Some advocates of civil rights are not advocates of a planned society
   ∴ Some believers in democracy are advocates of civil rights

7. No Democrats are Republicans
   Some Republicans are not isolationists
   ∴ Some Democrats are not isolationists
8. Some Germans are not Nazis
   All Nazis are supermen
   ∴ Some supermen are not Germans
9. All Republicans are protectionists
   All conservatives are Republicans
   ∴ Some protectionists are not conservatives
10. All beginning students in logic are students whose knowl-
    edge of the rules is superficial
    No beginning students in logic are persons without rational
    capacity
    ∴ Some students whose knowledge of the rules is superficial
    are not persons without rational capacity

Section VI: The Diagramming of Syllogisms

The diagramming of syllogisms in circles is an art which requires a thorough understanding of its principles, and, in some
cases, a more refined analysis of the logical forms than we have
as yet presented. This section will be devoted to this problem.

Let us restate our aims in diagramming arguments. We have
learned the rules to which a valid syllogism must conform. We
have learned the meaning of validity, viz.: a valid argument is
one in which it is impossible for the conclusion to be false when
the premises are true. We have also learned that if it is possible
to draw the circles in such a way that the conclusion might be
false though the premises are true, then the argument is invalid.
And one further point before we proceed: Though the diagrams
are not essential for proving validity, since the rules are sufficient for this purpose, the diagrams give us a visible or "geographical" pictures of the relations of the members of classes to
each other, so that we can see just why the argument is valid or
invalid.

The chief difficulty in diagramming is that some ingenuity
is often required to find a diagram which conforms to the premises and yet reveals that the conclusion need not follow. And
worse, the Euler circles, while accurate as far as they go, do not
adequately cover the full meaning of the A-E-I-O forms and do

not furnish us with a sufficiently good instrument for diagramming all possible syllogisms. We shall therefore now present a supplementary interpretation of the diagrams for the A-E-I-O forms and we shall then have an adequate tool for all syllogisms which use these forms.

1. The A-form.

"Ad < Bu." This tells us that all A is included within B. But it does not tell us that B is a larger class than A. B may or may not be larger. We shall now adopt a fundamental rule of procedure, namely, that we shall carefully distinguish between what we are sure of and what is doubtful. The A-form, then, tells us that the B circle is at least as large as the A circle, and perhaps larger. Stated in another way, it tells us that there is no A which is outside of B. Its proper diagram, then, should look like this:

The dotted line indicates that the B circle is at least as large as, perhaps larger than, the A circle. B may be larger than A, or B may be exactly the same size as A. The two possibilities may be represented by the following diagrams, in which the dotted line disappears:

Thus, when we are given "Ad < Bu," this may mean that the B circle is actually larger than the A circle, as in the interpretation: All men are animals. On the other hand, the two circles may be coextensive with each other, as in the interpretation: All men are rational animals. In this latter example, each class has exactly the same members. In considering the validity of any argument which uses the A-form, the circles must account for both possibilities, for if the argument is valid under one possible interpretation, and not for the other, then the conclusion does not necessarily follow. The syllogistic example cited earlier under Rule 5, page 181 would appear to be valid when diagrammed with Type 1 circles, but it is clearly invalid when we use Type 2 for both premises:

The class of men may be coextensive with that of "rational animals," and the class of "rational animals" may be coextensive with that of "moral agents." In a valid argument, on the other hand, the argument will be valid on either interpretation.

2. The E-form.

"Ad $\not<$ Bd." The Euler circles are entirely adequate for this form.

3. The I-form.

"Au $<$ Bu." Here again we must carefully examine the meaning of this proposition with respect to what we surely know. The I-form tells us that some members of A are within B, and vice versa. But that is all it tells us. It does not say that some of A is outside of B, for it leaves open the possibility that *all* of A is B. In ordinary speech, when one says "some" he usually means "not all," but this is not necessarily the case. A careful thinker, let us say, visits a foreign land such as the Melanesian islands, and notes that some of the natives eat betel. All the natives he has observed eat betel, but he cannot say that *all* natives do, and so he reports that *some* of them do, meaning "at least some, and possibly all." The I-form also allows for the possibility that all B are A, i.e., that all betel eaters are Melanesians.

The I-form should be represented by the following diagram:

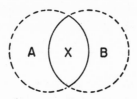

The solid lines indicate what we definitely know, or are sure of, namely, that some A are B. But the following possibilities may also hold in fact:

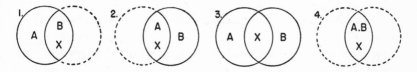

Note that the original solid lines marked "x" are present under each interpretation. The first means that all B are A; the second that all A are B; the third that some A are B, but also that some A is outside of B and some B outside of A; and the fourth that A and B are identical classes. (The dotted lines may be eliminated from each interpretation.)

4. The O-form.

"Au ⊄ Bd." We know for certain that some of A is outside of B. But it may be that *no* A's are B's. Our traveller is now among the Eskimos. He had heard that all Eskimos eat blubber, but the first Eskimos he observes do not eat blubber. He reports that "some do not." He does not know whether some do, or whether none do. He means "at least some Eskimos are not blubber-eaters, and possibly none are." This statement is also noncommital with respect to whether all blubber eaters are Eskimos, i.e., whether all B's are A's, etc. We shall represent the O-form by the following diagram:

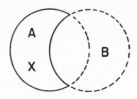

The solid lines indicate what we are sure of, marked by the "x." This new diagram may refer to the following factual situations:

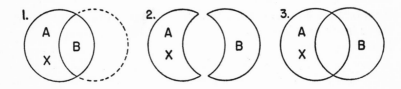

Here again the original solid portion marked "x" is present under each interpretation, i.e., each shows that "some A is not B." But the first interpretation indicates that some A is not B and that all B is A. This would be the case in "Some animals (A) are not dogs (B)" for all dogs are animals. The second diagram is equivalent to the ordinary E diagram. It indicates that, when interpreted strictly, "Some A is not B" *may* mean that "No A is B." The third interpretation indicates that some A is not B, that some A is B and that some B is not A. An illustration of the last situation is found in "Some men are not poets"; for some men *are* poets, and some poets are not men.

When the A-E-I-O forms are interpreted with the new diagrams, the dotted lines may be discarded for each interpretation. Note also that where the diagram requires it, "All A is B" may be represented by either

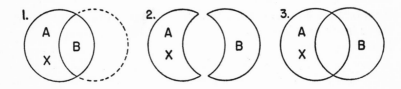

When we diagram arguments, we should use the simpler Euler circles where these are adequate. The special diagrams

should be resorted to only when necessary. Remember that we need find only one interpretation under which the conclusion might be false to prove an argument invalid. Try the possible interpretations until you can find an appropriate diagram (when you know from the rules that the argument is invalid).

We shall now illustrate the use and value of the new method. Assume that we have the following syllogism:

Ad < Bu

Cu ⊀ Ad

∴ Bu ⊀ Cd

This syllogism commits the fallacy of illicit major term. Let us try to diagram it with the Euler circles. We would then have the following diagram:

This diagram does *not* exhibit the invalidity of the syllogism, since it does not show that the premises might be true and the conclusion false. Rather, it appears to indicate that the conclusion is true, for some of the B circle is outside the C circle. We need a diagram which will show that these premises do not necessarily result in the conclusion presented.

Under our new method, we consider the possibility that the A and B circles are identical classes and that the O-form in the major premise can be exemplified by a diagram similar to 1 under the O-form above. If we use this O-form diagram and interpret A and B as identical classes, we will have the following diagram:

The new diagram graphically indicates that the fact that some C is outside of A and that all A is B does not necessarily prove that some B is outside of C.

Exercises

1. Draw circle diagrams for syllogisms 6–10 on pages 183–4. Use the ordinary Euler diagrams or the revised diagrams, whichever will suit your purposes. The problem in each case, to repeat, is to find a diagram that will indicate, by a geographical picture, that the invalid conclusion need not be true, even though the premises are true. In other words, try to find a picture which will show that the conclusion is *false*.
2. In drawing the diagram for the valid argument, Number 10, why is it impossible for the predicates of the premises to be identical in size?

Section VII: The Corollaries, Figures, and Moods

In this section we shall briefly discuss two matters of theoretical interest pertaining to the theory of the syllogism: the corollaries of the rules, and the figures and moods of the syllogism. Though these matters are of little or no practical value in the analysis of arguments, they have great aesthetic or purely contemplative intellectual interest.

1. The corollaries.

The five rules of validity are sufficient for the testing of the validity of all syllogisms. No other rules are necessary. These rules play a role in the theory of the syllogism somewhat comparable to that of the axioms in Euclidean geometry. The axioms of geometry are undemonstrated, or "primitive" propositions which are used to prove theorems. In a similar manner we may use the five rules to demonstrate derived rules or corollaries (theorems) and we may then use such derived rules in the testing of syllogisms. But the corollaries are not indispensable, since they contain no new principles. Our discussion of the manner in which they are derived, however, will furnish an interesting logical exercise in working out the implications of a deductive system.

Corollary 1. No valid conclusion may be drawn from two simple particular premises.

This corollary states that no conclusion can be validly derived from the combinations of two I-forms, two O-forms, or an I and an O. We already know that two O-forms are an impossible combination, since no conclusion follows when both premises are negative (Rule 3). Let us consider the other two possibilities.

Suppose that both premises are in the I-form. Then no terms will be distributed. The middle term will then be undistributed, and Rule 1 will be violated. Let us now suppose that we have an I and an O in the premises. Only one term will now be distributed (the predicate of the O). The distributed term must be the middle term to satisfy Rule 1. But the conclusion of the syllogism must be negative (Rule 4). If the conclusion is negative, then its predicate must be distributed. But both the major and minor terms were undistributed, so the major term cannot be distributed without violating Rule 2. We have thus proved that the corollary must hold on the basis of the rules.

There is, however, one apparent exception to the corollary we have just proved. Note that we proved the rule for "simple" particular propositions. This qualification must be explained. A particular proposition refers to *some* of the subject, i.e., less than all. But there are many different ways in which we may refer to less than all of the members of a class. We may say "a few," "one-half," or "most" S's are P's. All of these are interpreted as meaning "some," i.e., less than all. But a particular proposition beginning with "most," which means "more than one-half," is a "special" as distinguished from a "simple" type of particular, for which Corollary 1 will not hold. For consider an argument such as the following:

Most of the students in this college are students of Latin
Most of the students in this college are students of logic
Therefore, Some of the students of Latin are students of logic.

If more than half of the students study Latin and more than half study logic, then some students must study both subjects, since "most" means "more than half." A map diagram will illustrate the situation:

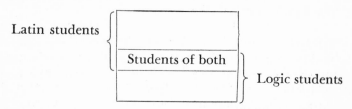

This syllogism is valid despite the fact that it appears to violate Rule 1 and Corollary 1. It is a special type of case, whose validity is based upon mathematical relations. The corollary will therefore hold for all particular premises except two premises beginning with "most." Unless specifically noted, however, we shall always refer to the simple type of particular propositions.

Corollary 2. If one premise is particular, then the conclusion must be particular.

If one premise is particular, then the other must be universal (Corollary 1). Both premises cannot be negative (Rule 3). This leaves the following possible combinations of premises: AI, IA; AO, OA; EI, IE. We must prove that each of these six combinations cannot yield a valid conclusion which is universal.

Let us consider AI, or IA. Can the conclusion be a universal? It cannot be E, for a negative conclusion would violate Rule 5. Nor can it be an A. For AI and IA contain only one distributed term, which must be the middle term (Rule 1). If the conclusion were an A, the minor term would be distributed, violating Rule 2.

Combinations AO and OA. The conclusion cannot be an A (Rule 4). Nor can it be an E, for the premises contain two distributed terms, one of which must be the middle term (Rule 1). An E-form distributes both subject and predicate, and at least one of these terms must have been undistributed in the premises. The same reasoning applies to the combinations EI or IE.

There are at least two other such corollaries, which we shall not prove; Corollary 3: The premises must contain at least one more distributed term than the conclusion, and Corollary 4:

No conclusion can be validly inferred from a particular major premise and a negative minor. As noted earlier these corollaries need not be used in testing the validity of syllogisms.

1. The figures and moods of the syllogism.

Syllogisms may be classified with respect to the position of the middle term in the premises, and with respect to the quantity and quality of the premises and the conclusion. The position of the middle term determines the *figure;* the *mood* is determined by the quantity and quality of the propositions. There are four possible figures, since the middle term may take four possible positions, viz.:

Figure 1	*Figure 2*	*Figure 3*	*Figure 4*
M . . . . P	P . . . . M	M . . . . P	P . . . . M
S . . . . M	S . . . . M	M . . . . S	M . . . . S
S . . . . P	S . . . . P	S . . . . P	S . . . . P

The moods are determined by the various combinations of A-E-I-O forms. When both of the premises and the conclusion are A-forms, the mood is called "AAA." The first letter stands for the major premise, the second for the minor, and the last for the conclusion. If the major premise is an A, the minor an E, and the conclusion an E, the mood is AEE.

Let us now consider the number of different combinations of moods and figures which are possible. How many are possible in Figure 1? Since there are four types of propositions, which may be arranged in three different ways in this figure, the number of possible syllogistic combinations is $4 \times 4 \times 4$ or 64. The same holds for the other figures, so there are 4×64, or 256 possible combinations. But not all of these combinations are valid. We may proceed to eliminate the combinations of premises which are invalid. Both premises cannot be negative (Rule 3). This eliminates EE, EO, OE, and OO. Both cannot be particular (Corollary 1), and IE is ruled out by Corollary 4. This leaves us with only eight possible combinations of premises which can yield valid conclusions in some or all of the figures: AA, AE, AI, AO, EA, EI, IA, and OA.

The next problem is to determine which combinations of premises are valid in each of the figures. For example, premises AA or AI cannot be valid in Figure 2, for the middle term is the predicate in each premise in that figure, and if the premises are affirmative, the middle term will be undistributed. We shall now state some special corollaries which determine the rules of validity for each figure, but we shall not prove these corollaries. Their proof will follow the general procedure we used in proving the general corollaries concerning validity.

Figure 1:

    Corollary 1. The minor premise must be affirmative.

    Corollary 2. The major premise must be universal.

Figure 2:

    Corollary 1. The premises must differ in quality.

    Corollary 2. The major premise must be universal.

Figure 3:

    Corollary 1. The minor premise must be affirmative.

    Corollary 2. The conclusion must be particular.

Figure 4:

    Corollary 1. If the major premise is affirmative, the minor must be universal.

    Corollary 2. If either premise is negative, then the major must be universal.

    Corollary 3. If the minor is affirmative, the conclusion must be particular.

The mediaeval logicians worked out a set of mnemonic lines to aid the student in memorizing the valid moods of each figure, viz.:

Barbara, Celarent, Darii, Ferioque prioris;
Cesare, Camestres, Festino, Baroko secundae;
Darapti, Disamis, Datisi, Felapton, Bokardo, Ferison habet;
Quarta insuper addit . . .
Bramantip, Camenes, Dimaris, Fesapo, Fresison.

The names in all these lines were invented, the instructions being in Latin. The first line gives us the valid moods in the first figure; the second, the valid moods in the second figure;

and so on. The italicized letters in each name indicate the mood. Thus a syllogism in Barbara is one having A-forms in premises and conclusion. The interested reader may wish to determine which moods are valid in each figure, with these suggestions as his guide. These classifications are of course unnecessary if our sole interest lies in the testing of syllogisms for validity, the five rules being sufficient for that purpose. The systematic organization of the rules and corollaries, however, has great theoretical interest, as indicating the nature of a deductive system, the subject of the concluding section of this chapter.

Section VIII: A Note on Deductive Systems

We are now familiar with the meaning of deduction. Granted certain premises we can deduce conclusions which necessarily follow from these premises. A *deductive system* refers to a collection or body of propositions which are so organized that some serve as the premises and the others as conclusions which necessarily follow from the premises. An example of such a deductive system is found in Euclidean geometry, a model for all such systems since 300 B.C. Euclid's premises, or "assumptions," include the following elements: (1) Undefined terms, such as "length" and "breadth," (2) definitions, such as the definition of a "line" as a "breadthless length," (3) axioms, or "common notions," [e.g., "Things equal to the same thing are equal to each other." "The whole is greater than any of its parts."] (4) postulates,* such as "All right angles are equal," and (5) rules of procedure, such as "It is possible to draw a straight line from any point to any other point."

From these assumptions Euclid deduces theorems, which follow from the assumptions as the conclusion follows from the premises of a valid argument. A famous example is the Pythago-

---

* Euclid's postulates differ from his axioms in that the latter are "common notions" which are "generally accepted" outside of geometry, whereas the postulates are introduced by geometry itself. Technically, the axioms are assumptions which are taken from outside the field of a given science, postulates those which are introduced by the given science; but we shall treat both as assumptions of the deductive system.

rean theorem: "The square formed on the hypotenuse of a right triangle is equal to the sum of the squares formed on the other two sides."

The relation of the rules of the syllogism to the corollaries resembles that of the assumptions to the theorems in the Euclidean system, the rules serving as assumptions (axioms or postulates) and the corollaries as theorems. This collection of propositions is thus a simple example of a deductive system.*

Some further comments on the nature of a deductive system may be helpful. (1) The postulates of an ideal deductive system should possess three characteristics: independence, consistency, and sufficiency. "Independence" means that the postulates should not be reducible to each other, for, if they are, then the reducible postulates would be theorems. "Consistency" refers to the fact that the postulates should not result in inconsistent theorems, and "sufficiency" means that they must be adequate to yield all the known truths concerning the set of propositions to which they are applied, i.e., all of the propositions in this set must be deducible from the postulates. (2) The postulates of a given system are not proved within that system. If they could be proved then they would be theorems rather than postulates. Whether they can be proved in some other fashion is simply irrelevant in the given system, the sole interest lying in the deducibility of the theorems from the assumptions. Thus, though Euclid's axioms and postulates seem "self-evident," this is not proof that they are true. It follows that *any* set of postulates may serve as the basis of a deductive system, but in practice the important systems are those in which the axioms are in "agreement" with the real world in some sense. A valuable system, moreover, is one which will yield significant theorems. (3) Finally, we should not think of the axioms as being first in the order of *discovery*. They are first, or fundamental, only in a logical sense, and are discovered *after* there already exists a collection of propositions forming the body of a science. The formal scientist, such as Euclid or Aristotle, then seeks for a

---

* For a more thorough discussion of these matters the interested reader should see M. R. Cohen and E. Nagel, *An Introduction to Logic and Scientific Method,* Harcourt, Brace and Company, 1934, Chapters 4 and 7; and J. N. Keynes, *Formal Logic,* 4th ed., The Macmillan Company, 1906, pp. 287 ff.

small number of assumptions from which the known truths concerning the subject matter may be deduced as theorems.

As we proceed in our introduction to logic we shall discuss other types of syllogisms. These, as we shall see, may be translated into the "Aristotelian" forms we studied in this chapter. But we shall also encounter other formal truths concerning deduction which cannot be reduced to the syllogistic form. This would appear to indicate that the whole of logic is not organized as a completely systematic formal science, and indeed this was the situation which characterized logic for two thousand years following Aristotle's work. Beginning in the nineteenth century, however, with the work of George Boole and other logicians, in particular the great work of Whitehead and Russell in their *Principia Mathematica* (1910–13), an important advance occurred in logical theory. Modern "symbolic" or "mathematical" logic has sought to demonstrate that *all* of the principles of logic may be proved on the basis of a small number of assumptions in an abstract deductive system. The exposition of the new logic, however, belongs to a more advanced work than the present one.

Chapter 9

SEMANTICS AND THE SYLLOGISM

Section I: The Need for Semantical Analysis

We have studied the rules of the syllogism and have learned how to distinguish a valid from an invalid argument. But though we now know the rules, our ability to analyze syllogisms is still very limited. This is true for two reasons: (1) Our analyses have been limited to examples presented in the schematic or artificial form suitable for the clearest possible exhibition of the structure of the argument analyzed, and (2) our analyses have been confined to arguments in which the propositions clearly indicated the relationships of the three terms to each other. It is easy to apply the rules when syllogisms are presented in such ready-made form, but in living discourse syllogisms are not presented in schematic form, nor are the terms always easily identifiable. In order to remedy these limitations and to acquire the ability to analyze arguments as they occur in everyday discourse, we shall investigate a number of semantical problems. We shall learn how to translate everyday language into its correct logical form, and we shall also study the principles of "equivalences" in propositions. Propositions stated in different forms may express the same meanings, and transformations from one form into another may be required for syllogistic analysis.

The need for further analysis of meanings will become apparent when we examine the following syllogism:

No unhealthy people are strong
All healthy people are non-alcoholics
∴ No strong people are alcoholics

This syllogism appears to contain five terms ("unhealthy people," "strong people," "healthy people," "non-alcoholics," and "alcoholics"), and thus it appears to violate the requirement that a syllogism must have three and only three terms. But, as we shall presently learn, the second premise may be translated into "All alcoholics are unhealthy people," since this proposition has identically the same meaning as the second premise. We now have only three terms, and a valid syllogism.

Section II: Sentences in Irregular Forms

A categorical proposition must be stated in one of the A-E-I-O forms. Such forms indicate the manner in which two classes are related to each other in inclusion or exclusion. In everyday discourse, however, propositions may not clearly indicate the relations of two classes to each other, and in such cases we must translate the sentences into the correct forms.

The necessity for this translation may be clarified by a somewhat farfetched analogy. The rules of the syllogism give us a kind of logical machinery for testing arguments. This logical machine may be compared with a stamping machine that impresses stampings on pieces of metal. The pieces are inserted into the machine, a lever is pressed, and out comes the stamped piece. But the machine will not accept any piece of metal. The metal must be of the proper size and shape for insertion into the machine. Now, our logical "machine" is one into which we insert arguments. After the argument is "inserted," we press the lever (the rules), and out comes the argument stamped "valid" or "invalid." But the logical machine also requires that the pieces (the propositions) must be in the proper form for insertion, and "proper form" here means that the class relationships must be clearly indicated. Thus every proposition must be stated in strict A-E-I-O form, with all of the constituent elements, such as the quantifier, the copulas, the signs of inclusion or exclusion, and the names of the two classes, in their proper places. The chart on the next page gives us the framework for each A-E-I-O form, with blank spaces which are to be filled in by the names of the subject and predicate classes.

		Traditional forms	Class terminology

A-form
- General : All _____ are _____or All _____ < _____
- Singular : X_____ is a _____or X_____ < _____

E-form
- General : No _____ are _____or All _____ ≮ _____
- Singular : X_____ is not a _____or X_____ ≮ _____

I-form : Some _____ are _____or Some _____ < _____

O-form : Some _____ are not ___or Some _____ ≮ _____

Every proposition must be stated in one of the forms shown above, for no others can be used in the analysis of categorical syllogisms. We turn now to the analysis of sentences as they are stated in everyday language. Such sentences may not be in the forms shown above, and we must learn how to make the proper revisions in order to shape the propositions for insertion into the logical machine.

1. Grammatical revisions.

Before we analyse a sentence into its class relations, we must clearly identify the subject and predicate. In "Little has been accomplished by fanatics" the subject is "fanatics." "Fanatics," we are saying, "are persons who have accomplished very little." In "All take great risks who put their eggs in one basket" the "who" modifies "all," and the sentence should read, "All persons who put their eggs in one basket are persons who take great risks." The copula ("are") now separates the subject from the predicate.

2. The missing quantifier.

We noted earlier that every logical proposition must have a quantifier and must therefore begin with "all," "no," "some," or, in the case of singular propositions, with the name of or reference to an individual thing or person. When no quantifier is stated, assume that the proposition is universal, unless it is quite clear from the context that "some" is intended. Where there is any doubt, assume that "all" is meant. Thus, in "College students are idealists" the speaker must be understood to mean "all." We are not certain that he meant "some." But in "Human beings live until the age of one hundred" it is obvious that "some" is intended.

3. The missing complement.

We noted earlier that the *completing complement* must be added to adjectives and other phrases in order to indicate classes. Thus, in "All lions are mild" the predicate term does not clearly indicate a class. "Mild" is not the name of a class. If it were, we would be able to point to its members, but we cannot point to a "mild." However, when we add the completing complement "creatures" or "animals," our sentence will clearly refer to two classes of things. The proposition must clearly indicate that the circle representing the subject can be drawn inside another circle representing the predicate, and each circle must name a class of nouns.

In a sentence such as "Communists are losing ground," "losing ground" is not a collection of nouns or things. We must add the complement "persons who are," and we then have the class: "persons who are losing ground." But do not add complements when classes are clearly designated, since the simplest adequate statement is the most desirable. Note, too, that the subject term may also require its complement, as in "The foolhardy are losers." Add "persons" to "foolhardy," and add the quantifier "all" and we get "All foolhardy persons are losers."

Exercises

Restate the following sentences so that the subjects and predicates will clearly refer to classes of things, i.e., groups or collections of nouns. Do not add complements to nouns. Where necessary, add expressions such as "things which are _____" or "persons who are _____," but where such simple words as "persons" or "things" are sufficient, you will simplify your statement by limiting yourself to a one-word complement. Also add the quantifier where it is missing.

1. Movies are entertaining.
2. She is a blonde.
3. The fish are biting.
4. Short skirts are on the way out.

    5. Bobby-soxers are disappearing.
    6. The members of the orchestra are tuning their instruments.
    7. The reflective are philosophers.
    8. The narrow-minded are prudes.
    9. Those who are loyal to their country are patriots.
    10. Blessed are the meek.
    11. All agree with me who are not ignorant of the facts.

4. The missing copula.

Many sentences omit the copula. We must supply it in such cases. Thus, in "Some fish fly" the copula is missing, and we must also add the complement to the predicate. The sentence will then read, "Some fish are flying creatures." Note that the operation of supplying the copula is always a two-fold one, since the completing complement will always be required for the predicate term and perhaps for the subject as well.

Another example: "Some ancient Oriental peoples worshipped the sun." We must supply the copula and add the complement so that the predicate will clearly indicate a class. Restated it reads, "Some ancient Oriental peoples are persons who worshipped the sun."

The following suggestion may be helpful to the student: Always identify the subject first, i.e., the complete subject. The copula should be stated immediately after the subject term. If you have difficulty in recognizing the subject in some cases, look for the main verb, and the subject will immediately precede it.

Exercises

Restate the following sentences by supplying the copula, complements, and quantifier when necessary. Express the copula in the forms of "are" and "included in the class of" ($<$). Be sure that the predicate is stated in the plural form. Draw circles for the last five items.

    1. Kangaroos jump.
    2. Wood burns.
    3. Grass grows.

4. Beginners make mistakes.
5. All atoms contain electrons.
6. Children like to play games.
7. Evolution accounts for design.
8. You contributed to our victory.
9. He ridicules others who has never accomplished anything worthwhile.
10. All agree with me who are not ignorant of the facts.
11. Socrates said, "Virtue is knowledge."
12. They jest at scars who never felt a wound.
13. The people scurried to shelter when they heard the approach of the bombers.

5. Exclusive propositions.

An exclusive proposition is one beginning with the words "only" or "none but." "Only men are priests." "None but adults are admitted." Such sentences do not clearly state the relationship of two classes to each other. "Only ——— are ———" is not a permissible form, and it will not be found in the chart on page 200. The subjects and predicates are not clear, and until they are it would be impossible to draw circles to represent these propositions or to fit them into our schedule of appropriate forms and yet retain the same meaning as the original statements.

Take the sentence "Only men are priests." How shall we draw the circles? Obviously we cannot draw a small circle representing men inside a large circle representing priests, for the sentence does not state that *all* men are priests. We therefore require a different type of translation. We require a restatement which can be diagrammed and which will have a meaning equivalent to that of the original sentence. The sentence can be translated into "All priests are men." This carries the meaning of the original sentence and is in proper class form. This simple example gives us our rule of translation: Whenever a sentence is in the form "Only (or none but) S is P" (where S stands for the subject and P for the predicate), we shall change the "only" to "all" and *reverse the order* of the subject and predicate. The exclusive sentence means that all of the members of the class denoted by the (original) predicate are included in the class represented by the (original) subject.*

A diagrammed statement of this type of translation may be helpful:

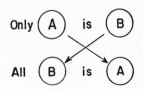

or

From the statement: "Only *fools* are *misers*"
We derive: "All *misers* are *fools*"

Exercises

Translate the following exclusive propositions into propositions revealing class relationships, by eliminating expressions such as "only" and "none but." The expression "none but" has exactly the same meaning as "only." Draw circles for the last two items.

1. Only B is C.
2. None but S is P.
3. Only sissies are cry-babies.
4. None but Democrats are New Dealers.
5. Only declarative sentences are propositions.
6. Only persons who suffer from inferiority complexes are persons who wish to dominate others.

More difficult types of translation are found in sentences in which the copulas and completing complements are missing. In "Only the discerning will understand" the sentence should first be stated in clear class terms. Add the copula and complements to the subject and predicate terms before transposing. We will then have a statement in the form: "Only discerning persons are persons who will understand." It is now easy to translate

---

* Some exclusive sentences may of course carry more meaning than is conveyed by our translations, as in a sergeant's order: "Only privates must report." This means that "all who must report are privates," but it may also mean that *all* privates must report. If this is the case, then the order is equivalent to two propositions: "Only privates must report," and "All privates must report."

into "All persons who will understand are discerning persons."

The procedure outlined below should be followed by the student until he becomes adept at this type of translation.

Step 1. The Copula: Examine the exclusive sentence and note whether the copula ("is" or "are") is present. If not, insert it.

Step 2. The Complements: The insertion of the copula requires the addition of a complement to the original predicate. You will now have a noun or substantive in the predicate signifying individuals who are members of a class.

Illustration: Assume that the original sentence is "Only the brave deserve the fair." Adding the copula and complementing the original predicate will give us "Only the brave *are persons who* deserve the fair."

Step 2a: Check the *subject* to determine whether it is stated as a class designating members. If not, add the proper noun-complement. In our illustration we must add "persons" after "brave," and our sentence will now read, "Only (the) brave *persons* are persons who deserve the fair."

Step 3. Transposition: We are now ready to transpose:

Only *brave persons*   are   *persons who deserve the fair.*
becomes

All *persons who deserve the fair*   are   *brave persons.*

Another example: "Only those who study this material carefully will master it." Following the first and second steps, we get "Only those *persons* who study this material carefully *are persons* who will master it." This then becomes, by Step 3: All *persons who master this material* are *persons who study it carefully.*

Exercises

Translate the following exclusive sentences into A-form propositions which clearly reveal the class relationships, following the steps indicated in the text. Use the symbol for class inclusion ($<$).

A. Restate by adding complements to the subject and predicate where necessary:

1. Only women are gossips.
2. None but gentlemen are deserving of the fair.

3. None but the imaginative are poets.
4. Only the narrow minded are censors.
5. Only the curious are wise.
6. None but good citizens are desirous of the general welfare.
7. None but those who put others at ease are really polite.
B. These restatements require adding the copula and complementing the predicate:
1. Only religious persons pray.
2. Only citizens can vote.
3. Only women bear children.
4. Only vulgar persons talk like that.
5. None but cowards die more than once.
C. Add the copula and complement subjects and predicates where necessary:
1. None but those who are neurotics are alcoholics.
2. Only those who suffer from inferiority complexes are aggressive.
3. Only the curious get burned.
4. Only the musical appreciate modern music.
5. Only those who can, do.

6. Negative sentences.

Every negative proposition must be restated as an E- or O-form. This will require the types of operations we have been using in this chapter, such as adding copulas and complements, etc. "No sparrows sing" must be restated as "No sparrows are birds which sing" or "All sparrows $\nless$ birds which sing."

Difficult problems occur with respect to sentences which begin with words such as "none" or "nothing." These should be restated as E-forms. Thus "None of the damned are happy" is restated as "No persons who are damned are persons who are happy" or "All damned persons $\nless$ happy persons." "Nothing human frightens me" requires the following steps in its restatement: (1) the quantifier is "no." (2) The subject is "human," completed with "things." (3) Add the copula. (4) Complement the predicate. The result: "No human things are things which frighten me," or "All human things $\nless$ things which frighten me."

We shall now examine a type of sentence which is ambiguous in its construction, i.e., amphibolous. Take, as example,

"All Polynesians are not easygoing." Note carefully that this sentence is not in strict E- or O-form. Its structural skeleton is "All _____ are not _____." No such skeletal form will be found in the chart on page 200. This means that the sentence does not assert a precise relationship between two classes, since there are only four ways in which this can be done. Because only sentences in the four structural forms will fit into our "logical machine," we must therefore find, if possible, an E- or O-form equivalent.

We shall adopt the convention that sentences which present the "All _____ are not _____" formation will be rephrased as O-forms, unless an E-form is obviously intended. Our example rephrased: "Some Polynesians are not easygoing persons." This rule is in accordance with customary usage. "All Germans are not Nazis" means "Some Germans are not Nazis," not "No Germans are Nazis." "All _____ are not _____" usually means "Not all _____ are _____," i.e., "Some _____ are not _____." But occasionally an E-form is intended, as in "All men are not immortal." This should be rephrased as "No men are immortal."

Exercises

Restate the following negative propositions in strict E- or O-form. State each E proposition in the two forms: "No S is P," and "All S ⊄ P."

1. All labor leaders are not idealists.
2. All the students in this class will not get A's.
3. Shostakovich's Fifth is not as great as Beethoven's Fifth.
4. No Englishmen make good coffee.
5. All that glitters is not gold.
6. None of the faint-hearted were present at our great victory.
7. The selfish individual is not a lover of his fellow-man.
8. Nothing artistic comes out of mere art.
9. Nothing which makes sense is beyond my comprehension.
10. None of those who violate the rules will receive special consideration.
11. All who proclaim devotion to ideals are not sincere.
12. No prejudiced person is included in the class of Christians.
13. What is not considered proper is not always wrong.
14. Plays cannot be judged by merely reading them.

7. Exceptive sentences.

In October, 1947, the Ford Motor Company, for the first time in its history, permitted smoking by employees during working hours. The announcement read, "All employees except women office employees may smoke." This is an exceptive sentence. It states (1) that all *employees who are not women office employees* are persons who may smoke, and (2) that no *women office employees* are persons who may smoke. Its correct translation requires both of these categorical propositions, the first in A and the second in E form.

Let us now symbolize this process. We shall introduce a new symbol "−", the sign of negation, to stand for "non-." Thus if WOE stands for "women office employees", "−WOE" will stand for "non-women-office-employees" or "employees who are not women office employees." Using "PMS" for "persons who may smoke," our exceptive proposition is translated symbolically as:

> A: All−WOE are PMS and
> E: No   WOE are PMS

In translating sentences which take the "All . . . except . . ." formation, note that the subject follows the word "except," and that the "all" refers to the members of a given group who are non-subjects. Using S for subject and P for predicate, we have "All −S are P" and "No S are P."

Another example: "All but the military were evacuated." The word "but" is equivalent to "except." "Military" is the subject, "persons who were evacuated" is the predicate, and the word "all" is understood to refer to "personnel who are non-military," so that we derive:

> A: All non-military personnel are persons who were evacuated;
> E: No military personnel are persons who were evacuated.

In using exceptive sentences in syllogisms, either the A or the E interpretation may be used as a correct (though incomplete) translation of such sentences. If the conclusion follows under *either* interpretation, the syllogism will be valid.

Exercises

Rephrase the following exceptive sentences as A-forms, by following the procedure outlined above:

1. No one is admitted unless on business.
2. All but the lazy pass this course.
3. All except those who repent will be damned.

Section III: Equivalent Propositions

Different sentences may express exactly the same thoughts and meanings. They will then express equivalent propositions. Thus the sentence "Hitler is dead" has the same meaning as "Hitler is not alive"; "No men are angels" has the same meaning as "No angels are men"; and "All just men are unprejudiced" means the same as "All prejudiced men are unjust." The three pairs of propositions we have just noted are examples of the logical processes called "obversion," "conversion," and "contraposition," the subject matter of this section. Though our immediate concern with these processes lies in the equivalences of language, we shall also note that these are also processes of reasoning, usually called "immediate inference." "Immediate" here means that we draw inferences from a single proposition, as distinguished from syllogistic, or "mediate" inference, in which we draw a conclusion concerning two classes because of their relation to a third class that "mediates" the inference.

The study of equivalent propositions has many values, not least of which is the realization that there is more than one way of stating the truth. In the search for truth it is not the specific words that count, but the ideas expressed. A difference in verbal formulation does not mean that there is a difference in meaning. We often find that apparent differences of opinion disappear when we learn that the difference is merely one of verbal formulation. This study will make us more keenly aware of equivalences in meanings, an awareness of which will be found indispensable in the analysis of many arguments.

1. Obversion.

Obversion is a process whereby we change a proposition into its equivalent by *changing* its *quality* (but not its quantity), and by *negating* its *predicate*. Examples: The obverse of "All men are fallible" is "No men are infallible." These two propositions have exactly equivalent meanings. Note that the obverse contains two negations. We changed the proposition from affirmative A to negative E, and we negated the predicate from "fallible" to "infallible." The basic principle underlying this process is that two negations result in a positive statement, similar to the "double-negative" rule in grammar. The child who says "I ain't got none" is, strictly speaking, saying that he does have some, though we will not usually mistake his meaning. "He did not fail to attend" means that he did attend. In algebra, too, we learned that the multiplication of negative numbers results in a positive number. The same principle also applies with respect to terms. The negation of "infallible" is "fallible"; the negation of non-combatant is "combatant."

The process of obversion is quite simple when we use class symbols. Only two steps are required in each case: (1) Change the symbol from $<$ to $\not<$ (or vice versa), and (2) place the symbol for negation ($-$) before the predicate. In this manner,

$$A < B \quad \text{becomes} \quad A \not< -B$$
$$A < -B \quad \text{becomes} \quad A \not< B$$
$$A \not< B \quad \text{becomes} \quad A < -B$$
$$A \not< -B \quad \text{becomes} \quad A < B$$

(Since the negation of a "negative term" results in a positive one, the negation of $-B$, or $--B$, will be written as B, as shown in the second and fourth examples.)

This is all that is required. There must be *no change in the quantity* of the propositions, but only in the *quality*. Thus a universal proposition remains universal, and a particular remains particular. When we use class symbols no changes will be required in the quantifiers, since the universals both use the quantifier "all." *The subject term must remain unchanged.* (The signs of distribution will of course be changed to indicate the change in quality.) The table below shows the manner in which all four types of propositions are obverted. Note that great care must be exercised when one obverts sentences in the traditional expressions of the propositional forms. In such expressions the quantifier of the universals changes from "all" to "no" (and vice versa), and the particulars require the change in the copula from "Some _____ are _____" to "Some _____ are not _____" (and vice versa).

Original A	Ad < Bu	All A are B	All men are mortal
Obverse E	Ad ≮ −Bd	No A are −B	No men are non-mortal
Original E	Ad ≮ Bd	No A are B	No liberals are appeasers
Obverse A	Ad < −Bu	All A are −B	All liberals are non-appeasers
Original I	Au < Bu	Some A are B	Some bankers are golfers
Obverse O	Au ≮ −Bd	Some A are not −B	Some bankers are not non-golfers
Original O	Au ≮ Bd	Some A are not B	Some Communists are not Russians
Obverse I	Au < −Bu	Some A are −B	Some Communists are non-Russians

When we obvert sentences in ordinary speech, difficulties may arise concerning the proper negation of the predicate term. We should negate by the prefix "non-," which expresses simple negation, rather than by prefixes such as "un-" and "in-" which often express antitheses, or words of contrary meaning. Consider "He is trustworthy" and "He is not untrustworthy." "Not untrustworthy," or the "not—un—" formation in general, appears to express a lack of certainty, though many people, especially the British, use this type of expression to express obversion. When the British communiqués from the war fronts announced that they "were not unsuccessful," they meant that they had been successful. To be safe, use the prefix "non-," though other prefixes may sometimes correctly express simple negation. Note also that the simple negation of "large" is "nonlarge," (*not* "small"); the negation of "rich" is "non-rich," (*not* "poor"). People may be "non-rich," though far from poor.

Exercises

1. Obvert the following:
   a. Some X is Z.
   b. No L is M.
   c. Some R is not S.
   d. All −A is −B.
   e. Some R is not −S.
   f. All puns are crimes.
   g. Some Chicagoans are gangsters.
   h. No planets are stars.
   i. Some books are not texts.
   j. Only A is B.
   k. Only the brave deserve the fair.
2. Obvert: Germany invaded Russia on June 22, 1941.

3. Are the following inferences justified? If not, which rule was violated?
   a. All volunteers are patriots. Hence, all non-volunteers are unpatriotic.
   b. All anonymous donors are wholly unselfish, so donors who sign their names are not wholly unselfish.
   c. All letter writers who refuse to sign their names are cowards. Therefore, no writers who sign their names are non-cowards.
4. It is a useful exercise to draw circles in order to see why the obverse has the same meaning as the original proposition. Thus, if "All A is B," then the area outside the B circle is "−B," and since no A is outside the B circle, it follows that "No A is −B." In the diagram:

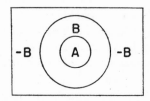

2. Conversion.

"No men are angels" has exactly the same meaning as "No angels are men." For obviously, if all men are excluded from the entire class of angels, then all angels must be excluded from the entire class of men. The two propositions are equivalent in meaning, though the order of their subjects and predicates is reversed. The subject of the first proposition has become the predicate of the second. The process whereby we pass from one proposition to another by reversing the order of the subject and proposition is called "conversion." This process is a legitimate one when the second proposition has the same quality as the first and when there is no "illicit distribution" of terms in the second proposition. When we apply this process to the A-E-I-O forms, however, we shall see that the results vary with respect to the equivalence of the original proposition to its converse. Let us look at each form separately.

The E-form. An E-form may be converted, as in the example above, into a new proposition exactly equivalent in meaning to the original proposition. If all of A is excluded from B, then all of B must be excluded from A.

The I-form. "Some Americans are Communists" also means that "Some Communists are Americans." The original sentence states that there are some individuals who are both Americans and Communists. Obviously, then, there are some individuals who are both Communists and Americans. This gives us the rule that an I-form can be converted into a converse that is exactly equivalent to the original sentence. If some A are B, then some B must be A. If circle A overlaps B, then circle B overlaps A.

The A-form. Can we convert "All dogs are animals" into "All animals are dogs"? Obviously not. "All A is B" cannot be converted into "All B is A." But an A-form proposition can be converted *by limitation.* "All dogs are animals" can be converted into "Some animals are dogs." "All A is B" can be converted into "Some B is A." * Thus the "conversion by limitation" of an A-form yields a *partial* converse. It is important to note, however, that conversion by limitation gives us a new proposition that is *not equivalent in meaning* to the original one.

The process of distribution will explain why A-forms cannot be converted simply, like E- and I-forms. An E-form distributes both terms, and so does its converse. In the I-form, both terms are undistributed; similarly in the converse. But in the A-form, the predicate is undistributed, and if we convert it simply (i.e., without limitation), the original undistributed predicate would be distributed in the converse, as in going from "Ad < Bu" to "Bd < Au." The general rule of conversion with respect to distribution is that the converse must not distribute a term that was undistributed in the original proposition (cf. Rule 2 of the syllogism). The fact that we have information concerning *some* members of a class does not warrant an assertion concerning *all* of its members. (There is, of course, no fallacy in stating less than we know, as when we have a distributed term in the premise and leave it undistributed in the conclusion.)

* The conversion of an A-form requires certain assumptions concerning the existential import of propositions. This problem will be discussed in Chapter 11, Section IV.

One further point. In formal logic we are interested in valid inferences. We have stated the rule that "All A is B" cannot be converted into "All B is A." But suppose we have an A-form such as "All triangles are three-sided figures." We know that this proposition can be converted without limitation into "All three-sided figures are triangles." This is because we *know* that this latter statement is true. The general rule that A-forms cannot be converted simply is a rule of formal logic, a rule telling us that we cannot convert "All A is B" into "All B is A" when we know nothing about the two classes except that all of A is included in B. We noted earlier that an A-form can be drawn in two ways:

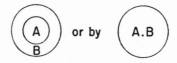

If we know that the latter circle can be drawn, then conversion without limitation is possible, but we need outside information in order to be sure that the two classes are identical. In the absence of such information, an A-form should not be converted without limitation.

The O-form. Can we convert "Some men are not priests" in to "Some priests are not men"? Obviously not. The rule: An O-form cannot be converted. To do so would result in an illicit distribution of the original subject term, for we would go from "Au ⋞ Bd" to "Bu ⋞ Ad." The subject A would be undistributed in the original and distributed in the converse.

Once again we note that outside information may tell us that the converse of an O-form *happens* to be true, as in the example: "Some students are not women." We also know that "Some women are not students." But the point is that if we *know* only that "Some A is not B," we cannot necessarily conclude that "Some B is not A." In formal logic we are interested in the necessary inferences that can be drawn from logical forms, and the rule of formal logic is that an O-form cannot be converted.

The following table summarizes the possibilities in conversion. Remember that only E- and I-forms convert into equivalent propositions, that A-forms convert by limitation only, so that the converse is not equivalent to the original proposition, and that the O-forms do not convert at all. Note also that the singular A- and E-forms are not usually convertible.

	E-form	I-form	A-form
Original	No A is B (Ad ⧼ Bd)	Some A is B (Au < Bu)	All A is B (Ad < Bu)
Converse	No B is A (Bd ⧼ Ad)	Some B is A (Bu < Au)	Some B is A (Bu < Au)

Exercises

1. Convert the propositions in Exercise 1 in the preceding exercises.
2. Are the converses of the following propositions justified?
   a. All Communists praise Stalin, so those who praise Stalin must be Communists.
   b. Since some Germans are not Nazis, it follows that some Nazis are not Germans.
   c. Some Indians are non-Hindus, so some non-Hindus are Indians.
   d. No New Dealers are conservatives. Then no conservatives are New Dealers.
   e. All movies are masterpieces, so some masterpieces must be movies.
3. Are the following examples of conversion formally justified? Are the converses true in fact? Explain your answer.
   a. All men are rational beings. Therefore, All rational beings are men.
   b. Some baseball players are not golfers, so some golfers are not baseball players.
   c. Some coins are not pennies, so some pennies are not coins.
   d. Some human beings are not professors, so some professors are not human beings.
4. Convert: Americans enjoy a higher standard of living than Europeans.
5. Of which error in conversion is Alice guilty, according to her logical friends in Wonderland?
      The Hatter asked, "Why is a raven like a writing desk?"
      Alice replied, "I believe I can guess that."
      "Do you mean that you think you can find out the answer to it?" said the March Hare.

"Exactly so," said Alice.

"Then you should say what you mean," the March Hare went on.

"I do," Alice hastily replied; "at least—at least I mean what I say—that's the same thing, you know."

"Not the same thing a bit!" said the Hatter. "Why, you might just as well say that 'I see what I eat' is the same thing as 'I eat what I see'!"

"You might just as well say," added the March Hare, "that 'I like what I get' is the same thing as 'I get what I like'!"

"You might just as well say," added the Dormouse, which seemed to be talking in its sleep, "that 'I breathe when I sleep' is the same thing as 'I sleep when I breathe'!"

(HINT: "I mean what I say" means "The things which I say are the things which I mean.")

3. Contraposition

The contrapositive of a proposition is the obverse of its converted obverse. To obtain the contrapositive we must perform three steps: obvert, then convert, then obvert once again. Let us illustrate this procedure:

Original	: All metals are conductors	Ad $<$ Bu
Step 1. Obvert	: No metals are non-conductors	Ad $\not<$ $-$Bd
Step 2. Convert	: No non-conductors are metals	Bd $\not<$ Ad
Step 3. Obvert	: All non-conductors are non-metals	$-$Bd $<$ $-$Au

This process may be applied to all A-form propositions, without exception. Note the symbols with which we begin and end: "Ad $<$ Bu" becomes "$-$Bd $<$ $-$Au." The contrapositive of an A-form is thus another A-form, with the original subject and the original predicate reversed in order and both negated. The contrapositive of "All S is P" is "All $-$P is $-$S." The contrapositive of "All wizards are magicians" is "All non-magicians are non-wizards." The student should learn how to perform this process in both the one step and in the three step procedure.

The contrapositive of an A-form is always equivalent in meaning to the orginal proposition. This must be the case, since the obverse of an A-form (Step 1), the converse of an E-form

(Step 2), and the obverse of an E-form (Step 3) are equivalent to the propositions which are obverted and converted. The contrapositive of an O-form also results in an equivalent proposition. Thus, "Some A is not B" is equivalent to "Some −B is not −A." The E-form yields a partial contrapositive and the I-form has no contrapositive. But we shall find little occasion to use contraposition except in the A-forms and will therefore not discuss this operation further.

Exercises

1. Exercises on contraposition: State the contrapositives of the following A-forms before you work out the three steps, and then prove your answer through the three steps:
   a. All men are mortal.
   b. All persons who fail in logic are non-studious.
   c. Only members are admitted.
2. On equivalence: Which of the following pairs are equivalent to each other? (The test of equivalence is whether or not you can translate back into the original proposition):
   a. All A are B and All −B are −A
   b. All A are B and All −A are −B
   c. All A are B and Some −B are −A
   d. All A are B and No −B are A
   e. Some A are not B and Some B are not A
   f. Some A are not B and Some −B are not −A
3. On equivalence: Match the numbered proverbs with the lettered ones on the next page. Do you regard the matched proverbs as having equivalent meanings?
   (1) It never rains but it pours.
   (2) Kind hearts are more than coronets.
   (3) Just as the twig is bent the tree's inclined.
   (4) Know thyself.
   (5) Carrying timber into a wood.
   (6) First come, first served.
   (7) Faint heart ne'er won fair lady.
   (8) A tempest in a teapot.
   (9) Don't put off until tomorrow what you can do today.
   (10) He who fights and runs away may live to fight another day.
   (11) Make hay while the sun shines.
   (12) Every man to his own taste.

(a) Discretion is the better part of valor.
(b) Troubles never come singly.
(c) A mountain out of a molehill.
(d) None but the brave deserves the fair.
(e) There's nothing so kingly as kindness.
(f) Strike while the iron is hot.
(g) Like father like son.
(h) One man's meat is another man's poison.
(i) Carrying coals to Newcastle.
(j) The proper study of mankind is man.
(k) The early bird gets the worm.
(l) No time like the present.
(From George W. Crane's "Test your Horse-Sense Quiz" in *The Chicago Daily Tribune*.)

Chapter 10

THE SYLLOGISM AND
EVERYDAY DISCOURSE

Section I: Syllogisms and Ordinary Discourse

We are at last ready to analyze syllogisms as they are stated in ordinary discourse. We have learned how to make the linguistic transformations that are required when the essential relations of subject and predicate are obscured by "irregular" forms of expression. We are now able to restate all syllogisms in the schematic form requisite for clear analysis.

We often reason in syllogisms in ordinary discourse, but such syllogisms do not usually follow the pattern of the schematic form. They are more likely to occur in such forms as the following: "Certainly, we ought to have military training for our youth. These are critical times, aren't they? And shouldn't we have military training in critical times?"

We shall analyze such syllogisms as these. We shall put the propositions into strict A-E-I-O forms, eliminating all unnecessary verbiage, rhetorical questions, etc., and then arrange the propositions in the schematic form we used earlier, with the premises first and the conclusion last. The above syllogism would then take the following form:

> All critical times are times when we ought to have
> military training for our youth
> The present time is a critical time
> ∴ The present time is a time when we ought to have
> military training for our youth.

The structure of this argument is now obvious, as is its validity.

In everyday discourse it is also customary to state an argument incompletely, because it seems unnecessary to state all the details. Someone tells us confidentially, "You know, all drunkards are short-lived. Well, poor John won't live very long." This argument is a syllogism in the form of an "enthymeme" (from two Greek roots meaning "in the mind"), i.e., part of the argument is unstated but understood. If we understand the speaker to mean that "John is a drunkard," we have a complete syllogism.

In this chapter we shall analyze syllogisms as they occur in ordinary discourse, using the linguistic knowledge we acquired in the previous chapter. As we noted earlier, the rules of the syllogism are easy to apply once we have properly analyzed the linguistic elements. But before we turn to the analysis of syllogisms, we must examine some special linguistic difficulties that arise in connection with the requirement that a syllogism must have three terms.

Section II: A Syllogism Has Three and Only Three Terms

The syllogism has been defined as an argument that has three and only three terms, but as yet we have not discussed the manner in which this requirement may be violated. Blatant violations do not usually occur in ordinary discourse. Thus, no one would be likely to argue in the following manner:

> All Englishmen eat roast beef with York-
> shire pudding
> Zoroastrianism is a Persian religion

Therefore,————?

Since these two propositions contain four terms, they could not serve as the premises of a syllogism. There would be no middle term. An argument having the appearance of a syllogism, but containing four terms, is usually said to involve the "four-term fallacy." In the strict sense, such arguments are not syllogisms, but it will be convenient to refer to them as syllogisms involving "the four-term fallacy."

Though the four-term fallacy seldom occurs in the crude form of the illustration, it often occurs in a more subtle way. The ambiguity of terms may conceal the fact that a supposed middle term is really no middle term at all, but a word with two quite different meanings. The middle term, in other words, may be used equivocally. Let us look at an example. A favorite argument among theologians, used to prove the existence of God, proceeds as follows:

> The events of nature are events subject to law
> Whatever is governed by law is governed by the decisions of a mind
> ∴ The events of nature must be governed by the decisions of a Mind (God).

We may ignore the slight shifts in terminology in this argument. We find that the middle term is "things subject to law." But this term is used equivocally, in two quite different senses. In the first premise it is used in its scientific sense. Scientists use the word "law" to refer to "the uniform occurrence of natural events in the same way under the same conditions." It is impossible to "violate" such a law, since a scientific law simply means a description which has no exceptions. When we turn to the major premise, however, we find that the word "law" is used in the legal sense of "a rule of action established by a governing body to regulate the actions of human beings." Such laws are *prescriptive*, whereas natural laws are merely *descriptive*. When we eliminate the ambiguity of the middle term, and substitute the two foregoing definitions for "things subject to law," we find the following argument:

> The events of nature occur in certain uniform patterns
> Whoever is subject to a rule of action established by a governing body is governed by the decisions of a mind
> ∴ The events of nature are governed by the decisions of a Mind.

Stated in this way, the four terms are glaringly obvious. But the four terms were not so obvious in the original argument, which had the appearance of a three-term syllogism because of the ambiguity of the word "law."

The student should examine every argument for possible violations of the three-term requirement. Note, however, that mere differences in terminology do not necessarily prove that four terms are used, as when synonymous expressions are used for the middle term, viz.:

> All anarchists are libertarians
> Those who believe that the state should be subordinate to the individual are opposed to the dictatorship of the proletariat
> ∴ All anarchists are opposed to the dictatorship of the proletariat.

In this argument the middle term is referred to by two different expressions: "libertarians" and "persons who believe that the state should be subordinate to the individual." Since both refer to the same referents, there are in reality only three terms. The term "libertarians" may be regarded as the subject of the major premise.

A merely apparent four-term fallacy may also occur when words of opposite meaning are used in an argument, as in

> All nurses are non-combatants
> All front-line fighters are combatants
> ∴ No nurses are front-line fighters.

In this syllogism we have apparent violations of both the three-term requirement and Rule 5. But here we note a fundamental "rule of courtesy" which should be given to all syllogisms: Do not assume that a four-term fallacy has occurred unless you have given the writer or speaker the benefit of every doubt. The reader should restate every syllogism as a three-term argument if this can be done without changing its meaning. When we give the last syllogism such courtesy, we find that the minor premise may be obverted into "No nurses are combatants," that there are thus only three terms, and that the syllogism is valid.

A different type of semantical violation of the three-term requirement is illustrated by the following example:

> All men are mortal
> All men are men
> ∴ All men are mortal.

Though this series of statements has the apparent form of a syllogism, there has been no reasoning from premises to a conclusion. The "conclusion" of this example merely repeats the first proposition. Thus it is not a syllogism, but for convenience we shall call it a "syllogism containing only two terms," or a "tautologous-terms syllogism." Another example, and a more interesting one, in which the tautologies are somewhat concealed, is found in the following:

>All good men are concerned with human welfare
>All virtuous men are good men
>∴ All virtuous men are concerned with human welfare.

Since "good men" and "virtuous men" are synonymous expressions, the "syllogism" contains only two terms, as in the previous example. On the other hand, a minor premise which analyzes the meaning of one of the terms will not result in such tautologies, as in

>All human beings know the difference between right and wrong
>All rational animals are human beings
>∴ All rational animals know the difference between right and wrong.

A synonymous definition in the minor premise will give us a tautologous-terms syllogism, but this will not be the case where the definition is an analytical one.

The four-term and two-term errors are semantical, rather than formal, in nature. The errors may be overlooked by carelessness in symbolization, as when we use the same symbol for different terms, or different symbols for the same term. We should therefore carefully check the language of every syllogism for possible violation of the requirement that a syllogism must have three and only three terms.

Section III: The Analysis of Syllogisms in Everyday Discourse

We shall now analyze syllogisms as they may occur in everyday discourse. The following procedure, which also sums up the types of linguistic transformations, will be of aid to the student in analyzing such syllogisms:

Step 1. The first step, and perhaps the most important one, is to correctly identify the conclusion of the argument. In Chapter 6, Section I, we noted that certain transitional words will serve as clues for the identification of the conclusion when the reader is in doubt. Thus, words such as "because," "for," and "since" always precede a premise and follow the conclusion.

Step 2. The next step requires the correct identification of the terms. This is often a difficult task. Examine the conclusion, and note its subject and predicate. If these are obvious it is usually easy to discover the middle term in the premises. If we symbolize the terms by the S-P-M method, we will have S and P and need only to find M. If the terms are not obvious, this will usually be due to the irregular language used in the propositions, and we must then apply the rules we have learned concerning linguistic revisions in order to exhibit each proposition in the strict logical forms shown in our table of possible structures on page 200.

Semantical revisions will be required when the argument uses rhetorical language, or rhetorical questions. These irregularities should be eliminated. Grammatical revisions may be required, as well as the supplying of missing quantifiers, copulas, and complements. Correct transformations and transpositions of exclusive, exceptive, and negative sentences may also be needed. The rules concerning equivalences may require application, as when obversion, conversion, and contraposition are called for.

The purpose of such revisions is to correctly identify the three terms of the syllogism. Very often it will be necessary to try out various hypotheses concerning the terms which were in the mind of the speaker until we find the correct ones. Above all, remember our rule of courtesy, that we should assume that the speaker had three and only three terms in mind, until we are reasonably convinced that this is not so. Minor variations in language should be disregarded, but important differences should of course not be ignored. When the author's meaning is in doubt, and you make assumptions concerning his meaning, state these assumptions explicitly.

Step 3. The syllogism should then be set up in the schematic form, with the conclusion last. All propositions should be stated in the class terminology, using the symbols $<$ and $\nless$.

Exercises

1. George Bernard Shaw must be a very wise man, for he is old, and we know that none but the old are truly wise.
2. Since only the lucky make strikes, I must conclude that I am a very unlucky bowler for I have not made a strike all winter.
3. Whatever is perceived by the senses is undoubtedly a fact. Then

the existence of the soul cannot be a fact, since no one has ever perceived the soul by the senses.

4. He that is of God hears God's words. You therefore hear them not, for you are not of God.

5. Many great men have done very poorly in their studies while they were at college. I got low grades last semester. Can it be that I am a great man?

6. Every scientist will agree that true theories are theories which are confirmed by experiments. Now, we know that carefully formulated scientific experiments have confirmed Einstein's theory of relativity. Therefore, it must be a true theory.

7. The attorney for the defence argued: "It is a rule of the company by which my client was employed as a signal operator, that express trains alone do not stop at his station. Now, the train in question stopped at his station, so he was undoubtedly correct in assuming that it was not an express train."

8. Decent newspapers cannot attain a wide circulation, for they decline to emphasize sensational material such as illicit love affairs and murders. We all know that papers which adopt such sensational methods invariably attain a wide circulation.

9. Nothing logical ever puzzles me, but some of these problems are illogical. That is why they puzzle me.

10. No political party is entitled to our moral allegiance unless it unqualifiedly renounces any attempt to advance the interests of a foreign power which seeks to destroy us. The "100% Americans for a 100% American" party is thus entitled to our moral allegiance, for it wishes to make America the strongest country in the world.

11. No unhealthy people are vigorous and some healthy people are overweight; hence, some persons who are overweight are not strong.

12. No unintelligent people are successful, so no successful people are alcoholics, for all intelligent people are non-alcoholics.

13. Roosevelt College lacks school spirit. Football teams foster school spirit. Consequently, Roosevelt College needs a football team.

14. The medical profession informs us that some stimulants are harmful to the human body. Everybody knows that all types of alcoholic liquor are stimulants; it follows, therefore, that some types of alcoholic liquor are harmful to the human body.

15. The Eskimos are the only people who eat nothing but meat, and it is found that all Eskimos have good teeth. So we may conclude that no people who eat only meat have bad teeth. (Thouless.)

16. A man is ennobled by the experience of finding himself faced by the choice between life and death. War provides the supreme situation in which men have to make this choice, so that if universal and perpetual peace could be attained, it would be at the price of robbing men of all ennobling experiences. (Thouless.)

17. Find a valid conclusion which would follow from the following premises: All of the incoming women freshmen at Indiana University disapprove of young men who neglect their studies in order to ride around in their flashy convertibles, and none of the incoming women freshmen at Indiana University seek to marry husbands who take the policies of either of the two major parties very seriously. Therefore?

18. All human beings are mortal, and all members of the genus homo sapiens are human beings, so all members of homo sapiens are mortal. (Does this example have three terms?)

19. All persons who believe in democracy believe in freedom of speech. You ask whether the Russians believe in freedom of speech? Certainly they do, if they are sincere when they tell us that they believe in democracy, and we may assume that they are sincere. (Does this example have three terms?)

20. The struggle for existence has resulted in evolutionary progress. Human beings desire evolutionary progress, so they ought to encourage the elimination of the unfit in human societies.

21. All Eskimos live in snow houses, and all people who like to live in snow houses would dislike our modern conveniences, so all Eskimos would dislike our modern conveniences.

22. The party to be headed by Henry A. Wallace has neither the organizational structure, the progressive philosophy, nor the support of the labor movement and other progressive groups in the nation, all necessary to the success of any progressive third party. History has proven conclusively that all attempts to build a political party from the top around an individual are predoomed to dismal failure. (From a statement issued in January, 1948, by the Chicago Industrial Union Council.)

23. Given the premise "All except the students with less than a 'C' average will graduate," which conclusions would follow from the following additional premises? "The Phi Betes do not have less than a 'C' average." "John will graduate." Construct the full syllogism in each case.

24. The *Digest* publishes what it considers the most interesting material that people want to read. Now, we know that an article doesn't have to be true in order to be interesting, and, since this

magazine tries to publish interesting stories, we may conclude that its articles and stories are not entirely true.

25. If an argument is valid, and the conclusion is false, then a premise must be false. If we assume this principle then I can prove the falsity of A. E. Housman's theory that good poetry can be recognized by "the thrill down our spine." (*The Name and Nature of Poetry*.) For though his own poetry is certainly good poetry, it does not send a thrill down my spine.

Section IV: The Enthymeme

"Roosevelt made mistakes, for he was only human." This sentence states a syllogism in the form of an enthymeme, which we define as an incompletely stated syllogism. Only part of the complete argument is explicitly stated, the remainder being "within the mind." Completed, the argument would look like this:

> All human beings make mistakes
> Roosevelt was a human being
> ∴ Roosevelt made mistakes

In everyday discourse we will find that syllogistic arguments are frequently stated in the form of enthymemes. In the example above it was unnecessary to state the major premise, "All human beings make mistakes," since it was obviously implied, and most speakers try to avoid "belaboring the obvious." Many arguments will be found to contain such unstated assumptions. Frequently, however, the assumptions are false or unjustified, and it is therefore important that we make our assumptions explicit, so that we may critically examine what is being assumed. This can be done only by completing the enthymeme. Otherwise we shall have another form of the fallacy of "begging the question."

Enthymemes may be classified into "Orders," to indicate the part or parts which are missing. There are four such Orders, as follows:

1. Major premise omitted.

The illustration above omitted the major premise. Another example: "This cough syrup should help me, for it helped a man in St. Louis. I read his testimonial." The major premise, "Whatever helped that man in St. Louis will help me," is assumed.

2. Minor omitted.

"Roosevelt will make mistakes, because all men make mistakes." The minor premise is missing here: Roosevelt is a man.

3. Conclusion omitted.

"All men make mistakes, and the President is a man." The conclusion is obvious, but unstated. Another example, as told by Thackeray: "An old abbé, talking among a party of intimate friends, happened to say, 'A priest has strange experiences; why, ladies, my first penitent was a murderer.' Upon this, the principal nobleman of the neighborhood enters the room. 'Ah, Abbé,' here you are; do you know, ladies, I was the Abbé's first penitent, and I may promise you my confession astonished him.' "

4. The minor premise and the conclusion are omitted.

This type is rarer than the others. It requires the *context* of a situation which indicates that an argument is intended. For example, assume that you are talking to a person whose boasting annoys you. You say, "Only an egoist boasts about his achievements." Your hearer will supply the minor premise and the conclusion. The complete syllogism will read as follows:

> All persons who boast about their achievements are
> egoists
> You are boasting about your achievements
> ∴ You are an egoist

The problem of validity in the enthymeme must now be considered. In all of the examples considered, we completed the enthymeme into a valid syllogism. But consider the following: "Why do I say that X is a communist? He's against the Marshall Plan, isn't he?" This is an enthymeme of the First Order, since the major premise is omitted. But what is the major? There are two possibilities: (1) All communists are opposed to the Marshall Plan, or (2) All persons opposed to the Marshall Plan are communists. It is likely that the first interpretation was intended, in which case the argument would be invalid, since the middle term would be undistributed. If the second interpretation were intended, then the argument would be valid, but the falsity of this premise would be quite apparent. When one is in doubt as to which interpretation is intended, the argument should be analyzed in terms of both possibilities. Note also that questions concerning the truth of a premise are not problems of formal logic, but of material logic.

Invalid enthymemes in other Orders will be quite obvious. The following is in the Second Order: "All Republicans believe in free enterprise, so you do not believe in free enterprise." This example violates Rule 2. A Third Order example: "All guilty individuals fail to pass the lie-detector test, and he failed to pass it." This argument contains an undistributed middle term.

Exercises

A. Complete the following enthymemes in strict categorical form. Each should be stated as a valid syllogism, unless it is obvious that an invalid argument was intended. State whether each is valid or invalid, and note the Order of the enthymeme. Linguistic irregularities should be handled as before. Note particularly, however, that the complete argument should have three terms, not four, five, or even six terms. It will be found helpful, in complying with the three-term requirement, to symbolize the subject and predicate of the conclusion by "S" and "P." Then find "M," but be sure that each term is stated in identically the same manner each time it is used.

1. This must be a good book—it was chosen by the Book-of-the-Month Club.
2. Fascists are enemies of the human race, so he is not an enemy of the human race.
3. Remark made to an aggressive person: "When anyone acts aggressively it usually means that he is suffering from an inferiority complex."
4. All Republicans are against the "police state" so you must be a Republican.

5. Naturally, I consider him an intelligent man. He's a Democrat, isn't he?
6. Generals are notoriously poor chess players. I also play the game badly.
7. All of the crows I have seen have been black, so crows must be black everywhere.
8. Don't take logic. You will have to work out a lot of exercises.
9. I don't see why I should be required to study Latin. Aren't all the worthwhile books translated into English?
10. We should have a separate Air Force command in this country. Doesn't England have one?
11. Women, as well as men, should be given high executive offices in our government, for government is nothing but national housekeeping.
12. Robespierre's enemies accused him of having identified the "enemies of the state" with his personal enemies. "I deny the accusation," he answered, "and the proof is that you still live."

B. State any set of two premises which will validly lead to the following conclusions (find a middle term):
1. John L. Lewis is opposed to dictators.
2. Some Germans are Christians.
3. Some payments for services rendered are not contemptible.
4. No logical exercises are too easy.
5. On rainy days, I dine alone.
6. Omar wished to remould this sorry scheme of things nearer to the heart's desire.

Section V: The Sorites

The sorites (rhymes with "nighties") is a series of syllogisms telescoped into one argument, as in the following:

> All young men are idealists
> All idealists are sensitive creatures
> All sensitive creatures are dissatisfied
> All dissatisfied creatures are unhappy
> ∴ All young men are unhappy

In this argument the first two premises lead to an unstated conclusion; namely, that "All young men are sensitive creatures." This unstated conclusion is then combined with the third premise, to yield the unstated conclusion that "All young men are dissatisfied," and so on. In other words, the conclusion of one syllogism is the premise of another, and all conclusions except the final one are unexpressed. The premises are so arranged that any two successive ones will contain a common term.

This form of the sorites is called the Aristotelian type. A second type, called the Goclenian sorites, proceeds in this way:

> All living things are mortal
> All animals are living things
> All men are animals
> ∴ All men are mortal

In the Aristotelian type the first premise contains the subject of the conclusion and the common terms of the premises appear first as a predicate and then as a subject. In the Goclenian type, the first premise contains the predicate of the conclusion, and the common term appears first as subject and then as predicate. Special rules for these sorites are as follows:

1. If negative premises are used, no more than one premise can be negative. In the Aristotelian sorites, it must be the last premise; in the Goclenian the first.
2. No more than one premise may be particular or singular. If such premises are used, they must come first in the Aristotelian form, and last in the Goclenian.

Every sorites, however, may be stated in either form. The Goclenian sorites may be translated into the Aristotelian type by proceeding backwards from the last premise.

Exercises

1. Construct a valid sorites having four propositions in which a negative premise is used. Then do the same with a particular premise.
2. Classify the following sorites with respect to its form. Is it valid?

The human soul is a thing whose activity is thinking. A thing whose activity is thinking is one whose activity is immediately apprehended, and without any representation of parts therein. A thing whose activity is immediately apprehended without any representation of parts therein is a thing whose activity does not contain parts. A thing whose activity does not contain parts is one whose activity is not motion. A thing whose activity is not motion is not a body. What is not a body is not in space. What is not in space is insusceptible of motion. What is insusceptible of motion is indissoluble (for dissolution is a movement of parts). What is indissoluble is incorruptible. What is incorruptible is immortal. Therefore, the human soul is immortal. (Leibniz, *Confessio Naturae Contra Atheistas,* translated by H. W. B. Joseph, *An Introduction to Logic,* The Clarendon Press, pp. 355–6.)

3. The following examples of sorites are taken from Lewis Carroll's *Symbolic Logic.* The analysis of these sorites will require a rearrangement of the premises, and the premises may require semantical transformations in order to get them into the requisite forms. Rearrange each as a valid argument:
   a. All babies are illogical.
      No one is despised who can manage a crocodile.
      Illogical persons are despised.
   ∴. No babies can manage crocodiles.
      (HINT: Write out the names of each term used in the sorites, and symbolize each by a letter. Then arrange the symbols in the proper order, etc.)
   b. No terriers wander among the signs of the zodiac; Nothing that does not wander among the signs of the zodiac is a comet; Nothing but a terrier has a curly tail. ∴. All creatures with curly tails are non-comets.
   c. Which conclusion may validly be derived from the following premises? All writers who understand human nature are clever; no one is a true poet unless he can stir the hearts of men; Shakespeare wrote Hamlet; no writer who does not understand human nature can stir the hearts of men; none but a true poet could have written Hamlet.
4. In the following case indicate the syllogistic reasoning involved in the decision of the Chief Justice. Then show how he applies the legal principle to the case.

On 21 April, 1928, the plaintiff, being a minor, entered into a contract with the defendant, by the terms of which he traded a Chevrolet truck, valued at $250, for a Dodge sport roadster, valued at $659.50. On 21 May, 1928, the plaintiff made a payment of $40.95 on his note. Thereafter the Dodge sport roadster was destroyed in a wreck; whereupon the plaintiff elected to disaffirm his contract, and now sues to recover $290.95, the sum of the value placed upon the Chevrolet truck at the time of the trade, to wit, $250 and the payment of $40.95 subsequently made on the note. Stacy, Chief Justice: When an infant elects to disaffirm a contract, relative to the sale or purchase of personal property, other than one authorized by statute, or for necessaries, what are the rights of the parties?

(1) An infant may avoid such a contract, either during his minority or upon arrival at full age . . .

(2) Upon such avoidance, the infant may recover the consideration paid by him . . . with the limitation that he must restore whatever part of that which came to him under the contract he still has . . .

(3) Where the infant parts with personal property, he may, upon disaffirmance, recover the value of such property, as of the date of the contract.

In the instant case the plaintiff is entitled to recover the $40.95 which he paid on his note, together with the fair market value of the Chevrolet truck at the time of the trade. (Collins v. Norfleet-Baggs, Inc., Supreme Court of North Carolina, 1929.)

Section VI: The Relations between Terms Generalized

We have now completed our discussion of categorical syllogisms involving the relationship of class inclusion. These syllogisms used propositions containing subjects and predicates interpreted in terms of classes included within or excluded from each other. In later chapters we shall study the compound types of propositions composed of sub-propositions rather than of terms. But before we leave the categorical type of syllogism we must note a special type which relates terms in relations other than that of class inclusion. Such syllogisms and the nature of "relations in general" will be our concern in this section.

Consider the valid syllogism:

A is older than B
B is older than C
∴ A is older than C

This syllogism cannot be analyzed by the methods we have hitherto employed. If we put each proposition into "class" form, we shall find four terms: "A," "things older than B," "B," and "things older than C." But the argument is valid, and we must now inquire into the rationale of arguments such as these.

Subject-predicate categorical propositions relate terms to each other, but in a very special way, by class inclusion. Hitherto we have translated all possible relations between terms into the relation of class inclusion. But this procedure, though satisfactory in a great many cases, is not adequate for arguments such as the one above, and it thus becomes necessary to find a more flexible tool for handling other types of relations. In order to do this we must generalize the notion of "relations" and find a wider principle which will cover both the relation of class inclusion and other types of relations.

When we assert "A $<$ B" we are saying that A is *related* to B in terms of class inclusion. We shall now use the symbol "(R)" for "related to," and we shall revise the previous symbolization to "A $(R_<)$ B." We may now assert new types of relations in the same manner. If we wish to say that A is older than B, we need not use the relation of class inclusion. We may use "o" for the relation of "older than" and symbolize the relationship as "A (R_o) B." This means that A is related to B in the relation of "older than." Similarly with other types of relations. The syllogism above may thus be symbolized as follows:

$$A \ (R_o) \ B$$
$$B \ (R_o) \ C$$
$$\therefore A \ (R_o) \ C$$

This type of argument may also be diagrammed, but not by circles. We may use a straight line to represent the different points on a line representing ages, from zero (o) to infinity (n), and we may then indicate the position of each term on the line, thus:

o　　　　　C　　B　A　　　　　n

The diagram shows us that if A is older than B and if B is older than C, then A must be older than C. This is not startlingly new knowledge, but it serves as a simple illustration of the manner in which we may picture relations other than class inclusion, in order to test the validity of arguments in which they are used.

It should be obvious that some relations will permit valid arguments, and that others will not. Thus, if we know that A is the lover of B, and that B is the lover of C, we can conclude nothing with respect to the relations between A and C, nor indeed can we conclude that B is the lover of A. The relation of "lover of" does not permit such inferences. This makes it necessary to classify all relations, so that we may know which types of relations will yield valid inferences, and which will not. The relation of class inclusion, as we well know, is a type of relation which permits valid inferences. We shall now examine the special characteristics possessed by a relation which make such inferences permissible.

We shall classify relations under two general heads, *symmetry* and *transitivity*, each of which has three subdivisions.

1. Symmetry.

The three sub-divisions are *symmetrical, asymmetrical* and *non-symmetrical*.

    a. Symmetrical relations:

This type of relation is defined as a relation such that if A has it to B, then B *must* have it to A. Examples: equal to, unequal to, different from, cousin of, playing cards with, etc. In each case if A has the relation to B then B has it to A.

    b. Asymmetrical relations:

Here, if A has the relation to B then B *cannot* have it to A. Examples: father of, older than, greater than, son of, at left of, etc. In each case if A has the relation to B then B cannot have it to A.

    c. Non-symmetrical relations:

Here, if A has the relation to B then B *may* or may not have it to A. Examples: Lover of, helper of. If A is the lover of B, B may or may not be the lover of A.

2. Transitivity.

The subdivisions are similar: *transitive, atransitive, non-transitive*.

    a. Transitive relations:

This relation is defined as a relation such that if A has it to B and B has it to C, then A *must* have it to C. The relation of "being older than" is such a relation, as are: equal to, ancestor of, class inclusion, etc.

    b. *Atransitive relations*:
        Here, if A has the relation to B, and B has it to C, then
        A *cannot* have it to C. Examples are: father of, greater
        by ½, etc.
    c. *Non-transitive relations*:
        Here, if A has it to B and B has it to C, then A *may* or
        may not have it to C. Examples are: lover of, unequal to.
These relations may also be combined as follows:

1. Transitive-symmetrical: equal to, contemporary of
2. Transitive-asymmetrical: greater than
3. Transitive-non-symmetrical: included in the class of
4. Atransitive-symmetrical: spouse of
5. Atransitive-asymmetrical: father of
6. Atransitive-non-symmetrical: nearest blood relative of
7. Non-transitive-symmetrical: cousin of
8. Non-transitive-asymmetrical: unrequited lover of
9. Non-transitive-non-symmetrical: lover of

    We shall now consider the importance of these relations
with respect to some inferences. "A < B, and B < C; therefore,
A < C" is a valid inference because class-inclusion is a transitive relation.* "Older than" is also a transitive relation, and
permits us to draw a similar type of inference. In other words,
it is our knowledge that relations such as "class-inclusion" and
"older than" are transitive relations which justifies us in drawing certain inferences.
    We may now generalize the reasoning involved in the sorites.
The Aristotelian sorites is a series of terms related by the transitive relation of class-inclusion. Thus if A < B, B < C, C < D,
D < E, then A < E. For purposes of further simplification, this
series of propositions may be stated as A < B < C < D < E.
Such a series is called a "chain of relations," and indicates that
any term at the left will be included within any term at its right,
since "<" is a transitive relation. In interpreting such a chain,
however, we should remember that it is a simplification of a

* Note, however, that this inference will hold only for general universals, and
not for singular propositions, since class-*membership*, as distinguished from class-
inclusion, is an atranstive relation. Where singular propositions are used in a
syllogism, as in the familiar "All men are mortal, Socrates is a man, etc.," the
inference rests on the principle that if every member of class A is a member of
class B, then any specified member of the first class must be a member of the
second class.

sorites, with the connecting links omitted. In *reading* it, we must supply the missing links, viz.: "A is in B, and B is in C, and C is in D, and D is in E."

We may also generalize our previous analysis of the relation of conversion. We found that the E- and I-forms were convertible. In our new language, we may say that the relations of "being wholly excluded from" and "being partially included within" are symmetrical relations, so that if A has one of these relations to B, then B must have it to A. But the A-form relation of "being wholly included within" is a non-symmetrical relation, and from this it follows that the A-form is not convertible simply. The generalization of relations also permits conversions which would not be permissible under class relations. Thus "married to" is a symmetrical relation, and symmetrical relations are always convertible. If "A is married to B," we may thus convert into "B is married to A." If we interpreted the original statement in class terms, its meaning would be substantially altered and its conversion preposterous. We may also now employ a new form of conversion, called "conversion by converse relation," when the relation is asymmetrical. Thus, "B is greater than A" converts by converse relations into "A is smaller than B." Similarly with "A is west of B" and "B is east of A."

We shall note further applications of these relations as we proceed. In particular, the importance of the transitive relation of "implication" will be emphasized. This relation, the most important relation in inference, will be discussed in the next chapter.

Exercises

Classify each of the following relations in terms of transitivity and symmetry. Which inferences are valid, which invalid? Why?

1. A is the employer of B, and B is the employer of C. So A is the employer of C
2. A is heavier than B, so B is lighter than A
3. As is the twin of B, so B is the twin of A
4. A is a member of the Chicago Chamber of Commerce, and the Chicago Chamber of Commerce is a member of the United States Chamber of Commerce, so A is a member of the United States Chamber of Commerce.

Chapter 11

THE RELATIONS
AMONG PROPOSITIONS

Section I: Relations with Respect to Truth and Falsity

This chapter is a kind of interlude in our general analysis of syllogistic forms. We shall continue our discussion of relations, but our interest will now shift from the relations of *terms* to the relations of *propositions*. We shall examine the relations of propositions with respect to their truth values. Our fundamental problem will be this: given a pair of propositions, under what conditions does the truth or falsity of one proposition determine the truth or falsity of the other? As an example of this kind of problem, consider the following propositions, designated by the letters "P" and "Q":

P: All nummulites are foraminifers
Q: No nummulites are foraminifers

These propositions refer to actually existing things.* Let us assume that the reader knows nothing concerning the truth or falsity of either P or Q. We may, nevertheless, discuss the relations of these propositions with respect to their truth values. Suppose we assume that one of these propositions is true. We can then draw inferences concerning the truth or falsity of the other. For example, if P were true, is it possible that Q might also be true? Obviously not. If P were true, Q would necessarily be false. P and Q cannot both be true. But both could be false, since they do not exhaust all the possibilities. Some nummulites might be foraminifers and some might not be. If the last situation prevails, then both P and Q would be false.

---

* Assumptions concerning the existential import of propositions will be discussed in Section IV.

We see, then, that it is possible to discuss the truth relations of propositions even though we do not know which, if either, is true. Our problem is to determine how the truth or falsity of one proposition affects the truth or falsity of another. Consider another example. Our friends Bill and Jim are arguing once again:

BILL: No union has ever been justified in calling a strike.

JIM: No union has ever called an unjustified strike.

Bill and Jim, we note, are extremists. We know that both are wrong, since some strikes are justified and others are not. But in considering the logical relations of these propositions to each other, we must disregard our "outside" knowledge, in the sense that we may happen to *know* that a proposition is true (or false). We must consider only the truth values of the propositions to each other. We must ask, Does the truth of one of these propositions necessitate the truth of the other? Could both be true? Could both be false? The answers to these questions in the pair of propositions asserted by Bill and Jim will be exactly the same as in P and Q above, since the two pairs of propositions illustrate exactly the same relations.

Would the reader say that Jim *contradicted* Bill's statement in our example? If so, then the reader would be mistaken, for the logician defines "contradiction" as a relation such that, if one proposition of a pair is true, then the other must be false, and if one of the pair is false, then the other must be true. This is not the relation which holds in the two pairs of propositions we have examined. The relation holding between P and Q in these pairs of propositions is called "contrariety."

Let us now consider a pair of contradictory statements:

P: Japan attacked on December 7, 1941.

Q: Japan did not attack on December 7, 1941.

Once again we note that we must disregard the fact that we know that one of these statements happens to be true. Our logical questions are: Would the truth of P necessitate the falsity of Q? If Q were false, would P necessarily be true? When the answers to both of these questions is Yes, then the relation between the pair of propositions under consideration is called "contradiction."

One more illustration of a logical relation:

P: Nero was not the most cruel of all the Roman emperors.

Q: Commodus was not the most cruel of all the Roman emperors.

Here we have a new kind of relationship between P and Q. Both of these statements may be true. Neither Nero nor Commodus may have been the most cruel of all the emperors. If P is true, Q may or may not be true, and the same if Q is true. But now note what may not be so obvious, that P and Q could not both be false. If P is false, then Q would necessarily be true; if Q were false, P would necessarily be true. For consider: If P were false, then it would follow that Nero *was* the most cruel emperor. Since only one individual can be entitled to this distinction, Q, which says Commodus was not the most cruel, would then necessarily be true. When propositions are related in this manner, the relation is called "subcontrariety."

We shall consider seven relations in all: independence, equivalence, contradiction, contrariety, subcontrariety, superimplication, and subimplication. These seven relations are all the possible relations which two propositions may hold to each other in terms of truth and falsity. We shall now analyze each type of relation in detail.

Section II: The Seven Relations

Relation 1. Independence.

The relation of "independence" means that two propositions have no bearing upon each other in terms of their truth or falsity. P: "Shakespeare wrote Hamlet" is logically independent of Q: "Betelgeuse has a diameter 300 times that of the sun." Though both of these propositions happen to be true, the truth or falsity of either determines nothing concerning the truth or falsity of the other. Their truth values are thus wholly irrelevant with respect to each other. Consider another pair: P: "Eskimos live in snow houses," and Q: "Eskimos like to live in snow houses." These are also independent, since from the truth or falsity of one of these propositions we could not necessarily conclude that the other is either true or false. As noted earlier we must disregard the actual truth or falsity of the propositions.

We shall define each type of relation by a table of "truth-values." The table for independence is as follows:

P true.....Q ?
P false.....Q ?
Q true.....P ?
Q false.....P ?

The question mark means "undetermined," i.e., we cannot know whether the proposition at the right side of the table is either true or false. The lines should be read as follows: If P is true, then the truth or falsity of Q is undetermined, etc. When propositions are independent, then both may be true, both may be false, or one may be true and one false. The truth or falsity of one has no bearing on the truth or falsity of the other.

Relation 2. Equivalence.

We have already learned the meaning of equivalences in propositions. We shall now define this relation: Two propositions are logically equivalent when the truth of one requires the truth of the other, and when the falsity of one requires the falsity of the other. In symbols:

P true.....Q true
P false.....Q false
Q true.....P true
Q false.....P false

Two equivalent propositions will always be true together, and false together.

Relation 3. Contradiction.

The logician defines contradiction in a precise manner. One proposition is the contradictory of another when the truth of one involves the falsity of the other and when its falsity involves the truth of the other. Both cannot be true and both cannot be false. The propositions P: "The golden Plovers are noted for their gregarious habits," and Q: "golden Plovers are not noted for their gregarious habits," fulfill the definition, and are thus contradictories. In symbols:

P true.....Q false
P false.....Q true
———————————————————
Q true.....P false
Q false.....P true

Both cannot be true; both cannot be false.

P: "All women are fickle," is the contradictory of Q: "Some women are not fickle." If P is true, then Q must be false. If P is false, then it must be the case that at least some women are not fickle, i.e., Q will be true. If Q is true, then P must be false, and if Q is false, then P must be true.

Relation 4. Contrariety.

This relation must be carefully distinguished from contradiction. P: "All women are fickle," and Q: "No women are fickle," are *not* contradictories, since both might be false. (Both *are* false, but we must ignore outside knowledge in considering the manner in which two propositions are related; it is sufficient to know that both *can* be false.) But note that if P were true, then Q would necessarily be false, and vice versa. P and Q are contraries. One proposition is the contrary of another when they are so related that both cannot be true, but both can be false. In symbols:

P true.....Q false
P false.....Q ?
———————————————————
Q true.....P false
Q false.....P ?

Both can be false; both cannot be true.

The propositions P: "Hitler was World Public Enemy Number 1," and Q: "Tojo was World Public Enemy Number 1," are contraries. Both could not be true, but both might be false. Mussolini, or some other individual, might have been World Public Enemy Number 1. If one of this pair of propositions is true, the other is false, but if one is false, then the truth of the other remains undetermined.

Contraries, it may be noted, do not exhaust all possible alternatives, whereas contradictories do. The contradictory of P in the last paragraph would be, "Hitler was *not* World Public Enemy Number 1."

Relation 5. Subcontrariety.

Consider the following propositions: P: "Some people in the United States are seven feet tall" and Q: "Some people in the United States are not seven feet tall." Let us examine these propositions in the light of the relations we have studied thus far. (Propositions should be called independent only as a last resort, when careful study indicates that none of the logical relations are applicable.) The propositions are obviously not equivalent. Are they contradictories? No, because both might be true. It follows also that they cannot be contraries, since two contraries cannot both be true. What precisely is their relationship?

Both can be true but *both cannot be false*. Consider: If P were *false,* we would then have to say that there were no people in the United States who were seven feet tall. If there are no such people, if follows that Q must be true. On the other hand, if *Q* were false, it would follow that *P* was true. When propositions have this type of relationship, they are called subcontraries. Both can be true, but both cannot be false. In symbols:

        P true.....Q ?
        P false.....Q true
        Q true.....P ?
        Q false.....P true

Both may be true, but both cannot be false.

Note again that "some are" and "some are not" are interpreted strictly by logicians. "Some are" means "and possibly all." "Some are not" means "and possibly none." If P is true, i.e., if some people *are* seven feet tall, we cannot conclude that some *are not.* The truth of P allows the possibility that some are not, but does not guarantee it. Similarly, if Q is true, i.e., if some people *are not* seven feet tall, we cannot conclude that some *are.* The truth of either proposition leaves it an open question as to whether or not the other is true.

The relation of subcontrariety should be carefully compared with and distinguished from contrariety. In the former both propositions can be true; in the latter both can be false. In subcontraries the truth of one proposition leaves the other undetermined; in contrariety the falsity of one leaves the other undetermined. In subcontraries the falsity of one proposition involves the truth of the other. In contraries the truth of one involves the falsity of the other.

An interesting example of subcontrariety is found in the following pair:

> P: Carnera is not the worst heavyweight fighter of all time.
>
> Q: Billy Conn is not the worst heavyweight fighter of all time.

The reader will find the definition applicable to this example. If it is false to say that Carnera *is not* the worst, then he *is* the worst. Q must then be true.

Relation 6. Superimplication.

Consider the relations of the following:

> P: All contemporary French novelists are Existentialists.
>
> Q: Some contemporary French novelists are Existentialists.

If P is true, then Q must be true. If P is false, Q is undetermined. For if it is the case that "all" of a group have a certain characteristic, then surely "some" must have that characteristic, but if we merely know that "all" do not have it, then "some" may or may not have it. In symbols:

> P true.....Q true
>
> P false.....Q ?

When two propositions are related in accordance with our table, the relation is that of superimplication. The reader will note that our table differs from the others in that it does not give us the truth values from the "Q" point of view. For the latter we must turn to the next relation, "subimplication."

Relation 7. Subimplication.

> P: Some contemporary French novelists are Existen-
> tialists.
> Q: All contemporary French novelists are Existen-
> tialists.

Note that this is a new relation, so that the "Q" sentence in the
former relation is now called "P," and vice versa. In this new
relation, if P is true, Q is undetermined, but if P is false, Q
must be false.

> P true.....Q ?
> P false.....Q false

If we know that "some" of a class have a certain characteristic, then "all" may or may not have it. But if even "some" do
not have it, it is impossible that "all" should have it.

Superimplication and subimplication are correlative aspects
of the basic relation called "implication." This relation differs
from the others in that it is not symmetrical. Contrariety, for
example, is a symmetrical relation. If P is the contrary of Q, Q
is the contrary of P. But "P implies Q" is not necessarily reversible into "Q implies P."

When one proposition *implies* another, the first (the implicans, or "implying proposition") is superimplicant to the second (the implicate, or implied proposition), and the second
proposition is subimplicant to the first. When one proposition
implies another, the four statements in the following tetrad
will hold:

(1) If the superimplicant is true, then the subimplicant must
be true.
(2) If the superimplicant is false, then the subimplicant may
be true or false.
(3) If the subimplicant is true, then the superimplicant may
be true or false.
(4) If the subimplicant is false, then the superimplicant
must be false.

The first two lines of the tetrad give us the truth values when
we take the implicans as primary; the last two lines when the
implicate is taken as primary.

An interesting example of the implicative relationship will be found in:

        P: All Eskimos have blue eyes.

        Q: No Eskimos have brown eyes.

Assuming that eyes can have only one color, then, if P is true, Q must be true, but if P is false, the truth or falsity of Q is undetermined. P is thus the superimplicant of Q since it fulfills the requirements of the definition. We may then look at the situation from the Q point of view, and we shall find that if Q is true, P is undetermined, but that if Q is false, then P must be false. Q is thus the subimplicant of P. This will become clear if you think about it for a while. If you don't see it, come back to it later.

In closing this discussion, we note that the relation of super-implication is the fundamental relation in the syllogism. Thus:

        P: All lemurs are mammals, and this animal is a lemur.

        Q: This animal is a mammal.

P is a compound proposition made up of two propositions, each of which might be the premise of a syllogism, and Q represents the conclusion of that syllogism. P implies Q, so that if P is true, Q must be true. The syllogism would be valid. But if either or both of the premises were false, Q might or might not be true. Thus we have P true, Q true; P false, Q ?. This is the relation of superimplication.

Exercises

Write out the tables of truth values for the various relations and keep the list before you. Identify the relations in the following pairs of propositions. Ask the following questions in each case: If P is true, is Q true, false or doubtful? If P is false . . . , etc.

    1. P: Halsey commanded the fleet in the Pacific.

       Q: Halsey did not command the fleet in the Pacific.

    2. P: Halsey was the sole commander of the fleet in the Pacific.

       Q: Nimitz was the sole commander of the fleet in the Pacific.

 3. P: No Polynesians eat cocoanuts.
    Q: All Polynesians eat cocoanuts.
 4. P: No Eskimos eat blubber.
    Q: Some Eskimos eat blubber.
 5. P: The Fifth is Beethoven's best symphony.
    Q: The Sixth is Beethoven's best symphony.
 6. P: The Fifth is not Beethoven's best symphony.
    Q: The Sixth is not Beethoven's best symphony.
 7. P: There is a book in this library which contains subversive ideas.
    Q: There is a book in this library which contains no subversive ideas.
 8. P: All Eskimos live in snow houses.
    Q: Some Eskimos do not live in snow houses.
 9. P: Halsey commanded the fleet in the Pacific.
    Q: Halsey was an excellent commander.
10. P: Swing music is first rate music.
    Q: Swing music is 4th rate music.
11. P: Some politicians are statesmen.
    Q: All politicians are statesmen.
12. P: Some of these exercises are easy.
    Q: Some of these exercises are not easy.
13. P: X is an artichoke.
    Q: X is a vegetable.
14. P: This book is not written in Chinese.
    Q: This book is not written in Japanese.
15. P: All Indians have blue eyes.
    Q: No Indians have green eyes.

Section III: The Square of Opposition

The term "opposition," as used in traditional logic, refers to the relations of propositions having the same subjects and predicates but differing in quality or quantity or both. The A-E-I-O forms may thus be "opposed" to each other when they embody the same subjects and predicates. We shall use the following group for illustrative purposes:

    A: All women are fickle
    E: No women are fickle
    I: Some women are fickle
    O: Some women are not fickle

No two of these propositions are independent of each other, since the truth or falsity of any one will involve truth values in the others. Nor are any two equivalent. But we shall find the other five relations exhibited among them. Thus, the A and O forms are contradictories, since their relation to each other fulfills the definition of contradiction which we stated earlier, namely, that if the truth of one of a pair of propositions involves the falsity of the other, and vice versa, then the relation is that of contradiction. E and I are also contradictories. A and E are contraries, since both cannot be true, though both can be false. I and O are subcontraries, since both could be true, but both could not be false. A is the superimplicant of I, and E of O. I and O are the subimplicants of A and E respectively.

The traditional logicians worked out an ingenious diagram called the "Square of Opposition," which embodies these oppositions, viz.:

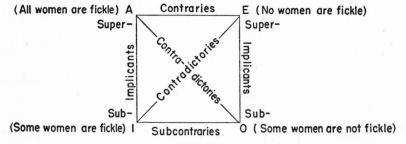

This diagram requires a word of explanation. The letters A-E-I-O at the corners stand for the propositions in the brackets, all of which have the same subjects and predicates. The diagonal lines connecting A and O, and E and I, marked "contradictories" mean that A and O are the contradictories of each other, etc. The line connecting A and E indicates that these are contraries, and the line between I and O that these are subcontraries. The vertical lines are marked "implicants," and the notations "super" and "sub" indicate that A is the superimplicant of I (E of O) and that I is the subimplicant of A (and O of E).

This diagram gives us an automatic device for detecting the relations of propositions *when they have the same subjects and predicates*. This limitation is very important for, as we already know, we may determine the relations between propositions which do *not* have the same subjects and predicates, as in relating "John is 6′ tall" to "John is 6′ 1″ tall." The relations of such pairs of propositions cannot be determined by the Square, for their predicates differ. But we know that they are contraries since they fulfill the definition of contrariety. The Square, then, does *not define*, but merely *illustrates* a limited application of the five relations.

The Square also has certain internal limitations. The universal propositions must be general, not singular, for singular propositions have no subimplicants. Furthermore, when we oppose singular A and E propositions to each other we find that the distinction between contradiction and contrariety disappears, as in "John is a great golfer" and "John is not a great golfer." Further possible limitations will be discussed in the next section.

Despite these limitations, however, the Square is useful for the purpose for which it was devised. It is also an interesting schematic exhibition of the five relations with respect to the A-E-I-O forms. When usable, it will be found very convenient for reference.

Exercises

The Square of Opposition should be used in working out these exercises.

A. Identify the relations among the following pairs:
1. P: Some women are not aviators.
   Q: Some women are aviators.
2. P: Some novelists are amoralists.
   Q: All novelists are amoralists.
3. P: Some politicians are crooks.
   Q: No politicians are crooks.
4. P: Some exercises in logic are not easy.
   Q: All exercises in logic are easy.
5. P: No Southern senators are Republicans.
   Q: Some Southern senators are not Republicans.
6. P: No Germans are pacifists.
   Q: All Germans are pacifists.

B. Complete the following chart, using T, F, and ? to symbolize
True, False, and Doubtful. For example, if A is true, then its
contradictory, O, must be false; its subimplicant, I, must be true;
and its contrary, E, must be false.

    If A is true, then I is ____, E is ____, O is ____.
      A is false, then I is ____, E is ____, O is ____.
    If I is true, then A is ____, E is ____, O is ____.
      I is false, then A is ____, E is ____, O is ____.
    If E is true, then A is ____, I is ____, O is ____.
      E is false, then A is ____, I is ____, O is ——.
    If O is true, then A is ____, E is ____, I is ____.
      O is false, then A is ____, E is ____, I is ____.

C. The propositions in the following group are stated in irregular
language. In order to place them on the Square, translations into
the A-E-I-O forms are necessary. In some cases it may be necessary
to obvert or convert them in order to obtain two propositions
with the same subjects and predicates. Identify the relations after
you have disposed of the linguistic problems.

    1. P: Only the brave deserve the fair.
       Q: Some persons who deserve the fair are not brave.
    2. P: None but geniuses write like that.
       Q: All persons who write like that are not geniuses.
    3. P: Nothing difficult displeases me.
       Q: Some things which displease me are not difficult.
    4. P: All men like jokes.
       Q: No persons who like jokes are men.
    5. P: Some novelists are moralists.
       Q: Some novelists are amoralists.
    6. P: Only the brave deserve the fair.
       Q: None of the brave deserve the fair.

D. Which problems on page 247 could have been answered by reference to the Square?

E. Prove by using the relations of contradiction and contrariety that
I and O cannot both be false, and that the falsity of I requires the
falsity of A.

F. Criticize the following:

    1. Granted that it is true that All wise men are mortal,
    2. then No wise men are immortal
    3. and No immortal beings are wise men.
    4. Hence it is false that Some immortal beings are wise men,
    5. and that Some immortal beings are not unwise men.
      But if this is false, it must be true that

6. All immortal beings are unwise men.
7. And that Some unwise men are immortal beings.
   (Creighton and Smart, *An Introductory Logic.* Copyright 1898, 1900, 1909, 1922, 1932 by The Macmillan Company and used with their permission.)
   (HINT: Are the terms properly negated, in the strict sense of contradiction?)

Section IV: The Existential Import of Categorical Propositions

Throughout our discussions of categorical propositions we have been making an unstated assumption concerning the existential import of propositions. We have assumed the existence of members of the classes referred to by such propositions. This assumption must now be made explicit for two reasons: (1) The careful thinker should be aware of the assumptions on which the validity of his reasoning depends, and (2) modern symbolic logic has shown us that the rules of inference of traditional logic sometimes depend upon certain unstated assumptions, and that the possibilities of valid inference are different if we use a different set of assumptions. This matter deserves some attention.

Modern symbolic logic adopts the convention that universal propositions do not affirm the existence of any individual members of classes, but that particular propositions do. This convention is tied in with the definitions of the A-E-I-O forms in the newer logic, viz.:

A: For any x, if x is an S then x is a P
E: For any x, if x is an S then x is not a P
I: There is an x such that x is an S and a P
O: There is an x such that x is an S and not a P

Note that the universals, in this interpretation, make no assertions that any S's exist. The A-form merely asserts that *if* anything is an S, *then* it would be a P. (If any being is a man, then that being will be mortal.) The E-form asserts that if anything is an S, then it is *not* a P. (If any being is a man, then he is not an angel.) The particular propositions, on the other hand, do assert that there are things which are S's, for each says "There *is* an x such that x is an S, etc."

Before we attempt to justify this new interpretation of the meaning of the A-E-I-O forms let us examine one of the consequences which follows from these definitions. It will now be illegitimate (without additional assumptions, to be examined presently) to deduce the truth of an I-form from the truth of an A-form (the relation of superimplication). Why is this? Examine the definitions of the A and I above. The A says that *if* anything is an S, then it is a P. The I: there *is* an x such that . . . In other words, we cannot derive an assertion concerning existence from a non-existential statement.

This point needs further clarification. We have heretofore assumed that "Some women are fickle" follows from "All women are fickle," but we are now told that this is an illegitimate inference. Nevertheless, the difficulty can be easily remedied if we recognize that the usual assertion that "All women are fickle" carries with it the tacit *assumption* that women exist. What we really mean, then, in making such an assertion, is something like the following: "If x is a woman, then x is fickle, and we assume that women exist" (or "If x is S then x is P, and assume that there are S's.") We can now infer that there *is* an x which is an S and a P, since there are S's and all S's are P's. Once we make the assumption of existence explicit, as an additional premise, the I follows from the A, as in the classical treatment of this matter. The importance of the new convention, then, is that we should be aware of the fact that we *have* made this assumption.

Let us now examine the justification for the new convention that universals should not be interpreted in an existential manner. Modern logic adopts this convention because of the undoubted fact that universals frequently refer to non-existential classes. As an example, examine the following A-form: "All world governments will bring more evil than good." We definitely do not mean that world governments exist, so that the interpretation "If there were a world government then it would bring more evil than good" renders our meaning more accurately. Similarly many significant universals in the physical sciences must be interpreted in a non-existential manner, as Newton's first law of motion ("All bodies free of impressed forces will persevere in their states of rest or motion in a straight line forever."), for there are no bodies free of impressed forces.

It is thus apparent that all universals do not assert existence. Since it is desirable to have a uniform rule which will apply in all cases, and since it is preferable to follow a strict interpretation which assumes as little as possible, modern logic interprets all universals as non-existential, and supplements with the assumption of existence, when this is appropriate. In practice, of course, many universals are meant in an existential sense, and it is unnecessary to make this assumption explicit in everday argument, but the point is that we should know what we are doing, and not draw inferences concerning existing things when this is impermissible.

It may interest the reader to note some further consequences of the new conventions with respect to some previous inferences. The conversion by limitation of an A-form will be incorrect without the explicit assumption of existence. Similarly, it will be illegitimate to deduce a particular from two universal premises, as in the following example:

> No world governments are perfect organizations
> All world governments are organizations which abolish national sovereignty
> ∴ Some organizations which abolish national sovereignty are not perfect organizations

This syllogism is invalid if we adopt the convention that particulars affirm existence, whereas universals do not. We have hitherto assumed that this would be a valid argument.

Another very important consequence of the new convention is the radically different interpretation of the Square of Opposition which is now required. I and O can no longer be derived from A and E, for reasons already noted. A and E are not necessarily contraries, nor are I and O necessarily subcontraries, since both of the former pair might be true, and both of the latter false. This somewhat startling consequence follows from the new assumptions. Take the I and O propositions: "Some ghosts are in this room" and "Some ghosts are not in this room." Each of these is regarded as false, on the ground that these particulars assert that ghosts actually exist, and this is a false assertion. The I-form asserts "There is a ghost in this room," and the O: "There is a ghost which is not in this room." Since both are false, their contradictories, A and E, must both be true. It thus follows that "All ghosts are in this room" and "No ghosts are in this room" are both *true*. For if we grant that there are no such things as ghosts, we will also grant that all of them are in this room, i.e., "all of them that there are" are in this room, namely, none. And we will also grant that none of them are in this room. Thus, under the new existential interpretation, both an I and an O with the same subjects and predicates may be false, and the corresponding A and E true.

But these difficulties do not arise when we assume the existence of the subjects of universal premises, as is the rule in the traditional logic. And this brings us to the very important problem of understanding what is meant by "existence." Both the classical and modern logic use the concept of "universes of discourse." This means that by "existence," in some cases, we may mean existence in the actual world of space and time. In other cases a special kind of "existence" is referred to, i.e., membership in a "universe of discourse" other than the real one. Thus a novelist or dramatist may create a world of his own in which his characters enjoy a special kind of being, and the same holds for the creatures of myths. We argue about the character of Hamlet, we say that it is correct to define a mermaid as "half woman, half fish," and when we say "Some fairies are wicked creatures," we definitely do not mean to affirm existence in the real world (though the proposition is particular), but we do affirm existence of a special sort for the denizens of the Grimm fairyland.

In other words, though particulars assert existence and universals do not, we must also be careful to specify the kind of existence referred to. Both "Some Greek gods were lustful" and "Some Greek gods were not lustful," when interpreted in terms of the universe of discourse of the Greek mythology, cannot both be false, just as in the universe of discourse of a ghost story our earlier I- and O-forms could not both be false. In such universes, the corresponding A- and E-forms could not both be true. (Nor can they both be true when we deal with actual existents.) On the other hand, "All angels are immortal beings" makes no assertion concerning existence, even in the universe of discourse of angelology, for it is a universal proposition. From such a universal we could not infer that "Some angels are immortal beings" unless we explicitly assume that angels do exist in that universe. If we make this assumption, then the inference would be justified.

Section V: The Traditional "Laws of Thought"

Traditionally, the so-called "Aristotelian Laws of Thought" have been regarded as basic in all reasoning. These laws have been formulated in two different ways, for things (or classes), or for propositions, as follows:

1. The Law of Identity: For things, the law asserts that "A is A," or "anything is itself." For propositions: "If a proposition is true, then it is true."
2. The Law of Excluded Middle: For things: "Anything is either A or not-A." For propositions: "A proposition, such as P, is either true or false."
3. The Law of Contradiction: For things: "Nothing can be both A and not-A." For propositions: "A proposition, P, cannot be both true and false."

These laws, though not the only principles used in reasoning, are certainly basic in the sense that all reasoning presupposes them. Note that these laws are really axioms, and not psychological laws which purport to tell us how we actually think. These are not scientific laws of nature, for they are frequently violated, as when people contradict themselves, or are inconsistent. When we think rationally, however, we always assume these axioms. We shall discuss the meaning and significance of these principles in connection with certain popular criticisms and misunderstandings.

1. The Law of Identity.

   a. For things. The Law of Identity asserts that "A is A." A book is a book, a cow is a cow. The reader's response to this may be, "Obvious, but why mention such trivialities." It may surprise the reader to learn that many contemporary writers, in particular the "General Semanticists," hold that the law of identity is a false and vicious principle. Count Alfred Korzybski, for example, in his *Science and Sanity* (p. 304) makes the sweeping claim that the mistaken belief in identity is responsible for many of the ills to which the spirit and flesh of modern man are heir, ills such as

> . . . unrest, unhappiness, nervous strain, irritability, lack of wisdom, and absence of balance, the instability of our institutions, the wars and revolutions, the increase of "mental" ills, prostitution, criminality, commercialism as a creed, the inadequate standards of education, the low professional standards of lawyers, priests, politicians, physicians, teachers, parents, and even scientists . . .

Because of his belief that the Law of Identity is responsible for these evils, Korzybski believes that the crucial need of the twentieth century is the formulation of a new non-Aristotelian logic which will reject the Law of Identity.*

Korzybski's basic criticism of the Law of Identity is that it is not true for a world that is in constant change. Things are in constant flux, he argues, so that nothing is ever the same from moment to moment. When we say that "a table is a table," we ignore the fact that the table *now* is different from what it was a moment ago. Hayakawa, in his *Language in Action,* as we noted in our earlier discussion of extension and intension, follows Korzybski's lead here. He asserts that "no word can ever have the same meaning twice" on the ground that the thing referred to has changed in the meanwhile and that our attitude toward it has also changed. Two answers may be given to this criticism:

(1) "The table *now* is different from what it was a moment ago." True, but unless words consistently referred to the same referent throughout a given unit of discourse, i.e., unless there was an identity in our meanings when we use words, communication would be impossible. When one speaks of a table, he means a table, and is understood to mean a table, for anything is itself and not some other thing.

---

* The remarks just quoted are directed toward arguments based on what Korzybski calls "the 'is' of identity." An illustration of what he has in mind is an expression such as "grass *is* green," interpreted to mean that grass is *identical* with green. This usage is indeed preposterous, and Korzybski quite properly objects to it. But the General Semanticists also generalize their attack against the law of identity, and reject it in the form in which we have stated it.

(2) The critics also confuse logical and physical identity. The problem here becomes a metaphysical one, involving the basic concepts of permanence and change. In the ancient world, the Greek philosophers first formulated this problem. Heracleitus, the philosopher of change, asserted that it was impossible for anyone to step into the same river twice, since the river was constantly changing. But Plato and Aristotle effectively criticized this doctrine of universal "flux" by noting that the statement "X has changed" requires that X retain its identity throughout the series of changes, for otherwise it would be impossible to say that X had changed. There is constant physical change in our universe, but also permanence or identity. The reader is undoubtedly a somewhat different person now from what he was before he began to read this discussion, but he must also be the same reader who began to read, for otherwise how could we say that *he* had changed? There can be no change except in relation to something that is constant.

b. For propositions. In the propositional formulation of the law of identity, we say that if a proposition is true, then it is true. This again is not so obvious as it appears, and the chances are that the reader will disagree when he learns what the law implies. Does the reader believe that a proposition can be "true for one man and false for another," or that "what is true in one age of history is false in another age"? If so, then he does not agree that the law is correct, for the law means that if a proposition is true, then it is true for all persons, in all times, and in all places. The reader may urge that the proposition "The earth is flat" was true in the middle ages, and false today. But, strictly speaking, "The earth is flat" was as false in the Middle Ages as it is today. Men *believed* that the earth was flat, but their belief was erroneous.

Another typical criticism of the law proceeds as follows: May not the time element, or the space element, make a proposition true for one time and place and false for another? For example, "It is cool today" may be true where we are, but false in the tropics, or false for us in July. But "It is cool today" is an incomplete statement of the speaker's meaning. If we state his meaning precisely, we would say something like the following: "The temperature is 41° F. at 1:15 P.M. in the shade at the

meteorological station in Chicago, Illinois on March 31, 1948."
If this statement is true, then it must be true for all time and
all places.

It is undoubtedly the case that men's beliefs differ, so that
what *seems* true to one man will seem false to another. Confidence in one's beliefs is not always justified, nor is certainty
always a guarantee of truth. We should remember that we may
be mistaken in what we believe to be true. Truth is an ideal
difficult to achieve, and in practice we may find it safer to be
satisfied with statements that a given belief appears to be
probable in the light of the available evidence. But if we know
the truth, then we know the truth.

2. The Law of Excluded Middle.

a. For things. Anything is either A or not-A, or anything is
either A or its contradictory. We may assert that anything in
the universe is either a piece of chalk or not a piece of chalk.
Contradictories always exhaust the universe of discourse to
which we refer. Thus, we may say of any color that it is either
red or not-red.

Some critics urge that this is vicious "either- or" thinking,
representing a "two-valued orientation" toward the world,
whereas the world requires a "multi-valued orientation." There
are, it is urged, infinite differences and degrees in things, so
that it is false to say "Either A or not-A." For example, we
should not divide men into two classes, the good and the evil,
for there is some evil in the best of us, and some good in the
most evil. The cartoonist Mauldin once illustrated the vice to
which the critics refer. He pictured one man carrying a sign
with the words, "Russia is never wrong." Another carried the
sign, "Russia is always wrong." Does not another alternative
exist? ask the critics. Must Russia be either always right or always wrong?

This criticism is based upon a confusion between contrariety and contradiction. The law of the excluded middle says
that anything is A or its contradictory. Thus, a man is either
rich or not rich, but the law does not assert that he is either rich

or poor. Similarly, either Russia is always right, or Russia is not always right.

b. For propositions. A proposition is either true or false. There is no middle ground between truth and falsity. Here again it is necessary to state a proposition precisely. "Either a street has been sprinkled or it has not been sprinkled." But suppose only part of the street has been sprinkled. Would our proposition then be both true and false? Not if we make it sufficiently precise. We usually mean that certain parts of the street have been sprinkled. In this sense, the proposition is true. If we meant that *all* of the street has been sprinkled, then the proposition would be false.

The failure to note the necessity for precision is responsible for the belief that some propositions are neither true nor false. "I am happy" and "We are enjoying prosperity" are examples of propositions which may be regarded as neither completely true nor completely false. But when the words are defined precisely, then, in some determinate respects the propositions will be either true or false. If we cannot define "happiness" or "prosperity," then we are not stating completely meaningful propositions, and truth or falsity apply only to meaningful propositions.

Another type of criticism is also based on the failure to define words precisely. B. B. Bogoslovsky, in his *Technique of Controversy,* cites the example of a beard in order to expose the alleged weakness of the law of the excluded middle. "Either Smith has a beard or he has not a beard." Now it is of course quite easy to distinguish between a beardless man and a bearded one, but where shall we draw the line which distinguishes one collection of hairs as a beard from another which is not? If 1000 hairs make a beard, and 100 do not, 999 will still constitute a beard and 101 will not. Shall we make 550 the dividing line and say that 549 hairs are no beard but that 550 are? This seems absurd because the word "beard" is never given a precise definition. But if a precise definition were required, then for any given collection we could say "beard" or "not-beard." In the same manner, the passing grade in a test may be defined as 60 or above. The student who makes 59 has failed, in terms of the definition, though there is certainly little difference in merit between a grade of 59 and one of 60.

3. The Law of Contradiction.

For things, nothing can both have and not have a given characteristic in precisely the same respect. This law asserts that nothing can be both A and the contradictory of A. A man cannot be both rich and not-rich at the same time and in the same respect. For propositions, we say that no proposition can be both true and false, in the same respects. The law of relativity tells us that an object may be moving for one frame of reference and at rest in another, but for any given frame of reference the object is not both moving and not-moving. It is perhaps needless to note that we are not always able to determine which of two contradictory propositions is true. But one must be true, and one false.

Exercises

A. Analyze and discuss the following items in terms of the preceding discussion:
  1. Every seven years the cells in a human body change completely. How then can a man's debts be held against him for more than seven years, since he is no longer the same man?
  2. Do the following items illustrate the law of identity?
    a. Those were the days when men were men
    b. Let us call a spade a spade
  3. What happens when an irresistible force meets an immovable object?
  4. According to the principle of contradiction, "animal" cannot be both vertebrate and invertebrate. But are not some animals vertebrate and others not?
  5. Are the following statements both true and false?
    a. Heavy objects fall at the same speed as light objects.
    b. Water boils at 212° F.
    c. Hamlet was a man.
  6. Does Aristotle use the principle of the excluded middle in the following quotation from his Physics?: "As every occurrence must be ascribed either to coincidence or to purpose, if the frequency of heat in the summer cannot be ascribed to

coincidence or chance, it must then be ascribed to purpose."

7. Is the law of the excluded middle applicable to statements such as "John loves Mary"?

8. Is it necessarily the case that a nation will either win a war or lose it?

B. Are the following remarks consistent with the discussion in the text?

There is a venerable law of logic called the "law of excluded middle" which states that A is either B or not B. Thus a piece of paper is either white or not white. This is obviously true, and I shall not deny its soundness as a law of pure logic. At the same time, we must notice that the kind of thinking embodied in this law may be dangerous and misleading when applied to a certain very common range of facts . . . All over human life we find properties which show continuous variation, and (just as in the case of white and black) we find this property obscured by the use of words implying sharp distinctions. "Sane" and "insane"; "good" and "bad"; "intelligent" and "unintelligent"; "proletarian" and "capitalist," are pairs of opposites which show this property of continuous variation . . . Any argument, therefore, which begins in some such way as follows: "A man must be either sane or insane, and an insane person is absolutely incapable of reasonable thought . . ." is a dangerous piece of crooked thinking, since it ignores this fact of continuity. (R. H. Thouless, *How to Think Straight*, Simon and Schuster, 1939, pp. 119, 123.)

C. In what respects do you agree with the following remarks from some "non-Aristotelian" writers? In what respects do you disagree? Do you find any misunderstandings of the laws of thought in these selections?

1. All people tend to think of things in terms of good and bad, black and white, hot and cold, God and Satan, rich and poor, etc. . . . Since this two-valued orientation underlies most of our thinking except in technological matters, the outcome of almost all disagreements is that both sides are pushed to irreconcilable extremes . . . Illiterates and "uneducated" people are by no means alone in their two-valued orientation; controversialists in intelligent magazines and in learned journals are similarly conditioned. The reader will recall, for example, the situation in which André Gide found himself after the publication of his *Return from the USSR*, in which he had recorded, with an artist's rigid self-honesty, his impressions of the Soviet Union. Thousands of anti-communists

clutched him to their bosoms as a brother, while thousands of his ideological allies gnashed their teeth at his "apostasy." For savages, for heresy-hunters like Mrs. Dilling, as well as for ideologically kosher intellectuals whether of the Left or the Right, there is no middle ground between black and white; it is *all* or *none*. This is what is meant, of course, by the "excluded middle" of Aristotelian logic. How far could modern engineering have got if we had thermometers which could give only two readings, "hot" and "cold" . . . ? (S. I. Hayakawa, "The Meaning of Semantics," *New Republic,* Aug. 2, 1939.)

2. *A is A.*

The characters of Aphrodite (a sow) *now* are different from those one second earlier or one second later. Not by much, but by enough to destroy the perfection of identity. A rocket is always the same rocket. True for words, but not for that nonverbal event in space-time which blazes in glory and falls a charred stick as we watch it; not for a mushroom full-blown today and underground yesterday; not for a rose, withered now and lovely a week ago; not for an ice cream cone five minutes in the sun; . . . We have no knowledge of anything in the real world which is not a process, and so continually changing its character, slowly or rapidly as men measure intervals.

Everything is either A or not-A.

The law of the excluded middle might read: "Every living thing is either an animal or a plant." It was so employed by biologists for centuries. We still play the game of twenty questions on the animal, vegetable, mineral basis. In recent years a number of organisms have been studied which defy the distinction. A class of living things has been observed whose metabolism under certain conditions follows the classification of "plant," under other conditions that of "animal." Thus Euglena, a little unicellular water organism, becomes green in abundant sunlight and behaves like a "plant." Remove the light, the green color disappears, and Euglena proceeds to digest carbohydrates like an "animal," rather than synthesizing them like a plant. . . . The law of the excluded middle is an unreliable guide to knowledge. The law of contradiction—Nothing is both A and not-A is equally unreliable. Euglena is both "plant" and "animal." (Stuart Chase, *The Tyranny of Words,* Harcourt, Brace and Co., pp. 228–30.)

3. The new reasoning is built on the experiences of a dynamic universe with motion as its essence, and with ceaseless change as its characteristic aspect, a universe conceived as a continuous succession of different but interrelated phases of one process which are all related to each other, and perpetually flow one into another. The logic of this reasoning must have as its foundation and root the law "A is B and non-B at the same time." Only such a Logic can be a reliable guide in a dynamic universe and can satisfy the modern mind, which realizes more actively than ever before that we live in a world always new and changing every moment. (B. B. Bogoslovsky, *The Technique of Controversy*, Harcourt, Brace and Co., p. 12.)

4. The Law of Contradiction is afflicted with a similar falsity. It says "nothing can both be and not be." But anything that can change or have a plurality of relations defies it. It can both be and not be with the utmost ease. It is at one time and not at another. Or in one respect, and not in another. Or in one place, and not in another. Or for one purpose, and not for another. Or in one context, and not in another. (F. C. S. Schiller, *Logic in Use*, Harcourt, Brace and Co., p. 38.)

5. In analyzing the Aristotelian codification, I had to deal with the two-valued, "either—or" type of orientation. I admit it baffled me for many years, that practically all humans, the lowest primitives not excluded, who never heard of Greek philosophers, have some sort of "either—or" type of evaluation. Then I made the obvious "discovery" that our relations to the world outside and inside our skins often happen to be, on the gross level, two-valued. For instance, we deal with day and night, land or water, etc. On the living level we have life or death, our hearts beat or not, we breathe or suffocate, are hot or cold, etc. Similar relations occur on higher levels. Thus, we have induction or deduction, materialism or idealism, capitalism or communism, democrat or republican, etc. And so on endlessly on all levels.

In living, many issues are not so sharp, and therefore a system which posits the general sharpness of "either—or," and so objectifies "kind," is unduly limited; it must be revised and made more flexible in terms of "degree." This requires a physico-mathematical "way of thinking," which a non-Aristotelian system supplies. (Alfred Korzybski, *op. cit.*, p. vii.)

Chapter 12

COMPOUND AND COMPLEX PROPOSITIONS AND SYLLOGISMS

Section I: Compound Propositions

We have concluded our study of categorical propositions and categorical syllogisms. We shall now examine compound propositions and compound syllogisms. The basic difference between the categorical and the compound proposition is that the former are made up of terms, the latter of propositions. Thus, "All men are mortal" has terms as its constituent elements. "If all men are rational beings, then a world community is a possibility" is a compound proposition, having two subpropositions as its constituent elements, namely, "All men are rational beings" and "A world community is a possibility." By analogy with chemical analysis we may think of categorical propositions as being composed of atoms, and compound propositions of molecules.

There are four types of compound propositions, each having a distinctive set of connective words, and each being made up of subpropositions, which we shall customarily symbolize by the letters P, Q, etc. Following is a list of the different types, with examples of each:

Hypothetical: *If* prices continue to rise, *then* the unions will ask for wage increases

Alternative: *Either* the nations will co-operate, *or* all will perish

Conjunctive: Capitalism is a free system *and* communism is an unfree system

Disjunctive: *Not both* can we limit freedom of speech *and* preserve our democracy

We shall study these compound propositions because they are customary forms of expression in logical discourse. We shall investigate the manner in which we draw inferences from such propositions. Each type will now be considered in detail.

Section II: Hypothetical Propositions and Syllogisms

1. The hypothetical proposition.

A hypothetical proposition is made up of two subpropositions connected by the words "if" and "then." In the example in the list above, these propositions are "Prices continue to rise" and "The unions will ask for wage increases." The first of these propositions is called the "antecedent," the second the "consequent." We shall symbolize these by the letters P and Q. The structural form of the hypothetical proposition may thus be exhibited as follows:

If $\dfrac{\text{P (antecedent)}}{\text{(Prices continue to rise)}}$ then $\dfrac{\text{Q (consequent)}}{\text{(The unions will ask for}}$
wage increases)

A hypothetical proposition thus takes the form "If P then Q." We shall also use the symbol ⊃, the sign of implication, to represent this type of proposition. "P ⊃ Q" means "P implies Q," or "If P then Q." Since P and Q stand for propositions, this form has the meaning "If the proposition P is true, then the proposition Q is true," or "If what P asserts is the case, then what Q asserts will be the case." Note also that when we wish to assert that a proposition such as P is true, we need simply say "P." When we wish to assert that it is false, we say "− P" ("not-P").

Let us now examine the precise meaning of "If P is true, then Q is true," or "If prices rise, then the unions will ask for wage increases." No assertion is made that either of the subpropositions is true. We have not said that prices will rise, nor have we said that the unions will ask for wage increases. The only assertion we have made is that the consequent will follow *if* the antecedent occurs. If prices rise, we have said, then the unions will surely ask for wage increases. They might, of course, ask for wage increases even if prices do not rise. But if we should find that the unions have not asked for wage increases six months hence, then we can be sure that prices did not rise, since if they did wage increases would have been requested. (Assuming, of course, that the proposition is true.)

The meaning of the hypothetical proposition thus involves six aspects:

1. No assertion is made concerning the truth or falsity of P taken alone.
2. No assertion is made concerning the truth or falsity of Q taken alone.
3. If P is true, then Q will surely be true.
4. If Q is not true, then P cannot be true.
5. If P is not true, then Q may or may not be true.
6. If Q is true, then P may or may not be true.

The relation of the antecedent to the consequent, it may be noted, is exactly the same as that of the superimplicant to the subimplicant in the relation of implication. If P is true, Q must be true. If Q is false, P must be false. But if either P is false or Q true, no necessary inference follows.

2. Hypothetical syllogisms.

The rules of validity of the hypothetical syllogism are based upon the meaning of the hypothetical proposition. We shall begin with an example of the so-called "mixed" type, which is made up of a hypothetical major premise, a categorical minor premise, and a conclusion. An example:

If a battleship is gray, then it has been painted (If P then Q)
         P   Q

The battleship Missouri is gray   (P)
              P

∴ The battleship Missouri has been painted   (∴Q)
              Q

We shall refer to the hypothetical premise as the "major premise," and to the second premise as the "minor." Note the latter carefully. It introduces a "special case," which corresponds to the "third term" of a categorical syllogism. Here it is "the battleship Missouri." The minor premise asserts that our special case has the characteristic stated in the antecedent of the major premise; hence, we say that the minor premise "affirms" th antecedent, and we symbolize the minor premise by "P." The conclusion affirms the consequent. But the minor premise might have informed us that the antecedent did not apply to the Missouri, i.e., that the Missouri was *not* gray, or that the consequent applied or did not apply to the Missouri. There are thus four possibilities; in our example only the first is shown.

The four possibilities in the minor premise give us four "figures" of the hypothetical syllogism, depending upon whether the minor premise affirms or denies the antecedent, or affirms or denies the consequent. Beginning in each case with the major premise "If P then Q," the minor premise may assert "P" or "−P," or "Q" or "−Q," which mean respectively, "P is true" (the antecedent of the major premise applies to this case, i.e., the Missouri), "P is false" for this case (or does not apply), "Q applies, or is true for this case," or "Q is false, or does not apply to this case." The four figures are as follows:

Figure 1. Affirming the antecedent:

If a battleship is gray then it has been painted	If P then Q
The Missouri is gray (affirms antecedent)	P
∴ It has been painted (affirms consequent)	∴ Q

Figure 2. Denying the antecedent:

If a battleship is gray then it has been painted	If P then Q
The Missouri is not gray (denies antecedent)	− P
∴ It has not been painted (denies consequent)	∴ − Q

Figure 3. Affirming the consequent:

If a battleship is gray then it has been painted	If P then Q
The Missouri has been painted (affirms consequent)	Q
∴ The Missouri is gray (affirms antecedent)	∴ P

Figure 4. Denying the consequent:

If a battleship is gray then it has been painted	If P then Q
The Missouri has not been painted (denies consequent)	− Q
∴ The Missouri is not gray (denies antecedent)	∴ − P

In these four figures, the name of the figure depends upon what the minor premise does. Note that "deny" is synonymous with "contradicts." A denial asserts the falsity of either antecedent or consequent. The minor premise will be symbolized by either P or −P, Q or −Q. The major premise of a hypothetical syllogism is always symbolized by "If P then Q" even if the propositions are "negative" ones, as in "If men are wise, then they are not afraid of death." In this case "they are not afraid of death" would be symbolized by Q, and a denial of this consequent, as in "they are afraid of death," would be symbolized by −Q.

We shall now examine the rules of validity of the hypothetical syllogism. (The concepts of distribution and class analysis are now irrelevant, since we are no longer dealing with terms.) The rules are as follows: Figures 1 and 4 are valid, and Figures 2 and 3 are invalid.

Figure 1. Affirming the antecedent:

The hypothetical proposition asserts that the consequent will be true if the antecedent is true. If the minor premise affirms the antecedent we may therefore properly affirm the consequent.

Figure 2. Denying the antecedent:

The major premise tells us that a ship will be painted if it is gray. It does *not* assert that it will be painted *only* if it is gray. The fact that the Missouri is not gray does not prove that it has not been painted; it may be painted in a different color, such as white. Thus this form is invalid.

Figure 3. Affirming the consequent:

The minor premise asserts that the Missouri is painted. But, for the same reasons as above, this does not permit us to conclude that it is gray. This form is also invalid.

Figure 4. Denying the consequent:

This form is valid. If the Missouri is not painted, then it cannot be gray, since only painted battleships are gray. The hypothetical proposition tells us that if the antecedent occurs, then the consequent will surely occur. But if the consequent is not the case, then the antecedent could not have occurred, for if it had, then the consequent would have occurred.

Exercises

A. State the figures of the following syllogisms and note whether they are valid or invalid:

1. If P then Q
   and −Q
   ∴ −P

2. If P then Q
   and Q
   ∴ P

3. If P then Q
   and −P
   ∴ −Q

4. If P then Q
   and P
   ∴ Q

B. Analyze the following syllogisms for validity. Write out each with the hypothetical major premise stated first, the minor premise second, and the conclusion last. Underline the sub-propositions of the major premise as P and Q, note whether the minor premise affirms or denies the antecedent or consequent, and then note whether the conclusion affirms or denies.

1. If a man can vote, then he is a citizen. John can vote, for he is a citizen.

2. If a sailor desires submarine duty, then he must be a brave man. But Bill cannot be a brave man, for he did not desire submarine duty.

3. If our country could not survive without a strong Britain, then we ought to help them. But there is no need to help them, for we can survive without them.

4. The prisoner was very nervous and we know that if he were guilty he would have acted in that manner, so we know that he must be guilty.

5. If men are not wise, then they will not show reverence for those matters which are beyond their understanding. In my classes in the social sciences and philosophy, I have noted that the instructors often confess to an inability to explain some things and yet they do not show reverence for those matters. Is this not sufficient to establish the fact that they are not wise?

6. If he had good taste, then he would not make wisecracks at inopportune moments. But since he does make them, he lacks good taste.

7. If this world is the work of a wise and beneficent Intelligence, it will exhibit evidence of wisdom and foresight. The most hardened skeptic is not able to deny that the world

does, as a matter of fact, exhibit evidence of wisdom and foresight. He should therefore admit that it is the work of such an Intelligence.

8. If all men were capable of perfection, then some would have attained it. But since no men have ever attained perfection, we may conclude that none are capable of it. (HINT: Does the conclusion *contradict* the antecedent?)

9. If some men were capable of perfection, then some would have attained it. But no men have attained perfection, so some men are not capable of it.

Section III: Special Aspects of Hypothetical Propositions and Syllogisms

In this section we shall note some special aspects concerning the meaning and form of hypothetical propositions and syllogisms.

1. Hypothetical syllogisms in ordinary discourse.

a. *Linguistic irregularities.*

In our study of categorical syllogisms we noted the necessity for the restatement of many propositions in order to make them fit into our "logical machine." Similar types of problems will be encountered when we analyze hypothetical syllogisms.

The hypothetical major premise must always be stated in the skeletal form: If P, then Q. The words "if" and "then" should be added when required. Some special types of irregularity will be frequently encountered: (1) Exceptive sentences, which use words such as "unless." Example: "Unless the fog lifts, the planes will be grounded." "Unless" is the equivalent of "if not," and we rephrase this sentence as "If the fog does not lift, then the planes will be grounded." (2) Words such as "when," "where," and "provided that" may be simply translatable into "ifs." Examples: "When we eliminate prejudice, this will be a better world." "Where science throws its searching light, ignorance disappears." "Provided that the weather is favorable, crops will be excellent." Each of these sentences should be rephrased by beginning them with "if" and adding "then" after the commas. (3) The consequent may be stated before the antecedent, as in "He will co-operate if we give him what he ask for." This should be restated as "If we give him what he asks for, then he will co-operate." Another, stated in exceptive form: "No wills are legal unless witnessed by two persons." This is restated as "If wills are not witnessed by two persons, then they are illegal."

b. Hypothetical enthymemes.

These incomplete syllogisms introduce no new principles. Hypothetical enthymemes must first be completed as syllogisms, and they will be valid or invalid. The following argument is in the First Order: "The unions asked for wage increases, so prices must have risen." The major premise is presumably "If prices rise, then the unions will ask for wage increases." If so, the argument is invalid. A Second Order example: "If the future is like the past, then men will be dissatisfied. They will be." The missing minor here is "The future will be like the past." It is valid.

In the statement "If Russia were a satisfied nation, then there would be no war, but Russia is not a satisfied nation" the conclusion is missing. The hearer is expected to conclude that there will therefore be a war. The completed argument will obviously be invalid, since the minor premise denies the antecedent. Difficulties may be encountered in Fourth Order enthymemes in which only the major premise is stated. The following is stated sarcastically: "Sure, the Republicans will save the country. All they have to do is to reduce the national debt by cutting taxes." This entire statement is the major premise of a syllogism: "If the Republicans will save the country, then they must reduce the national debt by cutting taxes." The hearer is expected to note that it is impossible to reduce the national debt by cutting taxes, so that it follows that the Republicans will not save the country.

Exercises

State the following arguments in the schematic form of the hypothetical syllogism and analyze for validity. Disregard all material other than the essential syllogistic structure.

1. They said that they would surely come if they could get a sitter, and I know that no sitters are available, so they will not come.
2. He said, "I shall come unless you hear from me by Saturday." We have not heard from him and Saturday has passed. We can conclude that he is coming.
3. If that isn't sound doctrine, then I don't know sound doctrine.
4. If adequate reasons exist for being hostile, if hostility is an adequate reaction to a situation, the assumption of a destruction instinct loses even the scant evidence it has for its support. (K. Horney, *New Ways in Psychoanalysis,* p. 127.)
5. Robert Filmer argued as follows, in his *Observations Concerning the Originall of Government* (1652): "The king is not proved a tyrant by evidence that he disregards the law, for, if disregard of law be tyranny, courts of equity and all exercise of the pardoning power are tyranny; and such is not the case."
6. If Jefferson and Lincoln were right when they said that all men are created equal, then no man should talk of tolerating another, since he has not the authority to do so. Neither has any group of men—a class, a nation, or a race—the authority to tolerate another group. Jefferson and Lincoln were right. Then let us not talk of tolerance. Equality is enough. Let us not consent to the existence of others. Let us assume it as we assume our own existence, and go on from there to live as justly as we can. (Mark van Doren, in *Harper's,* March, 1948.)
7. Is a science of values possible? Is it possible to establish the principles of good and evil on a scientific foundation? In his *No Compromise,* M. Rader considers a number of arguments which seek to prove that such a science is impossible. He writes:

The first argument we shall consider is based on the freedom of the will. It is maintained that men are endowed with a faculty of arbitrary choice which renders human life and its values too unpredictable for scientific treatment. The argument, if valid, would eliminate not only the value-sciences, but also psychology and sociology. The latter must also depend upon a certain constancy in human nature. If freedom is conceived as pure indeterminism, in the sense of

absolute chance, no science of human life is possible insofar
as freedom obtains. Hence, if psychology and sociology can
be scientific, this objection must be invalid. (M. Rader, *No
Compromise.* Copyright 1939 by The Macmillan Company
and used with their permission.)

(HINT: State the argument of the "free-willists" in syllogistic
form. Rader seeks to disprove the truth of their conclusion
by proving the falsity of their minor premise. State Rader's
argument in syllogistic form).

8. The following selection is taken from a discussion in which
the author is examining various popular answers to the question "What makes conduct right or wrong?" The author now
takes up the thesis that acts are right "because they are approved by a community."

We usually approve such conduct as is approved by the community to which we belong, and condemn whatever our
group condemns. May we not simply say, then, that morals
are *mores,* the customs of a given people? Obviously these
moral customs vary indefinitely.

> The wildest dreams of Kew are the facts of Khatmandu,
> And the crimes of Clapham, chaste in Martaban

According to this conception, there is no one universal
right and wrong; there are merely local and temporary standards, like the local spaces and times of relativity theory. Indeed, this view of morality is frankly relativistic. What is
right for us, as a member of our community, may be a sin for
a member of an alien group. It is a mortal sin for a Catholic
to commit suicide, but it is a glorious deed (under certain
circumstances) for a patriotic Japanese . . . To be moral is
simply to be true to the code of the group to which you belong.

This view of morality . . . makes . . . morality consist
in *conformity.* . . . It gives us no reason to think that the
particular code of our group is a *better* code than that of
some other group. It gives us no leverage by which to *criticize*
and *improve* the morals of our group. It allows no meaning
at all to the concept of moral *progress.* However superstitious
and stupid, or even cruel, the customs of our community are,
they are, by definition, what is right—for us. The unthinking

conformist is the moral man, the moral reformer is the immoral man—unless he converts his fellows to his view.

But we do not really believe this. We are all constantly criticizing the morals of our own group—not to say the morals of other peoples. And while a prophet is apt to be without honor in his own country during his lifetime, he is often rated by a later generation as the most moral man of his day, precisely because he rejected the inadequate moral code of his people. We all feel that moral judgments are more important than this definition of morality makes them out to be. (Durant Drake, *Invitation to Philosophy,* Houghton Mifflin Company.)

HINT: Use P for the thesis which the author discusses, and use Q for its consequences. The last paragraph states the author's minor premise. What is his conclusion? State the full syllogism.

2. The equivalences of categorical and hypothetical propositions.

A given proposition may be stated either as a categorical or as a hypothetical, and convey exactly the same meaning in either form. Thus, "If a battleship is gray, then it is painted" may be stated in the categorical form as "All gray battleships are painted." Similarly, "All students of literature are well-read persons" may be stated in the hypothetical form as "If a person is a student of literature, then he is a well-read person." Every hypothetical proposition is translatable into an equivalent A-form categorical, and vice versa. An E-form is equivalent to an A-form by obversion, and is hence also translatable, but particular categoricals do not have corresponding hypotheticals. Only universal general categoricals are equivalent to hypotheticals, singular propositions not being thus translatable. The schematic form of the translations may be shown as follows:

$$\text{All} \quad P \quad \text{are} \quad Q \quad (Pd < Qu)$$
$$\text{If it is a P then it is a Q} \quad (P \supset Q)$$

The value of the hypothetical type of expression is apparent when we seek to translate a hypothetical proposition such as "If prices continue to rise, then the unions will ask for wage increases" into its corresponding categorical. The categorical proposition must be stated in terms of class inclusion. P ⊃ Q must be stated as Pd < Qu. This can be done as follows: "All situations in which prices continue to rise are situations in which the unions will ask for wage increases." The hypothetical form of expression states the thought of this proposition more elegantly than does the categorical. Another value of the hypothetical form is that it emphasizes the "iffy" nature of a conditional proposition such as the one just cited. This use was also noted in our presentation of the definitions of the A- and E-forms in symbolic logic, in connection with the existential import of universal propositions. In Part Three we shall note the importance of the hypothetical proposition in scientific reasoning.

Exercises

1. Translate the following propositions from the categorical into the hypothetical form, and vice versa:
    a. All cats are lovers of solitude.
    b. No exercises in logic are easy.
    c. Express trains alone do not stop here.
    d. If a person is a radical then he is dissatisfied.
    e. If a person does not read then he is not well-informed.
    f. If statesmen will show self-restraint, then war will be averted.
2. Translate the four figures of the hypothetical syllogisms concerning the battleship Missouri into their corresponding categorical forms, and note the validity of each. To which fallacies of the categorical syllogisms do Figures 2 and 3 correspond?
3. Analyze the following syllogism in hypothetical form:
    It is a rule of the company by which my client is employed that express trains alone do not stop at his station. Since the train in question did not stop, how was he to know that it was not an express train?

3. The opposition of hypothetical propositions.

In this subsection we shall consider the possibilities of converting, contraposing, and contradicting hypothetical propositions.

a. Conversion.

Since a hypothetical proposition is equivalent to an A-form, it cannot be converted. "If x is a man, then x is mortal" cannot be converted into "If x is mortal, then x is a man." But the rule is a formal one, and means only that $P \supset Q$ cannot be converted into $Q \supset P$ in the absence of outside information. We learned earlier that when a subject class is identical with the predicate class, simple conversion of an A-form will be justified. Similarly with hypotheticals. "If a figure is three-sided, then it is a triangle" can be converted into "If it is a triangle then it is three-sided." But this is because we know that "if," in this case, means "if and only if." In other words, when we know that the antecedent is the exclusive condition of the consequent, then conversion will be justified. Phrases like "provided that" often refer to such exclusive conditions. Note also that when we know that we have a convertible major premise, all of the four figures will yield valid arguments.

b. Contraposition.

The contrapositive of a categorical A-form is equivalent to the original proposition. $Ad < Bu$ is equivalent to $-Bd < -Au$. The original terms are reversed and contradicted. Similarly with hypotheticals. The contrapositive of $P \supset Q$ is $-Q \supset -P$. In words, "If a man is wise then he is unafraid of death" contraposes into "If a man is afraid of death, then he is not wise."

c. Contradiction.

One proposition is the contradictory of another when the truth of one implies the falsity of the other, and vice versa. How would you state the contradictory of "If prices continue to rise, then the unions will ask for wage increases"? The form of this proposition is $P \supset Q$. When we carefully examine its meaning we find that it asserts *the impossibility of P being true and Q false*. To contradict it we must assert the *possibility* of P being true and Q false. Its contradictory would thus be "Prices will continue to rise and the unions will not ask for wage increases." This last proposition is of the conjunctive type, and requires a word of explanation.

A conjunctive proposition is one which simply joins two or more propositions by the connective "and." We shall henceforth use a dot (·) to symbolize "and." "P · Q" will thus be read as "P and Q" or "Both P and Q are true," "P · −Q" as "P is true and Q is false." Thus, if P ⊃ Q is our original proposition, then "P · −Q," which means "P is true and Q is false" is its contradictory. For, as we noted earlier, P ⊃ Q asserts the impossibility of P and −Q (P true and Q false). The contradictory asserts the possibility of P and −Q. We would *prove* our hypothetical proposition false if, six months later, we could show that prices had risen and the unions had not asked for wage increases.

Exercises

1. Are any of the following propositions formally convertible?
   a. If statesmen will show self-restraint, then war will be averted.
   b. If men are not free to express their opinions, then opposition smolders beneath the surface.
   c. If a person is not infected with the typhus bacillus, then he does not have typhoid fever.
2. Contrapose exercises a, b, and c.
3. State the contradictories of a, b, and c.

4. Pure hypothetical syllogisms and sorites.

Thus far we have analyzed mixed hypothetical syllogisms, in which the minor premise and conclusion were categorical propositions. But syllogistic arguments may contain hypothetical propositions exclusively. Such syllogisms are called *pure* hypothetical syllogisms. This form is illustrated by the following argument:

> If a man is young then he is an idealist   (P ⊃ Q)
> If a man is an idealist then he is sensitive (Q ⊃ R)
> ∴ If a man is young then he is sensitive   (∴ P ⊃ R)

The validity of this argument may be explained in two ways. (1) The three propositions may be translated into categoricals, in which case the validity will be obvious. (2) Implication is a transitive relation, so that if P ⊃ Q and Q ⊃ R then P ⊃ R.

A pure hypothetical sorites may be constructed in a similar manner, there being no limit to the number of propositions which may be used. Assume that we are given $P \supset Q$, $Q \supset R$, $R \supset S$, and $S \supset T$. Since implication is a transitive relation, P implies T. It is also obvious that any proposition in the series will imply any proposition at its right. The entire argument may also be stated in simplified form as $P \supset Q \supset R \supset S \supset T$; but, as we learned earlier, a chain of relations must not be interpreted as a single proposition. To do so would be meaningless, as we shall shortly learn. We should regard the chain as a simplification of an implicative sorites, with the links omitted. In reading it, we should supply the missing links, viz.: "P implies Q, and Q implies R, etc."

The contrapositive of the chain above is $-T \supset -S \supset -R \supset -Q \supset -P$. In other words, the contradictory of any proposition at the right, in the *original* argument, will imply the contradictory of any proposition at its left.

We may also note here that a pure hypothetical syllogism may be *followed* by a categorical proposition, as if we had added "John is a young man" to the syllogism with which we began this discussion. We could then draw the conclusion that "John is sensitive." The complete argument would then be a mixed hypothetical sorites.

Exercises

1. The following propositions are given as true: $A \supset X$, $S \supset M$, $Z \supset T$, $M \supset Z$, $X \supset S$. Put them together as a chain of implications. Then state the contrapositive.

   (HINT: The two propositions which appear only once are obviously the two ends of the chain.)

2. Analyze the following argument as a hypothetical sorites followed by a categorical proposition. Draw the author's conclusion.

   If our diagnosis is correct and if capitalism is doomed to die from the self-contradiction which grows and gnaws like a cancer within its body, we would seem to be faced with the necessity of abandoning the democracy which we love and choosing either the dictatorship that is fascism or the dictatorship that is communism. For capitalism, with all its evils, is the embodiment of democracy in economic form, and if the rights and liberties of private property are to be abolished in favor of bureaucratic ownership or bureaucratic regulation by the state, then those other rights and liberties which constitute the essence of human personality and without which the human individual would be degraded to the status of a bee in a hive or a cog in a machine, must be abolished also. (*The Ways of Things*, by W. P. Montague, Prentice-Hall, 1940, p. 628.)

(HINT: Symbolize the constituent propositions as follows: C: Capitalism is doomed, B: We will have bureaucratic ownership or bureaucratic regulation, F: We must choose the dictatorship of fascism or the dictatorship of communism, E: We must abandon economic democracy, P: We must abandon political democracy.)

Section IV: Alternative Propositions and Syllogisms

1. The alternative proposition.

Alternative propositions are compound, being made up of two constituent propositions joined by the connectives "either" —"or." "Either the nations will co-operate or all will perish." The subpropositions are called the first and second alternants. Using P and Q to symbolize these alternants, we find the following structure:

$$\text{Either } \frac{\text{P (first alternant)}}{\text{(The nations will co-operate)}} \text{ or } \frac{\text{Q (second alternant)}}{\text{(All will perish)}}$$

We shall symbolize the "either-or" relationship by "∨," and will read "P ∨ Q" as "Either P or Q" or "Either P is true or Q is true," or "Either P is the case or Q is the case," depending upon the sense of the proposition.

Let us now examine the meaning of an alternative proposition. When we say "Either P is true or Q is true," we assert that one at least of these propositions is true. We do not assert that either is false, leaving it an open possibility that both may be true. We simply say that at least one of these propositions is true. For example, we learn that a politician has been involved in shady dealings. We say of him, "Either he is a fool or he is a scoundrel." One at least, we say, must be true, and possibly both. He may be both a fool and a scoundrel. Similarly in the structural illustration above. We say that either alternative must hold, but we do not exclude the possibility that both will occur, i.e., that the nations will co-operate and also perish.

2. The alternative syllogism.

Alternative syllogisms are composed of an alternative major premise, a minor premise which affirms or denies one of the alternants, and a conclusion. There are thus four possible figures. The rules of validity of alternative syllogisms follow from the meaning of the alternative proposition. Since the alternative proposition asserts that one alternant at least is true, and possibly both, a valid argument results only when we deny one of the alternants and affirm the other. For if we are told that at least one of two propositions is true, and we learn that one of them is false, the other must be true. But if we learn only that one of them is true, no definite conclusion can follow concerning the other. It *may* be true, but it may not be. The alternative syllogism is thus valid when the minor premise denies; invalid when it affirms. Thus:

Affirming the first alternant:
Either X is a fool or he is a
   knave
X is a fool
∴ X is not a knave

Affirming the second:
Either X is a fool or he is a
   knave
X is a knave
∴ X is not a fool

These syllogisms are invalid. Both alternants may be true, or only one may be true. The major premise tells us only that at least one must be true, so that a definite conclusion following the affirmation of one alternant is unjustified.

Denying the first alternant:
Either X is a fool or he is a
   knave
X is not a fool
∴ X is a knave

Denying the second alternant:
Either X is a fool or he is a
   knave
X is not a knave
∴ X is a fool

These syllogisms are valid. Since at least one alternant is true, the denial of one requires the affirmation of the other.

Exercises

1. Complete the following alternative major premises in such a way as to get two valid syllogisms in each case:
   a. Either you are lazy or you are inefficient.
   b. Either you dislike me or I have offended you.
   c. Either Roosevelt or Ruin.
   d. Either the government will control the amount of money in circulation or we shall never succeed in avoiding boom and bust in the business cycle.
2. Analyze for validity: Either it is raining or it is not raining. It is raining. Therefore, it is not raining.

3. Special aspects of alternative propositions and syllogisms.

   a. *Normal and exclusive alternation.*

   In normal alternation, one at least of the alternants is true, and possibly both. The rules of the alternative syllogism are applicable to such propositions. But consider the following alternative propositions:

Contradictories: Either the workers will get wage increases or they will not.
Contraries: Either he was in Chicago or he was in New York yesterday at noon.

These are examples of "exclusive alternation," since both alternants cannot be true. In the first example, one of the contradictories must be true, the other false; in the second both of the contraries cannot be true, but we assume that at least one is true. An exclusive alternative proposition is defined as one in which at least one of the alternatives is true, but not both. When we have an exclusive major premise involving contradictories, or when we know from our outside knowledge that one of two contraries must be true, but not both, the alternative syllogism will be valid in all four figures. We may affirm in the minor premise and deny in the conclusion, or deny in the minor and affirm in the conclusion.

*b. The equivalences of alternative and categorical proposi-
tions.*

We learned earlier that every hypothetical proposition is
equivalent to an A-form categorical. Similarly, every alternative
proposition is equivalent to an A-form.

"All men are mortal" has as its corresponding equivalent alternative: "Either any being is not a man, or that being is
mortal." Note that we contradict the first term of the categorical. The schematic representation in symbols:

> Categorical: All   P   are   Q
> Alternative: Either x is −P or x is Q
>
> Alternative: Either   A or B
> Categorical: All   −A are B

To test the correctness of the equivalence of "Either a being is
not a man or that being is mortal" to "All men are mortal,"
consider the truth of our alternative proposition for everything
in the universe. The proposition states that one of the alternants, and possibly both, will be true for everything. Let us
apply it to a piece of chalk, a dog, and a man. The first alternant
is true for the chalk, since it is "not a man." Both alternants are
true for the dog, and the second is true for man.

Exercises

1. The following major premises are *known* to be exclusive alternatives. P ∨ −P; P ∨ R. Construct valid syllogisms in all four figures
   for each.
2. Restate the following propositions from the categorical to the alternative form and vice versa.
   a. All soldiers are brave.
   b. All high-ranking students are eligible for honors.
   c. Only the brave deserve the fair.
   d. Either you are over 21 or you will not be admitted.
   e. Either a man must tell the truth or he must multiply his lies.
3. Restate the following syllogisms in alternative form. Only the
   major premise will require restatement; the minor premise either
   affirms or denies.

   a. All Hoosiers are Americans and all Texans are Americans, so all Hoosiers must be Texans.

   b. All Hoosiers are Americans and no Texans are Hoosiers, so no Texans are Americans.

   c. Decent newspapers cannot attain a wide circulation, for they decline to adopt sensational methods, and we know that papers which adopt sensational methods attain a wide circulation.

3. Contradicting an alternative proposition.

The alternative proposition "P ∨ Q" asserts that *at least one* of the alternants is *true*. To contradict such a proposition we must assert that *both* P and Q are false. In symbols, −P · −Q is the contradictory of P ∨ Q. In words, "Either that child is ill or it has been spoiled" is contradicted by "That child is not ill and that child has not been spoiled."

Exercises

Contradict the following alternative propositions:

   a. A ∨ B, −P ∨ Q, R ∨ −S

   b. Either you are over 21 or you will not be admitted.

   c. Either the nations of the world will establish a world organization which completely eliminates all national sovereignties or the destruction of the world in a third war is absolutely inevitable.

4. The value of the alternative proposition.

The alternative proposition is an indispensable tool in scientific research. For example, a scientist is searching for the cause of a certain phenomenon. He will begin by marshalling his previous knowledge in the form of an alternative proposition: The cause of this phenomenon is either A, or B, or C, or D. He may then perform experiments which show that A, B, and D cannot be the causes. By this process of elimination (denying the alternants) he is left with the uneliminated C, and regards it as the cause. The success of this type of reasoning, valid though it is, will depend upon whether the major premise actually presents a complete or exhaustive list of all the possibilities. As we shall see in our discussion of scientific methods in Part Three, such assumptions are usually interpreted in terms of varying degrees of probability.

We must also note certain dangers which lurk in the formulation of alternative propositions. In popular thinking an "either-or" proposition often contains the assumption that contraries are contradictories. We say, "Either you are for us, or you are against us," "Either one is liberal or anti-liberal." But such thinking ignores the infinite degrees in attitudes. There are not merely two possibilities in such cases, but an infinite number of them. The same type of confusion often occurs in enthymemes in the alternative form. One may argue, "You can't identify a people with its government, so the German people cannot be held responsible for Hitler." This assumes the major alternative premise: "Either a people is identical with its government or it is not responsible for its government." But there are many degrees of "identification." A people is neither completely identifiable with its government, nor is it wholly irresponsible. As in many other such "polar" problems, the truth lies between these extreme positions. This problem was discussed earlier, as the reader may recall, in connection with the law of the "excluded middle."

Section V: The Conjunctive Proposition

We have already had occasion to note the nature of a conjunctive proposition in stating the contradictories of the hypothetical and alternative propositions. The conjunctive proposition is compound, since it is composed of two or more subpropositions joined by the conjunctive "and." "$P \cdot Q$" means that the propositions P and Q are both true. Note that the conjunctive proposition is true or false as a whole, so that if *either* of the constituent propositions is false, then the proposition will be false as a whole. The conjunctive proposition has no equivalent in any categorical form, nor is it the equivalent of any other compound proposition. Nevertheless, it has many uses in inference. We have already noted that the contradictories of the hypothetical and alternative propositions are stated as conjunctive propositions. The same holds for the disjunctive propositions which we shall shortly examine.

We shall also find that when we contradict a conjunctive proposition, the resulting contradictory is a disjunctive proposition. Thus, "P · Q" states that both P and Q are true. If we say that this proposition is false (as a whole) we say "It is not the case that both P and Q are true." In symbols, this will be stated as −(P · Q), which means that the conjunctive proposition "P · Q" is false, or "P and Q are not both true," or "Not both is P true and Q true."

Conjunctive propositions have other uses in inference. Since any two propositions may be joined together, we might state a familiar syllogism in the following manner: The proposition "All men are mortal *and* Socrates is a man" implies the proposition "Socrates is mortal." A conjunctive proposition is also required to state the meaning of a proposition such as "If, and only if P, then Q." This proposition is equivalent to "P ⊃ Q · Q ⊃ P." P implies Q and Q implies P. If we know that X is a Q we can conclude that X is a P, etc. The exclusive form of alternation may also be stated in the conjunctive form as "Either P or Q *and* Not both P and Q."

Section VI: Disjunctive Propositions and Syllogisms

1. The disjunctive proposition.

In "Not both can we reduce taxes and reduce the national debt" we find two subpropositions, called the first and second disjuncts, joined by the connectives "Not both" and "and." Using P and Q for the disjuncts, we find the following structure:

Not both $\dfrac{\text{P (first disjunct)}}{\text{(We can reduce taxes)}}$ and $\dfrac{\text{Q (second disjunct)}}{\text{(We can reduce the national debt)}}$

This proposition is symbolized by −(P · Q). It is the contradictory of the conjuctive proposition P · Q. To contradict a disjunctive proposition we simply remove the sign of negation and the brackets. Alternative readings of the disjunctive proposition are "Not both P and Q," "P and Q are not both true," "P and Q are not both the case," etc.

The meaning of the disjunctive proposition should be compared with the meaning of the alternative proposition. P ∨ Q means that at least one of the alternants is true, and that possibly both are true. −(P · Q) means that at least one of the disjuncts is false, and possibly both. In our proposition above we say that we cannot both reduce taxes and also reduce the national debt, but it is possible that we will accomplish neither, i.e., we may not reduce taxes and we may not succeed in reducing the national debt.

The disjunctive proposition is equivalent to a corresponding categorical. "All men are mortal" may be stated as "Not both can a being be a man and a non-mortal." The symbolic transformations are as follows:

> Categorical: All   P   are   Q
> Disjunctive: Not both is X a P and a −Q
>
> Disjunctive: Not both P and   Q
> Categorical: All   P are −Q

Note that the first "term" remains unchanged, the second is negated. A test of this equivalence may be shown by applying "Not both is a being a man and a non-mortal" to the piece of chalk, a dog, and a man. One at least of the constituent propositions must be false for everything, and possibly both. The first disjunct is false for the chalk, which is "not a man." Both disjuncts are false for the dog, and the second is false for a man.

The categorical equivalent of our illustrative proposition above will be "All situations (such as the present one) in which we reduce taxes are situations in which we will not reduce the national debt."

Exercises

1. State the contradictories of the following:
   a. −(A · B), −(−A · B), −(−A · −B).
   b. There will be no world government and there will be no third world war.

    c. It is impossible that a statesman should both protect his country's interest and sacrifice his country's interest.
2. State the equivalent categorical and disjunctive propositions for the following:
    a. All students of literature are well-read persons.
    b. All situations in which prices go up are situations in which the unions will ask for wage increases.
    c. Not both can we work hard and not succeed.

2. The disjunctive syllogism.

The rules of the disjunctive syllogism follow from the meaning of the disjunctive proposition. Since this type of proposition asserts that *at least one* of the disjuncts is *false,* and possibly both, a conclusion will follow only when we *affirm* one of the disjuncts. Since one at least is false, when we find that one is true, the other must be false. But when we find that one is false, then the other may or may not be true (or false).

The valid figures, which affirm one of the disjuncts:

$$-(P \cdot Q) \qquad\qquad -(P \cdot Q)$$
$$P \qquad\qquad\qquad Q$$
$$\therefore -Q \qquad\qquad\quad \therefore -P$$

The invalid figures, which deny one of the disjuncts:

$$-(P \cdot Q) \qquad\qquad -(P \cdot Q)$$
$$-P \qquad\qquad\qquad -Q$$
$$\therefore \ ? \qquad\qquad\qquad \therefore \ ?$$

We must also distinguish between normal and exclusive disjunction. In "Not both is Hitler alive and dead" we have exclusive disjunction, since one at least of the disjuncts is false, and both cannot be false. When we assume that we have an exclusive disjunction in the major premise, then the resulting syllogism will be valid in all four figures.

Exercises

1. Write disjunctive syllogisms in valid form with the following major premises:

     a. You cannot have socialism and retain economic freedom.

     b. Not both can anyone indulge in racial and religious discrimi-
nations and believe in the fatherhood of God.

2. Restate the following syllogisms in disjunctive form:

     a. All Hoosiers are Americans and all Texans are Americans, so
all Hoosiers must be Texans.

     b. All Hoosiers are Americans and no Texans are Hoosiers, so
no Texans are Americans.

3. The equivalence of disjunctive and alternative propositions.

Since the disjunctive proposition is equivalent to a corresponding alternative proposition, the special rules of validity
which we have spelled out in this section are, strictly speaking,
unnecessary. Many contemporary logicians do not treat the
disjunctive proposition as an independent form. For consider
its meaning once again: $-(P \cdot Q)$ says that one of the two disjuncts is false, and possibly both. But does this mean anything
except to say that "Either P is false or Q is false"? Thus,
$-(P \cdot Q)$ is equivalent to $-P \vee -Q$, i.e., P is false or Q is
false, and possibly both are false. After we perform this translation, the rules for the alternative propositions will apply to
$-P \vee -Q$, since the letters surrounding the "either-or" symbol
stand for *any* propositions. The rules of the disjunctive syllogism may thus be dispensed with. If, instead of using $-(P \cdot Q)$
for our major premise, we use $-P \vee -Q$, the minor premise
must *deny* one of the alternants, and this will require saying
"P" or "Q" since the denial of a negative proposition must be
stated in affirmative form. But it may perhaps be useful to the
student to have the spelled-out version of the disjunctive syllogism so that he may see more clearly why it is an unnecessary
form.

The corresponding alternative and disjunctive forms in
symbols:

       Disjunctive: $-(P \cdot Q)$ is equivalent to Alternative:
$-P \vee -Q$

       Alternative: $P \vee Q$ is equivalent to Disjunctive:
$-(-P \cdot -Q)$

Section VII: The Equivalence of Compound Propositions

We have seen that the hypothetical, alternative, and disjunctive propositions all have corresponding categoricals. A given categorical proposition may be stated in the three types, which must therefore be equivalent to each other. We shall now set forth the complete table of equivalences, so that we may see the manner in which each form may be translated into one of the others:

Categorical: All   *orioles*   are   *birds*   Ad $<$ Bu
Hypothetical: If x is an *oriole* then x is a *bird*   A $\supset$ B
Alternative: Either x is a *non-oriole* or x is a *bird* $-$A $\lor$ B
Disjunctive: Not both is x an *oriole* and a *non-bird* $-$(A $\cdot$ $-$B)

The reader should be able to translate any one of the three compound forms into the other types. In the previous section we showed how to translate a disjunctive into an alternative proposition. We shall now show only the manner in which we must translate alternative and disjunctive propositions into the hypothetical form. Since implication is a transitive relation and thus the basis of inference in chain arguments, or sorites, the following translations will be found extremely useful:

Hypothetical: A $\supset$ B
Alternative: $-$A $\lor$ B
Disjunctive: $-$(A $\cdot$ $-$B)

Alternative: A $\lor$ B
Hypothetical: $-$A $\supset$ B

Disjunctive: $-$(A $\cdot$ B)
Hypothetical: A $\supset$ $-$B

Let us now illustrate the manner in which these translations may be used in inference. Assume that we are given the following propositions as true: $-$Q $\lor$ R, $-$(R $\cdot$ $-$S), S $\supset$ T. We are given the problem of determining whether $-$T $\supset$ $-$Q is true. We proceed as follows: Our propositions must first be translated into hypotheticals, so that we can put them together as a sorites, or chain of implications. $-$Q $\lor$ R is equivalent to Q $\supset$ R, and so on. We shall then have the following chain: $Q \supset R \supset S \supset T$. The contrapositive of this chain is $-T \supset -S \supset -R \supset -Q$. We have now shown that $-T \supset -Q$ is true.

Exercises

1. Translate the following into hypothetical form, then state the contrapositive of each:
   a. $X \lor Y$, $-(T \cdot S)$, $-A \lor -M$, $-(-C \cdot -D)$
   b. Either Chamberlain was a foolish man or he sought to destroy the British Empire.
   c. Not both can a person put forth his best efforts and not succeed.
2. The following premises are given: $B \supset C$, $-C \lor D$, $-(D \cdot -E)$, $-F \supset -E$. Does it follow that $-E \supset -B$? Note that one of the premises must be contraposed in order to get it into the chain.
3. The following premises are given as true:
   $A \supset X$, $X \supset S$, $A \lor B$, $B \supset G$, $-(G \cdot Z)$, $T \lor O$, $-O \lor L$, $T \supset Z$
   a. Translate the non-hypotheticals into hypotheticals.
   b. Now state the series as a chain of implications. Eliminate the propositions which appear in pairs and find your end propositions. Where you find a proposition and its contradictory, contrapose a premise. Some "trial and error" may be required before you make the proper contrapositions.
   c. Now contrapose the entire chain.
   d. Are the following implications valid?
      (1) $-S \supset -Z$
      (2) $-S \supset -L$
      (3) $T \supset -A$
      (4) $X \supset G$
      (5) $-(-B \cdot -X)$.

Section VIII: Complex Propositions and Syllogisms

1. Complex propositions.

A complex proposition resembles a compound proposition in that its constituent elements are subpropositions, but in the complex proposition one or more of the sub-propositions are themselves compound. An example: If *price control will work*

(P), then either *the people must be willing not to buy in black markets* (Q) or *black markets must be ruthlessly stamped out* (R). This is a hypothetical proposition in which the antecedent is a categorical proposition, and the consequent a compound alternative proposition. Its structure in symbols: P ⊃ (Q ∨ R). Note the parentheses surrounding the symbols in the consequent of this proposition, to indicate that the major relationship is implication. These symbols are thus read as follows: "*If* P is true, *then* either Q or R is true." In the complex proposition (P ⊃ Q) ∨ R, the major relation is alternation, here with the compound P ⊃ Q as the first alternant. It is read as follows: *Either* P implies Q is true, *or* R is true." Its meaning is quite different from that of the first symbolic statement. Before we proceed, however, the importance of these parentheses must be explained.

In our study of ambiguity you may remember the exercise which asked, "How much is $3 \times 2 + 4$?" The question is amphibolous, but there is a rule in arithmetic which tells us to perform the multiplication before the addition. Now, suppose that we had written our first complex proposition above as P ⊃ Q ∨ R. This would also be ambiguous, since it might mean (P ⊃ Q) ∨ R, or it might mean P ⊃ (Q ∨ R). To avoid such ambiguity, we shall adopt the convention of using parentheses to indicate the compound subpropositions of complex propositions. In addition to the forms already noted, we shall use complex propositions in which conjunction is the major relationship, as in (P ⊃ Q) · (R ⊃ S). This is read as "P implies Q *and* R implies S." We shall, in general, limit our discussion to complex propositions in which the subpropositions are compound, but the next step in complexity is the formulation of propositions in which the subpropositions are complex. Such propositions will require special forms of bracketing, as in the following: [(P ⊃ Q) · (R ⊃ S)] ⊃ [(P ∨ R) ⊃ (Q ∨ S)]. This would be read as follows: If P implies Q and R implies S, then P or R imply Q or S. Statements of much greater complexity are of course also possible. Since restatement in the words of the English language will become extremely difficult after a certain point of complexity is reached, the advantage of working with symbols is quite apparent.

1. Use the convention of the parentheses to show the different possible interpretations of the following symbols, which stand for propositions: P · Q ∨ R, P ⊃ Q · R, P ∨ Q ⊃ R, P ⊃ Q ⊃ R, P ∨ Q · R ⊃ S.
2. Indicate how the last proposition might be interpreted as a complex proposition containing a complex subproposition.

2. Complex syllogisms.

Syllogisms may also be composed of complex propositions. Let us examine the complex hypothetical syllogism. The major premise may take any one of the following eight forms (among others):

(1)	(P · Q) ⊃ R	(5)	(P · Q) ⊃	(R ∨ S)
(2)	(P ∨ Q) ⊃ R	(6)	(P ∨ Q) ⊃	−(R · S)
(3)	(P ⊃ Q) ⊃ R	(7)	(P ⊃ Q) ⊃	(R · S)
(4)	−(P · Q) ⊃ R	(8)	−(P · Q) ⊃	(R ⊃ S)

With any one of these as the major premise, a valid syllogism will require a minor premise which either affirms the antecedents of the major, or denies the consequent. The former is a simple process, since we merely affirm the antecedent and then proceed to affirm the consequent. Note, however, that the antecedent must be affirmed in its entirety where it is conjunctive (Nos. 1 and 5) or hypothetical (Nos. 3 and 7), but this will not be necessary when it is alternative or disjunctive. The alternative form (Nos. 2 and 6) requires the affirmation only of one of the alternants, since the proposition asserts that the consequent will follow if at least one of the alternants is true, and in the disjunctive form (Nos. 4 and 8), we need only show that at least one of the disjuncts is false.

Before we proceed to construct syllogisms involving the denial of the consequent, note that such arguments will involve the denial (or contradiction) of compound propositions. For convenience in reference we shall list our previous analyses of the contradictories of such propositions:

Hypothetical:	P ⊃ Q	has as its contradictory:	P · −Q
Alternative :	P ∨ Q	has as its contradictory:	−P · −Q
Disjunctive :	−(P · Q)	has as its contradictory:	P · Q
Conjunctive :	P · Q	has as its contradictory:	−(P · Q)

We shall now state the complete syllogisms which result from denying the consequents in Nos. 5–8. (Nos. 1–4 are simpler, since only the antecedents are compound):

(5) (P · Q) ⊃ (R ∨ S)   (7) (P ⊃ Q) ⊃ (R · S)
    −R · −S   −(R · S)
    ∴ −(P · Q)   ∴ P · −Q
(6) (P ∨ Q) ⊂ −(R · S)   (8) −(P · Q) ⊃ (R ⊃ S)
    R · S   R · −S
    ∴ −P · −Q   ∴ P · Q

Exercises

Write the symbolic structures of the following syllogisms:
1. If price control were both morally desirable and politically feasible then the President would have insisted on keeping it. But since he did not, it was not both morally desirable and politically feasible.
2. If our lives are to be wholly unblemished with unhappiness, then we must both have our cake and eat it too. But since that cannot be, we shall not be completely happy in this world.
3. If you were either fairly intelligent or not lazy, then you would get to class on time. But since you don't, you are both lazy and unintelligent.
4. Zeno argued: In order to move, a body must either move in the place where it is or it must move in a place where it is not. But a body cannot move in the place where it is, for so long as it remains in the place where it is, then it is at rest in that place. And it is obviously impossible for a body to move in a place where it is not. Therefore it is impossible for a body to move at all.

3. Some special aspects of complex propositions and arguments.

(1) The contrapositive of a complex proposition involves no new principles. Thus, the contrapositive of (P ∨ Q) ⊃ (R ⊃ S) is (R · −S) ⊃ (−P · −Q). We reverse the antecedent and the consequent of the original proposition, and negate each of the original compound propositions. We require the contradictories of an alternative and a hypothetical proposition to perform this process in the illustration. (2) Equivalences among complex

propositions involving different major relations will also follow the principles we studied earlier. Thus (P ∨ Q) ⊃ (R ⊃ S) has a hypothetical major relation. Let us say that we wish to translate it into a proposition having an alternative major relation. We recall that P ⊃ Q translates into its equivalent alternative −P ∨ Q; i.e., we contradict the antecedent and leave the consequent unchanged. In the same manner, our complex proposition can be translated into (−P .−Q) ∨ (R ⊃ S). (3) Let us now examine the process of contradicting (P ∨ Q) ⊃ (R ⊃ S) as a whole. We recall that a compound hypothetical is contradicted by a conjunctive proposition in which the original consequent is denied, and so this proposition is contradicted by (P ∨ Q) · (R · −S).

Complex sorites and chain arguments require little comment. Examine the chain: (P · Q) ⊃ (R ∨ S) ⊃ −(T · U) ⊃ (W ⊃ Z). The reader is now aware of the ambiguity in such a chain if it were interpreted as one long proposition. But when we explicitly note that it is a chain which simplifies a sorites, so that it should be read as "P · Q implies R ∨ S, and R ∨ S implies −(T · U)" and so on, the ambiguity is removed. We may then state the contrapositive of this chain, making the same explicit proviso that it simplifies a sorites, viz.: (W · −Z) ⊃ (T · U) ⊃ (−R · −S) ⊃ −(P · Q).

Before turning to the exercises we shall note two laws of symbolic logic, and we shall then show how these laws may be used in the analysis of arguments. P ∨ R ∨ S, for example, may be combined into a complex proposition in which any two alternants may be regarded as constituting a compound alternative proposition which enters into a complex alternative; thus, P ∨ (R ∨ S). Another useful law, quoted earlier, states that [(P ⊃ Q) · (R ⊃ S)] ⊃ [(P ∨ R) ⊃ (Q ∨ S)]. This implication states that if P implies Q and R implies S, then P or R imply Q or S. These symbols might stand for the following implication in words: *If* he is a thief (P) implies that he is a scoundrel (Q) and he is an alcoholic (R) implies that he is a neurotic (R), *then* either he is a thief (P) or he is an alcoholic (R) implies that either he is a scoundrel (Q) or he is a neurotic (S).

The use which may be made of these laws may be illustrated by a very simple example. Assume that we are given the propositions "P ∨ Q ∨ R," "Q ⊃ S," "R ⊃ T", and we are asked whether "−P ⊃ (S ∨ T)" is true. Before we answer this question we must combine the propositions into a meaningful series of implications. We proceed as follows: P ∨ Q ∨ R may be restated as P ∨ (Q ∨ R), and this complex proposition is equivalent to the hypothetical −P ⊃ (Q ∨ R). We then combine Q ⊃ S and R ⊃ T into the conjunctive proposition (Q ⊃ S) · (R ⊃ T), since any two propositions may be combined into a conjunctive one. The second law tells us that the last conjunctive proposition implies (Q ∨ R) ⊃ (S ∨ T). We are now ready to put our propositions into a series of implications: −P ⊃ (Q ∨ R), and (Q ∨ R) ⊃ (S ∨ T), from which it follows that −P ⊃ (S ∨ T).

Exercises

1. State the contrapositives of the following:
   a. P ⊃ (−S · T)
   b. (P ⊃ Q) ⊃ (−R ∨ S)
   c. (P · Q) ∨ (R ⊃ −S)
   d. If price control is to work, then either the people must be willing not to buy in black markets or these markets must be ruthlessly stamped out.
   e. If C is the cause of E, then C is both the necessary and sufficient condition of the occurrence of E.
2. State the equivalent alternative propositions for the hypotheticals given above.
3. Contradict the items in Exercise 1.
4. The following premises are given: −A ∨ B, B ⊃ −(E · F), H ⊃ (E · F), N ⊃ K, O ⊃ L, −(−K · −L) ⊃ H. Put these propositions into a chain, and then state the contrapositive.
5. Given the following premises:
   a. Either democracy will triumph, or communism will triumph, or neither will triumph. (Symbolize by A ∨ B ∨ F.)
   b. The triumph of democracy implies that the U. S. will oppose Russian ambitions or that the U. S. and Russia will settle their differences. (A ⊃ (C ∨ D))
   c. If the U. S. opposes Russian ambitions, then the Republicans will return to power. (C ⊃ G)
   d. If the U. S. and Russia settle their differences, then a new party will come to power. (D ⊃ H)

e. If it is not the case that both the Republicans will not come to power and that a new party will not come to power then the Democratic party will be turned out of office. $(-(-G \cdot -H) \supset I)$

f. If either communism triumphs or neither democracy nor communism triumphs, then the U. S. will adopt a one-party system. $((B \lor F) \supset K)$

Arrange these premises in an ordered sequence of implications. If these premises are accepted as true, and some years hence it is the case that the Democratic party is not turned out of office, would it follow that the Democratic party is the only party in the United States?

Chapter 13

THE DILEMMA

Section I: The Meaning of Dilemma

A young man was considering the pros and cons of marriage. Being of a somewhat sombre and pessimistic turn of mind, his reflections took the following form: "If I get married, then I shall undertake grave responsibilities and worries. That's not so good. On the other hand, if I remain single, then I shall often be lonely without the companionship of some lovely woman. And that's not so good. What to do?"

This young man found himself confronted with a dilemma. A dictionary defines "dilemma" as

1. A situation, or the verbal formulation of a situation, in which we are forced to make a choice between equally undesirable alternatives; in other words, a perplexing predicament. 2. *Logic.* A form of syllogistic argument which presents us with two (or more) alternatives but which leads to unpleasant results, whichever alternative we choose.

This definition is satisfactory for our purposes. Note that the "perplexing predicament" may be one in which we must choose between equally desirable alternatives, as in the case of the child in Proust's *Remembrance of Things Past* who could not make up his mind when given the choice of two tempting kinds of dessert. For his alternatives were also undesirable: Whichever one he chose, he would lose the other. The definition also refers to the possibility of there being more than two alternatives. When there are three, we use the term "trilemma"; four, "quadrilemma." The word *lemma* comes from the Greek, meaning "something assumed."

Dilemmas are forms of argument which combine some of the forms of deductive reasoning we have already studied. They

constitute effective rhetorical devices that are frequently found
in ordinary discourse. But they do not constitute a new form of
proof.

Section II: The Analysis of Dilemmas

We shall now analyze a dilemma. The President, Senators,
and Congressmen are confronted with dilemmas whenever they
act on controversial legislation. Whichever way they act they
will lose votes. The dilemma arises when the alternatives are of
equal (or nearly equal) importance. Thus, when controversial
labor legislation comes to the president's desk, the president
may say to himself: "If I sign this bill, I will lose the labor vote.
If I veto it, I will lose the votes of those who believe this law is
necessary. But I must either sign or veto. Thus in either case I
shall lose votes."

This dilemma has the following structure:

If I sign this bill, then I will lose the labor vote, and
$\overline{\qquad P \qquad}$ $\qquad \overline{\qquad Q \qquad}$

If I veto this bill, then I will lose the votes of those who favor it
$\overline{\quad R \quad}$ $\qquad \overline{\qquad S \qquad}$

But either I sign this bill, or I veto this bill
$\overline{\quad P \quad}$ $\overline{\quad R \quad}$

Therefore, either I lose the labor vote or I lose the votes of those
$\overline{\qquad Q \qquad}$ $\qquad \overline{\quad S \quad}$

who favor the bill.
$\overline{\qquad\qquad}$

Gathering our symbols, we find:
If P then Q, and If R then S
But either P or R
Therefore, Either Q or S

Note the structure of the argument. It is made up of two
syllogisms in hypothetical form:

If P then Q   and   If R then S
P   or   R
Therefore, Q   or   S

These elements are combined in the following manner. The
major premise is a complex conjunctive proposition, made up

of two hypothetical propositions joined by the conjunctive "and." The minor premise is an alternative proposition in which the two antecedents of the hypotheticals in the major premise are affirmed. The conclusion, another alternative proposition, then goes on to affirm the consequents.

The dilemma should of course be stated in valid form. This requires that the antecedents of the major premise be affirmed, or its consequents denied. A dilemma in which the consequents are denied will take the following form:

> If P then Q and if R then S
> But either −Q or −S (or: Not both Q and S)
> Therefore, either −P or −R

In words: If you are careful then you will not unwittingly hurt the religious susceptibilities of others, and If you are considerate, then you will not do such things deliberately (If P then Q and if R then S). But you constantly hurt the religious susceptibilities of others, i.e., you do such things unwittingly or deliberately (Either −Q or −S). Therefore, you are either careless or inconsiderate (Either −P or −R).

Note that every dilemma assumes that an undesirable situation results from affirming the two antecedents or in denying the two consequents. The person presenting the dilemma states that an unwelcome choice is forced on an individual because of the undesirable character of both alternatives.

We may also note that there are other types of dilemmas. The type we have analyzed is called "complex," since the consequents and antecedents are different propositions. In a "simple" dilemma, either the antecedents are the same or the consequents are the same. Thus:

If P then Q and if P then R	If P then Q and if R then Q
and P or P (i.e., P)	But either P or R
Therefore Q or R	Therefore Q or Q (i.e., Q)

Section III: The Criticism of a Dilemma

Most dilemmas are formally valid, but every dilemma should be checked in order to determine whether the minor premise affirms the antecedents or denies the consequents. If it does not, then the dilemma is formally invalid. Few dilemmas are subject to this type of criticism. The typical objection to the statement that a dilemma exists is based upon material rather than formal considerations. The person who states that a dilemma exists is like a prosecuting attorney who argues that an individual is in a perplexing predicament from which he cannot escape. The defence to this argument is that the predicament merely *appears* to be embarrassing, on the ground that escape *is* possible. Whether escape is or is not possible depends upon the facts in the particular situation. In some cases it is, in others it is not. Some dilemmas are "impregnable." Let us now examine the three possible methods of escape from the "embarrassing predicament" which a dilemma may present.

1. Escaping through the horns.

The horns of the dilemma are the two alternants stated in the minor premise: "But either P or R." This implies that there are only two possibilities. But are these actually the only alternatives? If they are not, then we may "escape" through these horns by showing that there are other alternatives, such as T, etc. We then assert that P and R are not exhaustive of the possibilities, that we may escape the devil and the frying pan and not find ourselves in either the deep blue sea or the fire.

This form of attack cannot always be used. The young man contemplating marriage could not use this attack, since he must either remain single or get married. The alternatives exhaust the possibilities. But consider the following dilemma:

In 1940 President Roosevelt was highly concerned over the developments in the European war. He believed that it was in the interest of the United States to enter the war on the side of England. But if he advocated such a course of action the "isolationists" would accuse him of "war-mongering." He might then lose in the election to be held in that year, and the next administration might not recognize the danger to the security of the United States as clearly as he did. His dilemma:

> If I ask for intervention, the isolationists may take control.
> If I do nothing, Germany will win the war and endanger our security, etc.

But it was relatively easy to pass through the horns of this dilemma. "Asking for intervention" or "doing nothing" were

not the only possibilities. Roosevelt adopted measures of aid to
Britain which were "short of war," but exceedingly helpful to
England.

Our analysis may be generalized. It is impossible to slip
through the horns of a dilemma when the alternatives are genuine contradictories, since one or the other must hold, but it is
possible to slip through the horns when the alternatives are
contraries. In the last example the alternatives were contraries.
But one must be watchful of semantical problems here as elsewhere, and not mistake contraries for contradictories merely
because of the ambiguities of language. Consider the following
from Burnham and Wheelwright, *Philosophical Analysis* (Henry
Holt):

> Either it is right to kill another human being or it is not right.
> If it is right, murder is not a crime and should not be punished. If
> it is not right, there is no justification for putting anyone to death,
> which would only multiply wrongs. Thus, in either case, capital
> punishment cannot be defended.

The phrases "it is right to kill" and "it is not right to kill" are
not genuine contradictories, since the first phrase obviously is
used with the significance "for any reason whatsoever" and the
second with the significance "under certain circumstances." It
is thus possible to slip through the horns by saying "It is right
to kill under certain circumstances."

One final comment: Alternatives may be contradictories,
not because they are formally so, but because circumstances
make them so. Thus "sign the bill" and "veto the bill" are not
formal contradictories, since one might do nothing. But our
Constitution makes "doing nothing" equivalent to a veto under
certain circumstances and equivalent to signing under others,
so that there was no third alternative open to the President. No
escape between the horns was possible.

2. Taking the dilemma by the horns.

To "take a dilemma by the horns" means to deny the truth
of one or both of the hypothetical propositions stated in the
major premise. The major asserts: "If P, then Q; and if R, then
S." One may question or deny the fact that Q actually does

follow from P, or S from R. In order to contradict "P ⊃ Q" we
assert "P · −Q," i.e., P is true (or will occur) and Q is false (or
will not occur). Thus the dilemma may be a specious one, based
on false premises.

This form of attack might be used in the young man's dilemma. One might deny that marriage results in responsibilities
and worries, or single blessedness in loneliness. These, however,
are questions of material truth. Whether the premises are true
or false will depend on the facts of experience, not on formal
considerations.

3. Rebuttal, or the "counter-dilemma."

This form of escape is sometimes effective where the others
fail. Let us assume that the premises of the dilemma are true
and the alternatives exhaustive. Escape from the embarrassing
predicament may yet be possible. "A cloud may have a silver
lining" just as "every rose has a thorn." Choices involve sacrifices, but sacrifices often bring compensating gains. The counter-
dilemma emphasizes the silver lining. But, as we well know, it
is not true without exception that every cloud has a silver lining,
so this form of escape is not always possible. The facts of the
situation must be considered in each specific case.

Thus our pessimistic young man might be told to look at the
situation from a different point of view. "If you get married,"
we tell him, "you will not be lonely, and if you remain single
then you will avoid the cares and responsibilities of marriage."
Both alternatives now appear favorable, and his embarrassing
predicament has been eliminated. What we have done here is to
emphasize different aspects of the same factual situation. The
same facts may appear desirable or undesirable, depending upon
the point of view, as in the case of the child and his dessert.

The structure of the counter-dilemma will now be exhibited
in relation to the original dilemma:

Dilemma	*Counter-dilemma*
If P then Q, and if R then S	If P then −S and if R then −Q
But either P or R	But either P or R
∴ Either Q or S	∴ Either −S or −Q

The major premise of the counter-dilemma contradicts the original consequents and reverses their order. Note, however, that

the conclusion of the counter-dilemma is not the contradictory of the conclusion of the original dilemma. "Either I will have responsibilities or I will be lonely" is quite consistent with "Either I won't be lonely or I won't have responsibilities," since alternative propositions merely assert that one at least of the alternants is true. "P ∨ Q" and "−Q ∨ −P" (or "−P ∨ −Q") may *both* be true. Both *must* be true when the alternatives are exclusive; both *may* be true when we have normal alternation.

But not all counter-dilemmas are effective, nor indeed do all of them "make sense." Whether any one of the three attacks we have noted is effective will always depend upon the facts of the particular situation. An attack against a dilemma may be strong, or it may be weak. There are no rules which determine the effectiveness of an attack; your own common sense must be the judge.

Exercises

Complete the following dilemmas in proper form, underline the propositions, and use appropriate symbols. Note whether the dilemma is in valid form. Then determine whether the dilemma can be effectively attacked by one or more of the three methods of criticism. Be sure your criticism is a reasonable one, and justify your answer.

1. If you don't believe in the capitalistic system, then why don't you go to Russia to live? If you do believe in it then you should not criticize the manner in which it is operated. But either . . . , etc.

2. When the Caliph Omar ordered the destruction of the famous library at Alexandria, Egypt, he reasoned thusly: "If these books contain the same doctrines as those of the Koran, than they are unnecessary. If they contradict the doctrines of the Koran, then they are pernicious. Therefore, in either case, they should be destroyed."

3. Either the conclusion of a syllogism is contained in something already stated in the premises, or it is not. If the conclusion merely states something already given in the premises, then it adds nothing to our knowledge, and is useless. If the conclusion states something not given in the premises, then it is invalid. So every syllogism is useless or invalid.

4. If Voltaire had been a wise man then he would not have spoken irreverently of the Scriptures in jest. If he had been

a good man then he would not have done so in earnest. His
irreverent remarks brand him as either a fool or a scoundrel.

5. If God is benevolent, then He desires to prevent the suffering of helpless human beings. If he is omnipotent, then he
has the power to prevent such suffering. The fact that helpless human beings are suffering all over the world proves
that God either does not desire to prevent such suffering or
that He is unable to do so. (Epicurus.)

6. Either I am fated to pass my final exams or I am fated not
to pass my final exams. If I am fated to pass, then I shall
pass whether or not I prepare for them. If I am fated not to
pass, I shall fail whether I prepare or not. So, in either case,
study will be useless.

7. Either I am fated to pass this course or I am not fated to
pass it. If I am fated to pass I shall do so whether I do the
work correctly or not. If I am not fated to pass, the same.
So why study?

8. A chess player's meditations: If my opponent made that
move intentionally, then he was not wise; if unintentionally,
then he was not lucky. But as I have known him long
enough to know that he is neither wise nor lucky, I must
conclude that he made the move neither intentionally, nor
unintentionally. Which seems to put *me* in a dilemma, since
it must have been one or the other. (Costell.)

9. If human beings have free will, then they are not responsible
for their actions, since "free will" means "without cause,"
and actions which we do not cause are actions for which we
are not responsible. On the other hand, if we have no free
will, then our actions are caused by our personalities, and
we did not create our own personalities. So in that case too,
we are not responsible for our actions. Thus human beings
are never responsible for their actions and should never be
blamed (or praised) for anything which they may do.

10. A classical example of a counter-dilemma is illustrated by
the following tale concerning Protagoras, the famous Greek
sophist:
Protagoras, teacher of law and rhetoric, had agreed to give
Eulathus instruction in law, rhetoric, and argumentation
on the following terms: Eulathus was to pay half of the fee
in advance, and the remainder after he won his first case in
a court of law. Protagoras instructed Eulathus after receiving the down payment, but after the course was concluded
Eulathus showed no interest in the practice of law. After

waiting a reasonable time, Protagoras sued Eulathus for the balance of his fee, Eulathus conducted his own defence in the court. Protagoras presented the following dilemma to the judge:

"If the judge holds in my favor, then Eulathus must pay by judgment of the court, and if the judge holds in favor of Eulathus, then he must pay by virtue of our agreement, which requires that he pay when he wins his first case in court of law. But either the judge will hold in my favor or against me. Therefore in either case Eulathus must pay me."

Protagoras, however, had been an excellent teacher, and Eulathus was a shining example of the master's own method. Eulathus presented a counter-dilemma to the judge:

"If I win this case, then, by the judgment of the court, I do not have to pay Protagoras, and if I lose this case, then, by the terms of our agreement, I don't have to pay since I will not yet have won my first case. But either I win the case or lose it. Therefore, no matter how the decision goes, I need not pay."

11. The following "Philosophy of an Airman" (quoted in *The Principles of Reasoning*, D. S. Robinson) should be stated as a series of dilemmas:

If you fly well, there is nothing to worry about.
If you should spin, then one of two things may happen: Either you crash or you don't crash.
If you don't crash, there is nothing to worry about.
If you do crash, then one of two things may happen: Either you are hurt or you are not hurt.
If you are not hurt, there is nothing to worry about.
If you are hurt, one of two things may happen: Either you are badly hurt or you are not badly hurt.
If you are not badly hurt, there is nothing to worry about.
If you are badly hurt, then one or two things may happen: Either you recover or you don't recover.
If you do recover, then there is nothing to worry about.
If you don't recover you can't worry.

(HINT: Symbolize "there is nothing to worry about" by N; "you fly well" by W; "you spin," i.e., "you do not fly well," by −W; "you crash" by C; "you are hurt" by H; "you are badly hurt" by B; "you recover" by R. Use the complex form of the hypothetical proposition when necessary, and show that N is implied by all possibilities.)

Part Three

The Logic of Truth: Scientific Methodology

Chapter 14

TRUTH AND PROBABILITY

Section I: Deduction and Induction

In Part Two we studied the nature of formal reasoning, or deduction. A valid argument, we learned, is one in which the premises necessitate or imply the conclusion. Given certain premises, we deduce or exfoliate their implications. A valid argument is simply one having a certain form or structure, the truth of the premises being assumed or taken for granted. In Part Three we shall seek to determine the meaning of the assertion that a given proposition is in fact true. We shall examine the logical methods employed in determining truth, and we shall give particular attention to the methods of science, since scientific method is the human discipline which is most successful in the discovery of truth.

A distinction is sometimes drawn between "deductive logic" and "inductive logic," with the thought that these are two entirely different kinds of logic, and that science is exclusively concerned with the latter type. This distinction is misleading. Inductive reasoning seeks to establish true propositions concerning the facts of experience, based upon observations of such facts. Its ultimate goal is to find true generalizations of the highest generality. It develops methods, usually called scientific methods, for deriving such generalizations from experience. Deductive reasoning, on the other hand, merely exfoliates the consequences of our propositions and determines whether an argument is valid or invalid. But insofar as inductive reasoning seeks to *prove* any of its propositions, it asserts that the evidence is adequate to the conclusion, or that the argument is valid, and so it, too, must employ deductive reasoning. The notion that scientific method is nothing but the appeal to facts is therefore completely erroneous.

During the Middle Ages, before the rise of modern science, a widespread method of philosophers and scientists was to begin discussions by citing "the authorities" (i.e., principles drawn from the Scriptures, the writings of the Church Fathers, the works of the ancient Greek philosophers, particularly Aristotle), and then to apply these principles by deductive reasoning. These thinkers did not, in general, question the truth of their premises; they used their logical acumen to find contradictions and inconsistencies in the authorities, and to draw out new implications. But modern science is distinguished by two special characteristics. The first is its critical or questioning spirit, which refuses to accept any statement as true merely because the authorities say that it is true (or because someone claims that he has a "self-evident intuition" of its truth). The scientist asks for proof of all propositions. In the second place, science regards the appeal to the facts of actual experience as the ultimate test of the truth of any proposition. The mediaeval thinker did not regard the test of experience or fact as his ultimate guide. A Pisan professor of astronomy looked through Galileo's telescope, which revealed facts inconsistent with Aristotle's cosmology. But he thought it more likely that his senses deceived him, than that Aristotle was wrong. Thus there is an important contrast between deductive procedures, which begin with assumed principles, and scientific methods which appeal to the facts for truths; but, as we shall see over and over again, science also uses deductive reasoning. The ultimate goal of the scientist, moreover, is the organization of all knowledge into a deductive system, in which the special principles of all fields of investigation will be deducible from a few simple laws.

Though induction may furnish the ultimate grounds on which we base our premises, deduction is an indispensable aspect of science and all rational thought. The sciences of arithmetic, geometry, and other branches of mathematics are imposing structures which are purely deductive in nature. "Without deduction," as Chapman and Henle have said (*The Fundamentals of Logic*, Scribner, 1933), "we could prove nothing, science at its present stage of development would be impossible, and rational discourse would be a misnomer. We cannot acquire genuinely new truths by deduction; but we can, by its means, determine exactly what we mean, predict the future, and infer what the past must have been."

We shall therefore not dispense with the principles of deductive reasoning in our investigation of scientific methods. Nevertheless, we do have a new kind of problem: How do we establish the truth of a factual proposition? In the beginning of our study of logic we noted that we were to consider three problems: (1) the nature of meaning, (2) the nature of validity in argument, and (3) the nature of truth. We shall be concerned primarily with the third problem throughout Part Three.

Section II: Validity and Truth

"Valid" is an adjective which characterizes *arguments*. An argument is valid when the premises necessitate the conclusion. "True," on the other hand, is an adjective which characterizes *propositions*. A true proposition is one which "corresponds to the facts" or correctly describes the facts. We shall accept this definition of truth throughout our discussions in Part Three. Before we proceed further, however, let us summarize some of the things we have learned concerning the relationship of validity and truth.

We know that *if* the premises of an argument are true, and the reasoning valid, then the conclusion must be true. But when we analyze arguments for validity we do not concern ourselves with the truth of the premises; we assume that they are true, and we concern ourselves only with the form or structure of the argument. This means that we always presuppose an antecedent "If" or an "If it is true that" before all of the premises used in deductive reasoning whenever we assert that the conclusion is true. Thus, when we use syllogistic reasoning to prove the mortality of Socrates, we must be understood to mean the following:

(If it is true that)	All men are mortal
and (if it is true that)	Socrates is a man
Then (it is true that)	Socrates is mortal

In the same manner we might construct a valid argument in which we assume the truth of propositions which are known to be false. For example:

(If)	All Americans are heavy drinkers
(and if)	All heavy drinkers are Prohibitionists
Then it follows that:	All Americans are Prohibitionists

If the premises were true, then the conclusion would be true because the argument is valid in form. On the other hand, every
proposition in an argument may be true, and the structure invalid, as in:

>All Communists admire Karl Marx's *Das Kapital*
>Stalin admires Karl Marx's *Das Kapital*
>∴ Stalin is a Communist

The premises may be false, and they may validly imply a
true conclusion:

>All capitalists favor the abolition of private owner-
>ship of industry
>All Socialists are capitalists
>∴ All Socialists favor the abolition of private owner-
>ship of industry

But it is impossible that true premises should imply a false conclusion when the argument is valid in form. For this would
contradict our definition of validity, namely, that a valid argument is one in which the premises necessitate the conclusion, so
that the truth of the premises must necessitate the truth of the
conclusion.

These are some of the possible relations of truth and validity
when we assume the truth or falsity of the propositions used in
a syllogism. But our new problem is whether these propositions
are in fact true or false. Take the Socrates syllogism. We assumed in the major premise that all men were mortal. Most
persons would agree that that statement is in fact true. But is
it? Suppose we are asked for proof that this premise is in fact
true. How should we proceed? Two methods are possible. We
might deduce the truth of "all men are mortal" from other
premises, thus:

>All animals are mortal
>All men are animals
>∴ All men are mortal

If asked to prove that "All animals are mortal," we might
deduce this from the premises that "all living things are mortal,"
and "all animals are living things," and so on. But obviously,
such proof lives on borrowed premises, and we never rid ourselves of the qualification "provided the above premises are
true," and these premises themselves need proof. But we demand

that this deductive chain be broken, and that our deductions be based on a premise of which we can say, "This proposition is true—period." In the end our deductions must have a stop if we are not, in despair, to give up the search for truth. We require a non-deductive basis for our chains of reasoning. How shall we find it? We find it in our experiences. We believe that living things will die because they have died in the past. Is this conclusive proof that all living things will die in the future? No. We may be warranted in our certainty that some living things have died, but it can be only probable that what happened in the past will also happen in the future. Nevertheless, whether we say that our premise is true or probable, we seem to have found a means whereby we may break the deductive chain in the proof of a premise. Deduction is never absent in proof, but something new has been added, namely, the appeal to experience.

Section III: The Meaning of Truth

We have seen that the truth of the conclusion of a valid argument can have no greater certainty than the truth of its premises and that the validity of an argument is wholly independent of the truth or falsity of its premises. We also defined truth as "correspondence with the facts." We shall now examine some of the implications of this definition.

If a true proposition is one which corresponds to the facts, then a true proposition must be true for all men at all times and all places. This, indeed, was the conclusion we reached in our discussion of the "Laws of Thought." If a proposition correctly describes the facts, then it cannot be said to be a correct description for one man and not for another. Correctness is determined by objective considerations, upon the facts and the evidence. Truth is thus an objective, or public affair, and does not depend upon anyone's feelings.

The position stated above is opposed by "relativists," who hold that the truth of a proposition is relative to time, and place, and circumstance. Differences of opinion exist on all matters, says the relativist, and this is because each individual's ideas are based upon his own past experiences in a given environment. Since no two individuals have exactly the same experiences, truth will be different for each. We have already examined this position in some detail. Little need be said here, except to note a retort which may be made to the relativist: "If all ideas are the result of past experience, or 'conditioning,'" we may say to him, "then your relativistic theory is itself the product of *your* past experiences, and therefore not 'true' for any but those who have had your experiences." Thus this view appears to end in self-stultification.

Nevertheless, though the relativistic view must be rejected if our definition of truth is accepted, it does call attention to an important consideration, namely, that differences of opinion are often quite legitimate. The candid observer will be deeply impressed by the actual variety of opinions which men hold on all matters of real importance. Consider the differences of opinion on matters political, both at home and in the international sphere. Consider the differences with respect to religious truth, and consider the different interpretations of the events which lead to the breaking up of a friendship! But these differences of opinion do not mean that truth is relative. They mean only that no one may really *know* which of two interpretations is the correct one. We should say "This proposition is *true*" only when we *know*. In practice, however, our emotions, biases, and prejudices affect our judgments, and wishful thinking leads us into error. Self-righteous people will always think that they are right about everything, but truth depends upon the correspondence of a proposition with the actual facts.

We must therefore distinguish between the *truth* of a proposition and the *belief* we may have in its truth. The statement, "The earth is shaped like a flat disk and floats on water," is a false proposition because it incorrectly describes the facts, but it was once believed true. People were once ignorant of things we know today, and we are also beset by ignorance in many matters. But if we really know that a given proposition is true, then its truth will never change, provided that we state it with the proper precision and limit it to a specific area of investigation.

Here the reader may interpose an objection. Granted, he may say, that the relativistic view must be rejected, and that the truth does not change. Granted that it was false to say that the earth is flat. But how can we be certain that the earth is a spheroid? Perhaps *our* view is only an opinion, and later investigation may prove that *we* are wrong. In other words, how can we ever be sure that a given proposition does correspond with the facts? We made mistakes in the past and we may be in error today. The absolutes of today may be the untruths of tomorrow. Is not truth then an unattainable ideal, so that we can never be sure that we have attained it?

Questions such as these lead to a view which we shall call "probabilism," which holds that we can never be certain that we have attained the truth and that we must be content with varying degrees of probability. Certainty in factual propositions, it is held, is an unattainable ideal. Before we discuss this view further, however, we must clarify the notion of "degrees of probability," in relation to truth. Let us then think of truth and falsity as the two poles of a line, running from 0(zero), which stands for "absolutely false" to 1(unity) which stands for "absolutely true," viz:

0(.001)   .10   .30   .50   .70   .90   (.999)1
_____

This diagram indicates that when we are certain that a proposition is true, we say that it has a probability of 1; when we are certain that it is false, that it has a probability of 0. A probability of .50 means that we are wholly uncertain, leaning neither to truth nor falsity. Translating the specific degrees into their equivalents in ordinary expressions, we may say that .10 means "highly improbable"; .30 "improbable"; .70 "probable"; and .90 "highly probable." The percentages .001 and .999 stand for cases where we are "practically certain," allowing only for a very remote possibility that we are in error. These figures are of course only approximations.

The reader may have noted that the word "probability" has been used in two different senses, as meaning (1) some definite degree of probability, whether it be .10 or .90, and (2) "more than 50 per cent." The latter is the popular sense of the term, and means that something is more likely to happen than not. When we say "possible but not probable" we use the term in this sense. We shall use the word in both senses, but we will usually specify the degree when we use it in its broader sense. The context will also make clear which sense is meant.

Another clarifying remark before we proceed. An important distinction should be drawn between a probability judgment and the judgment that a proposition is true or false. A proposition is true or false regardless of whether we have the evidence available to us or not. Either the facts correspond, or they do not. But a probability judgment is always relative to the available evidence. For example, the statement, "Russia and Germany have signed a pact of friendship," was highly improbable to most observers in the light of the available evidence on August 23, 1939 immediately before the pact was announced to the world. The statement was true, but improbable in the light of the evidence which was known to outsiders. A well-informed foreign correspondent would have been justified in saying that the statement was improbable, even though a sufficiently astute observer might have predicted it on the basis of "inside information" concerning the motives of the principal actors in that political drama. Probability judgments will thus vary with every change in the evidence. We have indicated a case where a true proposition appeared to be improbable. Similarly, a false proposition may appear to be highly probable. Thus every probability judgment must be qualified by the words "in the light of the evidence which is available."

Let us now apply our diagram in estimating the strength of some of our beliefs. "Moses led the Jews out of Egypt." Would you say that this statement is absolutely true, and that error is inconceivable? Another: "The leader of Germany between 1933 and 1945 was a man named Hitler." Most of us would say "absolutely certain." But is it possible that the prevailing belief is based upon a gigantic hoax which was played upon the whole world? Such an interpretation is highly improbable, but is it *possible?* Let us press the point further. Is it possible for you to doubt whether you are reading these lines now? Is it possible that you are dreaming, and that your alarm clock may ring in a few minutes, waking you from your dream? Descartes, the seventeenth century French philosopher, believed that there was *only one* statement which he could not possibly doubt, namely, that he himself existed. For doubt, he said, implies the existence of a doubter. But he thought it possible to doubt everything else.

We return now to the point of view called "probabilism." The probabilist argues that no factual proposition can ever be absolutely certain. Take the proposition "People are living in Alaska at this moment." If we can conceivably be mistaken, he says, then we have not reached certainty, or "unity." The probability may be as high as .99 or even .999999 but it must be less than unity. Similarly in "There are lovers of boogie-woogie on the planet Mars." This has a probability of almost zero, but not quite; shall we say .00000001? If the probabilist is correct, then we can never be sure that any proposition concerning the world is true or false in a conclusive sense. We must always allow for the possibility that any belief, no matter how certain it may appear, may turn out to be in error.

The probabilist view is based upon two chief arguments: (1) Human beings have made mistakes in the past even when they were most confident that they had discovered the truth. They may be mistaken today. (2) All perception involves interpretation and inference.

The second argument refers to the fact that when we perceive a table, for example, we *see* a brown-colored patch of a certain shape, and then we *interpret* this patch as a table. Interpretation is thus involved in perception, and the interpretation may be mistaken. Thus, the traveler on the desert who "sees" an oasis in the distance may be seeing only a mirage. The radio listener may "hear" the burning of wood in a campfire, and the sound of a man walking through the snow. But it was only the crumpling of cellophane and the crunching of soapflakes in a projection booth. Human beings may also suffer from delusions and hallucinations. Under the influence of alcohol a man may falsely believe that he sees bats flying around in his room. These are some striking examples of "observations" which are mistaken.

We shall not explore, much less attempt to dispose of, the metaphysical or epistemological issues raised by the probabilist point of view except to note some of the arguments which a critic of this view might advance. With respect to the first argument, that our past mistakes are a reason for present doubt, does not the probabilist regard it as absolutely certain that we have made such mistakes in the past? If we are not certain that we have made mistakes, we admit the possibility that we have never been mistaken in any matter whatsoever and that our judgments were always absolutely true. But surely it is certain that we have made mistakes. Similarly, if we are told that "no knowledge is certain," the speaker contradicts himself, for he asserts that at least one proposition is certain, namely, the proposition just quoted.

With respect to the argument concerning perception, the critic might urge that some perceptions must be absolutely veridical, for otherwise we could not know that hallucinations were errors. Thus, when we are in a normal state of health and sobriety, we are simply not mistaken in our everyday judgments concerning the existence of the chairs and tables around us. Such observations, on the "common sense" level of experience, furnish the basis of all of human knowledge and also enable us to distinguish between correct and incorrect perceptions.

Doubt would thus appear not to be warranted in some cases, the critic might continue, but in others it may be not only proper but obligatory. The important distinction is between the easy cases and the difficult ones, i.e., between cases where interpretation and inference involve the possibility of error and those in which they do not. The theories of a physicist concerning the structure of the atom are probable rather than certain, for error is possible here, but when the physicist takes a pointer reading which indicates +.745 the physicist is certain *that he is taking a pointer reading* and that the number he is looking at is somewhere between .6 and .9. When there is the slightest possibility that we may be mistaken, let us modestly admit it. But we *know* of at least one person in the world who had parents, and we know that it is false to assert that "all grandfathers can run around the circumference of the earth in less than 10 seconds." And would it not be rather odd for one to say, "The available evidence makes it highly probable that I was not drowned ten years ago, but I must admit the possibility that I may be mistaken"?

Finally, the critic might urge, the statement that one proposition is more probable than another is itself not merely probable, for otherwise we should find ourselves saying that "it is probable that it is probable that it is probable" ad infinitum. It is more probable that there is life on the planet Mars than that there are beings there who enjoy boogie-woogie and bebop. When we say "more probable" we mean just that, and not that it is probably more probable.

We shall close this long discussion with a few general remarks. For practical purposes we assume that some propositions are true, rather than merely probable. In any case, in a given investigation we must assume the truth of a host of propositions whose truth is not in question in that particular investigation. But at least some of these assumptions may themselves be questioned in later investigations. This is the point of view of the scientist, who is, in general, concerned with matters involving probability rather than certainty. The scientist is satisfied with verification which gives high probabilities. But even though certainty is not attainable in scientific problems, this does not mean that "one opinion is as good as another." Beliefs based on good evidence are more likely to be true than not, and our concern in all cases will be to determine on what evidence our beliefs are based. The fundamental question, one which will be raised over and over again, will be: WHAT IS THE EVIDENCE?

Section IV: The Meaning of Empirical Probability

Thus far we have indicated some of the ways in which we apply judgments of truth and probability. We shall now examine the *meaning* of probability judgments. But first we must distinguish two types of probability, the *empirical* and the *a priori* (pronounced ā′ prī·ō′rī). "Empirical probability" means the probability which is based upon past experience, as that alcohol will probably cause intoxication. Thus far all of our illustrations have been of this type. A priori means "in advance of experience," or "prior to experience." Mathematics is an a priori science, for we know in advance of seeing the beasts that two kangaroos plus two kangaroos will add up to four kangaroos. A priori probability is essentially a branch of mathematics, and its applications can be calculated mathematically with complete precision and exactness. It is most conveniently illustrated by games of chance. Thus, since there are 38 slots on a roulette wheel, a player's chances of getting a given number are 1/38. The probabilities may be calculated in advance of experience if we assume that the wheel is so constructed that there is an equal chance that the ball will fall on any number. The basic formula for all probabilities is $p = f/n$, in which p stands for probability, n for the total number of possibilities, and f for the "favorable" event, or the event which we seek to measure. Probability may also be defined by $\dfrac{f}{f + u}$ in which u stands for the unfavorable events.

Mathematical or a priori probability is a deductive science whose rules are clear and results precise, granted certain assumptions. This type will be considered in more detail later. The remainder of this section will be devoted to the meaning of empirical probability (also called "experiential"). In this type we find a general absence of mathematical exactitude, though here too, as in a priori probability, we shall use the fraction f/n. We shall now be satisfied with rough approximations to the fraction. As examples, consider the probabilities that there will be another war within the next ten years, or a reversal in business during the next two years. Exactly how probable are these predictions? Exactness is unattainable, but surely some predictions are more sensible than others. We might say that we did not know the exact probability of a turn in the business cycle, but that its probability was less than .9 and more than .1. In any case, as it has been well said, empirical probabilities are "the very guide of life." A successful adjustment to the world around us requires that one should know how to "bet" on the future: to know which events are more likely to occur than others. The wise man can predict better than the uninstructed man. Justice Oliver Wendell Holmes had this view of probability in mind when he described himself as a "betabilitarian." Our confidence in our predictions or beliefs, he said, is indicated by the manner in which we would be willing to bet.

When we speak of an event as probable in the empirical sense we mean that it is more likely to occur than not. "More likely to happen than not" must be clarified. When we say that it is probable that any redhead will be hot-tempered, that Shakespeare wrote the plays attributed to him, that the theory of evolution is more probable than the "special creation" theory, or that it is probable that Caesar crossed the Rubicon, in what senses do we mean "more likely to happen than not"? When an agent of the FBI finds a man in the possession of the ransom bills paid to a kidnapper who is still at large, what justifies him in believing that it is probable that the holder of the ransom notes is guilty of the crime?

All of these examples, as we shall see, use the basic concept "in most cases," though it is also possible to reach a rough approximation to specific percentages of the probabilities. Let us begin with the redheads and hot tempers. (Our figures are purely imaginary). If we say it is probable that any redhead is likely to be hot-tempered, we mean that *most* are, so that there is a greater-than-even chance that any one taken at random will be hot-tempered. Or we might state the percentage, by stating that 60 out of 100 are hot-tempered. This would mean a probability of .6. We might use the f/n fraction, thus: $\dfrac{RH^{ht}}{RH}$ which puts all redheads into the denominator and redheads possessing the special characteristic into the numerator.

In the same manner, we reach conclusions concerning the probability that the holder of the ransom money is the kidnapper. (The police, of course, will generally follow any clue, no matter how small the probability may be.) But the problem of "in most cases" is somewhat more complex when we consider the probability of a historical proposition.

When we say that it is highly probable that Caesar crossed the Rubicon, it may appear that the concept "in most cases" is inapplicable, for surely we do not mean that he did so "in most cases." Nevertheless, our concept is applicable here also. What we mean when we say that such judgments are probable is something like the following: "Whenever we have had evidence in quantity and quality like the evidence which supports the proposition 'Caesar crossed the Rubicon,' then, in the great majority of cases, the occurrence of the event attested to has been confirmed in all subsequent investigations." Our fraction f/n in this case may be represented by $\dfrac{E^t}{E}$ in which the denominator "E" stands for all cases in which we have had this kind of evidence (in quantity and quality) and "E^t" for all cases in which such evidence has turned out to be reliable, and the proposition attested to, true. A similar analysis applies to a prediction that another war will occur within a given limited period of time, say 25 years. We ask, "How often have situations like the present one developed into wars during such a period of time?" Comparisons of present situations with past ones will of course be complicated by the presence of new factors, and new experiences and attitudes; but there are also similar factors present. Though our judgment will be anything but mathematically precise, nevertheless, the wise man is more likely to reach a correct estimate of the probability than the uninstructed man. We must also take into account our present, and perhaps future, inability to predict human behavior with precision, since the variables are exceedingly various, and this, too, will affect our judgment. But our estimate of the probability of war will depend on our evaluation of the f/n fraction.

One further complication. In some cases we may find a wholly uniform experience, as when we find that all zebras have stripes, and know of no exceptions. Our f/n fraction will now equal 1, since the numerator and denominator will have the same size. But we must qualify our prediction concerning future observations of zebras by also considering the following question: What is the probability, on the basis of past experiences with observations of this type, that a generalization without exceptions will prove to be absolutely true?

We know that at one time all observed swans were white and then black swans turned up in Australia. Thus, though the probability that *all* zebras (both the observed and the unobserved) are striped, may be high, it is far short of unity. In any case, it cannot be determined with the exactness of mathematical probability.

In other words, empirical probabilities are always based on past experience. The type of thinking described herein is also used by insurance actuaries, who must estimate the probabilities with respect to life-expectancy. If, in a given area, we find that 9500 of 10,000 individuals of the age of 30 live to their fortieth years, then the probability that any individual at random in this area of the age of 30 will reach 40 is .95. As conditions change, insurance rates change, but this is the basis of the predictions. The great Lloyds institution in London will generally furnish insurance on *any* future event, using these theories of empirical probability as its guide. Though the race does not always go to the fastest horse and the best jockey, it usually does.

Section V: Probability and the Syllogism

We shall now examine the manner in which probability judgments are related to the problems of validity in syllogistic reasoning. The rules of validity are very much like the rules of mathematics. The product of 26×26 is 676. If a student answered this problem with 675, his answer would be completely wrong, though very close to the truth. We shall find a similar situation with respect to validity. An invalid argument may also be "quite close" to validity. Though validity is either attained completely or not, nevertheless some invalid arguments may be better than others, just as 675 would be a better answer in the arithmetic above than would be 179.

Let us begin with a *valid* argument in which the word "probably" enters. Thus:

> If a person has red hair, then he is probably hot-tempered
> Smith has red hair
> ∴ Smith is probably hot-tempered

Now examine the following argument:

> If a theory is true then it will be confirmed by experiment
> The theory of relativity has been confirmed by experiment
> ∴ The theory of relativity is (probably) a true theory

In this syllogism the minor premise affirms the consequent. Is the argument "saved" by inserting the word "probably" into the conclusion? Now, there is no question that the argument is an invalid one without the word "probably," but most persons would agree that the argument, valid or invalid, is a satisfactory one for the scientist. Why is this? And why is it that the following argument cannot be "saved" by the use of "probably"?

> All Chinese drink tea
> X drinks tea
> ∴ X is (probably?) Chinese

We cannot say "probably" here. Let us explore this problem.

In our discussion of formal logic we learned that validity was determined by form and structure and that we were to ignore our outside knowledge. But we are now interested in material (or actual) truth as distinguished from formal truth, and our actual knowledge becomes relevant. We noted earlier that an A-form proposition could not be converted simply, without limitation. But we may happen to know that the simple converse of a given A-form is true as a matter of fact. If we know this then we may assert our knowledge. For example, the following syllogism is invalid:

> If a figure is a triangle, then it is three-sided
> This figure is three-sided
> ∴ It is a triangle

But we also know that "All three-sided figures are triangles." If we add or substitute this as a premise, then our argument is valid. The point is that if all we know is that "A is a B," we cannot conclude that "All B's are A's," but if we know more, then we can use our knowledge.

Every A-form proposition such as "All A are B" can be converted into "Some B are A." But "some" is a very vague quantifier. It covers all quantities from "more than none" to "just short of all." Take the following proposition: "All true theories are confirmed by experiment." Normally, it converts into "Some theories confirmed by experiment are true." But if we know that the great majority of theories confirmed are true theories, then we may say "Most confirmed theories are true." And this is equivalent to "If a theory is confirmed by experiment, then it is probably true."

We may now restate our syllogism above, using our actual knowledge, and say:

> If a theory is confirmed, then it is probably true
> The theory of relativity is confirmed
> ∴ The theory of relativity is probably true

When the major premise of an invalid argument of the original type can be converted either simply (i.e., without limitation) or into a major containing the word "most" or "probably," then we may derive a probable conclusion validly. The next three examples will help clarify this rule:

(1)
> All communists eat food
> Joe Doakes eats food
> ∴ Joe is a communist

(2)
> All communists favor the abolition of private property
> Joe favors the abolition of private property
> ∴ Joe is a communist

(3)
> All communists follow the Russian foreign policies with complete consistency
> Joe follows the Russian foreign policies with complete consistency
> ∴ Joe is a communist

All of these arguments contain undistributed middle terms. But they have varying degrees of merit. The material problem here is the manner in which we may convert their major premises. In Number 1 we may say, "Some (a small minority) persons who eat food are communists." In Number 2 we may say, "Some (a larger minority) persons who favor the abolition of private property are communists." (Socialists are not communists.) In Number 3 we may say, "The overwhelming majority of persons who follow the Russian line are communists." Thus the conclusion in Number 1 has a probability close to zero, in Number 2 it is too uncertain to warrant the conclusion, but in Number 3 the conclusion is very highly probable, even though it is not conclusive.

In other words, many invalid arguments may be transformed into valid arguments containing conclusions which are probable when we know that the major premise may be converted into a proposition which states a probability.

Section VI: A Priori Probability

We return now to the discussion of a priori, or mathematical, probability. Probabilities in this field are worked out on a purely formal basis by deduction from certain axioms and assumptions. Strictly speaking, this field of thought is a branch of mathematics, rather than of logic, but we consider it here in order to add to our understanding of probability and because it furnishes a splendid example of a deductive system which exfoliates the implications of basic axioms.

When a coin is tossed in the air, we say that the probability that the coin will fall heads uppermost is $\frac{1}{2}$. This probability is known before we toss a coin, and it is unnecessary to toss coins to determine it. In fact, tossing coins is wholly irrelevant to the a priori probabilities. This is because we make certain assumptions and deduce their consequences in a purely formal manner. We assume that the coin will fall when tossed, that it will not fall on its edge, that it is so balanced that it will not have a tendency to fall on one side rather than the other, and that it is not controlled in any way. If these assumptions are made, then there are two possibilities, each of which is equally probable. Using the fraction f/n, we find that one of two possibilities is favorable, and the probability is $\frac{1}{2}$. In the same manner, and with similar assumptions, we find that the numbers on a die give us six "equiprobable" possibilities. The probability of getting a given number, such as a "4," is thus $\frac{1}{6}$. The probability of getting a spade from a deck of 52 cards is $\frac{13}{52}$.

The deductions we make in this field simply exfoliate the meaning of our assumptions. Experiments are unnecessary in determining our meanings. "If there are two equiprobable possibilities and one is favorable, then our chances are one in two." But a new question now arises: Are *actual* coins perfectly balanced? To say that they are is an empirical judgment of which we cannot be absolutely certain. Nor can we be certain, in general, of lack of manipulation. Crooked gamblers, as is well known, load the dice in their favor. But we do find, when large numbers of coins are tossed, that they fall as we should expect them to in accordance with the a priori probabilities. The variations from the norm are negligible in large numbers, and we may assume that coins are perfectly balanced in fact. Thus, when we throw a coin 1000 times, we should expect to get somewhere in the neighborhood of 500 heads and 500 tails.

Let us be perfectly clear as to the meaning of a priori probability. It gives us a calculus of chances. It does not tell us that heads and tails will fall in equal amounts, but merely that that is the most likely possibility. The coins might all fall heads, since this is a conceivable possibility, but the odds against such an occurrence are fantastically high. But it might occur. The chances against four bridge players all getting "perfect" hands, each with single suits, has been estimated as 1 in 2,235,197,406,-895,366,368,301,560,000. Such a combination of hands may not occur in thousands of years of playing, or it may occur twice tomorrow, but the probability is that it will occur once in the number given above. In the long run, the a priori probabilities do tend to occur, but in any case, these are the expectations. But note that there is no "law of averages" which controls probabilities. It is not certain that there will ever be four perfect hands, though it is probable that there will be if sufficient hands are played.

The failure to understand the nature of a priori probability is responsible for an error which is usually called "the gambler's fallacy." Let us assume that we intend to toss a coin 1000 times. The first 20 tosses turn up tails. How would you bet on the next toss, provided you were sure that the coin was a fair coin? The gambler's fallacy is the assumption that there is a better than even chance that the next toss will fall heads, on the ground that heads are "overdue." The assumption is that the "law of averages" must fulfill itself, that there must be 500 heads and 500 tails in 1000 tosses, so that the heads must now make up for lost time. But coins have no memories of past tosses, nor do they have consciences. The odds on the twenty-first toss are exactly the same as on any other. The a priori probability is always $\frac{1}{2}$ on any toss.

If the objection is raised, "But isn't it probable that 1000 coins will fall in the proportion of 500 each?," the answer is Yes.

"Then won't the heads have to make up their due proportions?" To this the answer is No. A priori probabilities refer to the future only. If the first 20 tosses show tails, we must then revise our expectations as to the total results when the 1000 tosses will have been completed. Since there are 980 tosses to go, with a probability of 490 heads and 490 tails, the probability for the total (including the 20 tosses) will be 490 heads and 510 tails.

Coins never "make up" for past performances. Nor do dice or roulette wheels. The only sensible inference when 20 tails fall in a row is the possibility that the coin is not perfectly balanced, so that the greater probability would then lie in favor of tails. Or the coin may have been manipulated. But even a fair coin may fall tails 20 times in a row.

In the next section we shall examine some theorems which follow from the fundamental principles of a priori probability.

Section VII: The Calculus of Mathematical Probabilities

We shall now work out some of the interesting applications of a priori probability as applied to complex events. This subject is dealt with in mathematics under the title "Theory of Combinations and Permutations." Our basic formula is f/n but we shall deal with matters in which it is difficult to determine the total possibilities. Once we do that, the rest is easy.

Let us start with a simple problem. What are the chances of getting two heads in a row (or two heads with two coins)? We must first consider the total number of possibilities. Two coins may combine with each other in four different ways. Using "H" for heads and "T" for tails, the four possibilities are: H-H, H-T, T-H, and T-T, in which the first letter stands for one coin, the second for the other. We shall call this list our "table" for two coins. Since there are four possibilities and H-H appears once, the chances of getting two heads is one in four, or $1/4$. Now another problem. What is the probability of getting *at least one* head? There are four possibilities, in three of which we will find at least one head. The probabilities are $3/4$. The probability of getting *only one* head is $2/4$, since only H-T and T-H satisfy the last requirement.

Let us now examine the manner in which we work out similar problems in connection with two dice, where the possibilities are much more complex, since two dice may combine with each other in 36 different ways. The six numbers on one die may each combine with each of the six numbers on the other. The following is our table for two dice, in which the first number stands for the number which appears on the first die and the second for the number which appears on the second:

TABLE FOR TWO DICE

6–6	5–6	4–6	3–6	2–6	1–6
6–5	5–5	4–5	3–5	2–5	1–5
6–4	5–4	4–4	3–4	2–4	1–4
6–3	5–3	4–3	3–3	2–3	1–3
6–2	5–2	4–2	3–2	2–2	1–2
6–1	5–1	4–1	3–1	2–1	1–1

The probability of getting two 6's is thus $\frac{1}{36}$, since there are 36 possibilities, only one of which is favorable. The probability of getting a combination which totals 7 is $\frac{6}{36}$, since the following combinations total 7: 6–1, 5–2, 4–3, 3–4, 2–5, and 1–6. The probability of getting a 4 is $\frac{3}{36}$, since there are only three combinations which total 4: 3–1, 2–2, and 1–3. Since there are 6 ways in which to make a 7 and only 3 in which to make a 4, it is exactly twice as easy to make a 7 as it is to make a 4. In 36 throws, 7 will probably appear 6 times and 4 only 3 times. The "odds" in favor of 7, as compared with 4, are thus 2 to 1.

We shall now examine the theory which underlies the calculation of the probabilities of complex events from the knowledge of their components. There are three different types of combinations of events, which we shall call "Exclusive," "Independent," and "Dependent" (or "Combined").

1. Exclusive events.

Exclusive events are events which are strictly alternative, or "exclusively alternative." If one such event occurs, then the others cannot occur. When a coin is tossed, "heads" and "tails" are strictly alternative events; since both cannot occur, one excludes the other. Similarly the numbers on a die are strictly alternative, since only one can appear.

To determine the probability of getting one of two or more strictly alternative events, i.e., of getting either heads or tails on a coin, or either 5 or 6 on a die, or either 2 or 3 or 4 on a die, we add their separate probabilities. The respective probabilities of these combinations are: 1 ($\frac{1}{2}$ plus $\frac{1}{2}$), $\frac{2}{6}$ ($\frac{1}{6}$ plus $\frac{1}{6}$), and $\frac{3}{6}$ ($\frac{1}{6}$ plus $\frac{1}{6}$ plus $\frac{1}{6}$).

Note that when we have mutually exclusive events, "either x or y," and add all of the probabilities together, the total will be 1, or unity. The probability of getting either 1, or 2, or 3, or 4, or 5, or 6 on a die is thus 1. The probability that *some* number will appear is "unity." Similarly the probability of getting at least one of the 36 combinations with two dice, or at least one of the four combinations with two coins is also 1. The probability of getting 5-6 or 6-5 is $\frac{2}{36}$, since each of these combinations has a probability of $\frac{1}{36}$. The probability of getting T-H or H-T is $\frac{1}{4}$ plus $\frac{1}{4}$, and so on.

2. Independent events.

Two events are independent when the occurrence of one has no effect on the occurrence or non-occurrence of the other. Thus the probability of getting a head on one coin has no effect on the getting of a head on the other coin. What is the probability of getting two heads? Since these events are independent, we multiply the separate probabilities: $\frac{1}{2} \times \frac{1}{2}$ is $\frac{1}{4}$. The probability of getting three heads in a row is $\frac{1}{2} \times \frac{1}{2} \times \frac{1}{2}$ or $\frac{1}{8}$. The probability of getting two 6's is $\frac{1}{6} \times \frac{1}{6}$ or $\frac{1}{36}$. These are the probabilities of favorable events. We may also compute the probability of the unfavorable event. The chance of getting an unfavorable event is $1 - f/n$. If we know the probability of the favorable event, we may subtract it from 1, since $1 - f/n = u/n$, in which "u" means "unfavorable." f/n plus u/n will always equal unity. The probability of not getting a 6 with one die is thus $1 - \frac{1}{6}$ or $\frac{5}{6}$. The probability of not getting a 6 with two dice? The chances of not getting a 6 on each is $\frac{5}{6}$. Since the events are independent, we multiply the separate probabilities and we have $\frac{5}{6} \times \frac{5}{6}$ or $\frac{25}{36}$.

3. Dependent or combined events.

The typical problem here is one such as this: What is the probability of getting at least one head with two coins? These events are not independent, since we do not require heads on both. A head on the first coin will settle the issue, so what happens on one coin affects what we require on the other. These are not strictly alternative events which cannot both occur. Thus we can neither add nor multiply. The events are called "dependent" because what we need on the second coin depends upon what we get on the first.

Let us shift the problem to a different one. What is the probability of getting *only one* head? Two combinations satisfy this requirement: T-H plus H-T. These combinations are strictly alternative events. For the probability of either one, add the separate probabilities: $1/4$ plus $1/4$ is $1/2$. This is the probability of only one head. Now, the problem of getting *at least one* head means that we can also use H-H. This is also strictly exclusive of the others, and we add its probability ($1/4$) to the previous probability, so that the probability of getting at least one head is $3/4$.

This problem may also be solved in a simpler manner by subtracting the probability of the unfavorable event from 1. The remainder will give us the favorable event. Thus, if we want at least one head, the unfavorable event would be "no heads." The probability of no heads is obtained by multiplying the probability of no heads on the first coin (tails) by no heads on the second coin (tails). The probability of "no heads" is thus $1/4$ ($1/2 \times 1/2$). Then subtract $1/4$ from 1 and we have $3/4$, the same as before. The favorable plus the unfavorable event always add up to unity.

The same methods apply to two dice. In order to find the probability of getting *at least one* 6, start with the simpler problem of getting only one 6. Two possibilities satisfy this problem. We must get "no 6" on the first and a 6 on the second, or vice versa. Let us use the symbol X for "no 6." The two favorable possibilities are thus X-6 and 6-X. These are strictly exclusive so we must add their separate probabilities. The probability of X is $5/6$, that of 6 is $1/6$. We then have X-6

($\frac{5}{6} \times \frac{1}{6}$) plus 6-X ($\frac{1}{6} \times \frac{5}{6}$). This gives us $\frac{5}{36}$ plus $\frac{5}{36}$ or $\frac{10}{36}$. For *at least one* 6 we may also use the combination 6-6. It probability is $\frac{1}{36}$. The probability of getting *at least one* 6 is thus $\frac{11}{36}$. To confirm this result consult the table of dice.

By the indirect method, we must subtract the possibility of getting no 6's from 1 and we will then have the probability of getting at least one 6, since "no 6" is the contradictory of "at least one 6." By the law of the "excluded middle" either we will get "at least one" or "none at all." f plus u equals 1. To get no 6's we must get "X" on both dice. These probabilities are multiplied: $\frac{5}{6} \times \frac{5}{6}$ or $\frac{25}{36}$. The probability of getting at least one 6 is thus $1 - \frac{25}{36}$, or $\frac{11}{36}$.

There are of course many more difficult problems in the calculus of probabilities, but we have indicated the general theory and some of the important theorems.

Exercises

A. *The Distinction between Validity and Truth.*
    Judge Jerome Frank has attacked what he calls "the slavish adherence of lawyers to that instrument of reasoning which was worshipped by all men of the Middle Ages—formal logic." To illustrate his point, he writes,

    The school board of Seattle is reported to have insisted that all teachers, as a condition of procuring employment in the Seattle schools, should sign a contract by which they would agree not to join a teacher's union. Suppose that a suit were brought to compel the school board to hire teachers without imposing this condition. If a court were to decide such a suit in favor of the school board, an analysis of its opinion would show that its reasoning was apparently based upon a "fundamental principle." The court would argue that one who is under no duty to enter into a contract with another may stipulate any condition he pleases as a condition to entering into a contract. This principle the court would take as its major premise. It would then state, as a minor premise, that the school board is under no duty to enter into a contract with any particular teachers . . .
    This method of syllogistic reasoning, which is that of formal logic, is the method used by the courts today. Because of its use,

the court's conclusions appear inescapable and inevitable. This seeming machine-like certainty, however, is artificial and conceals a fatal weakness. For a decision against the school board might have been rendered, and, if so, could have been justified, with reasoning which would have seemed similarly inevitable. The court could have argued thus: Officials administering the trust of public office may not unreasonably discriminate between applicants for employment . . . (There is your major premise.) To deny employment to a teacher because he refuses to agree not to join an organization of teachers is an unreasonable discrimination. (And there is your minor premise.) . . . The weakness of formal logic is now exposed. The court can decide one way or the other and in either case can make its reasoning appear equally flawless. Formal logic is what its name indicates; it deals with form and not with substance. The syllogism will not supply either the major premise or the minor premise. The "joker" is to be found in the selection of these premises. (Jerome Frank, *Law and the Modern Mind,* Coward-McCann, 1949, pp. 65–6.)

Defend formal logic against Frank's criticism.

B. *The Meaning of Truth.*

1. Is the author of the following selection somewhat inconsistent in his relativism?

   The old illustration that 2 + 2 equals 4, whether one be sick or well, should be finally exploded. A number has more concreteness, because of the definite character of its associations, than a visual image or auditory sensation, but the process of perception is similar and the agreement or disagreement as to the nature of the impression is dependent equally upon the state of the body and mind at the time of perception. To a man suffering with paresis, 2 and 2 may make 11 or 7 or 5, just as to a man afflicted with toothache, a fascinating novel of genuine quality may be dull and of little value. (V. F. Calverton, *The Newer Spirit,* Liveright, 1925.)

2. A relativist argued: "A person's conception of what is true depends upon the manner in which he was conditioned by his environment and group customs. Western peoples thus have one set of conceptions, such as a reliance upon the methods of science, but Eastern peoples have a different kind of standard. They rely on mysticism as the source of truth.

Thus there can be no 'absolute' truth, for every 'truth' is such only for those who have been conditioned to accept it. We criticize them, but they have an equal right to criticize us." Discuss.

3. A relativist says, "All American school teachers, without a single exception, are members of the Communist Party." This statement, he argues, is true *for him*. If you disagree, he says, you mean only that the statement is false *for you*. Discuss.

4. Pyrrho, the ancient Greek sceptic, dogmatically denied the possibility of human knowledge, either with respect to the senses, morals, or logic. Pyrrho's disciples, it may be recalled, refused to mourn him after he died, on the ground that they could not be sure that he was dead. Distinguish "probabilism" from Pyrrhonic scepticism.

C. On *Empirical Probability and Syllogisms.*

1. How would you answer the sorcerer in the following?

   Dr. Livingstone was trying to dissuade an African sorcerer from his fetishistic ways of invoking rain. "You see," he said, "that after all your doings, it sometimes rains, and sometimes does not, exactly as when you do nothing at all."
   "But," replied the sorcerer, "it is just the same with you doctors. You give the patient remedies, and sometimes the patient gets well, and sometimes he dies, exactly as when you do nothing at all." (A. Wolf, *Exercises in Logic and Scientific Method.* Copyright 1939 by The Macmillan Company and used with their permission.

2. Analyze the following in terms of its probability-syllogisms. Was Holmes' success more amazing in some cases than in others?

Our visitor bore every mark of being an average commonplace British tradesman, obese, pompous, and slow. He wore rather baggy gray shepherd's check trousers, a not overclean black frock-coat, unbuttoned in the front; and a drab waistcoat with a heavy brassy Albert chain, and a square pierced bit of metal dangling down as an ornament. A frayed top hat and a faded brown overcoat with a wrinkled velvet collar lay upon a chair beside him. Altogether, look as I would, there was nothing remarkable about the man save his blazing red head and the expression of extreme chagrin and discontent upon his features.

Sherlock Holmes' quick eye took in my occupation, and he shook his head with a smile as he noticed my questioning glances. "Beyond the obvious facts that he has at some time done manual labor, that he takes snuff, that he is a Freemason, that he had been in China, and that he has done a considerable amount of writing lately, I can deduce nothing else."

Mr. Jabez Wilson started up in his chair, with his forefinger upon the paper, but his eyes upon my companion.

"How in the name of good fortune, did you know all that, Mr. Holmes?" he asked. "How did you know, for example, that I did manual labor? It's as true as gospel, for I began as a ship's carpenter."

"Your hands, my dear Sir. Your right hand is quite a size larger than your left. You have worked with it and the muscles are more developed."

"Well, the snuff, then, and the Freemasonry?"

"I won't insult your intelligence by telling you how I read that, especially as, rather against the strict rules of your order, you use an arc and compass breastpin."

"Ah, of course, I forgot that. But the writing?"

"What else can be indicated by that right cuff so very shiny for five inches, and the left one with the smooth patch near the elbow where you rest it upon the desk."

"Well, but China?"

"The fish which you have tattooed immediately above your wrist could only have been done in China. I have made a small study of tattoo marks, and have even contributed to the literature of the subject. That trick of staining the fishes' scales of a delicate pink is quite peculiar to China. When, in addition, I see a Chinese coin hanging from your watch-chain, the matter becomes even more simple."

Mr. Jabez Wilson laughed heartily. "Well, I never!" said he. "I thought at first that you had done something clever, but I see that there was nothing in it after all." (A. C. Doyle, *The Red-Headed League*.)

D. *On A Priori Probability*.

1. "I haven't seen John's new convertible, but the probability that it is red is $\frac{1}{2}$, since there are only two possibilities: it is red or not-red." Criticize.

2. What is the probability that the next birth in your neighborhood will be a boy? What assumptions did you make? Are they true?

3. Which hand is it more difficult to acquire in a bridge game, a hand containing 13 spades, or a hand containing Q, 10, 4 of spades, J, 9, 7 of hearts, 10, 8, 4 of diamonds, and Q, 6, 5, 2 of clubs?

4. A baseball player has made only one error in 200 chances. What is the probability that he will field the next chance without an error? What would the probability be if he had fielded 200 chances flawlessly? Would it make any difference if we assumed that the next chance would be a normal one and the player was alert? Does this problem involve empirical or a priori probabilities, or a combination of both?

5. You draw marbles from two bags labelled A and B. The first ten drawn from A are all red; the first 70 drawn from B are all blue. Each bag contains 100 marbles. Is it possible to state the probability (a) that all the marbles in A are red? (b) that all in B are blue? Is the probability empirical, a priori, or both?

6. Captain Marryat, in the novel *Peter Simple*, tells us of the midshipman who, during a battle, stuck his head through the first hole made in the side of his ship by an enemy cannon ball, because, he said, "by a calculation made by Professor Inman, the odds were 32, 647 and some decimals to boot, that another ball would not come in at the same hole." (H. A. Larrabee, *Reliable Knowledge*.)
Comment on the midshipman's reasoning.

7. It is sometimes argued that if six chimpanzees were set to work pounding six typewriters at random for millions of years, they would in time write the works of Shakespeare, since all possibilities would be realized if they were given enough time. They would write much nonsense of course, but by mere chance they would be likely to hit the keys necessary to write anything whatsoever. Do you agree?

8. In his books, *New Frontiers of the Mind* and *The Reach of the Mind,* J. B. Rhine, Director of the Parapsychology Laboratory of Duke University, claims to have established the reality of clairvoyance, or the awareness of objects without the use of the senses. A series of "extrasensory perception," or "ESP" tests, was conducted in which subjects were asked to identify concealed cards. A simplified 25-card deck was devised, containing only five variations in design—star, rectangle, cross, circle, and wavy lines. Subjects were then asked to identify the cards as they were placed face down on a table.

On the basis of chance, the probability is that a subject will score an average of five hits per 25 cards. According to Professor Rhine, one subject scored an average of 6.85 hits per run of 25 cards for more than 3500 runs; another scored an average of more than 18 hits per 25 through a series of 74 runs through the deck, one of these runs giving a perfect score of 25 and several above 20. These facts, says Professor Rhine, have strongly established the case for clairvoyant extrasensory perception, since a perfect run should occur only once, according to one calculation, in over 298,023,223,876,-953,125 times! The odds are 100 to one that no one will average 8 or better for even three runs in succession, and 10,000 to one that no one will average 5.77 cards in 100 runs. Nevertheless, according to a reported poll taken among 352 psychologists in 1939, only 5 accepted ESP as established, with only 26 considering it "likely."

Do you believe that the case for ESP has been established, granted that the *facts* cited above are true?

E. *The Calculus of Mathematical Probabilities.*

1. Compute the probabilities of the following: (a) 4 heads in a row, (b) three 6's in a row, (c) a 4, 5, or 6 with one die, (d) one head in 3 throws.

2. A man argued that since the probability of throwing a 6 with one die was ⅙, the probability of throwing a 6 with two dice was ²⁄₆, with 3 dice, ³⁄₆; with 4 dice, ⁴⁄₆; with 5 dice, ⁵⁄₆; with 6 dice, ⁶⁄₆; with 7 dice, ⁷⁄₆, etc. Point out his error.

3. When we toss 3 coins, there are 8 possible arrangements of the 3 coins: 1 of 3 heads, 1 of 3 tails, 3 of 2 heads and 1 tail, and 3 of 2 tails and 1 head. What is the probability that you can toss at least 2 heads with the 3 coins?

4. The possibilities with 4 coins are 16 in number: 1(4 heads), 4(3 heads, 1 tail), 6(2 heads, 2 tails), 4(3 tails, 1 head) and 1(4 tails). What are the probabilities that you can toss at least 2 heads with 4 coins?

5. A checker keeps tab on the numbers which fall on a roulette wheel. There are 38 numbers, so that the probability is that each number will fall 50 times in every 1900 revolutions of the wheel. The checker finds the results for the first few numbers after 1900 revolutions: number 1(48), number 2(55), number 3(47), number 4(79), number 5(43), number 6(14), number 7(51), number 8(49). Would this information

be relevant to the making of a bet on any of these numbers?

6. A slot machine has three wheels with 20 characters on each wheel. Only one character on each wheel shows the jackpot symbol. What are your chances of hitting the jackpot if the machine is not "rigged"?

7. Five cards are dealt to you from a pack of 52. Four of your cards are hearts. What is the probability that the top card in the deck is a heart?

8. Five cards are dealt to you once again. You have no ace or 9. What is the probability that the top card is either an ace or a 9?

9. Compute the probabilities in the dice game known as "craps." Instructions and rules follow:

    a. The "shooter" wins if he throws a combination totalling 7 or 11 on the first throw, and loses if he throws 2, 3, or 12 on the first throw.

    b. If some other number is thrown, such as 4, the shooter must then throw another 4 before he throws a 7 to win. If he throws 7 before 4, he loses.

    c. The possibilities for the various numbers are as follows:

Number	Ways of making	Combinations
2	1	(1–1)
3	2	(1–2, 2–1)
4	3	(3–1, 1–3, 2–2)
5	4	(4–1, 3–2, 2–3, 3–2)
6	5	(5–1, 4–2, 3–3, 2–4, 1–5)
7	6	(6–1, 5–2, 4–3, 3–4, 2–5, 1–6)
8	5	(6–2, 5–3, 4–4, 3–5, 2–6)
9	4	(6–3, 5–4, 4–5, 3–6)
10	3	(6–4, 5–5, 4–6)
11	2	(6–5, 5–6)
12	1	(6–6)

$\overline{36}$ possibilities

    d. Compute the chances of the shooter's losing. The shooter may lose on the first throw by throwing a 2, 3, or 12, and he may lose after throwing a 4, 5, 6, 8, 9, or 10 on the first throw. Since the probabilities of throwing (and losing) in these different combinations are strictly alternative, the separate probabilities should be added.

    e. Special attention should be given to the probabilities

of loss when a number from 4 to 10 is thrown. Suppose that 4 is thrown. This number will probably be thrown 3 times in 36 throws. (See the middle column above.) We must now compute the probability of *losing* when 4 is thrown on the first throw. There are twice as many possibilities of making a 7 as there are of making a 4, since 4 occurs $\frac{3}{36}$ (3 times in 36) and 7 occurs $\frac{6}{36}$ (6 times in 36). In 9 attempts to make a 4 before a 7 the shooter will probably succeed three times and fail six times. He will lose six times out of nine, or $\frac{2}{3}$ of the time. Thus the probability that any shooter will lose via the number 4 is $\frac{3}{36} \times \frac{2}{3}$. (He will throw "4" $\frac{3}{36}$ of the time, and if he does, lose $\frac{2}{3}$ of the time).

f. Compute the probabilities for losing via the other numbers in the same manner, add the probabilities together, and you will have the shooter's chances of losing. Subtract this fraction from 1 and you will have the shooter's chances of winning.

g. It will be found convenient to translate all your fractions into fractions having a denominator of 990.

Chapter 15

HYPOTHESES AND
SCIENTIFIC METHOD

Section I: Concerning the Proof of a Proposition

If a proposition corresponds with the facts, then it is a true proposition. This definition of truth is pleasingly simple, but difficulties arise when we seek to apply it to actual cases. The proposition "I have a $1000 bill in my wallet" is false, for it obviously does not correspond to the facts, but such correspondence or lack of correspondence is not so easily determined in propositions such as Einstein's famous statement that "the universe is finite but unbounded." Our basic question in this chapter will be, How do we determine whether a proposition does or does not correspond to the facts? We shall emphasize the manner in which the scientist answers this question, for scientific method is the most trustworthy method for testing the truth of propositions. Our discussion, however, will aim only at delineating the logical essentials of the method and we shall avoid entering into the details of the highly developed techniques which are used in elaborate research. We shall also seek to emphasize aspects of the scientific method which have some relevance to everyday thinking. The difference between the careful thinker in ordinary affairs and the scientist who develops reliable methods of inquiry is, as we shall see, one of degree rather than kind. It has been said that every man has something of the poet and lover in him. We may add that he is also something of a scientist.

Our present concern is with the methods of proof which may be used in testing the truth of a proposition. The basic problem here arises when we ask, Is proposition "P" true? Now, there are two ways in which the investigation into the truth of a proposition may be initiated. "P" may be a familiar "truth" which we suddenly decide to question. Most of us, of course, never raise such questions, especially where matters of "common knowledge" are concerned. Such ideas are regarded as immune from criticism, and false ideas enjoy long lives. Prejudices abound with respect to the activities of groups about which we know very little, such as Wall Street bankers, liberal political organizations, and racial and religious minorities. But the great thinkers in each generation question the basic presuppositions or assumptions of their times. Such men see problems in "accepted truths" that others take for granted. Questions may also result in scientific revolutions, as when Einstein questioned the accepted definition of "simultaneity." But more typically, propositions become candidates for testing by scientific methods, when they are advanced as suggestions for the solutions of problems. A typical scientific problem is the search for the cause of a disease, as in cancer research. The cause of this disease is as yet unknown. Many hypotheses are suggested, i.e., propositions in the form "X is the cause." These propositions are then subjected to careful testing for their truth or falsity.

We have just noted the two ways in which our basic question arises. It is also important to note that there are two general methods of proof which may be used in determining the truth or falsity of a proposition. These are the direct and the indirect methods. By direct proof we shall mean proof by simple observation; by indirect proof, cases in which logical reasoning, as well as observation, is required. To illustrate: The proposition "There are four yachts in the harbor" may be verified by direct observation. We see the yachts, and seeing is believing. (At least usually.) But there are many propositions which cannot be verified in this manner—statements concerning past events, for example. We cannot see Caesar crossing the Rubicon today, nor can we "see" a gas expanding when heated, since the gas is invisible to the eye. In such cases indirect methods of proof are required. The proposition "A gas expands when heated" is tested by heating gas in a cylinder. We see the piston moving up. Such indirect proof requires logical reasoning in addition to observation. We must deduce the consequences which will follow if our proposition is true, and we then experiment to determine whether these consequences actually occur. Our reasoning takes the following form:

> If gas expands when heated, then the piston will move up when the gas is heated
>
> The piston did move up when the gas was heated
>
> Therefore, it is true (or probable) that gas expands when heated.

We note that our reasoning has taken a syllogistic form. Though the syllogism is invalid, it justifies a highly probable conclusion.

The indirect method of proof is a very useful one in science. The secrets of nature are not always open to inspection by the naked eye, nor does the microscope always reveal them. Many of the significant propositions in science cannot be verified directly. We therefore ask what observable consequences will follow if the proposition is true. This is deduction. We then go to observation to find out if these consequences do in fact occur. Science thus involves both observation and logical reasoning, or empirical and rational elements. Observation, of course, is the indispensable prerequisite of all truth concerning matters of fact and experience, and it is the ultimate ground of all truths concerning nature. But we could not go very far without the aid of logic.

Section II: Problems, Facts, and Hypotheses

All investigation begins with questions or problems. Philosophy, Aristotle said, begins in wonder. So does science. The testing of the truth of a proposition begins with the question, Is it true? All reflective thinking, as John Dewey has insisted over and over again, is a problem-solving activity. Reflective thinking differs from daydreaming, reverie, and other non-logical forms of thinking in that it explores and analyzes the conditions which will resolve a difficulty. When the smooth tenor of untroubled existence pursues its placid course, we do not think reflectively. We must have something to think about, a problem which requires solution.

A motorist driving his car on a good country road pays a minimum of attention to the mechanics of his car and keeps alert for wandering livestock, but if he has no problems he indulges in reverie. Suddenly he notices that a cow is standing in the middle of the road, eating loose alfalfa which had fallen on the road from a farmer's wagon. If he cannot drive off the road, he must remove the cow. He has a problem, and must think reflectively to find a solution. One solution might be to remove the alfalfa from the road. This is a practical problem which requires removing the obstacle to the motorist's progress toward his destination. But other types of problems might have occurred to him while driving. He might have noted that the gasoline trucks drag iron chains on the ground after them, and he might have wondered why they do this. This would have been a theoretical problem for him, as distinguished from the practical one. This distinction between practical and theoretical problems also characterizes two types of scientific problems, those concerned with the practical conditions of human welfare, and those which are concerned primarily with the enlightenment of the human mind. Problems concerning the chemical constitution of the stars, or Copernicus' problem concerning the relationship of the earth to the sun were primarily theoretical problems. But reflective thinking, in any case, always starts with a problem.

Our emphasis on the role of the problem in reflective thinking will help us to understand the nature of scientific method. In particular it will help us to see the inadequacy of a conception of science fostered by nineteenth century positivism, which thought of science as a fact-collecting agency. This view regards the scientist as a man who goes out into the field of nature with a notebook, jots down the description of what he observes, classifies his material, and then draws generalizations. But this view is inadequate, for at least two reasons. First, the world is full of a bewildering variety of things. What shall we note, and what shall we ignore? Effective observation of such variety must have a purpose; one must know what to look for. We must go to nature with questions or problems, and the scientist must note the facts relevant to his problems. In the second place, "the facts" are not items which can always be directly observed, so that when we say "Look at the facts," there may be nothing to see. These two criticisms require further discussion.

1. Observation requires hypotheses.

Significant observations do not usually occur unless we are looking for something. In looking at a painting, or listening to music, or reading a book, the trained observer, i.e., the man who is familiar with the field, will observe infinitely more than the untrained person. The artist, said Leonardo da Vinci, sees what others catch only a glimpse of. He knows what to look for. In the same manner, no scientist makes observations without a plan of observation. He starts with a problem, e.g., the nature of the rock formations in an area. He examines the rocks with some definite goal in mind. He develops a suggested solution of some specific problem. Such suggested solutions are called "hypotheses," the working tools for the solution of problems. He has a "theory" as to how the rocks are formed, and he then looks for proof, or verification of his hypothesis.

Looking must have a purpose, to determine whether certain specific things are or are not present in nature. A detective needs a clue, and the scientist needs a working hypothesis which will be confirmed or rejected by the facts. If a hypothesis is refuted, the scientist must then revise or even abandon that hypothesis, and try out a new one. "How odd it is," said Charles Darwin, the father of modern evolutionary theory, "that anyone should not see that all observation must be for or against some view, if it is to be of any service." On another occasion he said, "No one can be a good observer unless he is a good theorizer."

Significant observation requires that we look for something specific, that we have a "point of view." But this method also involves a pitfall. There is the danger that a preconceived notion concerning the facts will lead to a biased point of view. The observer may then see only what he wishes to see, in line with his wishful thinking. He may not note the negative instances, or exceptions to the rule he seeks to verify. Further, the observer must also pay a certain price for the advantages of the hypothesis. He will usually ignore significant facts having a bearing on problems in which he is not interested. An anecdote concerning Darwin will illustrate this. Darwin and a fellow scientist visited a region in England searching for certain fossils in which they were interested. They were not aware of the glacial theory at the time of their visit, and they completely ignored the glacial markings on the rocks among which they worked. Years later, Darwin revisited this region and was astonished to discover how clearly marked were the glacial ridges on the rocks. He had not noticed them earlier because he was not looking for them. Modern archaeologists have recognized this aspect of selective observation and have accordingly established a methodological rule when new excavations are opened up. The archaeologists who discover ancient monuments or buildings will not excavate them completely, but will leave part of the "find" untouched, for they may otherwise ignore important clues which a later generation will be aware of, in the same manner as Darwin became aware of the glacial markings.

2. What are "the facts"?

We have noted the importance of selective observation, centering around a problem, in our first comment on positivism. The second inadequacy in the positivistic view is that the facts cannot be directly observed. When we are told to "base our ideas on the facts," the question arises, "What are the facts?" This is the very problem we are trying to solve. The distinction between a hypothesis and a fact is often a tenuous one. Just what is a "fact"?

The word "fact" has several senses. We shall note two important ones. When we say that a true proposition corresponds with the facts, we use the word "fact" for those existences in space and time which are what they are, independent of our theories, our knowledge, and our beliefs about them. These "facts" are simply there, awaiting our discoveries of them. In a second sense, however, "fact" means an established truth. We use the word "fact" in this sense when we say that "it is a fact that the earth is round." But at one time this view was regarded as a fantastic hypothesis, since most persons believed that the roundness of the earth involved the absurd consequence that the people in the antipodes (the other side of the earth) would have to walk upside down, like flies on a ceiling. What was once regarded as a "wild theory" is now accepted as a fact because the evidence overwhelmingly supports the hypothesis that the earth is round. The difference between what is called "hypothesis" and what is called "fact" (in the second sense) is thus one of degree only. Hypotheses become facts when the evidence becomes sufficiently convincing. The popular distinction between "fact" and "opinion" points to a similar distinction. An opinion is a theory, the evidence for which is wholly inconclusive. When we prove our opinion, it becomes a fact.

When it is said that we should "go to the facts," this second sense of "fact" is overlooked. The facts cannot be known until we have formulated and verified hypotheses concerning them. Not all facts can be directly observed. Very complicated deductions and mathematical calculations are required to test hypotheses concerning the internal structure of the atom. An observer in a physicist's laboratory watching an experiment might see the physicist watching the needle in a galvanometer. The reading is + .745, and this reading may confirm a hypothesis concerning the atoms. But there was no direct observation of the facts. When Copernicus formulated his heliocentric theory concerning the revolution of the planets around the sun, he rejected the geocentric notion that the earth is motionless, with the sun, moon, and stars revolving around it every 24 hours. Did he merely observe the facts? No. Direct observation tells us that it is the sun which is in motion. But we now say that it is a fact that the earth moves.

Note also that there may be an element of hypothesis even in what we think of as direct observation. We see stars in the heavens. What we actually see are gleaming specks of light. We interpret these specks of white light as stars because of our hypotheses. I see a friend on the street, walk up and slap him on the back, but alas! I have annoyed a stranger. I acted on a hypothesis, which erroneously interpreted the facts. Interpretation is always somewhat hazardous, involving a leap into the unknown. Similarly, the desert traveler who "sees an oasis," sees an image, but his image does not correspond to anything in the real world.

The central element in scientific thinking is thus problem-solving, and the hypothesis is the central tool in such thinking. The word "theory" is sometimes used synonymously with hypothesis, though theory also has a specialized meaning in the physical sciences, where it refers to the fundamental principles underlying a science. The "atomic theory" is used in this latter sense, since the atomic theory underlies various branches of the physical sciences.

We shall now turn to the analysis of scientific method to examine the manner in which the scientist proceeds in his search for the solution of problems.

Section III: The Logical Analysis of an Example of Scientific Thinking

The following example of scientific thinking is an abridged version of an incident in A. J. Cronin's novel, *The Citadel* (Grosset and Dunlap, pp. 57–60):

Andrew tore open the envelope. It was a message from Dr. Bramwell:

Come round at once. I want you to help certify a dangerous lunatic.

·   ·   ·   ·   ·

Andrew threw on his things in three minutes. Accompanying him down the road, Annie told him as best she could about Emrys. He had been ill and unlike himself for three weeks, but during the night he had turned violent and gone clean out of his mind. He had set upon his wife with a breadknife. . . .

·   ·   ·   ·   ·

"Acute mania." Bramwell rolled the words over his tongue with tragic grandeur. "Acute homicidal mania. Clear evidence, I think!"

"It sounds pretty bad," Andrew answered slowly. "Well! I'll take a look at him. . . ."

He went over to Emrys, and at first he hardly recognized him. His face seemed swollen, the nostrils thickened, the skin waxy. . . .

Andrew spoke to him. He muttered an unintelligible reply. Then, clinching his hands, he came out with a tirade of aggressive nonsense. . . . [1] . . . . A silence followed. Andrew felt that he ought to be convinced. Yet, inexplicably, he was not satisfied. Why, why, he kept asking himself, *why* should Emrys talk like this? Supposing the man had gone out of his mind, what was the cause of it all? He had always been a happy, contented man—no worries, easygoing, amiable. Why, without apparent reason, had he changed to *this?* [2]

There must be a reason, Andrew thought doggedly; symptoms don't just happen of themselves. Staring at the swollen features before him, puzzling, puzzling for some solution of the conundrum, he instinctively reached out and touched the swollen face, noting subconsciously, as he did so, that the pressure of his finger left no dent in the edematous cheek. [3]

All at once, electrically, a terminal vibrated in his brain. [4] *Why* didn't the swelling pit on pressure? Because—now it was his heart which jumped!—because it was not true edema, but myxedema. [5] He had it, by God, he *had* it! No, no, he must not rush. Firmly, he caught hold of himself. He must not be a plunger, wildly leaping to conclusions. He must go cautiously, slowly, be sure!

Curbing himself, he lifted Emrys' hand. [6] Yes, the skin was dry and rough, the fingers slightly thickened at the ends. Temperature —it was subnormal. Methodically he finished the examination, fighting back each successive wave of elation. Every sign and every symptom—they fitted as superbly as a complex jigsaw puzzle. The clumsy speech, dry skin, spatulate fingers, the swollen inelastic face, the defective memory, slow mentation, the attacks of irritability culminating in an outburst of homicidal violence. Oh! the triumph of the completed picture was sublime. [7]

Rising, he went down to the parlor. . . . "Look here, Barmwell—" . . . "I don't think we ought to certify Emrys" . . .

"In my opinion Emrys is only sick in mind because he's sick in body. I feel that he's suffering from thyroid deficiency—an absolutely straight case of myxedema." [8]

The *Citadel* incident will now be analyzed in order to show how scientific thinking typically follows eight steps, or phases, in the solution of a problem. We shall begin with an outline of the eight steps, and then show how each is a phase of the problem in *The Citadel*. Frequent reference back to the example will help the reader in following the discussion. (The numbers in the example refer to the steps.)

The Eight Steps

(1) The preliminary data which suggest the problem.
(2) The formulation of the problem.
(3) Observation of facts relevant to the problem.
(4) The use of previous knowledge.
(5) The formulation of the hypothesis.
(6) Deduction of the implications of the hypothesis.
(7) Testing of the hypothesis.
(8) Conclusion: The hypothesis is confirmed or disconfirmed.

1. The preliminary data which suggest the problem.

Andrew does not trust Dr. Bramwell's opinion, suspecting that it may be the result of a "snap judgment," based upon a superficial examination of the facts. He decides to "take a look" at the patient and notes certain peculiarities in the man's behavior.

2. The formulation of the problem.

Why, Andrew asks himself, does Emrys act in this manner? The formulation of this problem initiates the process of reflective thinking, or problem solving.

3. Observation of facts relevant to the problem.

Andrew now seeks for facts which may be connected with his problem. He notes that his finger leaves no dent in the flesh.

4. The use of previous knowledge.

This step is not consciously formulated in Andrew's mind, and will be discussed in connection with the next step.

5. Formulation of the hypothesis.

A hypothesis is a suggested solution of a problem. Andrew's hypothesis is that "Emrys has myxedema." But where did the hypothesis come from? Obviously, only a trained investigator could have thought of this hypothesis, based on his previous knowledge (Step 4). It is a generalization of medical science that patients suffering from myxedema will have edematous flesh, or, stated hypothetically: "If a patient has myxedema, then he will have edematous flesh." The hypothesis came to Andrew's mind "like a flash" because he did not consciously formulate this bit of knowledge, but it was there. Andrew went from "He has edematous flesh" to "He has myxedema." His reasoning was syllogistic, in the form of an enthymeme, with the major premise omitted. The syllogism, spelled out, follows:

> Emrys had edematous flesh (Step 3)
>
> If one has myxedema then he will have edematous flesh (Step 4)

∴. Emrys has myxedema (Step 5)

His reasoning proceeds from the observed fact (the minor premise), through the rule (major premise), to the hypothesis (conclusion). The syllogism is invalid, since it affirms the consequent, but the conclusion is probable, since the major premise could be converted into "If one has edematous flesh, then one probably has myxedema."

Note, however, that Andrew regards the hypothesis as merely a tentative solution until he has further evidence or proof. He now desires to test his hypothesis, and we proceed to the next step.

6. Deduction of the implications of the hypothesis.

This step is also not formulated consciously in Andrew's mind. His thoughts may have taken this pattern: "I must test my hypothesis. But how? This thing must be reasoned out, so I need an indirect proof. I must deduce the consequences of my hypothesis. If my hypothesis is true, what further facts should I observe in the patient? He should have spatulate fingers, etc., etc." Once more we find a hypothetical proposition, in which the hypothesis is the antecedent, and the deduced implications the consequent. Thus:

If Emrys has myxedema   then he will have spatulate fingers, etc.

   (the hypothesis)   (the deduced implications)

The purpose of deducing (or exfoliating) the implications of the hypothesis is that we will then have a definite prediction that certain observable facts will be found, if the hypothesis is true. We can then perform a test to determine whether these predicted facts are actually present. Step 6 is obviously dependent upon our previous knowledge, as was Step 4. We are now ready for the test.

7. Testing of the hypothesis.

Andrew finds the predicted facts by further observation.

8. Conclusion: Confirmation or rejection of the hypothesis.

The hypothesis in this case has been confirmed. If the observations in Step 7 had been negative, then either further analysis or a new hypothesis would have been required.

Note that Steps 6–7–8 also form a unit of syllogistic reasoning, like Steps 3–4–5. Step 6: "If he has myxedema, then he will have spatulate fingers." Step 7: "He has." Step 8: "Therefore, he has myxedema." Once again, we can only say "probably." But the probability of the hypothesis has now been increased greatly for it rests on stronger evidence. The probability of a patient's having a particular disease increases, other things being equal, with the number of the observed symptoms.

If the hypothesis had been *disconfirmed* by negative evidence, our syllogism would then have been in the fourth figure. If Step 7 had shown that Emrys did *not* have spatulate fingers, etc., then Andrew would have concluded that he did not have myxedema. Does this mean that a negative experiment gives us certainty rather than probability? No, for we cannot be certain that our premises are absolutely true, nor even that our deductions are infallible. A negative experiment, however, gives us a more conclusive proof than a positive one. It is often possible that some other hypothesis might also account for the known and observed facts, but if the deduced facts are *not* present, then that particular hypothesis cannot be true, with the qualifications above noted. When a hypothesis is proved false, we must return to Step 3 and make a fresh start in the search for a new one. We shall now summarize our discussion in terms of the eight steps:

(1) Emrys talks unintelligibly, etc.
(2) Why does he act in this manner?
(3) His flesh is edematous.
(4) (If he had myxedema, then his flesh would be edematous.)
(5) Hypothesis: He has myxedema.
(6) If he has myxedema, then he will have spatulate fingers, etc.
(7) He has spatulate fingers, etc.
(8) Conclusion: He has myxedema.

Section IV: Some General Aspects of the Phases of Scientific Thinking

We shall now discuss the eight steps in greater detail, noting some qualifications in order to avoid an oversimplified conception as to the nature of scientific method. Comments will be made upon each step in turn.

1. The preliminary data which suggest the problem.

Problems may be practical, arising out of an obstruction to our desires, or they may be theoretical. In the latter case it is some peculiarity in the observed facts which gives rise to the problem. But there are also cases where the "preliminary data" are not present, as when, during the last war, the federal government called upon the chemists to produce formulas for synthetic rubber and for a substitute for quinine.

2. The formulation of the problem.

A problem should be formulated as precisely as possible, for we shall fumble aimlessly in seeking to solve a vaguely defined problem. Will Rogers once remarked that both he and Bernard Shaw knew that the world was all wrong, but that neither of them knew just what was the matter with it. To know that something is "all wrong" may pose a problem, but not one which can be attacked efficiently. The problem may require analysis through breaking it down into its parts, and some observation may be required before the precise nature of the problem becomes evident. Only those with previous knowledge, moreover, can formulate problems precisely.

3. Observation of facts relevant to the problem.

The purpose of observation is to find the relevant facts which will suggest a clue or hypothesis for the solution of the problem. Effective observation thus depends upon previous knowledge, since only such knowledge will enable us to determine which facts are relevant. In some cases, of course, the pre-

liminary data may give us sufficient facts for the suggestion of
the hypothesis.

Observation is an art, and an art is an activity which requires
skill. Normal sense organs and mental alertness are both indispensable. But only trained observers are able to make the fine
discriminations which are required in many situations. "The
hand is quicker than the eye" calls attention to this difficulty, as
does the motto of the U. S. Army Camouflage Division: "Seeing
was believing." In a famous instance Japanese airmen were able
to detect camouflage netting designed to simulate the foliage
roof of the jungle because the camouflaged region lacked the
jungle odors. The netting was then impregnated with jungle
odors. But no matter how skilled observation may be, we should
remember that it is not infallible.

4. The use of previous knowledge in selecting hypotheses.

This requires not only knowledge, but the ability to use it
at the right time and place. No rules or recipes can substitute
for insight and imagination in hitting upon the right hypothesis. The great scientist resembles the great artist in his ability to
see relations which were never before dreamed of. In the *Citadel* case, Andrew merely applied a previously known generalization to the case before him. But in great scientific discoveries
such generalizations are not available. Thus, Kepler's problem
was to describe the motions of the planets. He formulated the
hypothesis that they moved in ellipses, and not in circles, as had
previously been believed. He was, of course, familiar with the
properties of ellipses but it required great imagination to relate
these figures to the motions of the planets.

5. The hypothesis.

We have discussed the hypothesis as the working tool in the
solution of problems. A good hypothesis is one which successfully solves the problem for which it suggests a solution. In
thus functioning .successfully, the hypothesis must do certain
things. First, it must *account for the facts which are already*

known. This means that, before we put it to the test of proof, it should account for the facts which have been observed in the specific investigation at hand, and it should be consistent with our previous knowledge. In the *Citadel* case, Andrew's hypothesis met this first requirement, for the hypothesis of myxedema accounted for the observed fact that Emrys' flesh was edematous.

Our first requirement, however, calls for judicious interpretation. Great scientists sometimes appear to show a bland disregard of "the facts." Let us examine the instructive illustration afforded by Mendeleev, the great Russian chemist who discovered the law of the periodicity of the chemical elements. Mendeleev formulated a hypothesis which did *not* account for all of the facts. In 1869, the year in which he formulated his hypothesis, 63 chemical elements had been isolated, but these elements had no apparent logical relationships to each other. Mendeleev believed that if the elements were arranged in groups according to their atomic weights, then their other properties could be explained as periodic functions of their atomic weights. But two of the elements, tellurium and gold, could not be fitted into the suggested pattern, for their atomic weights were not in accordance with his hypothesis. His attitude may be summed up as "So much the worse for the facts." He argued that the atomic weights of these recalcitrant elements had been miscalculated, and it later turned out that he was correct. Mendeleev did not, of course, think that a hypothesis could be true if it were not in accordance with the facts; he simply had the boldness to predict that "the facts" were not really facts. The student of the history of science will find that many scientists are reluctant in giving up plausible hypotheses despite negative experiments. When a scientist hits upon a novel explanation that appears to give a new insight into the laws of nature, he may hold tenaciously to his hypothesis despite the consideration that his hypothesis does not account for all of the known facts. His faith in his idea may be so great as to justify him in disregarding hostile facts on the ground that it is in the facts, and not in his idea, that error resides. In the end, the facts reign supreme, but there may be legitimate controversies as to just what they are.

A second requirement of a good hypothesis is that it should be *verifiable* in terms of the facts. We should be able to prove it or disprove it. In the typical case, a prediction is made that certain facts will be observed, and we either observe these facts or we do not. Andrew made such a prediction. His verified prediction corroborated his hypothesis and strengthened its probability. Predictions are particularly impressive when they predict facts the existence of which would otherwise have been unknown. Einstein, for example, predicted that if his hypothesis of relativity were true, the sun would deflect the path of a ray of starlight. He predicted a deflection of 1.75 seconds. The verifying experiment showed a deflection of 1.65 seconds. No deflection had previously been suspected.

Though a good hypothesis should be verifiable by observation, this does not mean that a hypothesis which cannot be so verified is worthless. A speculative hypothesis concerning the origin of the solar system has a measure of probability when it accounts for the known facts, and it is stated in such a way that its implications *might* be observed under the appropriate conditions. A legitimate working hypothesis always involves the possibility of its being proved *or disproved* by the occurrence or non-occurrence of observable events. If this condition is not present, then the suggestion is only a pseudo-hypothesis. As an illustration of such a pseudo-hypothesis consider the thesis that all human choices are motivated by the desire to achieve the greatest amount of pleasure and the least amount of pain for oneself. An interesting popular exposition of this thesis, called "psychological hedonism," will be found in Mark Twain's *What is Man?* This thesis is not a hypothesis, since it is not possible to disprove it by a crucial experiment. For no matter what evidence we present against it, the proponent of the thesis will say that the evidence proves his point, even when we cite the martyr who goes to the stake for his religious beliefs. No distinction is made between the type of evidence which would support the thesis and the type which would disprove it. This is another example of "begging the question" or "arguing by definition."

Typically, a hypothesis is verified after its consequences are deduced. This is the rule when the facts which suggest the hypothesis are few. In such cases it must be held only tentatively until further proof is available. This was Andrew's position at Step 5. But in some cases the available facts may be so numerous (or convincing) that a given hypothesis which accounts for all of them may be highly probable *without further deduction of its implications.* For example, the reader may arrive at his home one evening and find his rooms in a state of disarray, the dresser drawers pulled out, clothing strewn on the floor, and his prized oil paintings gone. These immediate observations make the hypothesis "My home has been burglarized" highly probable, without the necessity for deducing its implications and making a prediction. The observed facts present a relatively "complete picture," and every observed fact points in the direction of the hypothesis. In such situations we use the principle of "converging evidence." The hypothesis "H" accounts for the evidence, made up of facts a, b, c, d, e, f, etc., and all of these facts "converge on" the hypothesis. This situation may be represented by a diagram:

All of the facts point in one direction. Predictions may also be made, but in cases of this type the original hypothesis is probable without further deductions, for it satisfactorily accounts for a host of observed facts. The problem is thus "solved" when we reach Step 5.

The principle of the convergence of evidence is used extensively in the historical sciences, including human history, geological history, evolution, and in criminal trials involving the use of circumstantial evidence. Note, however, that in a criminal trial the problem of verification may be different for the police, on the one hand, and for the jury on the other. The jury will be given the dossier of facts built up slowly and painstakingly by the police. The jury must "account for" these facts. But the police, in amassing their evidence, worked with clues which served as tentative or working hypotheses; they deduced the consequences of these hypotheses until they finally built up a case for presentation to the jury. The evidence for the prosecution will then be presented in its entirety to the jury, and the jury will be asked to decide whether the hypothesis "X is guilty" does or does not satisfactorily account for or explain all of these facts. When all of the evidence points in one direction, with each fact appearing to point at the accused with the tacit accusation "Thou art the man," the hypothesis that he is guilty will have a high probability without the necessity of making further predictions.

A third requirement for a good hypothesis is that it should be *simple*. This means that, other things being equal, where two hypotheses explain a given set of facts, and where each is verified by prediction, the simpler of the two should be preferred. Copernicus used this principle in advancing his hypothesis—that the earth moves around the sun—when he pointed out that the science of astronomy would be greatly simplified if the sun, rather than the earth were taken as the center in determining the movements of the planets. "Ockham's razor," a maxim attributed to William of Ockham, the mediaeval philosopher, tells us that "entities should not be multiplied beyond necessity." There are also cases, of course, where no choice between two rival hypotheses, on the ground of simplicity, is possible. The two theories of light now used by physicists afford a good illustration of this point. Newton's corpuscular theory and Huyghen's wave theory explain the known facts equally well. Both are equally "simple." In such cases, as Sir William Bragg once remarked, "We have to work with both theories. On Mondays, Wednesdays, and Fridays we use the wave theory; on Tuesdays, Thursdays, and Saturdays we think in streams of flying energy quanta or corpuscles."

It should be noted, however, that "simple" is a vague term. The hypothesis that "God is the cause of all things," including every movement of your body, is a "simple" explanation in one sense, but not at all simple in another, since it requires special explanations as to why He caused each particular motion of your body. The more complex physiological explanation of these movements in terms of muscular contractions is thus the "simpler" of the two hypotheses.

6. The deduction or exfoliation of the implications of the hypothesis.

Little need be added to our earlier discussion. Knowledge and imagination are both required for the proper deduction of the implications of a hypothesis. Ideally, we should seek for consequences which will follow *only* if the hypothesis is true, but this is not always possible. We also noted earlier that Step 5 may close the investigation; Step 6 and the remaining steps will then not occur.

7. Testing the hypothesis.

When consequences are predicted in Step 6, we proceed to test for the presence or absence of these consequences. This is the role of Step 7. We make further observations, i.e., we observe to see whether the consequences do or do not in fact occur. We may perform an experiment in our test, or we may let nature take her own course. An experiment, as Susan Stebbing has said, is simply "a deliberate observation in the light of a definite expectation as to what will be observed." An experiment often involves special forms of apparatus, but these are not indispensable. In any case both experimental and non-experimental observation are forms of observation.

8. Conclusion.

Step 6 states the consequences which follow from the hypothesis. When the test (Step 7) confirms these consequences and when we draw the conclusion that the hypothesis is true, we have an invalid syllogism which is "saved" by adding the word "probably." But when Step 7 negates the consequent of Step 6, the syllogism is a valid one. This gives us the rule that a negative experiment has a higher probative value than a positive one, but even a negative experiment can give us no more than probability. As noted earlier, we have no guarantee that our major premise was absolutely true, nor that our testing procedure was flawless, at least in complicated problems. Errors may have crept into our calculations, and relevant factors may not have been analyzed properly. An interesting example of a negative experiment which contained such errors is found in the experiments of Bishop Needham during the eighteenth century. At that time biologists were concerned with the question as to whether life can be generated spontaneously from non-living matter. Spallanzani, an Italian priest, performed experiments to prove the theory of biogenesis, i.e., that all living things have parents, including germs. He sterilized a liquid, put it into a sealed flask protected from the dusts of the surrounding air, and found that his liquid remained sterile. Unless it was exposed to the air it remained free of germs. Needham, an English priest, sought to disprove the theory of biogenesis. He boiled a liquid, thus sterilizing it, put it into a flask, and plugged the top tight with a cork. After a period of time he found germs in his flask. This appeared to him to be a convincing refutation of the theory of biogenesis, since if living things are reproduced only by other living things, there should have been no germs in his flask. But germs *were* present, so the theory appeared to be disproved. Spallanzani, however, showed that Needham's experiment was worthless since his flask had not been properly sealed. The germs were able to push their way through the porous cork into the flask.

The use of negative cases gives us a syllogism in which the consequent is denied. This type of reasoning is also used in the form of argument called the "Reductio ad Absurdum," in which we "reduce to the absurd," i.e., we prove a proposition by showing that its contradictory is absurd, or false. We take the contradictory of the theory we wish to prove, deduce its implications, show that these implications are absurd, and we have then disproved the contradictory of our original theory. If its contradictory is false, it must be true. As an example, suppose that we wish to prove that the moon is uninhabited. We proceed as follows:

1. Assume the contradictory of H, or H′, as true: The moon is inhabited.
2. Deduce the consequences of H′: If the moon is inhabited, then its creatures live without air. (These implications are based upon our knowledge.)

3. It is impossible for living creatures to live without air. (Denies the consequent.)
4. Therefore, H' must be false.
5. Therefore, H must be true (for H is the contradictory of H').

Note that Steps 1–4 in this proof correspond to Steps 5–8 in our previous notation. The Reductio, of course, gives us no greater certainty than the certainty of the premises in Steps 2 and 3.

One final point. In some problems, several different hypotheses may occur to the mind of the scientist. Step 5 will then be formulated as an alternative proposition, e.g., "The cause of X is either A, or B, or C, or D." We then deduce the implications of each, and test each. If all but one are eliminated, the remaining hypothesis is probably the cause. This is not conclusive proof unless we can be certain that the four hypotheses exhaust all the possibilities, i.e., that no other hypothesis can explain the facts, in addition to the other reservations which are required.

Section V: Supplementary Comments on the Eight Steps

The aim of our eight-step analysis is not psychological analysis but logical analysis. We have sought to clarify the roles of observation, hypothesis, deduction, and testing in the solution of scientific problems. Our analysis may not be exemplified in every detail in any given case of scientific thinking. There may be a telescoping of the steps, as in the *Citadel* case, and new variations may be added, but in general these eight steps will appear. In poetry, similarly, we find that few poets adhere with rigidity to a given rhythmical pattern, such as an iambic pentameter. This may be the basic rhythm, but the meaning of the words in a line of verse often requires accents which depart from the strict scanning of the meter. But underlying the departures, there is a definite pattern. So it is with scientific method.

Our pattern requires certain modifications when we deal with purely rational problems, as in mathematics, chess, or puzzles. The important thing in such problems is the suggestion of hypotheses and the mental elaboration of their implications. Observation is incidental to deduction. We deduce consequences in the mind and accept or reject these implications.

Some examples: In a chess game, I explore the possibilities. I wish to capture my opponent's Queen. It occurs to me that I can attack successfully if I move my knight to KB5. Now, if I move my knight, then he will move here, and I will then move there, and he will do this, and I will do that, etc. Then I note that my position will be weakened, without compensating gains, and try another possibility. Puzzles and "brain-twisters" give us similar types of problems. Suppose we had the following problem presented to us:

$$(A) \quad . \qquad . \quad (B)$$
$$. \qquad . \qquad .$$
$$(C) \quad . \qquad . \quad (D)$$

Copy these dots on a sheet of paper, ignoring the letters. Then draw four straight lines, without removing your pencil from the paper, and without retracing any lines, so that the lines will go through all of the nine dots. The reader will now try out various hypotheses, by the trial-and-error method, and may shortly conclude that all of the obvious suggestions are impossible. A sense of defeat is typical at this point. The reader may now be given a helpful hint: The instructions permit a line to extend out beyond a series of dots. This hint suggests new hypotheses. But there are no rules which will guarantee success in working out such problems. Imagination in selecting fertile hypotheses is of the essence. But we must also persist in trying out new hypotheses and deducing the consequences of each possibility. (The solution of our problem will now be given: Start at the dot near A, and run the line out beyond B. Then come back through the middle dot between B-D and the middle dot between C-D to a point below C. Then up to A and back to D through the center dot.)

Our general pattern may be varied in yet another way. In working out a problem we may find that new problems are generated by our investigations. We will then have a primary problem and subsidiary problems. When a patient visits a physician, the physician's primary problem is that of curing the patient. But before the physician can formulate a hypothesis for the cure, he must diagnose the patient's illness. This becomes the subsidiary problem, and the physician must work through the eight steps toward a solution of this problem. The solution of the problem of diagnosis then becomes the third step in the primary problem of cure. In this case the subsidiary problem appears in connection with the *observation* of the relevant facts.

The subsidiary problem may also occur at other stages, as in the *proper formulation* of the *hypothesis*. Let us use a famous murder mystery as our example. A dead child was found in a field outside of a large city. A preliminary problem concerned the cause of death. The hypothesis of murder was easily verified by the condition of the body. The next problem is the primary one: Who committed the murder? We shall now set forth the steps in the solution of this problem, omitting some of them for simplification:

2. Primary problem: Who committed the murder?
3. Observation: A clue is found in a pair of glasses.
5. Hypothesis: The owner of the glasses is the murderer. But a hypothesis must be specific, and so we take up a subsidiary problem:
   2. Who is the owner of the glasses?
   3. Observation: Careful examination of the type and make gives us the name of the manufacturer. The manufacturer informs us as to the dealers who handle these glasses in the vicinity of the murder. A list of customers is then obtained: A, B, C, D, etc.
   5. Hypothesis: Either A, B, C, D is the owner of these glasses.
   6. If D was the owner, then he was in the woods on the day of the murder. (We assume that we have eliminated A, B, and C)
   7. D was in the woods.
   8. D is probably the owner of these glasses.
5. The hypothesis is restated: D is the murderer.
6. Deducing the implications: If D is the murderer, then fur-

ther incriminating evidence will be found connecting D with the murder.

7. Testing the hypothesis: We find such incriminating evidence.

8. Conclusion: D is (probably) the murderer.

Similarly, the problem of *verification* may raise a subsidiary problem. A classical example of an ingenious experiment which verified an important hypothesis in physics will be found in Galileo's *Two New Sciences* (Northwestern University Press). Galileo (1564–1642), the great Italian physicist, was interested in the fall of bodies through space. His famous experiment, in which he dropped weights from the top of the Leaning Tower of Pisa, showed that the speed with which bodies fall to the earth does not depend upon their weight, provided that we neglect the resistance of the air. He also knew that the speed of falling bodies increases as they approach the earth. He assumed that the increase in speed occurred in accordance with a general law of nature. He now became interested in the manner in which the change of speed occurs, i.e., just what is the law of a falling body? Two suggestions came to his mind. The first was that the speed increased with the *space* traveled, i.e., that the speed was proportional to the distance a body falls through space. (The greater the distance, the greater the speed.) He rejected this hypothesis. He then tried a second suggestion, that the speed varied with the *time* of the fall, so that the change in velocity would be proportional to the time interval. He deduced the consequences of this hypothesis and found that they were not self-contradictory. He then sought to test the new hypothesis, which he formulated as follows: The speed of a falling body increases in direct proportion to the time of the fall. But it was impossible for him to test this hypothesis directly, for he had no instruments with which to measure the speed of fall. He then deduced the implication that the *distance* fallen would be proportional to the square of the time taken. In other words, the distance traversed after two seconds should be four times as great as after one second; after three seconds, nine times as great, and so on. But how was he to test this consequence? He then set up two kinds of apparatus with which he could measure distance and time. He set up an inclined plane, with a smooth groove, and rolled a ball down the groove. For the measurement of time, he used a large vessel of water, which trickled through a pipe into a small glass. He then permitted the ball to roll one quarter of the length of the incline and measured the time elapsed by the quantity of water which flowed into the glass. The ball was then rolled the full length of the incline, and now there was twice the former amount of water in the glass. In other words, in double the time there was four times as much distance. In this way he discovered that "the spaces traversed were to each other as the squares of the times." When the time factor was multiplied by three, the space factor was multiplied by nine, and similarly for all other quantities.

Section VI: The Problem of Verification in History and the Law Courts

In this section we shall consider some problems in assessing the value of evidence in historical investigations. We shall also consider the problem of proving the guilt of an accused person in a court of law, since this, too, is a historical investigation involving the truth of propositions concerning past events.

In general, the historian is concerned with three types of logical problems. He must verify specific propositions concerning specific events: Did Caesar cross the Rubicon? He seeks for explanations of important events: Why did the British government go to such lengths to appease Hitler? What were the fundamental causes of the Revolutionary, Civil, and World Wars? A third problem is the search for a general law of history. The Marxian thesis that economic or materialistic causes are responsible for the fundamental happenings of history is an example of one hypothesis in the last field. We shall be concerned, in what follows, with the first problem, concerning the verification of specific propositions. We shall simply note that the method of "proof" in the two latter fields usually involves the principle of converging evidence, and the search for a pattern of explanation which will place the relevant facts in an intelligible order. Though conclusive proof for such explanations is an unattainable ideal, each hypothesis will usually be of value in pointing to some significant factor which might otherwise have been overlooked. Limited as the theory of economic determinism may be in explaining history, it has nevertheless revealed a causative factor which is of great importance in countless situations.

Let us now turn to propositions concerning specific events in the past. The first obvious point is that the past cannot be inspected directly. Each past event is a unique event which cannot be repeated again in exactly the same form. The problem is: Did such and such an event occur? The only basis on which we can answer this question is in terms of the evidence. Every such proposition must be regarded as a hypothesis, as a candidate for proof, and will have a varying degree of probability depending upon the quality and quantity of the evidence which supports it. Authority, "what everybody knows," and rumor are not evidence. How does the historian assess his evidence in proving such hypotheses?

The historian uses observation of the remains of the past— monuments, inscriptions, and other tangible objects. He also finds the writings of past men and women who were witnesses of events or who reported hearing about such events. These reports constitute the memory of the human race. The Greeks rightly made Memory the muse of history. Two important types of problems arise when we consider the writings of the past. The first question is: Is the document genuine, i.e., was it written by the person purporting to have written it? The original document may have disappeared, and we must use a copy. Is the copy a correct one? The second question concerns the competence of the witness: Who is the witness? Was he a reliable person who could be trusted to tell the truth? Even if we grant that he was not a liar, did he have special biases which might distort his judgment and lead him to give distorted testimony? Was he a competent observer who would be likely to give an accurate story of what he witnessed? To what extent do independent witnesses give substantially similar accounts of the same events? Was the witness suggestible, so that he would be likely to be easily led by a questioner? And so on.

Was Jonah a historical character? Can we be absolutely certain of his existence because he is mentioned in the Bible? Can the Bible be mistaken in this particular instance? What is the evidence on which you base your judgment? According to the Moslems, the Koran was revealed to Mohammed by God, "sent down" through the Angel Gabriel, thus making him the true and final prophet of God's will. The pious Mohammedans are absolutely certain that this event occurred, but the historian asks, What is the evidence, and how reliable is it? The Mohammedans also report many miracles, i.e., violations of the natural order of cause and effect in the world. Such reports are based upon the testimony of witnesses, but the belief that this testimony is true is a hypothesis, which must be supported by adequate evidence. One must also consider other hypotheses, e.g., that the witness was mistaken. The scientific thinker judges the evidential value of such hypotheses by the principle of probabilities. Which is the more likely, that the witness was mistaken or that the miracle occurred? The scientist does not dogmatically deny the occurrence of unusual events merely because they do not fit into his preconceived theories, but he asks for the evidence in each case. It is, of course, not strange that most people believe in the miracles of their own religions and disbelieve in those of the other fellow's, since religion calls forth our deepest emotions. But the scientific attitude is that the occurrence of historical events should be judged on the basis of reason and logic, rather than emotion.

Similar problems occur in the law court during investigations into criminal charges. The lawyer distinguishes two kinds of evidence: circumstantial evidence and the testimony of witnesses. Circumstantial evidence refers to evidence associating an individual with a crime, such as fingerprints, part of his clothing, his possession of the loot, and so on. Neither type of evidence can give more than probability of varying degrees. Let us look at an example of circumstantial evidence. A streetcar conductor was robbed and murdered. A mask and hood were found at the scene of the crime. The police suspected that N was the murderer, for the following reasons: N was identified by a witness as having been seen running away from the locality of the crime shortly after it presumably occurred. When the police searched his room they found thread of the same kind as that in the mask. They also found hair-tonic having the same odor as that of the hood. Four days after the murder, N attempted to leave town without bothering to collect his unpaid wages from his employer. People who knew him told the police that he had mentioned the possibility of his holding up a streetcar conductor. The watchman in the plant where he worked reported that his .32 caliber revolver, the type with which the conductor was killed, was missing for several days before the murder was committed. N's shift at the plant started at 6 P.M., but on the night of the murder he did not report until 1:15 A.M. N's defence was that he had decided to take a walk on the night in question; that when he was near the scene of the crime a man ran by saying that there had been a murder, and so he ran too. Now, the evidence in this case is very powerful and convincing, and establishes a high probability of N's guilt, but it does not give certainty. It is *possible* that N was innocent, despite this evidence, i.e., even if all the facts cited are true. We should remember, too, that circumstantial evidence is based upon the reports of investigators, and these reports may be mistaken. Evidence may even be "planted." But when we consider the evidential value of testimonial evidence we also find only probabilities, not absolute certainty. Witnesses may be honestly mistaken, and they may also commit perjury. Even the confessions of individuals are subject to some doubt. Innocent persons have "confessed" in order to shield others; confessions may be extorted by illegal means, such as torture or drugs; and there are always the neurotics who rush in to confess to sensational crimes.

In a trial-at-law a witness presents his testimony on "direct" examination. His testimony is then subject to cross-examination. A witness is, in general, permitted to testify only as to matters which he himself saw or heard. Hearsay evidence, i.e., statements made on the basis of what someone told the witness are excluded, not because such evidence is irrelevant, but because it does not permit of the safeguard of cross-examination. Witnesses may also be called to throw doubt on the credibility of a witness' testimony.

Probability, in other words, is all that can be hoped for, whichever type of evidence is used. The question is, How good is the evidence (whether it be circumstantial or testimonial)? Though laymen hold circumstantial evidence in suspicion, lawyers and logicians are more acutely aware of the possibilities of error in testimony. But neither type should be esteemed or disparaged in a wholesale manner. Further, if certainty of proof were required, few, if any, accused persons could be convicted. We should also note that the courts establish different standards of proof for civil and criminal cases. In a civil case, all that is required is that one party prove his case by a preponderance of the evidence. But in a criminal charge, the state must prove a person guilty "beyond a reasonable doubt." This means that no "reasonable man" would doubt that the accused has been proved guilty. The hypothesis, in other words, must have a very high probability before conviction is justified. Certainty is not required.

Exercises

A. *The Analysis of Scientific Thinking: The Eight Steps.*

The following account of the discovery of the cause of pellagra by Dr. Joseph Goldberger is based upon the story as told in Chapter 11 of Paul de Kruif's *Hunger Fighters* (Harcourt, Brace and Co.). De Kruif's material is freely adapted in what follows.

In the second decade of the twentieth century an old disease called "pellagra" had become epidemic in the southern states. The disease was also endemic, i.e., its occurrence was confined to some localities and not others. One village might be affected; a neighboring one not. Pellagra is characterized by gastric disturbances, skin eruptions, and nervous derangement. Medical opinion at the time inclined to the belief that the disease was caused by an unknown microbe. Dr. Goldberger was sent to Mississippi by the U. S. Health Service to find a way of eliminating the disease. His work in discovering the cause of pellagra was quite remarkable, especially in view of the fact that he worked without the aid of specialized laboratory equipment.

Goldberger's problem: What is the cause of pellagra? He observed the fact that the sufferers were always in contact with other victims. Since this is the consequence which would be expected if the disease were caused by microbes, i.e., it would be "catching," he adopted the tentative hypothesis that the disease was caused in this manner. He then reasoned that if microbes were the cause, persons in close contact with the victims should catch the disease. But in the first hospital he visited, he found that the orderlies, nurses, and doctors who were in close contact with the victims never caught the disease. This led him to discard the hypothesis that the disease was caused by germs. It was now necessary to find and try out another hypothesis. He continued his observations. He found that only the poor suffered from the disease. He noted that the victims' diet consisted of corn-meal mush, hominy grits, and like foods, but practically no milk or fresh meat. On one occasion, while visiting an orphanage, he noted that only the children in the 6–12 age group had the disease. In investigating this point he found that the children under six were given milk and the children over twelve were fed meat. The orphanage's funds were limited, so they skimped on the food of the 6–12 group, who were too young to work (and so did not "deserve" meat) and who were beyond the "baby" stage, the stage when milk was regarded as essential. This fact suggested the hypothesis that a diet lacking in milk and fresh meat was the cause of the disease. He then reasoned out the consequences of this hypothesis, namely, that remedying these deficiencies in diet would cure the disease. He secured a sufficient amount of milk and fresh meat for the children at the orphanage. All cases of pellagra disappeared.

INSTRUCTIONS:
Analyze this account in terms of the eight-step analysis. Two complete analyses will be required: first, of the discarded hypothesis, and then of the confirmed one.

B. *Hypotheses in Criminal Cases: Circumstantial Evidence.*

In 1932 the Lindbergh baby was kidnapped and murdered. Bruno Richard Hauptmann was arrested after paying for gasoline at a filling station with a banknote which had been part of the $50,000 ransom. During his trial and after the verdict of "guilty," Hauptmann protested his absolute innocence, and insisted, even at the very last moment before he was executed, that he had had nothing to do with the crime. He also asserted that he had no knowledge of any person or persons who may have been involved in the crime. The evidence against him was purely circumstantial. No witnesses testified to having seen him at or near the scene of the crime when it occurred. Following are some of the items of circumstantial evidence presented by the prosecution to prove his guilt:

1. When arrested, Hauptmann had $20 of the ransom money in his pockets, and concealed under a board in his garage was an additional $14,600. (His defence was that this money, identified as the ransom money, had been left in his possession for safe keeping by a friend named Isador Fisch, just before Fisch left for Europe, where he died.)

2. Hauptmann had been in the habit of keeping a personal financial record up to the time of the kidnapping. This record showed that he possessed about $5000 in 1932, this amount including a used car and some stock. Federal agents accounted for expenditures of $35,000 after the ransom money had been paid. Hauptmann opened accounts with several stockbrokers and lost about $9000 in the stock market. He bought a new car, sent his wife to Germany, and went to Florida and on hunting trips. He quit his job during March, when the kidnapping occurred, and his wife quit her job in a bakery shortly thereafter. During the period of these large expenditures he was unemployed.

3. The kidnapper's ransom notes indicated that the author was a German, as was he. An expert identified the ransom notes as being in Hauptmann's handwriting.

4. The handwriting on a note left in the nursery after the kidnapping was the same as that of the ransom notes. These notes were sent to Dr. J. F. Condon, a retired school-principal, who acted as the intermediary. Dr. Condon arranged to meet the writer of the notes in a cemetery, where he paid him the ransom money after receiving the baby's sleeping garment as proof that the recipient of the money was the kidnapper.

5. Condon testified that Hauptmann was the man with whom he sat on a bench at the Woodlawn cemetery, and to whom he later paid the ransom at St. Raymond's cemetery. Lindbergh identified Hauptmann's voice as that of the man in the latter cemetery.

6. The lumber used to make the kidnap ladder was traced to the National Mill Work and Lumber Co., in the Bronx. Hauptmann had worked there, and bought lumber there. He was an expert carpenter. Part of the ladder was also made from wood ripped from his attic floor.

7. The nails used in the ladder were found to have the same microscopic defects as nails found in Hauptmann's home.

8. Paper like that of the ransom notes was found in his home.

9. The print of a wrapped foot outside the Lindbergh home was similar to Hauptmann's footprint. So was the footprint of the man who received the ransom.

10. Ground marks beneath the baby's bedroom indicated that the kidnapper may have injured his leg. Hauptmann walked with a cane for a few weeks after the crime, and was treated by a doctor later.

11. He worked near the Lindbergh home shortly before the kidnapping.

12. An automobile seen near the Lindbergh home shortly before the kidnapping was of the same make, color, and model as Hauptmann's.

13. A taxi driver identified Hauptmann as the man who gave him $1 to deliver a note to Dr. Condon.

14. He revealed a reluctance to answer questions, and gave surly responses, such as "Leave me alone."

15. He had a criminal record in Germany before coming to the United States.

16. In his testimony he stated that he lent $2000 to Fisch. Previously he had said that Fisch gave him the ransom money for safe keeping.

17. Dr. Condon's telephone number and address were written on the back of a closet door in his home. When asked where he got the number, he said that he copied it from an ad in a newspaper. It had never been published.

18. The number of a ransom bill was also found on the back of a closet door. He said that this number had been given him by Fisch, at a time before the time he had previously said that he had met Fisch.

Questions:

1. If you were a member of the jury, would you regard the evidence as proving Hauptmann guilty beyond a reasonable doubt?

2. Exhibit the steps in problem-solving from the point of view of the police, from the time the first clue is found, until their entire dossier has been built up.

3. Show why, from the point of view of the jury, the hypothesis that Hauptmann is guilty need only account for the evidence which is presented to it.

4. Which items of the evidence did you consider most cogent?

5. Show how this case illustrates the principle of "the convergence of evidence."

C. *Hypothesis in Criminal Cases: Testimonial Evidence (The Sacco-Vanzetti Case).*

This case was a *cause célèbre* during the 1920's. Two anarchists named Sacco and Vanzetti were convicted of murdering Parmenter and Berardelli in a payroll robbery. They pleaded their complete innocence. The trial and conviction occurred during the so-called "Red Hysteria" in 1919. Following are some excerpts from Justice Felix Frankfurter's book *The Case of Sacco and Vanzetti* (Little, Brown and Company, 1927):

So far as the crime is concerned we are dealing with a conventional case of payroll robbery resulting in murder. At the trial the killing of Parmenter and Berardelli was undisputed. The only issue was the identity of the murderers. Were Sacco and Vanzetti two of the assailants of Parmenter and Berardelli, or were they not? This was the beginning and the end of the inquiry at the trial; this is the beginning and the end of any judgment now on the guilt or innocence of these men. . . .

The character of the testimony of the five witnesses who definitely identified Sacco as in the car or on the spot of the murder demands critical attention.

Splaine and Devlin were working together on the second floor of the Slater and Morrill factory, with windows giving on the railroad crossing. Both heard the shot, ran to the window, and saw an automobile crossing the tracks. Splaine's identification of Sacco, as one of the occupants of this escaping car, was one of the chief reliances of the prosecution. Splaine, viewing the scene from a distance of from 60 to 80 ft. saw a man previously unknown to her, in a car traveling at the rate of from 15 to 18 miles per hour; she saw him only for a distance of about 30 feet, that is to say, for from one and a half to three seconds; and yet she testified:

"The man that appeared between the back of the front seat and the back seat was a man slightly taller than the witness. He weighed possibly from 140 to 145 pounds. He was muscular, an active looking man. His left hand was a good sized hand, a hand that denoted strength."

Q.—"So that the hand you said you saw where?" A.—"The left hand, that was placed on the back of the front seat, on the back of the front seat. He had a gray, what I thought was a shirt,—had a grayish, like navy color, and the face was, what we would call a clear-cut, clean-cut face. Though here (indicating) was a little narrow, just a little narrow. The forehead was high. The hair was brushed back and it was between, I should think, two inches and two and one-half inches in length and had dark eyebrows, but the complexion was a white, peculiar white that looked greenish." (R. 114–5.)

Q.—Is that the same man you saw at Brockton? *A.*—It is.
Q.—Are you sure? *A.*—Positive.

The startling acuity of Splaine's vision was in fact the product of a year's reflection. Immediately after Sacco's arrest the police, in violation of approved police methods for the identification of suspects, brought Sacco alone into Splaine's presence. (R. 121, 130.) Then followed in about three weeks the preliminary hearing at which Sacco and Vanzetti were bound over for the grand jury. At this hearing Splaine was unable to identify Sacco:

Q.—"You don't feel certain enough in your position to say he is the man?" *A.*—"I don't think my opportunity afforded me the right to say he is the man." (R. 132.)

When confronted with this contradiction between her uncertainty forty days after her observation and her certainty more than a year after her observation, she first took refuge in a claim of inaccuracy in the transcript of the stenographer's minutes. This charge she later withdrew and finally maintained:

"From the observation I had of him in the Quincy Court and the comparison of the man I saw in the machine, on reflection I was sure he was the same man." (R. 133.)

Questions:
1. (The evidence cited here is only a fraction of the total.) How convincing do you regard the testimony of Mary Splaine?
2. What conclusions, if any, do you draw with respect to the comparative value of circumstantial evidence and testimony?
3. Do you have an opinion on the probable guilt or innocence of these men? On what evidence is your opinion based?

D. *The Problem of Evolution.*

What is the origin of all the myriad forms of life found on the earth? The theory of evolution holds that during countless ages of development, all forms of life originated by descent through gradual or abrupt modifications from earlier forms which trace back to the most rudimentary organisms. The theory of "special creation" holds that all of the living beings were created by God in their present forms, the present species being lineal descendants of the originally created species.

The evolutionist presents evidence from various fields of investigation, briefly summarized as follows:

1. Paleontology: Rocks contain fossils. The "record of the rocks" reveals that the oldest rocks show only the more elementary forms of life. The older fossil-bearing rocks contain only fishes and plants. As we proceed through the later rock strata we find a greater complexity and variety of living forms. The evolutionist also notes the fact that no fossil has ever been found in a "wrong" rock stratum.

2. Geographical distribution: Isolated regions show striking differences in their forms of life, e.g., the Australian kangaroo.

3. Comparative anatomy: There are anatomical similarities in various large groups of living creatures. The arms of man, the forelegs of the dog and frog, the wings of birds are all based on the same structures. The blood of related species, as man and the ape, shows chemical resemblances.

4. Embryology: "Ontogeny recapitulates phylogeny." This means that the stages in the development of an individual organism "summarize" the historical stages in the development of the species. Thus some warm-blooded animals pass through the "fish stage" in their embryonic development.

5. Vestigial organs: Human beings and other living things have organs which are vestigial, i.e., of no use today, but presumably inherited from evolutionary ancestors who had them and found them useful. The vermiform appendix is the most striking example.

6. Breeding: By cross and selective breeding, animals and plants are produced which differ greatly from previously known varieties.

The argument of the special creationist is positive and negative. Positively, that it is in accordance with the Word of God as revealed in the Book of Genesis. Negatively, that evolution is "incredible," or that its proof is not conclusive. He points to various gaps in the evolutionary record, to the fact that breeding has not produced a new species, and so on.

Questions:
1. Which of the two rival theories do you regard as the more probable? Why?
2. Do you regard evolution as a theory or a fact? Why?

3. How does the special creationist account for the various types of evidence presented by the evolutionist? In this respect, which of the two hypotheses is the simpler?

4. "Special creationists use a double standard of criticism; a severe one for the theory of evolution, and an uncritical one for their own theory." Comment on this statement.

E. Did Shakespeare Write "Shakespeare's Plays"?

Very little is known concerning the life of William Shakespeare. The available facts, however, indicate that he was a man of lowly origin and scant schooling. It has therefore been regarded as incredible that such a man could have written those plays which reveal as remarkable a genius as the world has ever known. Controversies over the authorship of the plays have raged for many years. From time to time the names of other writers have been suggested for the honor of authorship, such as Sir Francis Bacon, Marlowe, Raleigh, and others. The most recent candidate for the honor is one Edward de Vere, the 17th Earl of Oxford. The case for de Vere has been presented by Louis P. Bénézet, in his *Shakspere, Shakespeare, and de Vere* (Granite State Press, 1937).* Bénézet holds that the author of these plays must have been a man with certain characteristics. The writer of the plays, he says, must have been (1) a student of the classics, (2) an aristocrat of feudal ancestry, (3) a warrior, (4) one versed in the law, (5) one with skill in music, (6) one familiar with Italy and France, (7) a member of the Red Rose family, (8) one careless of money, (9) one who was known to be a poet aside from the "Works of Shakespeare," (10) one closely associated with plays and players, (11) one the facts of whose life fit with the self-revelations of the sonnets, (12) one who was known to be a playwright apart from the "Works," (13) one who "bore the canopy," and (14) one whose associations with the Earl of Southampton were so close that he would feel free to dedicate works to him.

The problem: Who wrote these plays? There are several hypotheses. The hypothesis that a given individual is the author, says Bénézet, implies that he had the fourteen characteristics. Bénézet holds that few of these requirements fit Bacon. In Shakespeare's case, if the author of the plays is regarded as the William Shakespeare who died in Stratford-on-Avon in 1616, only No. 10 may hold, he contends. But he says

---

* Discussed in greater detail by Frye and Levi, *op. cit.,* Chapter XVII.

that all fourteen requirements are fulfilled by de Vere, and he therefore regards that hypothesis as established. A strong point in de Vere's favor is the fact that he was a poet and that his extant poetry is written in a style bearing many similarities to the style of the Shakespearean sonnets. To the question, why did he not sign his name to the plays?, Bénézet cites the aristocratic conventions of the time that practically prohibited individuals of Oxford's rank from acknowledging that they published verse and plays.

Other reasons given for rejecting Shakespeare's authorship are the facts that his death appeared to have attracted no notice in Stratford or in London, and that the Shakespeare who died in Stratford requested that the following lines be engraved on his tomb:

Good friend for Iesus sake forbeare
To digg the dust encloased heare
Blest be ye man yt spares thes stones
And curst be he yt moves my bones

These lines do not bear the mark of genius.

On the other side of the case we may cite Ben Jonson's remark, in the dedicatory poem to the First Folio of 1623, that "he loved Shakespeare this side of idolatry." Ben Jonson was the most powerful literary figure among Shakespeare's contemporaries.

Questions:
1. Show how Bénézet uses the principle of the convergence of evidence.
2. Do you regard his hypothesis as verified in terms of the evidence? Why, or why not?
3. If your answer to the last question is negative, whom do you regard as the author of Shakespeare's plays? Why?

F. *A Historical Problem.*

A historian, studying the policies of the Communist party of the United States, finds the following facts: After the first world war until 1935 the party vigorously attacked American "capitalists" and all other political groups, including liberals, progressives, and non-communist radicals. The moderate Socialists were denounced as "social fascists" and referred to as "Enemy No. 1" as late as 1933–4. In 1933 Hitler came to power in Germany and destroyed the German Communist party. In

1935 the American Communists decided to collaborate with Socialists and other democratic parties in a "Popular Front" against Nazi-ism and Fascism. The Catholic Church was also invited to join the united front. This policy was coincident with the same policy adopted by the Communist International at its 1935 Congress. On August 23, 1939 the Soviet Union and Nazi Germany signed a non-aggression pact, and the Soviet Union thenceforth gave Germany diplomatic support in its war against the western powers. The American Communists ceased their campaign against fascism and sought to prevent American aid to Britain and France in their war against Hitler. They denounced as "war-mongers" those who wished to aid England and France in what the Communists referred to as the "imperialist war." On June 22, 1941 German armies invaded Russia. Thereafter the Communists denounced fascism and gave their whole-hearted support to the American war effort in what they called "the people's war." The leader of the American Communist party, Mr. Earl Browder, now defended American "big business" against criticism from liberal groups, and in his book *Teheran* (International Publishers 1944), he pledged the support of the Communists to the capitalistic system in the United States: "We declare in advance our understanding that the democratic-progressive camp to which we adhere will adopt the defence of 'free enterprise,' that we understand this term as a synonym for capitalism as it exists in our country, and that we will not oppose it nor put forth any counter-slogans."

In 1946 the American Communists attacked the leaders of the United States and its capitalistic system, denouncing them as the enemies of mankind.

Questions:
1. Which hypothesis would you suggest as the best explanation for the twistings and turnings or the "divergations and tergiversations" of the policies of the American Communist party during these years? How probable do you regard your hypothesis? Can you suggest a second hypothesis which would also explain the known facts?
2. Did you use the principle of converging evidence? Can the method of prediction be used in problems such as this one?
3. Can a problem such as this one be explained by the theory of "economic determinism," which holds that all political decisions are based upon economic factors? Can this theory predict an event before it occurs?

G. *The Problem of Relevant Evidence in Historical Problems.*

If you were interested in finding the answers to the following questions, what types of evidence would you consider relevant?

1. Did Moses lead the Jews out of Egypt?
2. Did Moses write the Pentateuch (the first five books of the Old Testament)?
3. Was Jesus a historical character?
4. Did Homer write the *Iliad* and the *Odyssey?*
5. Was Abraham Lincoln assassinated by John Wilkes Booth?
6. Is the Mohammedan religion the true religion for all mankind?
7. Is Hitler alive?

H. *Prove the following propositions by using the Reductio ad Absurdum method:*

1. The earth has the shape of a spheroid.
2. President Truman was not in league with Stalin.
3. The interests of capital and labor are not identical.
4. The rule "Thou shalt not lie" should not be followed without any exceptions whatsoever.
5. Wall Street bankers did not dictate income tax legislation.

Chapter 16

CAUSE AND EFFECT: THE "EXPERIMENTAL METHODS"

Section I: The Significance of Causal Analysis

When the ancient poet Virgil said, "Happy is he who knows the causes of things," he was in agreement with the more modern Sir Francis Bacon who proclaimed that "Knowledge is power." For, in large measure, man's power and control over nature has its origin in man's understanding of the causal connections of natural events. It is unnecessary to catalogue the achievements of modern science, including nuclear fission, to prove the importance of knowing the causes of things. Suffice it to say that our knowledge that germs are a cause of diseases has enabled us to come near to eliminating diseases such as tuberculosis; and that it is through knowing causes that we can often produce at will such effects as we consider desirable. Our search for that better world that will meet the heart's desire depends in great part on our knowing the appropriate causal patterns. If we knew the causes of cancer, business depressions, and war we might make progress in eliminating these evils.

So much for the importance of understanding the causal relation. Before we proceed, let us consider a basic question: Do all things have causes? If a motorist should suddenly hear an unfamiliar ticking sound in the motor of his car while cruising on a highway, his immediate response would be that something is wrong, that *something is responsible* for the unfamiliar noise. Our motorist has made the assumption that there is a cause of the noise. Now, this assumption, that nothing happens without a cause, is a basic assumption of rational thinking. We assume the existence of a world in which invariant order prevails, in which things "don't just happen by themselves." We say that there must be a reason for everything; even though we don't know what the reason is. Science does not know the cause of cancer, but that there is some cause for cancer is beyond doubt. We may despair of ever unravelling the causes of such a complex event as war, but even when we despair of finding an explanation we are certain that such causes must be present.

We assume then, that something is responsible for every event in experience, that nothing happens without a reason. But it was not always thus. The Greeks did not assume that every event has a cause. Aristotle believed that Nature's laws were not uniform, that some things occurred by mere "chance," that Nature acted in a certain way only "for the most part." A. N. Whitehead, in *Science and the Modern World,* proposes the interesting thesis that our modern scientific view of universal causation and invariant law is due to the influence of mediaeval theology. The theologians believed that there was a sufficient reason for every smallest detail in the universe, since an omniscient, omnipresent, and omnipotent God would let nothing— even the fall of a sparrow—happen except in accordance with His Will. Whitehead argues that science adapted the theological view that all things have meaning and significance into the scientific assumption that there are natural causes for all events. But however the matter may be explained, modern science accepts the principle of "universal determinism," which simply means that every happening has a cause or reason, i.e., that everything happens because of some previous happening. "Chance" and "luck" are not regarded as objective aspects of the world which is pictured by science. It is not "luck" whether the coin falls heads or tails; its fall depends entirely on the velocity with which it is spun, the pressure of the air, etc. The word "chance" is simply a name for our ignorance of the precise conditions which are present. Further, if the deterministic view is true, then "free will" in human behavior is a myth, since human conduct also has its reasons or causes. Such, at any rate, is the assumption of the scientific psychologist.

A distinction between two types of causes may be noted here. In Plato's *Phaedo,* which describes the last hours of Socrates in his prison cell, Socrates discusses (among other matters) the problem of causation. For example, what was the cause of his sitting in his cell at that particular moment? Some philosophers, Socrates tells his friends, would say,

that I am now sitting here because my body is made up of bones and muscles . . . that I am able to lift my bones at the joints by the contraction or relaxation of the muscles, and this is why I am sitting here with my legs bent. They would have a similar explanation of my talking to you, in terms of air, sound and hearing . . . forgetting the real cause, which is that the Athenians saw fit to condemn me, and that I have thought it best to remain here and undergo my sentence. It may be said, indeed, that without bones and muscles and the other parts of the body, I cannot execute my purposes. But to say that I do as I do because of them, and that this is the way in which mind acts, and not from the choice of the best, is a very careless and idle mode of speaking. I wonder that they cannot distinguish the cause from the condition.

Socrates is here distinguishing between physical causes and purpose-as-cause. Aristotle used the term "final cause" for purpose-as-cause. Why are you wherever you are now? Because your muscles contracted in a certain manner? Or because a purpose brought you here? That is the distinction which Socrates makes. This distinction warns us that when we are concerned with finding the causes of things we should not limit our search to some particular kind of cause, and exclude all others.

Section II: The Definition of "Cause" and "Condition"

Exactly what do we mean when we say that "Alcohol causes intoxication"? We mean that there exists an invariant relationship between the alcohol and intoxication such that, upon the occurrence of imbibing the alcohol (under specified conditions and in appropriate quantities) intoxication will invariably follow.

To begin with, we shall distinguish the term "condition" from that of "cause." There are two types of conditions: necessary and sufficient. A necessary condition is an event or circumstance which must be present in order to get a certain result or effect, but which is not sufficient in itself to "produce" the result. A lighted cigarette or match is thrown into a bush by a camper. A forest fire results. Was the match the cause? But sup-

pose that the leaves had been damp because of a recent rain.
There would then have been no fire. The dryness of the leaves,
we say, was a *necessary condition* for the fire; but dry leaves are
not a *sufficient* condition, by which we mean "sufficient to produce the result." But was the match sufficient to produce the
result, since it required dry leaves in order to act as the cause?
And what shall we say of oxygen in the air, which is also a
necessary condition for combustibility? Similarly, we say that
a people's dissatisfaction with its circumstances is a necessary
condition for revolution, but not sufficient to produce one. We
say that draughts are the cause of colds, but unless there were
germs in the body there would be no colds. It thus appears
to be important to distinguish conditions from causes. Let us
now define these terms more precisely.

a. Necessary conditions.

A necessary condition (symbolized by N) is one whose presence is necessary or indispensable to the occurrence of the effect
(symbolized by E). Without N, no E. Without germs, no colds.
If a person has a cold, then he has the germs. But germs are not
sufficient to cause a cold, for many persons have the germs without having colds. The relation of a necessary condition to an
effect is identical with that of the antecedent to the consequent
in an exclusive proposition: Only if N, then E. Since an exclusive proposition may be converted without limitation, we may
also say: If E, then N. There are four ways of showing the relationship of N to E:

(1) If N occurs (or is present), E may or may not occur. (N . . . E?)
(2) If N does not occur, E will not occur. $(-N . . . -E)$
(3) If E occurs, N must be present.   (E . . . N)
(4) If E does not occur, N may or may not be present.$(-E . . . N?)$

Note that when N is the necessary condition for E, N has the
relation of subimplicant to E, and E the relation of superimplicant to N.

b. Sufficient conditions.

A sufficient condition (symbolized by S) is one which can, by
itself, produce the result, or effect, but which need not be pres-

ent for the effect to occur. Thus, a specified quantity of cyanide of potassium is sufficient to produce death, but death may be produced by other causes, such as drowning. If S, then E. But this proposition cannot be converted into "If E, then S." S is now the superimplicant of E; E the subimplicant of S:

(1) If S is present, E occurs	(S......E)
(2) If S is absent, E may or may not occur.	(−S....E?)
(3) If E occurs, S may or may not have occurred.	(E......S?)
(4) If E does not occur, S did not occur.	(−E...−S)

Now, a *necessary* condition does not adequately satisfy our notion of "cause" (symbolized by C). A cause should fulfill the relationship "If C then E." Nor does the *sufficient* condition adequately fulfill this notion, for if C is the cause of E, then we should be able to say that if E occurs, C must have been present, or "If E, then C." The sufficient condition fulfills the former requirement, the necessary condition the latter one. By cause we mean "the necessary and sufficient condition." Before we analyze such conditions, however, it is necessary to call attention to a certain vagueness in the notion of a "sufficient" condition. We usually assume the presence of certain necessary conditions when we speak of sufficient conditions. Further, this notion leads to the concept of the "plurality of causes," i.e., that a given effect may have more than one cause, as when we say that death may have been caused by poison, or drowning, or many other things, but that any one of these things is sufficient to produce death. But this is perhaps a somewhat loose way of speaking, since the effect produced by poison is not identical with that produced by drowning. Instead of describing the effect in both cases by "D," should we not say "D^p" and "D^d"? Certainly a coroner finds different kinds of evidence in the two cases. In other words, the plurality of causes will hold only when we analyze the effect in a general rather than in a precise manner.

c. Necessary and sufficient conditions.

To fully satisfy our notion of the causal relationship we need a combination of necessary and sufficient conditions, so that we may say "If C then E, and if E then C," or "If and only if C, then E." "C," in other words, stands for *necessary and suffi-*

cient conditions. When C occurs, the effect will always follow, and where we find the effect we can be sure that C was present, viz.:

(1) C . . . . E
(2) −C . . . . −E
(3) E C
(4) −E . . . . −C

There are now no cases where C is present and E absent, or vice versa. When two events have this relationship, then C is the cause of E.

For illustration, let us return to the match and the forest fire. Was the match the cause? Can we say "If a match is thrown into underbrush, then a forest fire will always occur?" Obviously not. Without the necessary conditions of dry leaves, and certain atmospheric conditions, there would be no fire. The cause of the fire is the total combination of various factors and conditions, so that we should say, "A forest fire is caused by the igniting of dry leaves under specified meteorological conditions."

Thus causal analysis is a complicated affair and becomes a cumbersome undertaking when we try to determine the total set of conditions which are necessary and sufficient. This ideal is seldom attained in any but the physical sciences. In the social sciences the strict notion of "cause" is an almost impossible one to apply, and may appear to be an unattainable ideal. What are the causes of juvenile delinquency, or divorce, or wars? Think of the host of conditions which are necessary, though not sufficient, for such effects. And yet the interest in and the search for causes are indispensable, for we do seek to determine the conditions which will produce the effects we desire, or which will eliminate those we dislike. The notion that "something is responsible for every happening" is one of the foundations of the quest for knowledge.

In popular speech the word "cause" is often used in a looser, though quite adequate, manner. This is illustrated in the concept of legal responsibility, which would hold the careless camper responsible for the forest fire, since he "caused" it with his lighted match. Such statements presuppose, without making the presuppositions explicit, that all of the necessary conditions were present. Further, his act was one under human control; it was a sudden and dramatic change in the situation which existed prior to the fire, and it initiated the sequence of events which led to the occurrence of the fire. Note also that the legal sense of cause cannot be superseded by a "scientific" explanation in some cases, as in describing the cause of death in a fight. The average man will be satisfied by what he saw: "A series of severe blows to the head was the cause of death." The physician may describe the cause as "a coronary thrombosis induced by paralysis of the muscles of the heart." But the latter analysis does not answer the question as to legal responsibility.

An important distinction which must be noted here is that between "proximate" and "remote" causes. A stone falls from a building under construction and kills a passer-by below. What was the cause of his death? The stone? Gravitation? The strong wind which blew the stone off a ledge? Or a careless workman who left it there? The contractor who hired this careless workman? The architect who hired the contractor? The wife of the man who ordered the building in order to satisfy her social ambitions? The parents of the wife for bringing her into the world? This analysis, which reminds us of the old verses, "For the want of a horseshoe the battle was lost," points to the earlier conditions which are responsible for the present conditions, so that ultimately we must go back to the beginning of things for a complete causal explanation. In practice, however, we consider the proximate causes. We do not seek for the total set of conditions which lead to the effect, but only for those which, when present, will always bring the effect into existence.

Section III: The Discovery and Testing of Hypotheses of Causal Connection

The logician's primary interest is in the study of scientific techniques for *testing* hypotheses of causal connection, rather than in methods for *discovering* the causes of things. Discovery always requires imagination and sometimes scientific genius, but testing is more a matter of applying rules, though genius may be required in difficult cases. No rules or recipes will enable us to *find* the cause of cancer, for the best scientific brains in the biological sciences are baffled by this problem.

But by applying rules we can *test* hypotheses of causal connection, and say that certain factors are *not* the causes.

When the problem is one of discovering a causal connection, previous knowledge is a necessary condition for the suggestion of appropriate hypotheses. Thus only a trained physiologist can suggest a likely cause of cancer. But knowledge is not a sufficient condition. The great scientist may be likened to a great poet in his ability to see new analogies and connections in things supposedly unlike, for this ability is also the secret spring of the poet's metaphors. Thus, it took imagination to suspect that the pollen of ragweed was a cause of hay fever, that the "child-bed fever" of the mothers of new-born infants was due to germs brought to them by physicians who had just come from sick patients, and that the presence of germs in previously sterile liquids came from the dust of the outside air. Rules cannot substitute for the flash of insight of the scientific imagination.

In the instances cited, imagination was required to find the cause in order to remove it, and thus eliminate the effect. But the scientist also needs imagination to discover the causal relations which will *produce* a desirable effect. Here, also, hypotheses of causal relations are required. During the last war the United States could not import natural rubber and our scientists had to learn how to produce synthetic rubber. We also learned how to produce the atomic bomb. Edison worked painstakingly for a long period of time to find the proper filament for his incandescent bulb. Or scientists may seek for serums to combat diseases. Ehrlich tried out hundreds of hypotheses in search of his "magic bullet," a cure which would kill certain deadly microbes called trypanosomes. The six-hundred-and-sixth hypothesis worked, and "606" became the effective cure for the "disease of sin," syphilis. Ehrlich seems to have used the trial-and-error method, but imagination was also required in order to try out dioxy-diamino-arsenobenzol-dihydro-chloride from among the enormous number of substances the world contains.

We have drawn a distinction between the discovery and the testing of hypotheses of causal connection. The formulation of the hypothesis requires "discovery." After formulation, it must be tested. The discovery comes in Step 5 in our analysis of scientific thinking. Its implications drawn, we then test. Imagination is required for the proper application of all the steps, but in this chapter we shall study the rules for testing, since there are no rules for discovery. The problem of discovery is, What is the cause? In testing we ask, Is H the cause? In the typical problem of discovery we find that various hypotheses will be suggested: H, H', H'', or H'''. We then have a testing problem. We must eliminate the false hypotheses. If we eliminate all but one, this establishes some probability that it is the cause, but the formulation of the alternative hypotheses was not a product of the testing procedure.

One further point before we turn to the "experimental methods." A necessary and sufficient condition gives us the relations: CE, $-C-E$, EC, and $-E-C$. The formula states a *generalized relationship*. But usually we find causal relationships in particular instances. Thus, a man frequently suffers from a temporary swelling of his upper lip. His physician assures him that his lip is not infected, and tells him to watch his diet, since he may be allergic to certain foods. Subsequently his lip swells again. He thinks back to determine what he ate just prior to the swelling. It was X, he thinks. But he is not sure. On a later occasion he again eats X and awaits the swelling. It appears. He then avoids X, and the swelling never recurs. His hypothesis was verified by a prediction and may be regarded as well-confirmed. But may he *generalize* the causal relationship between X and "swelling of the lip"? Does this rule apply only to himself, or to others as well? Does it apply to himself under certain conditions or under all conditions? The problem of generalizing such connections involves the problem of "inductions," or generalizations, to be studied in the next chapter.

Section IV: The "Experimental Methods"

By "experimental methods" we mean certain rules for *testing* hypotheses of causal connection, or more generally, of any statements of invariant connections. "Experimental" here does not necessarily refer to laboratory experiments but to deliberate observations in testing hypotheses. Our discussion will be based upon the formulation of the experimental methods in John Stuart Mill's classic *System of Logic*. Mill worked out the "canons" of five methods, which he called the Methods of Agreement, Difference, Joint Method of Agreement and Difference,

Concomitant Variations, and Residues. We shall follow Mill's titles, except for the Joint Method, but we will restate his definitions and his treatment of the canons.

The basic form of the reasoning involved in these canons may be stated as follows: After a hypothesis of causal connection has been suggested, such as "C is the cause of E," we formulate the hypothetical proposition: If C is the cause of E, then we will find the basic relations CE, −C−E, EC, and −E−C. The tests are designed to determine whether these relations are present or not. If they are, it is probable that C is the cause of E; if not, we may eliminate C as a possible cause.

1. The Method of Agreement.

The following case will illustrate this method. An epidemic of typhoid fever occurs in a small town. Among the individuals stricken are A,B,C,D, and E. The Public Health authorities wish to discover the cause, and investigate the relevant events which occurred just prior to the occurrence of the disease. Such events, or conditions under which the effect occurred, and among which we may find the causal condition, will be called the "antecedent factors," symbolized by lower case letters. The following information was gathered:

ANTECEDENT FACTORS

INSTANCES	WATER SUPPLY	MILK	VEGETABLES	OYSTERS	EFFECT (TYPHOID)
Case A	Tap (a)	Dairy (d)	Yes (v)	Yes (o)	.....Occurred
Case B	Tap (a)	Condensed (c)	None	Yes (o)	.....Occurred
Case C	Bottled (b)	Dairy (d)	Yes (v)	Yes (o)	.....Occurred
Case D	Bottled (b)	Dairy (d)	Yes (v)	Yes (o)	.....Occurred
Case E	Tap (a)	None	Yes (v)	Yes (o)	.....Occurred

To simplify our discussion of this case we shall gather the symbols in the table:

$$
\begin{array}{llllll}
\text{A.} & a & d & v & o & \ldots\ldots & E \\
\text{B.} & a & c & & o & \ldots\ldots & E \\
\text{C.} & b & d & v & o & \ldots\ldots & E \\
\text{D.} & b & d & v & o & \ldots\ldots & E \\
\text{E.} & a & & v & o & \ldots\ldots & E \\
\end{array}
$$

(The *effect* also occurs in a contextual situation, but we shall ignore such elements in order to simplify the problem.)

Note that previous knowledge was necessary for the gathering of the items classified in the table, i.e., that the cause of the typhoid might be found in factors such as a,b,c,d,v, or o. No cognizance was taken of the types of clothing worn by these individuals, nor of their occupations, since these items are known to be irrelevant. A preliminary hypothesis, that the source of typhoid will be found in liquids or substances in contact with liquids, is an indispensable requirement for the gathering of this *relevant* data. The range of possible culprits thus becomes greatly narrowed. This ground work is necessary before we can apply the rules.

The rules, once again, will test each of the antecedent factors in order to determine whether any one of them is the cause. If any factor fulfills our definition of a cause, it probably is the cause; if not, we will eliminate it. The rules thus have two aspects, negative and positive. Negatively, we seek to eliminate false causes, and positively, to identify the correct cause. After we eliminate a number of factors we assume that the cause will be found among the remaining factors. If we eliminate all but one, it is probably the cause. We shall begin with the negative aspect of the rule.

a. The Negative Method of Agreement.

Our first task is to eliminate factors which cannot be the cause, using the rule "No factor can be the cause in whose absence the effect occurs." Thus, if we examine the hypothesis that a is the cause, we will find $-a\ldots E$ in cases C and D, i.e., a does not occur in these cases, but E does. But the definition of a cause requires $E\ldots C$ and $C\ldots E$ in all cases; hence the present rule. If "a" were the cause it should be found wherever E occurs. It does not, so we eliminate it. Similarly, using this principle we can eliminate b, since the effect occurred in cases A, B, and E in b's absence, and so on with all the other factors except o. Note that the negative method never tells us what the cause is, but only what it is not.

b. The Positive Method of Agreement.

We now examine the factor or factors not eliminated. The

positive formulation tells us what the cause *is,* by the following rule, "If, in two or more cases where an effect occurs, we find that one and only one of the antecedent factors is common to all of the collections of antecedents, then that factor is probably the cause." * We find that only *o* is common to all the sets of conditions preceding the effect, so *o* is probably the cause. The instances *agree* in possessing this factor alone.

Our illustration is, of course, a highly simplified case. It would be advisable to take a laboratory analysis of the oysters before drawing any conclusions, for it is obvious that the oysters are not the cause, but rather the presence of the bacillus in the oysters. This is an important point, and it teaches us that this method can give us no more than probability because of the possibility of crude analyses. There may be some unknown factor in the probable or ostensible cause, and this unknown factor may be the true cause. Search for such unknown factors begins when an exception to a previous generalization is discovered; e.g., it may have been believed that oysters were the cause of typhoid until a case of typhoid without the eating of oysters occurred. Progress in science comes through the discovery of exceptions to such generalizations.

Another point: If our laboratory analysis shows that the oysters are not contaminated, our original conclusion must be rejected, and this will require re-analysis of the known factors or a search for additional antecedents. On re-analysis we may now find that the tap water was the cause, for the vegetables in cases C and D may have been washed in tap water.

2. The Method of Difference.

We begin with a new illustration. Susan suffers from a skin irritation and inflammation of her face. This irritation occurs after she uses face powder. We assume that the powder is the cause, but Susan wishes to use face powder, and she desires an analysis of the powder in order to determine whether some one ingredient in it is the true cause of the irritation. A chemist friend finds that the powder contains six ingredients: talc, kao-

---

* Or an indispensable part of the cause. This qualification will apply throughout the following discussions.

lin, magnesium carbonate, zinc oxide, ochre (for coloring), and perfume. The chemist suspects that the perfume is the cause, and performs an experiment. He prepares a batch of face powder containing only the first five elements. He then divides this batch into two parts, to one of which he adds perfume. Susan now tries the face powder without the perfume (Batch 1) and finds no after-effects. She then tries powder with the perfume added (Batch 2) and finds that the irritation recurs. She concludes that the perfume is the cause of the irritation.

Let us now set up this experiment in schematic form:

Batch 1	talc(t)	kaolin(k)	mag. carb.(m)	zinc oxide(z)	ochre(o)		No irritation
Batch 2	talc(t)	kaolin(k)	mag. carb.(m)	zinc oxide(z)	ochre(o)	perfume(p)	Irritation occurs

Gathering the symbols, we have:

Batch 1: t, k, m, z, o   ..... no E
Batch 2: t, k, m, z, o, p ..... E

Let us now see how the rules apply to this case.

a. The Negative Method of Difference.

We wish to eliminate the non-causal antecedents. We apply the new rule, "No factor can be the cause in whose presence the effect fails to occur." We know that t cannot be the cause, for the effect failed to occur when it was present. Here also we apply our definition of a cause, which requires $-C \ldots -E$, and $-E \ldots -C$. If the causal factor is present, the effect should be, and vice versa. But in this case we find $t \ldots -E$. In the same manner we will eliminate all other factors except p. Note how this new rule differs from the Negative Rule of Agreement. There we worked with cases in each of which E occurred. Here we have two cases, in one of which E did not occur. But in both types of negative methods we are told what the cause is not, rather than what it is.

b. The Positive Method of Difference.

The reader should refer to the symbols in reading the positive rule, "If a case in which an effect occurs, and one in which it does not occur, are exactly alike except for the presence or absence of a single factor, the effect occurring when that factor is present, and not occurring when it is absent, then that factor is probably the cause."

The rule tells us that p is the cause. This was a successful case of proof, but we did have a good hypothesis to work with. Our conclusion, however, is only probable. It is possible that Susan is allergic only to some kinds of perfumes, i.e., those which contain a particular ingredient, and that it is really this ingredient which causes her irritation. But this method of testing is a very efficient one, precise and convincing, especially in a laboratory, where all of the relevant factors can be strictly controlled. It is aptly called the "laboratory method," or the method of "control experiment"; i.e., one of the two situations is the "control," so that we may determine the precise effect which follows from varying a single factor in the other.

Many simple examples will illustrate the method. A drop of iodine is added to a glass of water. We say the iodine is the cause of the brown color, because all of the factors in "water uncolored" and "water colored" were the same except for the introduction of the drop of iodine. Another: a man is shot through the heart and dies. The only difference between the man alive at 3:15 A.M. and dead an instant later is the bullet in his heart.

It is extremely important to note the factor of relevance in applying the positive rule, since no two situations are ever *exactly* the same. Time has elapsed, for one thing. But only relevant factors need be considered. Also note that the factor identified as the cause may not be a completely sufficient condition, but may require the presence of other factors as necessary conditions.

3. The Joint Method.

This method is of little importance, since it introduces no new approach. It is a makeshift which may be employed when the other methods are not immediately applicable. (Our discussion departs considerably from Mill's treatment!)

Let us assume that in the typhoid example of the Method of Agreement there were two factors, rather than one factor, common to all cases—e.g., individuals A, B, C, D and E had all been to the circus where they had all drunk pink lemonade. Assume, too, that no laboratory analyses are available. We cannot then say whether the oysters or the pink lemonade is the cause, but we can eliminate the other factors by the negative method of agreement, since the effect occurred in their absence. The problem now is to eliminate either the oysters or the lemonade, since our hypothesis has become "Either oysters or lemonade is the cause." We should then seek for additional cases, to determine whether there were other individuals who had drunk the circus lemonade or eaten the oysters and suffered no ill effects. If we find such we can eliminate one of these factors by the Negative Method of Difference, and this leaves the other as the sole cause. This procedure suggests that the Positive Method of Agreement should always be supplemented by one of the negative methods, for greater assurance.

4. The Method of Concomitant Variations.

A manufacturer of cosmetics uses newspaper advertising to sell his products. He wishes to test the hypothesis that larger ads sell more goods. He had previously used a 400-line ad. He now runs a larger one in different cities, keeping all factors constant except the size. These constant factors are such things as similarity of newspaper coverage, the use of pictures, written material, and composition. As a check on the effectiveness of the advertising he includes within each ad a coupon asking the reader to send it in for a free sample. The results:

        City A: 400-line ad brought in 500 coupons
        "   B: 500-line "   "   " 580   "
        "   C: 600-line "   "   " 640   "
        "   D: 700-line "   "   " 695   "
        "   E: 800-line "   "   " 725   "

The manufacturer concludes that within certain limits he will get increased sales with an increase in the size of the ads.

Let us now set up our example in symbols, using n for newspaper coverage, p for pictures, w for written material, c for composition, "ls" for lines, and "E" for coupons:

        City A: n p w c 400 ls........500 E
        "   B: n p w c 500 ls........580 E
        "   C: n p w c 600 ls........640 E
        "   D: n p w c 700 ls........695 E
        "   E: n p w c 800 ls........725 E

This example illustrates the principle of "concomitant variations"; i.e., when the factor of advertising lineage varies by
increase in size, the effect (numbers of coupons) varies by increase in number. The canon: If we find that a certain factor
varies in concomitance with variations in the effect, then that
factor is probably the cause of the variations in the effect.

The great value of this method as compared with the others
lies in its ability to handle *degrees*. In the methods of Agreement and Difference, typhoid and skin-irritation were either
present or absent; by the method of variations we can determine
just *how much* of a variation in the cause will produce a given
variation in the effect. Another of its values is that it may be
usable in instances where no other method is applicable. If we
wished to test the hypothesis that the moon is the cause of the
tides, it would be impossible to use the positive method of difference, since that method requires that we use a situation in
which the causal factor does not occur. The moon cannot be
removed. But the variations show the causal relationships: The
closer the moon to the seas, the higher the daily tides, and vice
versa.

Concomitant variations may be either direct or inverse. By
direct variation we mean the type we have illustrated, where an
increase in the cause is accompanied by an *increase* in the effect,
and vice versa. In inverse variation, an *increase* in the factor is
accompanied by a *decrease* in the effect, and a *decrease* by an
increase, as in "The larger the production of goods, the smaller
the unit-cost of the items produced (within limits)," and vice
versa.

The two forms may be shown by symbols, in which the plus
signs refer to larger amounts of the factor or the effect; the minus
signs to lesser amounts. A letter shown without a plus or minus
sign refers to the amount which is taken as "standard," i.e., some
established measure of quantity, viz.:

Direct variation	Inverse variation
a b c− .... E−	a b c− .... E+
a b c .... E	a b c .... E
a b c+ .... E+	a b c+ .... E−

The examples we have used represent ideal situations in that
all other factors have remained constant. But the method may

also be applied in an unideal situation, as in the following:

a   b−   c− d   e . . . . . E+
a− c++ e   f   b+ . . . . . E− −
m   f+   b− a− c+ . . . . . E−

Only *c* varies concomitantly with E.

We shall add a brief comment on the relation of the method of concomitant variations to the "functional" method. A function, as used in mathematics, means a quantity whose value is dependent upon some other quantity, illustrated by the relation of the circumference of a circle to its radius. If we know either, we can compute the other. The ancient philosopher Pythagoras discovered that the pitch of a plucked string on a musical instrument is a function of its length; thus the length of the string on middle C of a piano is twice as long as that of the octave above, and half as long as the one below. These are examples of perfect "concomitant variations," where the variations are in exact and proportionate correspondence. But these functions do not state causal connections. Thus, some concomitant variations indicate causal connections whereas others do not. A causal connection involves an asymmetrical sequence of events in time, in which the cause *precedes* the effect. There is no such temporal sequence in some functions. We may call such non-causal functions "pure functions."

Modern science, in its search for invariant relations, finds non-functional causal laws, functional causal laws, and non-causal or purely functional laws. An example of the latter is Newton's law of gravitation: "Every particle of matter attracts every other particle of matter with a force directly proportional to their masses and inversely proportional to the square of their distances." This means that each chair in this room simultaneously attracts every other chair to itself, but in no sense is one a "cause" of the others.

5. The Method of Residues.

Let us assume that the "man from Mars" visits the earth after World War II. He is puzzled by the enormous enrollments in American colleges and universities. He studies the causes of college attendance, such as the desires to get ahead in life (g), to enrich one's knowledge and cultural background (k), to improve one's mind (m), to enlarge the circle of one's friends (e), and to have a good time (t). But these reasons existed before the war and do not account for the much larger post-war attendance. He also notes that the caliber of the faculties (f), the laboratory equipment (l), and the campus attractions (c) are substantially the same as they were before the war. There must therefore be some additional and as yet unknown factor which accounts for the very large enrollment.

The man from Mars began with a knowledge of the causes of a "normal" enrollment, and found that he could eliminate these as the causes of the excess attendance, so he must seek for the unknown factor which is the cause of the excess. A more thorough examination of all relevant factors is required. He finds that business conditions (b) have improved, but this will account for only a small part of the excess. The man from Mars now discovers the existence of Public Law 346, the so-called "GI Bill of Rights"(GI). He assumes that he has exhausted the field of the relevant factors; he knows that all of the factors except the GI bill account only for an approximately normal enrollment, and he concludes that the remaining factor accounts for the excess.

In summary form, using E for "enrollment" and 100E for "total enrollment":

The effect to be accounted for: 100E (normal: 50E)
The known factors (g,k,m,e,t,f,l,c,b) account for: 55E
Some unknown factor must account for 45E
The only other factor is GI
Therefore, GI accounts for 45E

This is application of the Method of Residues. Mill stated the canon as follows: "Subduct from any phenomenon such part as is known by previous inductions to be the effect of certain antecedents, and the residue of the phenomenon is the effect of the remaining antecedents."

The method is a useful one, though it is, strictly speaking, only an application of deductive reasoning. We assume a knowledge of the causes of the "normal" to begin with, and then apply a kind of logical arithmetic. The same method is used in the following simple example: The candy in a box weighs one pound, fourteen ounces, but the box of candy weighs two pounds. Some other factor accounts for the two ounces, namely, the box. We assume that there are no other relevant factors. Of course, the method itself does not suggest which factors are relevant.

An example from the history of science is the Curie discovery that radium is the cause of the high radioactivity of pitchblende. In the early stages of the investigations into radioactivity, it was found that the radioactive emissions of substances were proportional to the amount of uranium present in them. Let us use the symbol "r" for a "radioactive unit." In terms of this unit, a gram of uranium oxide (88 per cent uranium) gave off 88r, and a gram of uranium nitrate (47 per cent uranium) gave off 47r. It was assumed that uranium in pure form would give off a maximum emission of 100 units.

The Curies then found that a gram of pitchblende emitted radioactive units in the neighborhood of 10,000 units, or several thousand times as much as uranium oxide and uranium nitrate. The Curies knew that pitchblende contained the following components: U(uranium), Th(thorium), Pb(lead), and O(oxygen). They also knew that only uranium among the elements listed could produce radioactivity, and, since it constituted only 5 per cent of pitchblende, it could account for only 5r. They therefore sought the cause of the high radioactivity in some element hitherto unknown, but which must be present as its cause. They then discovered radium(Ra), which constituted only .0001 of pitchblende, but which was responsible for its high radioactivity.

The method of residues was applied as follows: Pitchblende is the cause of 10,000r. (Our figures are of course approximations.) The known factors, U, Th, Pb, O, can account for only 5r, so some unknown factor must account for the remainder. After further analysis we find the presence of an additional factor in pitchblende: Ra. Ra accounts for the remainder.

Section V: Causality in the Social Sciences

We have discussed some of the difficulties which arise in applying the experimental methods in the physical and biologi-

cal sciences. These difficulties are multiplied enormously when
we seek for causes in the psychological and social sciences.
This is because human behavior, the subject matter of these
sciences, is vastly more complex than is the career of a germ.
Human actions are not indefinitely repeatable, and the variables
involved are exceedingly large.* To take one example, a
causal analysis requires that we isolate one factor and trace the
results when this factor is absent or present. Apply this method
to the problem of juvenile delinquency. Can we find a situation
in which one and only one factor is found among all of the
antecedents, or two situations in which all the factors except
one are alike?

These are the difficulties, and they appear insuperable to
some social scientists. These scientists argue that social science
should abandon the search for causes, and limit itself to a
search for "tendencies." † As an example of this method, let
us assume that we find that the rate of delinquency is greater
in the slums than it is in the "better" residential areas. This will
indicate a "tendency" for slum children to turn to crime. This
does not mean, we are warned, that living in the slums is the
cause of crime, nor even an indispensable part of the cause. But
such knowledge is useful insofar as it indicates that we may
lessen the incidence of delinquency by eliminating the slums.

Is it impossible to find the causes of human behavior? Shall
we agree with the criminologist who said, "Sociologists know
nothing whatsoever concerning the cause of crime, and probably
never will"? Is it futile to hope that we will some day find the
cause of wars, since it is "inconceivable" that we shall ever
find a cause "C" such that, whenever it is present war will follow, and never in its absence? The answers to these questions
should not be prejudged. It requires an excessive boldness to
assert that social scientists will *never* discover the causes of human behavior. And certainly only on the assumption that there
are such causes will we ever find them, if they exist.

In any case, the experimental methods and their tests will
apply to hypotheses of social causation insofar as social scientists

* It may be argued that there are other differences, too, such as "human freedom." This problem, however, raises issues of a metaphysical nature, and cannot
be discussed here.

† "Tendencies" involve the use of statistics, to be discussed in the next chapter.

advance such hypotheses. Statements of "tendencies" are simply modest ways of indicating causal hypotheses. The methods, of course, give us the ideal relations, and it is too much to expect that this ideal should be exemplified when we test hypotheses of social causation, but it is always useful to know just how far short of the ideal we have fallen. The cautious social scientist will be careful not to out-talk his knowledge and to assume that he has found the cause where none is known. On the other hand, the negative tests may be very useful to the social scientist in helping him to eliminate *false* hypotheses. Thus, we know that fiendish torture is *not* an efficient way of eliminating juvenile delinquency. Such negative knowledge concerning causes is also of value.

Section VI: The Fallacies of Causal Analysis

A fallacy is an error of reasoning in an argument which claims to be valid. In this section we shall discuss some typical fallacies which arise in the application of the experimental methods. Though all such fallacies involve improper analysis of the factors in the given situation, we shall divide the errors into special types.

1. The "Post Hoc" Fallacy.

A cause always precedes its effect in time. But mere temporal succession is no proof of a causal relation. "Post hoc" is an abbreviation of the Latin expression *post hoc, ergo propter hoc* (after this, therefore because of this). Its form: "X occurred, then Y occurred; X came before Y; therefore, X is the cause of Y." We assume that one thing is the cause of another merely because it precedes it in time. Some examples: In 1940, during the presidential campaign, Wendell Willkie charged that the New Deal was destroying the greatness of the United States, since the birth rate had gone down noticeably between 1932, when the New Deal took over, and 1940. Another: "Hoover was elected president in 1928. In 1929 we had the worst stock-market crash in our history. Just put those two facts together." But the mere fact that one event follows another is no proof that there is any causal connection between them.

The fallacy is not always so easily detected. Thus, in 1947 the coal miners went out on strike, and the next day the newspapers reported that a number of steel-making furnaces had been shut down. The public assumed that the strike was the cause of this shut-down. But steel furnaces are shut down regularly for cleaning and repairs. The fact of temporal priority does not prove causal connection.

The Post Hoc lies at the basis of many superstitious beliefs. A baseball team wins on a day when the manager neglects to shave. He refuses to shave the next day and thereafter as long as the winning streak lasts. Thirteen people sit down to dinner. One of them is killed. Ergo, the number 13 is unlucky, and barber shops skip the number on their chairs, apartment hotels call the thirteenth floor "No. 14," etc. An old story ascribes the superstitious injunction against "three on a match" to the fact that three soldiers once lighted their cigarettes on one match, and thereupon the third man was killed by an enemy sniper.

2. Identifying a Necessary Condition with the Cause.

The cause of an event is often confused with one of its necessary conditions. Thus, a young man desires economic security. He learns that surgeons enjoy good incomes, so he becomes a surgeon. Can we say that his desire for a good income was the cause of his becoming a surgeon? But other young men also knew the facts concerning surgeons but became accountants, or lawyers, or civil servants. A good income may be a necessary condition before some persons will enter a given profession, but it is not the cause which explains why any given individual enters any specific profession.

3. The Fallacy of Emphasizing Irrelevant Factors.

This title has a very broad coverage, but we shall note only two typical forms. This fallacy results from applying the rules of the experimental methods without considering the importance of relevance.

When we apply the Positive Method of Agreement we should beware of assuming that a factor is the cause merely because it is apparently the only factor which is common to all of the antecedents. Careful analysis, and the criterion of relevance are indispensable. What may happen when this warning is neglected is illustrated by the case of the man who made a study of the conditions antecedent to his getting drunk at various parties which he attended. He found that he had been drinking bourbon and soda, scotch and soda, rye and soda, gin and soda, rum and soda, brandy and soda, and vodka and soda. Since soda was the only factor common to all of the antecedents, he concluded that he had found the cause of his intoxication, and at the next party he insisted on drinking his whisky straight.

Another form of this error will be found in applying the method of concomitant variations. Though the fact that two things vary concomitantly lends some probability to the existence of a causal connection between them (or that some third factor may be the cause of both), such variation is not proof. Thus we might find that the rise and fall of bank deposits in New York banks is in precise variation with the rise and fall in the number of semicolons on the editorial page of the *New York Times*. The concomitant variation is irrelevant. In general, we should not assume that variation proves a causal connection unless there is some reason, independent of the variation, to suspect this relationship.

4. The Fallacy of Neglecting Relevant Factors.

Errors in this connection result from a failure to apply the rules of the experimental methods. The Positive Method of Agreement tells us that if we find only one factor common to all of the antecedents, it is probably the cause. This means that we must not neglect to observe negative instances. But it is a common error to note only the instances which confirm our opinions and to ignore those which are contrary to them. The exception, it should be noted, does *not* "prove the rule"; it overthrows the rule.*

Another form of the error results from failing to apply the

---

* For several variant interpretations of the expression, "The exception proves the rule," see H. W. Fowler, *Dictionary of Modern English Usage.*

Positive Method of Difference properly. This requires that all relevant factors be the same except one. We often find a striking difference between two situations (one resulting in a given effect, the other not), and we assume that this striking difference is the cause. But if other factors in the two situations are dissimilar, this is a dangerous assumption. There may be some degree of probability in such arguments, but they are far from conclusive. An example may be found in Frederick Hayek's *Road to Serfdom*. Hayek argues that government planning resulted in fascism in Germany; therefore, if our government plans, we too will be on the "road to serfdom." But we must remember, in assessing the probability of his conclusions, that the conditions and the people of the United States differ very greatly from the conditions and people of Germany.

5. The Reversing of Cause and Effect.

This may be called the "putting the cart before the horse" fallacy. What appears to be the cause may be the effect, and vice versa. Thus, in a region where the climate is very severe, we find that the people are possessed of rugged physiques. We assume that the climate is the cause of their ruggedness. But it may be that only those possessed of such physiques were able to survive. Another example: It is argued that the movies are the cause of the low cultural taste of the public. The motion picture industry retorts that it merely gives the public what the public wants, so that the low taste is responsible for the movies which are made. Which is cause, which effect? This illustration, it may be noted, is also an example of "reciprocal," or "cumulative," or "interdependent" causation. The factors are in reciprocal relation, mutually affecting each other. Thus the movies may further debase a public taste that was already low. This process is sometimes called the "vicious circle." On the other hand, as Gunnar Myrdal has noted in *An American Dilemma*, the vicious circle also has its opposite, which we may call the "beneficial circle." If the movies improve, the public taste will improve, and the movies will then become still better.

Exercises

A. *Symbolical Statements.*

The following exercises illustrate the experimental methods. Explain your answers to the questions, and formulate your statements in the language of the appropriate method.

1. Apply the Positive Method of Agreement to the following group of six collections of antecedents of the effect (E). Which factor among these antecedents is probably the cause of E? Why?

   (1) a b c d e f . . . . . . E
   (2) b c d e f g . . . . . . E
   (3) c d e f g h . . . . . . E
   (4) d e f g h i . . . . . . E
   (5) e f g h i j . . . . . . E
   (6) f g h i j k . . . . . . E

2. Why can the cause not be identified in the following group, in terms of the same method?

   (1) a b c d e f . . . . . . E
   (2) b c d e f g . . . . . . E
   (3) c d e f g h . . . . . . E
   (4) d e f g h i . . . . . . E
   (5) e f g h i j . . . . . . E

3. Now apply the Negative Method of Agreement to Group 1. What specific knowledge does this give you with respect to factor *a*? Why? Now apply the method to *b* and so on through the list of factors. Then do the same for Group 2.

4. Apply the positive method of Difference to the following group. What is the probable cause? Why?

   (1) a g h t x w l p n y . .   E
   (2) y p w t g l a x h . . −E

5. Why is the Positive Method of Difference inapplicable to the following?

   (1) a g h t x w l p n y r s m o . . .   E
   (2) a h t o y v r s p x g l m w . . . −E

6. Apply the Negative Method of Difference to the factors in Group 4. What specific information does this give you with respect to factor *a*? *g*? and so on? Then do the same for Group 5.

7. Can the Negative Method of Difference be applied to Groups 1 and 2? Why or why not?

8. Explain why the following additional information would be useful in connection with Group 2, using the Joint Method.

(6) b c d f a . . . . . . —E
(7) g d c b f . . . . . . —E

9. Use the Method of Concomitant Variations to find the probable cause in the following "unideal" situation. Is the variation direct or inverse? Why?

(1)	a	b	c	d	e	f	. . . E
(2)	a—	b	c+	d+	e	f	. . . E+
(3)	a+	b	c—	d—	e	f—	. . . E—
(4)	a++	b	c++	d+	e	f++	. . . E++
(5)	a+	b—	c—	d—	e—	f	. . . E—

10. Which factor is the cause of what, in the following?

a b c d and e account for 100 E.

(*a* accounts for 13E, *b* for 17E, *d* for 19E, and *e* for 21E.)

B. *Examples of the Use of the Experimental Methods.*

Analyze the reasoning in the following examples and exhibit the structures of the arguments in the appropriate schematic forms.

1. In the previous chapter we analyzed Goldberger's discovery that pellagra was a consequence of a lack of milk and fresh meat in the diet. But many scientists believed that his proof was inconclusive, and they inclined to the microbe theory. Goldberger then established further proofs of his hypothesis by the use of the experimental methods. He was granted permission to try out a dietary experiment at one of the state's prison farms with convicts who volunteered for this purpose. Twelve convicts lived on a diet chosen by him for six months, after which time they were given their freedom. These men were isolated from the others and fed almost nothing but white bread, corn pone, grits, sweet potatoes, salt pork, cane syrup, and cabbage for six months, beginning in April, 1915. After several months of this diet these men became listless; they began to develop severe abdominal pains, and they finally developed skin eruptions of the pellagra type. No other convicts in the farm suffered from such disorders.

But many cautious scientists were still not satisfied. Perhaps the convicts did not really have pellagra, they said. Or perhaps they suffered a recurrence of former cases of pellagra. Perhaps chance microbes had gotten into these men alone. And despite the fact that persons in contact with the sufferers did not catch the disease, the fact remained that the victims *always were in contact* with other victims. So perhaps the disease was caused by a microbe after all. Goldberger decided to put the microbe hypothesis to a conclusive test. He and his assistants injected the blood of pellagra victims into themselves, and even ate small portions of the excreta of these diseased persons. They suffered no ill results except for a temporary discomfort. He had now satisfactorily proved that the disease was not caused by microbes.

Goldberger had discovered the cause of the disease and how to eliminate it. His final problem was to find an inexpensive cure, for not every sufferer can be fed the comparatively expensive diet of milk and fresh meat. By chance, in experimenting with dogs, he discovered that two ounces of yeast per day will constitute a satisfactory substitute for milk and meat in pellagra treatment. (Positive Method of Difference, Negative Method of Difference.)

2. The planet Neptune was discovered in September, 1846, by two astronomers, the Englishman, J. C. Adams, and the Frenchman, U. J. J. Leverrier. Working independently of each other, these astronomers were sure that the actual orbit of the planet Uranus, supposedly the outermost planet in the solar system, could not be accounted for by the gravitational attraction of the known heavenly bodies. Its orbit was not what it should have been on the assumption that the sun and the inner planets were the only forces influencing its motion. These astronomers formulated the hypothesis that the actual motion could be accounted for only on the assumption that Uranus was being attracted by another planet whose orbit was exterior to its own. Leverrier then estimated the probable position of this unknown planet in terms of the force which it presumably exerted on Uranus, and the stars in this region were then carefully searched with a telescope. Star-charts then showed that one of the "stars" changed its position from night to night. A new planet had been discovered. (Method of Residues.)

3. The French scientist, Louis Pasteur, laid the foundations of the modern science of bacteriology. He had proved that liquids containing organic matter, called "putrescible liquids," will never show the presence of micro-organisms if they are completely protected from the outside air after being sterilized by intense heat. He then wished to prove that the presence of organisms in such liquids is due to exposure to the dusts of

the outside air, rather than to the air as such. (He believed that the invisible organisms in the outside air cling to dust particles.) To prove his hypothesis he arranged an ingenious experiment. He used two flasks, both of which had open ends to permit entrance of the air, but he curved the neck of one of these flasks downward, after sterilizing the fluid within it. The liquid in this flask remained pure. He also performed other experiments. He exposed ordinary flasks to the air in various places, in laboratory cellars, in the streets of Paris, in the country, and in the high Alps. These experiments showed that as the air was freer of dusts, the less was the degree of putrescence in his liquids. (Positive Method of Difference, Method of Concomitant Variations.)

4. Pliny the Elder, the ancient Roman author of the *Natural History,* disproved the claims of the astrologers in the following manner: "If a man's destiny is caused by the star under which he is born, then all men born under that star should have the same fortune. But masters and slaves, and kings and beggars are born under the same star at the same time." (Negative Method of Difference.)

5. "You say that the capitalistic system is the cause of imperialism, which you define as the desire to extend the territory of one's country. But I can cite some noncapitalistic countries which are imperialistic in this sense, so capitalism cannot be the cause." (Negative Method of Agreement.)

6. Ignaz Phillipp Semmelweiss (1818–1865) is one of the great originators of antiseptic surgery. His great achievement was his discovery of the cause of puerperal (child-bed) fever, an affliction of women, originating at childbirth. Semmelweiss was attached to the Vienna General Hospital as assistant professor in charge of the maternity ward. This ward had two divisions. In one, the First Division, the medical students were instructed. In the Second Division women were trained to become midwives. During the six-year period prior to 1846 the average deaths per thousand births was 99 in the First Division, 33 in the Second. Why this difference? Semmelweiss set to work on this problem.

Various suggestions were made. Such factors as climate, overcrowding, and the fact that unmarried women came to these charity wards were suggested. But these were obviously not the cause, since these conditions prevailed in both divisions. It was then suggested that the fear which women had of coming into the First Division was responsible for the high rate in that division. But Semmelweiss argued that their fear was an effect, not the cause, since the high mortality preceded the fear. Could it be the difference in sex of the attendants? This was absurd. Could it be the fact that women in the First Division were delivered on their backs; the women in the Second Division on their sides? He tried out this hypothesis, and ordered side deliveries in the First Division, with no change in the death rate.

Then one day one of his colleagues received a wound on a finger from the knife of a student who had come from the dissecting room. The colleague sickened and died. Semmelweiss noted that his symptoms were very much like those of puerperal fever. The hypothesis occurred to him that childbed fever is wound infection or blood-poisoning, that the women were infected by the hands of the students who attended deliveries after coming from the dissecting room. Though these students washed their hands in soap and water, he was sure that some of the germs must remain on their hands. He ordered the students to wash their hands in chlorinated lime water. Just prior to the institution of this practice, the mortality rate was 122 per thousand. Before the end of the year it had fallen to 30, and at the end of two years it was 12. The rate of deaths in the Second Division remained unchanged. (Negative Method of Agreement, Positive Method of Difference.)

C. *Problems in the Application of the Experimental Methods.*

1. On a radio program an ex-convict described how unpleasant his boyhood homelife had been, so that he ran away from home and was thus led into a life of crime. Do you think that this man's unhappy childhood was largely responsible for his becoming a criminal? Why or why not?

2. A farmer wished to test the agricultural value of lime. He plowed up two plots of ground, applied a coat of lime to one and planted corn in both plots. In the lime plot he planted yellow corn; in the other, red corn. He cultivated the lime plot five times after the corn was up; the other three times. The lime plot yielded ten bushels per acre more than the other. Why was this a poor experiment?

3. Farmer Brown had poor crops last year, though his neighbors had fairly good crops. His neighbors say that the cause of his poor crops was his failure to attend church regularly. How would you test this hypothesis?

4. Galen, the ancient Greek physician, anticipated the methods of the lie-detector tests. One day, when he was feeling the pulse of a female patient, a visitor entered and remarked that he had just come from seeing the famous Pylades dance. Galen noticed that the patient's pulse quickened. Galen suspected that she was in love with Pylades. The next time she came in he had a friend come in to say that he had seen another dancer perform, and on another occasion, a different dancer was mentioned. No quickening of the pulse occurred. On the fourth occasion the name of Pylades was mentioned again, and again her pulse quickened. What, if anything, had Galen proved? (Wolf.)

5. In 1926 E. Haldeman Julius, publisher of the "Little Blue Books," published a translation of Victor Hugo's play *Le Roi s'Amuse*, under the title *The King Enjoys Himself*. Eight thousand copies were sold in that year. In 1927 the title was changed to *The Lustful King Enjoys Himself*, and 38,000 copies were sold. Which hypothesis do you suggest to explain the remarkable increase in sales? Which method will you use in testing your hypothesis? (Clarke.)

6. A scientist wished to test two hypotheses concerning the cause of the "flavor" which tobacco has; namely, (1) it is due to the sense of taste, and (2) it is due to the sense of smell. The scientist smoked a cigarette, keeping his nostrils closed while he did so. He found that the cigarette had no taste. What had he proved? By what method?

7. In 1946 a Chicago newspaper reported an interview with Peter Sorenson, an old-time creameryman, concerning the butter shortage in the city grocery stores at that time. "It's just simple arithmetic," he said. "You get five pounds of butter out of 100 pounds of milk and the OPA says the most you can charge is 54¢ a pound. That's $2.70. The cheesemaker gets 10 pounds of cheese out of the same milk, but that cheese retails for 49¢ a pound, or $4.90—$2.20 more than the butter. So, the cheesemaker gets the milk and that's why there's no butter. Blame it on the OPA." Sorenson had a solution for the butter shortage. "Take off the price ceiling." "Sure, butter will go to 75¢ a pound," he said, "but you'll be able to buy it. That's the only way to cure it. Let supply and demand run it. Soon there will be plenty of butter and the price will come down." In which respects do you think Sorenson's theories of causation were adequate or inadequate?

8. In a psychological experiment described by T. G. Andrews in his *Methods of Psychology* (J. Wiley, 1948), it was desired to test the hypothesis that practice in memorizing increases the ability to memorize. This hypothesis was too general to permit of a specific test, and so it was modified into the more precise question: Does practice in memorizing certain prose passages increase one's ability to memorize certain lines of poetry?

A group of subjects were chosen for the experiment. The following principles were used in selecting these subjects. (1) The group was a homogeneous one (all were college students). (2) All were given a preliminary test to determine their ability to memorize certain lines of poetry. (3) The group was then divided into two subgroups, each with the same average ability as determined by the pretest and with equal variability in each subgroup.

One subgroup, the experimental group, was then given practice in memorizing prose passages. The control subgroup received no practice. Both groups were then given the same test to determine their abilities in memorizing certain lines of verse. The results:

	Preliminary test	*Practice*	*Poetry test*
Experimental group:	Grade 62	Yes	79
Control group:	62	No	66

What does this experiment prove? Why were the three principles of selection necessary?

9. In his essay "Some Psychological Postulates for Peace" (in Harrison, Mander and Engle, *If Men Want Peace,* The Macmillan Co., 1946) Edwin R. Guthrie discusses the problem: What causes wars? He raises the question as to whether there are conditions which make nations prone to war, just as there are conditions in a forest which make the forest prone to fires, such as the dryness of the wood. He then suggests that we shift the problem to the causes of belligerency, and continues:

There is one widespread notion of the causes of belligerency that a psychologist must regard as silly and mistaken. This is the belief

that nations are prone to war when they are driven by hunger or
need. But hungry men are not belligerent. It is hard to interest them
in glory or in conquest, or even in revolt. They will listen atten-
tively only to talk of food. And they will not exert themselves particularly even to get food. Outside the walls of a Chinese city there
encamped, according to one account, some two hundred thousand
starving peasants. Into the city, which was on a trade route, came
large shipments of grain on their way to a more distant market. The
starving thousands died quietly and without violence. During the
great Irish famine, families lost members by starvation though the
proprietor's share of the potato crop was in the cabin untouched.
During the Russian famine, starving folk lined the banks of the
Volga, occasionally in the presence of a red soldier who was adequate to guard a storehouse of grain which was government property. The French revolution, often misunderstood because of Marie
Antoinette's famous "Why don't they eat cake?" was a revolution of
the best-fed peasants in Europe. They were not hungry. They were
full of the fighting energy that only food and freedom from want
can give. . . .

An economy of plenty is one of the conditions of belligerency,
(but) it is only one feature of the situation that makes nations ripe
for war. There are other and more complex determiners. . . . The
second requirement of belligerency lies . . . in the existence of a
large body of youth for whom the culture can easily provide food
and shelter but for whom there are open no adult roles. These
youth provide the manpower, the energy, the enthusiasm for conquest, invasion, political revolution, adventure, and coloniza-
tion . . .

Something more than the pressure of a new generation on a
static state of occupation is required. That something more lies in
the possession of a military tradition. Military roles must be part of
the literature and song of a nation. In Germany, Hitler could not
have created these out of whole cloth. He could only cultivate intensely what already had familiar expression in German tradition.

> Which hypothesis concerning war does the author seek to dis-
> prove? Which does he attempt to prove? How successful do you
> consider his argument?

D. *The Fallacies of Causal Analysis.*

> The following group of fallacies contains examples of each
> type. We noted five types, but discussed two forms of types 3
> and 4, making seven in all. The five types are:

(1) The "Post Hoc."
(2) Identifying a Necessary Condition with the Cause.
(3) The Fallacy of Emphasizing Irrelevant Factors.
    a. The Irrelevant Common Factor.
    b. Irrelevant Concomitant Variations.
(4) The Fallacy of Neglecting Relevant Factors.
    a. The Neglect of Negative Instances.
    b. The Neglect of Differences.
(5) The Reversing of Cause and Effect.

Note the fallacy or subfallacy in each case, and explain your answer.

1. The height of the hem-line of women's dresses is caused by general business conditions. You will find that the dresses are short during periods of prosperity and long during depressions. Thus, the 1920's was the period of short dresses and prosperity. During the depression of 1932 dresses were long. During the period of wartime and post-war prosperity they were short. The "New Look" of long dresses came in with the post-war recession.

2. Samuel Grafton in the *New York Post,* replying to a campaign speech by Mr. Thomas E. Dewey in Cheyenne, Wyoming, in 1940, pointed out that the latter "abounds in quaint comparisons between what it cost the government to do so-and-so in 1938 and what it cost in 1802 . . ."; and then pointed out that, according to Valentine's Manual of the Common Council of the City of New York for 1864, there were only two rape cases during the year. "But for the year 1939, with Mr. Dewey as prosecutor, there were 73 rape cases in the courts. Why this appalling increase in rape under the administration of Mr. Dewey?" (As quoted in H. A. Larrabee, *Reliable Knowledge,* Houghton, Mifflin Co., 1945.)

3. During the war years of World War I, the Federal government operated the railroads and the roads had financial deficits each year. The advocates of private control argued that this experience proved the inefficiency of federal control, for the roads had earned money before the war, when they were under private control.

4. To which error is Sir Francis Bacon calling attention in Aphorism 45 of his *Novum Organum?*

And therefore it was a good answer that was made by one who, when they showed him hanging in a temple a picture of those who had paid their vows as having escaped shipwreck, and would have him say whether he did not now acknowledge the power of the gods—"Aye," asked he again, "but where are they painted that were drowned after their vows?" And such is the way of all superstition, whether in astrology, dreams, omens, divine judgments, or the like; wherein men, having a delight in such vanities, mark the events where they are fulfilled, but where they fail, though this happens much oftener, neglect and pass them by.

5. You can't fight great wars without armaments. You will find that the armaments of the great powers increased greatly in amount during the 1930's. War followed as a natural consequence of their having the instruments of war at their disposal, so we may conclude that armaments are the cause of wars.

6. When we examine the majors of students who rank high scholastically we find that all of the Latin majors rank in this group. This is conclusive proof that the study of Latin improves the mind.

7. H. L. Mencken in his early years, attended Professor Knapp's Institute. He reports that the professor had a great contempt for the public schools.

Every time there was a hanging at the city jail . . . he referred to the departed, not by his crime but by his education, which was invariably in the public schools. No authentic graduate of F. Knapp's Institute, he let it be known, had ever finished on the gallows. (H. L. Mencken, *The Days of H. L. Mencken,* A. A. Knopf, 1947.)

E. *The Fallacies of Causal Analysis: Miscellaneous Examples.*

Analyze this group as before. Explain your answer in each case.

1. I felt miserable before I took those pink pills. But now I feel fine.

2. In the early years of the twentieth century it was argued that wages in the United States were higher than they were in England because the United States had a protective tariff, whereas England had no system of "protection."

3. "My men were in the trenches when they saw a fearsome sight. The dreaded green-colored gas came rolling toward them. Soldiers were running about in the gas and falling. I said to my men: 'There is no use in trying to escape. Let us sing a hymn.' We stood up and sang 'Abide With Me.' The

poison gas disappeared, and not one of my men was harmed."

4. Since polar bears with white fur are found only in the arctic regions of year round snow and ice, we may assume that it is the coldness of these regions which is responsible for the whiteness of their fur.

5. Old man Jones recently celebrated his ninetieth birthday. He ascribed his longevity to the fact that he drank a pint of beer every day.

6. All of the students in a logic class did consistently well on four tests. On the fifth test everyone failed. A student sought the cause of the failures. He found that some students had prepared for this test by studying in solitude; others had studied in groups. Some had studied in silent rooms; others had studied with the radios on. But in all cases he found that the students had studied until 1:00 A.M. He concluded that the common factor, studying until 1:00 A.M. was the cause of the failures.

7. Certainly I believe in magic. I saw a magician operating with an empty hat. He said "abracadabra," and a rabbit appeared. I carefully noted that the only difference between the hat empty and the hat filled with a rabbit was the utterance of the magic formula.

8. It was during the middle of my freshman year at high school that I noticed that my grades in the weekly "exams" took a sudden drop. Study as hard as I might, I could not raise my low average. I could not account for this drop, for I studied just as hard as ever. Now I am not what you might call a superstitious fool; but I could not help going backward in my mind and searching for some recent event or change of habit that could possibly coincide with the beginning of my change from the high to a low grade. It was not long before I discovered the desired coincidence. I had, up to the date of my 'drop,' been riding to school by the subway train. But on the very Friday I had received my first low grade I had met a friend with whom I had ridden to school on a surface car. As I found this route shorter and more convenient I continued to use it, and was still using it at the time of this strange discovery. On the very next day I returned to the subway route and the very next Friday my grade rose from a "50" of the previous week to a "90." A foolish coincidence, you will say; but it has influenced my actions in spite of myself. Every day I go out de-

termined to try the surface cars just for the fun of it, but
some unseen instinctive force impels me to seek the subway
route. Even now, while attending the University, I walk
every day a distance of almost half a mile to get a subway
train, rather than take the surface car which runs right by
my house. But every now and then I meet some friends, who
also attend the same college and live on the same street; and
I am compelled for companionship's sake to ride with
them when they take the surface car. Invariably on such a
day I have poor luck in all my work. For instance, I often
upset apparatus in my chemistry laboratory when I ride on
the subway; but the damage is never so great as when I use
the surface route. What would you call such a coincidence?
(A. M. Tozzer, *Social Origins and Social Continuities,* pp.
254–5. Copyright 1926 by The Macmillan Company and
used with their permission.)

9. An English writer noted that those among the English poor
who had cows were the most industrious, so he argued that
the way to make the others industrious was to give them
cows.

10. Henry Ford: "If you will study the history of almost any
criminal, you will find that he is an inveterate cigarette
smoker."

11. A Chicago newspaper in 1936: "In 1928 there was a total of
$5 billions in new financing of domestic corporations. In
1929 there was $8 billions, and in 1930 there was $5 billions.
In 1933 the New Deal established the Securities Exchange
Commission and what was the result? In that year there was
only $161 millions, not billions. Abolish the SEC and we
shall again have financing in the billions."

12. John and Jim grew up together and were graduated from
the same high school. John went to college and was graduated with honors, while Jim became a salesman. Today Jim
earns $6000 per year while John, who has become a high
school teacher, earns $3000. This proves that a college edu-
cation is not a good investment.

Chapter 17

THE NATURE OF
INDUCTIVE REASONING

Section I: The Meaning of Generalizations

A generalization is a statement to the effect that something is always the case; in the simplest form, "All A's are B's," or "All crows are black." Generalizations are an indispensable element in life. We guide ourselves in our daily activities by generalizations, and we would find it difficult to move a single step without them. When we are hungry, we eat food because we know that food is nourishing and that it will satisfy hunger. We know that fire will heat, that it will burn, and that it will boil water. We know that alcohol intoxicates. But these generalizations should be stated more precisely and with the proper qualifications before we assert them as true. Thus, only some kinds of food are nourishing. And even such a generalization as "Water boils at 212° F." requires the qualification: "under certain conditions of atmospheric pressure." When these variables and qualifications are asserted precisely, many generalizations may be asserted as true.

In our previous discussions we frequently noted the important role which generalizations play in our reasonings. Generalizations typically form the major premises of our syllogisms: "All men are mortal," "If P, then Q," etc. Hypotheses are suggested by generalizations, as in the *Citadel* case. Causal laws, which tell us that X is the cause of Y, and functional laws, which tell us that X is a function of Y are also generalizations.

Before we proceed further, an important qualification to our definition of generalizations must be noted. A statement in the form "All A's are B's" is a generalization only when all

415

of the A's have *not been observed.* "All crows are black" refers to the unobserved as well as to the observed crows. This
statement is a genuine generalization. By a generalization, then,
we mean a statement that something is always the case when
this statement is based upon an incomplete observation of the
facts of experience. Generalizations in this sense are called "inductions" by logicians, but the two words are usually used inter-
changeably. Let us now look at a different type of statement:
"All the chairs in this classroom are brown." If this statement
is based upon our observation of each and every chair in the
room, then it is not a generalization in our sense. It is nothing
but a *description* of things which have been observed. Though
cast in the form "All A's are B's," we shall call such statements
"quasi-generalizations." Aristotle used the expression "perfect
inductions" for these quasi-generalizations, but in our terminology they are not genuine generalizations or inductions.

Three fundamental questions concerning generalizations or
inductions are: (1) By what process do we arrive at generalizations? (2) Is the process of reasoning valid? (3) Are generalizations true? Let us look at these questions:

(1) We begin with a simple example. I visit the Brookfield
Zoo near Chicago, and see a panda. I note that he has rings
around his eyes. I then visit the New York zoo and find other
pandas with rings. I then visit Tibet and China and see more
pandas, all with rings around their eyes. I then generalize: "All
pandas have rings." The reasoning proceeds as follows: "All the
observed cases of pandas (p1, p2, p3, p4, . . . pn) have rings.
. . . Therefore, all pandas have rings." Note that we conclude
that all pandas have rings on the evidence that all the observed
cases have rings. The jump from the *observed cases* to the generalization concerning *both* the *observed* and all of the *unobserved cases* is called the "inductive leap." We shall use the
symbol → for this inductive leap. Our reasoning may thus be
represented by: "All the observed P's are R's → All P's are R's."

(2) Is our reasoning valid? Obviously not. "All of the observed cases" represent only a fraction of all cases, past, present,
and future. We have therefore drawn a conclusion concerning
all on the evidence of *some.* This is a violation of the funda-

mental rule that we cannot distribute an undistributed term. Note again that the sentence "All the chairs in this room are brown" does not involve an inductive leap, since it is not a generalization.

(3) Is our generalization concerning the pandas *true?* All observed cases have rings, and no cases without rings have been observed. It is true so far as we know. But this does not guarantee that all future pandas will be found to have rings around their eyes. Nor that all existing pandas have such rings. Nevertheless, our generalization may be said to have a measure of probability, the degree of probability depending upon factors which we shall presently examine.

Induction differs from deduction in that the former process permits us to make assertions on the basis of things observed in our experience, whereas in deduction we merely reason from known or assumed truths to their consequences. But induction also involves inference, and all inference is deduction. Our inductive leaps are based upon a concealed assumption, and we shall find a syllogism when we examine the assumption carefully. When we move from "Some pandas have rings" to "All have," we assume that what is characteristic of some will also be characteristic of all. The syllogism:

>   If all of the observed pandas have a characteristic,
>   then all will have it
>   All of the observed cases have rings
> ∴ All pandas have rings

This is a valid syllogism, but its major premise can have only a measure of probability. The specific problem of inductive logic, then, is to determine by what principles and standards we can assess the probability of such major premises.

Section II: The Truth or Probability of Generalizations

The process of induction involves a generalization from some to all, from the observed cases to all cases (the observed and the unobserved). The inductive leap is a leap in the dark to the unobserved cases of the present, future, and past. The observed cases are regarded as a sample of all the cases. A buyer of cloth takes a sample from a bolt, and the sample is regarded as a fair or representative sample of the whole (or of the unobserved portions). Similarly with a buyer of wheat who takes sample handfuls from a carload. The induction can be relied on if the sample is a fair one. The big problem, then, is to assess the fairness of the sample. If the sample is fair or representative, then the generalization will be highly probable; if not, not.

But before we discuss the probability of inductions, we must note certain distinctions in the types of inductions. Inductions may be classified in two ways: as referring, on the one hand, to *indeterminate* groups of things, or to *determinate* groups; and in a second classification we shall divide inductions into the *uniform* and *statistical*. We shall now examine these two distinctions.

Every induction goes from some to all, from the observed sample to the whole collection. The generalization concerning the pandas makes an assertion concerning an *indeterminate* group, by which we shall mean a group whose membership is indefinite, or "infinite," in size. There are no known limits to the total membership of the panda group, for pandas have existed since time immemorial, we have observed only a fraction of those existing today, and there are pandas yet to come. But compare the induction when we take a sample of wheat from a carload. Here we generalize concerning *this* carload, a *determinate* group whose membership has definite limits. But this case also represents genuine induction, since here, too, we find the inductive leap from some to all. We say, "The observed grains have X characteristics → all the grains have the same characteristics (in this carload)."

Our second distinction refers to *uniform* and *statistical* inductions. On the one hand we may find a uniformity in the sample. *All* of the observed pandas have rings. We then generalize and say, "All without exception" have rings. In a statistical induction, on the other hand, we find that a certain *proportion* in our sample has a certain characteristic. We study 1000 cases of childbirths, and find that 52 per cent of the children are males. This fact does not constitute a generalization in itself, since it is merely a description of what has been observed in a

sample collection of cases. But if we should make further observations, studying other collections of cases under different
conditions, and at different times and places, and should find
that our percentage is confirmed under any and all conditions,
we may generalize and say, "52 per cent of all births are males."
We have now made the inductive leap from some to all, but
instead of finding that all of the observed cases have a certain
uniform characteristic, we find that all of the observed collections of cases (or the one large varied group) show that a certain
proportion of individuals have a given characteristic. Our generalization then asserts that all large collections of cases will
show the same proportion.

We may also combine our two distinctions. Uniform generalizations may be made for indeterminate or determinate groups
(the pandas and the wheat), and we may make statistical generalizations which deal with indeterminate or determinate groups.
The generalization concerning childbirths is a statistical generalization which refers to an indeterminate group. A statistical
induction dealing with a determinate group is illustrated by a
poll of public opinion, such as the Gallup poll, which examines
the opinions of a sample group of individuals, usually about
3000 persons. The pollsters find a certain division of opinion in
the sample, then generalize and tell us that the opinions of all
adult Americans (75,000,000 persons) will divide as the sample
did. In this case we deal with a determinate group, the American people existing at a specific time. The childbirth generalization concerns an indeterminate number of children existing
anywhere or at any time. But in all of the various types, be it
noted, we find the inductive leap, from the observed cases to
all cases. In this chapter we shall be concerned primarily with
uniform generalizations. Statistical generalizations will be considered further in the next chapter.

We now return to the problem of the probability of generalizations. We shall consider such generalizations as the following: Pandas have rings; water is composed of H_2O; all men are
mortal; typhoid fever is caused by the typhus bacillus; the volume of a gas is a function of the temperature and the pressure;
and every particle of matter attracts every other particle of
matter with a force proportional to the product of their masses

and inversely proportional to the square of their distances. How probable are such generalizations, and on what principles do we assess their probabilities?

The important question concerning the probability of an induction involves the dependability of the sample. Is it fair? Is it representative of the whole collection of cases we are considering? Can we be sure that all cases yet to be examined will be like those we have examined? A number of factors will influence our judgment of the fairness of a sample and hence of the probability of an induction:

1. The number of cases.

Other things being equal, the number of cases on which the generalization is based will affect its probability. The generalization that all pandas have rings will be less probable if our sample consists of 10 cases than if it is based upon 100 cases, and similarly with all generalizations. The enumeration of cases is basic in all induction.

But enumeration of cases is only one of the factors which determine the fairness of a sample and hence of the degree of probability of a generalization. When a generalization is based upon enumeration *alone*, i.e., on nothing more than that all of the observed cases have a characteristic in common, we shall say that such generalizations are based upon "simple enumeration." Simple enumeration is the weakest type of evidence for a generalization. Its weaknesses were noted by Sir Francis Bacon:

The induction which proceeds by simple enumeration is childish; its conclusions are precarious, and exposed to peril from a contradictory instance; and it generally decides on too small a number of facts, and on those only which are to hand.

This condemnation is perhaps too sweeping, but the weakness of such generalizations is generally recognized. Our lack of confidence in inductions based on simple enumeration may be illustrated by an imaginary case. If, on our next visit to Tibet, we should find a panda without rings around his eyes, we would be surprised, but we should not consider the instance incredible. We would immediately revise our generalization and say, "Most pandas have rings around their eyes." But, as we shall see in a moment, we are less ready to abandon inductions based on grounds other than simple enumeration.

2. The homogeneity of the cases examined.

When we take a sample of a carload of wheat, we are confident that the quality of the whole will be like that of the sample. But if we should take a sample carton of cherries from a carload our assurance would not be so high. Why is this? Because cherries differ from each other in quality much more than do grains of wheat. Grains of wheat are known to be more homogeneous when taken from a given area than are cherries, with respect to the qualities important for commercial uses. The homogeneity of the individuals in a collection, then, appears to answer our question as to how we determine whether a sample is a fair one. If we *know* that a class of things is homogeneous, then we can be sure that our sample is a fair one.

But, the reader may ask, is this not circular reasoning, since we *assume* that a whole class is homogeneous, and this is something we can never be sure of so long as there are unexamined cases? We must admit that the use of the principle of homogeneity does require this assumption. Nevertheless, homogeneity is a factor in induction, and the assumption will be more or less probable depending upon our past experiences with the class in question. Some characteristics are probably homogeneous, others not. Thus, on a visit to South America we note in the first cases examined that the Indians have a distinct tint to their skin and that they eat greasy foods. We regard the tint as a more homogeneous characteristic than eating habits, and we will be more confident that all will have the same tint than that all eat greasy foods. But these assumptions can be no more than probable.

3. The careful analysis of the cases.

When we turn to examples of inductions in the exact sciences, we are struck with a great contrast to the cases we have examined thus far. It is certainly a safer induction to say that the speed of a falling body increases in direct ratio to the time it falls than it is to say that all pandas have rings. Newton's law of gravitation is an induction with a much higher probability than that all crows are black. If we found a ringless panda in Tibet, as noted, we should be surprised and interested in our discovery. But if we should find that unsupported objects do not fall to the earth in Tibet, we should doubt our senses. Why is this? Why are the inductions of the exact sciences more probable than those concerning the blackness of crows or the spottiness of leopards and panthers? Our third factor supplies the answer: such inductions involve a careful analysis of the cases examined. When we use the experimental methods, for example, we carefully examine the instances. When we use the Positive Method of Agreement we must not only find the uniform presence of a certain antecedent, but we must find this to be the case no matter how the other surrounding factors are varied, under any and all conditions. In a control experiment the probability of our results can be very high. Simple enumeration is of comparatively little worth in such cases.

Thus a chemist may conclude that he has discovered a new law of nature on the basis of two or three experiments (or samples), whereas thousands of instances will give a much lesser probability to inductions concerning leopards and their spots. Furthermore, the chemist can produce the effect he desires at will, or prevent the effect at will. When the cause is present, the effect occurs; when not, not. Thus the methods of experimentation studied in the previous chapter furnish us with inductions with a very high probability. But there is yet another factor affecting the probability of inductions, viz.:

4. The systematic organization of knowledge.

The aim of science is not the mere accumulation of true propositions concerning reality. Its ultimate aim, rather, is to find an explanation of the entire "system of nature" and of the structure of the universe. The ideal of science is to integrate all known truths into a system of truths in the form of a deductive system, in which all subsidiary laws and their applications can be deduced from a few simple basic laws. The science of mechanics is such a system. With Newton's law as the basis for the system, we can deduce the other laws of mechanics in exact mathematical terms. The different parts of Nature's jig-saw puzzle are seen to fit together in a beautiful harmony. The over-all system explains the particular laws, and the parts of the system support the whole. In the social sciences, of course, this ideal is as yet only a remote vision, except in economics, which resembles mechanics in that it assumes certain basic axioms (concerning human behavior) and then deduces the consequences which will follow *if* these axioms are actualized in reality. All of the principles of economics are thus organized into a deductive system.*

The deductive nature of the exact sciences gives us an additional factor in the probability of inductions. For when a chemist discovers a new compound, his induction is supported not only by the evidence which he has before him, but he knows that his discovery can also be deduced from the general laws of chemistry. He experiments along lines suggested by the general laws and his results follow from them. Myriads of experiments support those general laws. His experiment also involves the factor of careful analysis. Let us use a simple illustration of this principle. We know that all machines wear out in time. Let us assume that this principle is based upon the enumeration of cases, the homogeneity of the cases examined, and the careful analyses of all cases. At a later stage we formulate the generalization that "All men are mortal." This induction is also based upon the first three factors. But there is something more. We also know that a human body is a machine, so that the mortality of men also follows by deduction from the first generalization. In a similar manner the law concerning machines may be deduced from higher generalizations, and so on. All such general-

---

* When predictions are made on the basis of deductions from postulates, however, the probability of these predictions will depend upon the extent to which the actual situation corresponds to the ideal situation assumed by the postulates. Thus in *applied,* as distinguished from *pure,* economics we have no assurance that we have taken account of all of the ways in which an actual economic situation may depart from the system assumed by the postulates.

izations give mutual support to each other and increase the probability of any induction within the system.

We may therefore distinguish between two types of generalizations, which we shall call "isolated" and "integrated." An isolated generalization is one which stands alone, without receiving the support of others. Pandas and their rings are an example. There are no laws of nature which require that pandas should have rings. An integrated generalization, on the other hand, is one which is supported by other generalizations and which in turn supports them. This explains why we should be so shocked if we found that a basic law of physics, such as gravitation, did not hold in Tibet. For we should then have to discard, not merely that particular law (for a law is not really a law if it has a single exception), but we should also have to discard a host of other laws which are integrally associated with that one. Our structure of knowledge would topple into ruins. This is the basic reason why scientists are sceptical concerning reports of miracles. If God had ordered the earth to stop rotating in order to increase the daylight for Joshua, such an action would have played havoc with the entire solar system. We may now also understand our confidence in the generalization that all men are mortal, or that they will die before they reach a certain anniversary of their births. We can do more than point to a given enumeration of cases. We can point to the fact that all living things die and deduce the fact that men, as living beings, must also die. We can point to the fact that human organisms are also physical machines, and that all machines must eventually wear out because of friction.

We have noted some of the factors which determine the "fairness of a sample" and which explain why some generalizations have a much higher probability than others. But in the end, it is the evidence of experience which controls our judgments of the probability of inductions, and experience always comes back to the enumeration of cases. We always go from the evidence that X has happened in some cases to the generalization that it will happen in all. Though we use deduction to support an induction, as in factor 4, the basic inductions of the "system" also go back to the enumeration of cases, and rest upon supporting generalizations which also use that principle. In practice, however, the generalization which is based upon the four factors will have a higher probability than one based upon enumeration alone, or upon what we call "simple" enumeration.

Section III: The Justification of Inductions

The probability of a specific induction depends upon the number of cases examined, the homogeneity of the instances, the varying times and places in which we have observed the instances, the careful analysis of the observed cases, and the supporting generalizations. But the basic justification for *any* induction rests on a general principle which we have not yet considered. This is the principle of the "uniformity of nature." Whenever we say that an induction is probable, we assume that the future will be like the past, that similar causes will have similar effects, and that the structure of the world will remain unaltered in certain fundamental respects.

The principle of the uniformity of nature thus lies at the foundation of the principles of empirical probability and of science. Without it there could be no prediction whatsoever.

This fundamental principle, however, cannot be proven conclusively, since it is impossible to guarantee what the future will be like. We can never be absolutely certain that the future will be like the past. But, it may be asked, though this principle is not certain, is it not highly *probable,* since all of recorded history confirms it? This justification for the principle would involve circular reasoning, for we would use the principle in the very act of justifying it, i.e., every statement of probability assumes the principle. The principle, then, cannot be proved. It is simply accepted as an unproved assumption or postulate of science.

Though the principle of the uniformity of nature is only a postulate, this does not mean that there is any reason to reject it. The following remarks of Hans Reichenbach indicate the attitude of the scientist towards his assumption:

To renounce the assumption of induction would be necessary only if we knew that the assumption is false. But that is not the case—we do not know if it is true or false. And that is quite another matter! Without believing that the assumption is true or false, we are still justified in defending it in the sense in which we make a wager. We want to forsee the future, and we can do it if the assumption of induction is justified—and so we wager on this assumption. If it is false, well, then our efforts are in vain; but if we use the principle of induction, we have at least a chance of success. (Journal of Philosophy, Vol. XXXIII (1936), p. 157. Cited in H. L. Searles, *Logic and Scientific Methods,* The Ronald Press, 1948.)

The principle of the uniformity of nature is also assumed, be it noted, whenever we seek to explain the events of prehistory, or of any events not observed by human beings. We might be able to *describe* the past without this principle, but we would not be able to *explain* it. For whenever we seek to *explain* past events, we assume that what is today was also then. We assume the regularity of nature: that the uniformities of today prevailed in the past. When we find a tree with one hundred rings we infer that it is one hundred years old; when we find ancient rocks of the Paleozoic Age we assume that they were formed as rocks are formed today. We believe that the earth is millions of years old on the basis of such reasoning. Limestone is built up at the bottom of the ocean floor by slow processes today, and we assume that the limestone of the past was also built up by the deposits of foraminifera on the ocean's floor. We then compute the length of time it must have taken to build up the rock crust of the earth. Though these explanations are not guaranteed to be absolutely true, we regard them as most probable because of our postulate that nature is uniform in many respects.

Section IV: Analogy and Scientific Method

In this section we shall examine a method of inference which is closely related to induction. This is the method of analogical reasoning which, like induction, draws inferences concerning unobserved entities on the basis of what has been observed. Both involve the "inductive leap." Analogical reasoning, however, uses a type of analysis which differs from that used in induction. Let us look at an example taken from Thomas Reid, the eighteenth-century Scotch philosopher:

We may observe a very great similitude between this earth which we inhabit, and the other planets, Saturn, Jupiter, Mars, Venus, and

Mercury. They all revolve around the sun, as the earth does, although at different distances, and in different periods. They borrow all their light from the sun, as the earth does. Several of them are known to revolve around their axes like the earth, and, by that means, must have a like succession of day and night. Some of them have moons, that serve to give light in the absence of the sun, as our moon does to us. They are all in their motions, subject to the same law of gravitation, as the earth is. From all this similitude, it is not unreasonable to think that these planets may, like our earth, be the habitation of living creatures. There is some probability in this conclusion from analogy.

We shall criticize this argument in due course. But first let us note its structure. To simplify the argument, let us assume that Reid mentioned only one planet, which had all of the characteristics he mentioned. He compares this planet to the earth. He finds that both revolve around the sun (r), both borrow their light from the sun (b), both revolve around their axes (a), both have moons (m), and both are subject to the law of gravitation (g). Now, he continues, the earth also has life (l); therefore, it is probable that the planet also has life.

We shall exhibit the structure of this argument in symbolic form. We note that a thing or situation (A) has characteristics r, b, a, m, g, and l. We then find a thing or situation (B) which has r, b, a, m, and g. B thus resembles A in having five common characteristics. A also has a sixth characteristic. We infer that B will also have the sixth characteristic. This is reasoning by analogy. "B resembles A in certain observed respects; therefore it will also resemble A in the as yet unobserved respects." Such reasoning involves a process similar to the inductive leap, and the conclusion can be only probable at best. We move from similarity in *some* respects to similarity in *all* respects. Note also the enthymeme which is present in such reasoning, for we assume the major premise: "Anything which has the characteristics r, b, a, m, and g will also have the characteristic l."

The distinction between analogy and induction has been well stated by the English logician, W. E. Johnson: "Induction is understood to depend primarily upon the number of instances known to be characterized by a certain adjective; while the force of analogy depends upon the number of adjectives

which are known to characterize a certain instance." This means
that in induction we observe a number of instances, i.e., individuals such as pandas, and "leap" from a finding concerning
the observed instances to an inference concerning the unobserved instances. Thus:

Panda₁ has rings
Panda₂ has rings   ⟶   All pandas have rings
Panda₃ has rings
Etc.

In analogical reasoning, on the other hand, we deal with two
things or situations having adjectives in common. One of these
things has an additional observed adjective. We infer that the
other will have the additional adjective though it has not been
observed, thus:

Earth has r, b, a, m, g, and l
Planet has r, b, a, m, g   ⟶   Planet also has l

The distinction between the two methods may be illustrated
by simple examples: When we reason from the fact that all of
the honeydew melons we have eaten had a certain flavor, to the
conclusion that *all* have the same flavor, we reason inductively.
(From the fact that a number of instances were characterized by
a certain adjective, we infer that all will be so characterized.) In
analogical reasoning, on the other hand, we reason as follows:
"Honeydew melon A has a certain shape, color, odor, and flavor.
B resembles A in its shape, color, and odor. Therefore, B will
resemble A in flavor." (From the fact that A and B have a certain number of adjectives in common, we infer that they will
have another adjective in common.) The two methods are also
interrelated, for an induction will be strengthened when its instances are highly analogous, and an analogy will be strengthened by a number of previous instances in which the inference
was justified. But the two methods are logically distinct.

The problem of determining the probability of an analogical argument is similar to that of determining the probability
of an induction. The four criteria we studied earlier will be
applicable here, in approximately the same manner. Thus, the
probability of analogical argument will depend in part upon
the number of resembling characteristics. Other things being
equal, the greater the number of resembling characteristics, the

stronger the inference. But the other criteria such as homogeneity, careful analysis, and the relation to a deductive system of knowledge will also determine probabilities here. Most important of all in these arguments, however, is the absence of important "negative analogies," i.e., respects in which B is dissimilar to A. Thus, the following situation would not justify the inference:

A has v, w, x, y,   and z
B has v, w, x, y, n $\longrightarrow$ z

The presence of the dissimilar negative characteristic n may destroy the possibility of B also having z. This is also the crucial weakness of Reid's analogical argument. He pointed to several resembling features between the earth and the planets, but there is an important negative analogy which destroys his argument: On all of the planets except Mars, the temperatures are such that life, as we know it, would be impossible. With respect to Mars, however, the argument undoubtedly has some probability, the degree of probability depending upon many other factors which Reid did not consider.

Section V: Analogy and Argumentation

Analogies play an important role in scientific reasoning, but they also have many other uses. They are coins of intellectual currency in everyday argumentation, where we frequently encounter the "argument from analogy." They are also useful in non-argumentative discourse when we seek to prove nothing, but only to describe or illustrate. We shall comment briefly on these two latter uses before considering the use of analogy in argumentation.

Analogy is widely used in literary discourse when a vivid description is desired. The use of similes and metaphors involve comparisons, and every comparison is an analogy. In a simile the comparison is explicit: "Life, like a dome of many-colored glass, stains the white radiance of eternty." In a metaphor the comparison is implicit, as in speaking of "the raging sea," or "the ship of state." Bacon uses analogy for description when he writes: "He that hath wife and children hath given hostages to fortune; for they are impediments to great enterprises, either of virtue or mischief." Bacon is not trying to prove anything in this sentence; he is merely likening a married man to a general whose favorite officers are in the custody of the enemy. Analogies are also used for the purpose of illustration or instruction when greater clarity of meaning is desired. Historical situations can be made more vivid by comparing them with contemporary situations. "Why did Brutus assassinate Caesar?" "Well, suppose that Goering, Hitler's close friend, had been a decent man, and had decided to save Germany from dictatorship by assassinating him; that would be analogous to what Brutus did, or thought he was doing." Analogies are often used in writings which seek to popularize the explanation of scientific concepts for the layman. Thus E. N. daC. Andrade, the English physicist, explains the differences between a solid, liquid, and gas by picturing the different motions of the molecules in each:

> In a solid, the molecules can be pictured as a crowd of men all doing physical exercises—"the daily dozen"—without moving from the spot where they stand. . . . In a liquid the molecules can be pictured as a swarm of men gathered together in a hall at a crowded reception; they are tightly wedged, but each one works his way through the others, with many a push and apology. . . . For a gas we have to think of a large open space on which men are walking without looking where they are going; each man continues in a straight line until he bumps into someone else, when he abruptly starts off again in a different direction. (E. N. daC. Andrade, *What is the Atom?* Harper and Brothers, 1926.)

These illustrations show the use of analogies in non-argumentative forms, where no proofs are attempted. But note that an analogy which is used for description or illustration may subsequently be used in an argument, as if Bacon, for example, were later to use his analogy in attempting to prove the undesirability of marriage under certain circumstances.

We shall now examine the "argument from analogy." This argument may use the simpler types of analogies which we studied in the previous section, but it may also involve the use of analogies between *relations*. The remainder of this section will be devoted to the analysis of "relational analogies." Let us illustrate by an example which also shows the context in which one such argument might originate: A legislature, let us say, is considering the question as to whether the private communications between a priest and penitent should be "privileged" in a law court, so that a priest may not be compelled to testify as to communications made to him in confidence. The legislature finds that communications made as between husband and wife, doctor and patient, lawyer and client, are granted this immunity. An argument from analogy may then be constructed, as follows: The priest-penitent relation resembles the doctor-patient relation in the following respects: The communications are made in the expectation that they will be held in the strictest confidence (c); it is socially desirable that the communicators should have trust in the communicatees (t). The doctor-patient relation is entitled to "privilege" (p). Therefore, the priest-penitent relation is entitled to "privilege."

The structure of a relational analogy is thus exactly like that of an analogy between two things, except that instead of saying, "A is like B in some respects, therefore:—," we say, "The relation of A to B is like the relation of C to D in some respects; therefore:—." In the example given we say that the relation of a doctor to his patient is like the relation of a priest to his penitent in two respects; therefore, it resembles it in a third. In other words: The doctor-patient relation has c and s and p. The priest-penitent relation has c and s; therefore, it also has p.

Let us now examine another relational analogy as it might appear in an everyday argument:

The colonial system is a boon and not a curse to mankind. It is right and proper for advanced nations to control undeveloped nations until the latter become more advanced. Will not everyone agree that it is right for parents to control their children until the latter reach the age of discretion, which we call maturity or adulthood?

Before we judge the soundness of this argument, we should analyze its structure. We shall accordingly set forth the steps which should be followed in order to exhibit the structure of such arguments as clearly as possible, viz.:

(1) The argument should first be stated as clearly and simply as possible in hypothetical form, omitting all rhetoric and irrelevancies: "If it is right for parents to control their children

until they mature, then, by analogy, it is right for advanced nations to control undeveloped nations until the latter mature."

(2) We should then find the two pairs of terms whose relations are regarded as analogous. One pair is "parents: children";
the other is "advanced nations: undeveloped nations." Using
the first letters of these words as symbols, we see that the analogy
is P : C : : A : U, or $\frac{P}{C} : : \frac{A}{U}$; i.e., P is to C as A is to U.

(3) We should now seek to find the adjectives or characteristics which are alleged to be common to both relations. These
similar characteristics may be stated explicitly, or they may be
implied. The latter holds for this argument. Apparently the
writer finds the following characteristics in both relations: the
relation of a superior to an inferior with respect to power(s);
the relation of a mature entity to an immature one, in terms of
the ability to adjust to contemporary civilization (m).

(4) What now, is the additional characteristic possessed by
the parent-child relationship which is alleged to apply to the
other pair? This is obviously moral approval (a). The former
relationship is regarded as morally right.

(5) The argument should now be diagrammed symbolically:

The P : C relation is characterized by s and m and also
by a.

The A : U relation is characterized by s and m. Therefore, also by a.

After stating the argument in this manner, its structure is
clear and its weaknesses, if any, will be exposed. The chief basis
for criticism of analogical arguments is the finding of significant
differences or negative analogies between the two relations.
There may be similarities between two relations, but if the differences outweigh the similarities, the argument from analogy
has little or no worth. Does our illustration have any significant
negative analogy? Yes. In the parent-child relation, the control
is exercised for the benefit of the child, rather than for the
parents. In the colonial system the advanced nation has been
typically concerned with its own interests, rather than with the
interests of the colony. There are honorable exceptions, but
this is the general rule.

Thus we must add a sixth step to our analysis:

(6) Look for the negative analogy. If it is present, the argument fails. In our example, self-interest (n) characterizes the A : U relationship, so that the two relations are *not* similar in all significant characteristics except the inferred one.

Since the argument from analogy can only give us a measure of probability, at best, our analysis will determine only the *degree* of probability which the argument possesses. The determining factor in all problems of material logic will be our knowledge of the actual facts in the situation under discussion.

Section V: Some Fallacies of Inductive Reasoning

The process of induction gives rise to numerous problems and difficulties. Certainty is impossible in this field, and error is frequent. But in considering the "fallacies," or forms of unjustified inference in the field of induction, we are not concerned with sheer error, but with some typical forms of bad reasoning against which we may guard ourselves. Error will appear despite the sound use of careful methods; we are now concerned with some representative types of careless reasoning.

1. Hasty Generalization.

We refer here to the process of generalizing too hastily. This usually occurs when we use the method of simple enumeration. We generalize too much in everyday thinking, on insufficient evidence. We neglect to note negative instances. We "jump to conclusions." "All women are poor drivers" and "All Los Angelenos drive recklessly" are usually based on a few highly selected samples. The young lady who said "Gentlemen prefer blondes" knew that she was popular with men and that she was a blonde.

Prejudice is a chief cause of hasty generalizing, since it leads us to stress the few instances which confirm our prejudices and to ignore all exceptions. Thus the prejudiced person notes that a small number of union members went on strike during the war and asserts that "All union members are unpatriotic." Minority groups suffer from this tendency of the prejudiced to magnify

the exceptional and unfavorable behavior of some of their members. Another reason for this error is the desire to attract attention to oneself by exaggeration, a not-too-subtle form of exhibitionism. If one were to say that some politicians are crooks, no one would pay any attention to him, since it is well known that politicians are not saints. But the statement that "All politicians are crooks" immediately attracts notice. Goethe once said that it is easy to be brilliant if one respects nothing, not even truth.

A careful thinker will not make assertions which out-run his evidence. He will refrain from asserting generalizations unless he has a sufficient number of instances or a carefully controlled experiment as evidence. This does not mean that generalizing is improper, for some generalizations are highly probable. Let us be careful to avoid jumping to the conclusion that because some generalizations are bad, all are bad.

2. The Fallacy of "Oversimplified Generalizations."

This error is traditionally known as the "Fallacy of Accident," or "Dicto Simpliciter." The latter phrase comes from the Latin, *a dicto simpliciter ad dictum secundum quid*. It refers to our taking a generalization or *general principle* in a simple, unqualified sense, when it should be qualified. We take as our major premise a generalization which is true in general, but not in all cases, and apply it to one of the types of cases to which it should not be applied. Example: The generalization "Every man has a right to keep his own property" is true in general. But if we should proceed to argue that "Therefore, the state has no right to condemn my land in order to build a public road across it," we would be applying the generalization to a case to which it does not apply. By and large, we have the legal right mentioned, but it is subject to qualifications. The state retains the right of "eminent domain," which permits the state to "condemn" land for public purposes upon the payment of a reasonable price therefor. Another example: "The representatives of Congress should be drawn from all classes in the community. There are mystics in the community. Therefore, some congressmen should be mystics." The reference to "all classes"

should not be taken in an unqualified sense. In these arguments the generalizations which are used as the major premises are not false when properly qualified. Every man does have a right to his own property, *under certain conditions;* Congress *should* represent all *politically significant* classes in the community. But the major premises in arguments involving the Fallacy of Accident fail to make these necessary qualifications.

Note the difference between the Hasty Generalization and this fallacy. By "Hasty Generalization" we refer to the process of drawing a generalization on the basis of insufficient evidence. Example: "I saw two cars driven badly today; both were driven by women; so all women are poor drivers." In Accident we begin with an oversimplified generalization and then apply it to a case to which it is not meant to apply. In the one fallacy, the Hasty Generalization is the end-result or conclusion; in Accident the generalization is the major premise of the argument.

3. The Converse Fallacy of Accident.

In the Fallacy of Accident we begin with a principle which is true in general but which does not apply to a specific case. In the Converse Fallacy we begin with a principle which is true only in exceptional cases and then apply it generally. The following is an example of Accident: "It is always wrong to tell a lie. The theater manager lied to the audience when he told them that the star had taken sick and that the show was cancelled. He knew that the theater was on fire. Therefore, he committed a moral wrong." The absolute admonition against lying should be qualified, for it does not apply to such cases. But now suppose that someone were to read this discussion and argue as follows: "It is morally right for a theater manager to lie in order to achieve a good result. Therefore, it is not wrong to tell a lie in order to achieve a good result. Therefore, it is not wrong to tell a lie." The exceptions to the prohibition against lying are very special cases which qualify a general principle; but we should not generalize the exception into an unqualified rule. In Accident we use a principle which is true in general, but not in a special case. In the Converse Fallacy we use a principle which is true only in a special case, but not in general.

Hasty Generalization and the Converse Fallacy of Accident
are very similar: nevertheless, we should carefully note a distinction between them. This may be made clear by the following examples. (1) A man suffered from shock. A drink of whiskey
proved beneficial to him. Now, on the basis of this instance, it
would be a hasty generalization to jump to the conclusion that
whiskey is always beneficial in cases of shock. (2) Let us now assume that it is established that whiskey is beneficial in all cases
of shock, i.e., it is beneficial under certain circumstances. If we
inferred from this that whiskey is beneficial under any and all
circumstances, we would commit the Converse Fallacy of Accident. The distinction is that in the Converse Fallacy of Accident
we go from the fact that P is true under certain circumstances
to the conclusion that P is true under any and all circumstances.
In Hasty Generalization, on the other hand, we go from the fact
that one (or a few) A's are B's to the conclusion that all A's are
B's. Both fallacies occur, of course, only when the inferences are
illegitimate.

4. Composition and Division.

These are two fallacies having a converse relationship. Let
us look at examples.

Composition: Each of the football players on the All-Star
team is the best player in his position in the entire country.
Therefore, the All-Star team is the best team in the entire
country.

Division: The Chicago Bears football team is the best team
in the country. Therefore each player on the Bears team is the
best player in his position in the country.

In Composition we go from the parts to the whole, and assume that the qualities possessed by the parts must also characterize the whole. This is not an inductive fallacy in the strict
sense, but it may be confused with such fallacies. Composition
is also a linguistic fallacy in some cases, as when we go from a
statement concerning *all* of the parts taken severally and indi-
vidually to a statement concerning *all* of them taken together
as a whole. But the fact that the individual members of a group
possess certain characteristics does not justify us in concluding

that the whole will possess a similar characteristic. Groups possess characteristics as groups which the individual members do not possess. A group may be an "organic whole" in which the interrelationship of the parts is responsible for its character. An operatic production may have the greatest stars, but a cast made up of male and female prima donnas may show a deplorable lack of teamwork, and the production may not be as good as many in which the lesser stars work well together. Similarly, a cake made up of the best ingredients may not be the best cake. Water is made up of hydrogen and oxygen but its qualities are different from the characteristics possessed by its ingredients. Division is the reverse error. The fact that a whole has certain characteristics does not justify us in concluding that the parts will have the same characteristics.

Exercises

A. Are the following, examples of induction? Why or why not?
  1. I have read this book and examined every page, so I am safe in asserting the generalization: "All of the pages in this book are white."
  2. Since all of the pages in this book are white, we are safe in assuming that many books have white pages.
  3. In the plebiscite, 99 per cent of the voting population voted "Yes."

B. In the following group of inductions, (1) show how each goes from "some" to "all," and (2) classify each in terms of the distinctions between the determinate and indeterminate, and between the uniform and the statistical:
  1. Ragweed is the cause of hay fever in persons of a certain allergic type, so all persons of that type will be allergic to ragweed.
  2. In all of the observed cases, the volume of a gas is a function of the temperature and pressure, so we may assert this function as a law.
  3. In the sample we have taken, 50 per cent of the people said they would vote Republican, and only 40 per cent said they would vote Democratic, so you may be sure that the country will divide that way at the election.
  4. In the sample examined, one-third of the people were ill-housed, so the same proportion will hold for the country as a whole.

5. All of the students in my class are hard workers, so I assume that all of the students in this college are hard workers.

6. Practically all the people I have known prefer a free society to a totalitarian society, so I assume that the same characteristic will hold for practically all of the human race.

C. How would you answer Mill's question, from his *A System of Logic*, Vol. I, page 363? "Why is a single instance, in some cases, sufficient for a complete induction, while in others, myriads of concurring instances, without a single exception known or presumed, go such a very little way towards establishing a universal proposition? Whoever can answer this question knows more of the philosophy of logic than the wisest of the ancients, and has solved the problem of induction."

D. Distinguish the induction from the analogical argument in the following and show how the "inductive leap" is involved in each:

1. I enjoyed Arthur Koestler's last novel. The reviews say that his new one also deals with a significant current issue and shows philosophical insight, so I am sure that I will enjoy it too.

2. I enjoyed Koestler's first four novels so I am sure that I will enjoy his fifth.

E. Are the following analogies used as arguments or illustrations?

1. Plato, *Republic*: "Are dogs divided into hes and shes, or do they both share equally in hunting and in keeping watch, and in the other duties of dogs? Do we entrust to the males the entire and exclusive care of the flocks, while we leave the females at home, under the idea that the bearing and suckling of their puppies is labor enough for them? No, they share alike in the various duties, the only difference being one of strength. Then, since the difference between men and women consists only in the fact that men beget and women bear children, women ought to follow the same pursuits which men follow, and they ought to receive the same education and training."

2. Herbert Spencer likened the State to an individual organism. The nerve trunks running by the side of the arteries, he said, are like the telegraph wires which run by the side of railways. The organs of the nervous system, which form the apparatus of external action, and the organs of the alimentary system, concerned with the assimilation of food, he likened to the organs of the governmental system, which serve for external action, and to the organs of the industrial system which serve for internal life.

3. An agnostic visited the laboratory of an astronomer and became interested in a mechanical model of the solar system which he saw there. The machine was so contrived that it showed how the various planets moved in their orbits around the sun. "Who made this ingeniously contrived mechanism?" he asked the astronomer. "No one made it," was the answer. "But that is impossible," said the agnostic, "for a machine must have a maker." "Well, then," was the astronomer's reply, "how can you assert that this gigantic machine which we call the universe, did not have a Maker?"

F. *The Analysis of Relational Analogies.*

The following analogical arguments should be analyzed in terms of the 6-step procedure as used in the example on pages 432–3. This procedure, in summary form, is as follows:

(1) State the argument in the form of a hypothetical proposition, with the accepted facts stated as the antecedent and the inferred analogy as the consequent, e.g.: "If it is right for parents to control their children, then, by analogy, it is right for advanced nations to control undeveloped nations."

(2) Find the two pairs of relations, viz.: $\frac{P}{C} : : \frac{A}{U}$. (If there are more than two pairs of relations, choose one pair for your analysis.)

(3) Find the common adjectives or characteristics in your pairs. In the example cited above we found that these were "s" (the "superior-inferior" relation) and "m" (the mature-immature relation). In symbols:
   The P : C relation has s and m
   The A : U relation has s and m

(4) What is the additional characteristic of the P : C relation, which is inferred to hold for A : U? In the previous example, it was "a" (moral approval).

(5) The analysis of the argument should now be stated as follows:
   The P : C relation has s, and m, and a
   The A : U relation has s and m. Therefore, it also has a

(6) Are there any negative analogies, symbolized by "n"?

1. Democratic elections are foolish. Are children capable of selecting their own teachers?

2. If a doctor is justified in deceiving a sick patient, if there is no harm in telling the children about Santa Claus, if a stage manager in case of fire behind the scenes ought to deceive

the audience so as to avert a panic, it is only logical to conclude that there is no wrong in cribbing at an exam. (Castell)

3. A determinist argued that it was absurd to show moral indignation toward our fellow human beings because of their
cruelty, their injustice, their pride and self-love, and their
callousness. Like the lower animals and inanimate objects, he
said, human beings follow the law of their natures. They are
what they are because of the environmental causes which
make them what they are. To be angry with them, then, is
like being angry with the stone for falling or with the flame
for rising.

4. Henry George: "We would hold it a crime if a transatlantic
liner were not brought to a stop by a signal of distress from
a mere fishing smack. Yet a miner is entombed alive, a
painter falls from a scaffold, a brakeman is crushed in cou-
pling cars, a merchant faces financial ruin, and organized society leaves widow and child to bitter want or degradation."

5. Wasn't it a tragic waste of our resources when the New Deal
plowed under every third row of cotton? Then isn't it a
tragic waste to plow under every third child by birth control?

6. Bacon, *The True Greatness of Kingdoms*: "No body can be
healthful without exercise, neither natural body nor politic:
and, certainly, to a kingdom or estate, a just and honorable
war is the true exercise. A civil war, indeed, is like the heat
of a fever; but a foreign war is like the heat of exercise, and
serveth to keep the body in health; for in a slothful peace,
both courages will effeminate and manners corrupt."

7. Newell Dwight Hillis: "The canvas Raphael painted has en-
dured for three centuries. But has God ordained that the
canvas shall be preserved while the artist has fallen into dust?
Is 'In Memoriam' more than Tennyson? Is St. Paul's Cathe-
dral more than Sir Christopher Wren, its architect? Is the
leaf to live, while the tree dies? Reason and conscience whis-
per, 'It cannot be. If thoughts live, the thinker cannot die.
To suppose that death ends all is intellectually as absurd as
it is morally monstrous.'" (Cited by Costell.)

G. *The Fallacies of Induction.*

We discussed five fallacies of induction: Hasty Generalization,
Accident, the Converse Fallacy of Accident, Composition, and
Division. In the group below you will find one example of each:

1. Thrift, since it enriches the individual, can hardly fail to
benefit the community.

2. You are inconsistent. You say that you enjoy jokes, but now, when the joke is on you, you say that you do not enjoy it.

3. It is wrong to limit the work-week to 40 hours. During the war the men in my outfit were required to work 24 hours a day when necessary.

4. Three times during the past month I have read about paroled convicts who committed new crimes. This proves that "once a criminal, always a criminal."

5. Every nation seeks to perpetuate its existence, so that it is unthinkable that any statesman would sacrifice his country's existence for the welfare of others. It is therefore unthinkable that any individual can sacrifice his own existence for the welfare of others.

H. *Miscellaneous Fallacies of Induction.*

1. Whatever is the cause of evil is itself an evil. Religion has caused much evil in the world, such as wars and persecution. So religion is an evil thing.

2. You should not major in philosophy, for then you may become a philosopher, and what kind of world would we have if everyone was a philosopher? Who would do the menial jobs?

3. I have talked with a number of Chinese laundrymen, and they do not seem to be men of high culture. So I conclude that the Chinese people do not have much culture.

4. It is always right to help a friend. It is therefore quite proper to offer bribes in order to secure the election of a friend.

5. What you bought yesterday you eat today. You bought raw meat yesterday, so you must eat raw meat today.

6. The steelworkers will benefit from an increase in their wages. So will the automobile workers. So will the bricklayers and everybody else. So we could easily have universal prosperity if a wage increase were given to everybody.

7. You say that you believe in socialism, and if socialism means anything at all, it means equality of wealth. You have more wealth than the average. Why don't you begin by giving it away until you are down to the average?

8. Napoleon got along on only five hours of sleep, so that is all the sleep anyone really needs. (Show how this example may illustrate two of the fallacies.)

9. I have noted that Edison, Ford, and other successful men did not have college educations. Evidently most famous men

did not have college educations.

10. Under the conditions of war it is morally justifiable to kill one's enemies. Therefore totalitarian governments are wholly justified in killing their political enemies.

11. Whatever you have not lost you still have. You have not lost your horns. Therefore you still have them.

12. An abundance of work is a sure sign of industrial prosperity. We should therefore welcome wars, earthquakes, tornadoes, hurricanes, fires, and sabotage, for all of these create a great deal of work.

13. Any laws, customs, or institutions that are found in all prosperous countries, but never found in any backward countries, must be beneficial. Why worry, then, about slums, public debts, suicide, high divorce rates, gangsters, etc?

14. All Indians walk single file. How do I know that? I once saw an Indian walk that way.

I. *Some Special Types of Problems.*

In each of the following paradoxical statements and arguments there is an assertion which should be limited in its scope. Find this assertion in each example.

1. You are not what I am. I am a human being. Therefore, you are not a human being.

2. He who calls you a man speaks truly. He who calls you a fool calls you a man. Therefore, he who calls you a fool speaks truly.

3. There are exceptions to every rule. But this statement is itself a rule, so there must be exceptions to it. So if the rule is true it must also be false.

4. All generalizations are false, including this one.

5. Epimenides, the Cretan, said, "All Cretans are liars." If this were true, then Epimenides was also a liar, since he was a Cretan. If he was a liar, then his statement is a lie, so we may conclude that Cretans are not liars. If they are not liars, then we may believe Epimenides. Then it must be true that all Cretans are liars. But if so, then Epimenides is also a liar, etc.

6. Improbable events happen almost every day. But what happens almost every day is a very probable event. Then improbable events must be very probable events.

Chapter 18

STATISTICS

Section I: The Need for Statistics

Is the divorce rate high in the movie colony in Hollywood? The reader will probably answer this question with an emphatic Yes, but the question may be raised: How does the reader know? By what he has read in the papers concerning *Forever Amber* and Artie Shaw and the movie stars? It is well to remember, however, that items concerning prominent persons receive a disproportionate amount of publicity and that judgments based upon "what everybody knows" may be snap judgments. Has the reader ever consulted the statistics on this matter? If the reader is interested in knowing the answer to our question, then he should consult the statistics concerning the divorce rate per thousand of population in Hollywood, the rate for the rest of the United States, and he should then compare these rates with each other. "High" is a comparative term, and means high in comparison with some standard. Does the United States as a whole have a high divorce rate? In comparison with which standard? With the rest of the world? With our own country 100 years ago? In any case, only the statistics can give us answers which are something more than mere guesses.

A college administration is interested in establishing admission standards in order to limit admission to students who can perform the work satisfactorily. One of the deans proposes that an entrance examination be given to all applicants. Applicants in the lowest percentiles of those who take such a test, he contends, are highly unlikely to pass their freshman courses. A few will pass, he admits, but the great majority will not. How does he know this? He cites the fact that colleges using such examinations have found a high *correlation* between a student's success on the examination and his subsequent success in his college work. To say that a correlation exists does not mean that every student who does well on the entrance test will do well in his college work, and vice versa. It does not mean that there is a "one-to-one" relationship, or an exact correspondence between the two variables, but only that in a large group there is a definite *tendency* for students who do well in one variable to do well in the other. In general, the better a student does in his entrance examination, the better he will do in his college work. A correlation also establishes a definite probability that any student who gets a certain score on the entrance examination will have a given chance of success.

Our illustrations point to the frequent need for numerical information concerning groups. Statistics is the science that deals with the collection, classification, and evaluation of large masses of numerical or quantitative facts concerning groups. Statistical information is indispensable in such varied fields as business analysis, meteorology, insurance rates, opinion polls, education, population trends, and many others. Statistics is a very complex and highly developed science, but we shall touch on only a minute portion of its principles and problems. In this chapter we shall discuss the methods of statistics in relation to some of the logical problems we have dealt with in the preceding chapters, in particular to descriptions of facts and inductions. For statistics is an indispensable method for *describing* large masses of data, and statistics enables us to draw *generalizations* or inferences which would not be possible without such descriptions.

Section II: Statistical Descriptions

We shall now consider some aspects of statistical descriptions, leaving the examination of statistical inductions until later. To begin with, we note a broad division which may be made between two types of statistical descriptions. As an example of one type, assume that we desire a "picture" of the yearly incomes of Americans. We know that Americans receive different incomes, but there is an enormous amount of "raw data" here, and we would like to know how these incomes break down

into various classifications so that we may have a clear picture
of the distribution of such incomes. How many receive less than
$1500 per year? How many between $1500 and $2500, etc.? The
statistician's "frequency tables" give us this type of information.
He may also give us a convenient *summary* of this classified material in the form of "averages" or statements of "central tendencies."

In the example given above, the description involved only
one characteristic, namely, incomes. But we may also desire a
description which shows the relationship of two or more characteristics to each other, as in our earlier illustration of the relationship between entrance examinations and college grades. We
desire to know whether the extremes in one case are the same as
the extremes in the other, and whether those falling in the middle of one group are the same as those in the middle of the
other. Such descriptions deal with more than one variable.

Our discussion of statistical descriptions will thus divide
into two parts, into descriptions which deal with one characteristic or variable, and those which deal with more than one. We
shall devote special attention to one example of each type,
namely, averages, which deal with one variable, and correlations, which deal with more than one. Averages, or statements
of "central tendencies," will be discussed in Section III. In Section IV we shall discuss "measures of dispersion," which are very
useful in connection with statements of central tendencies. Correlations will be examined in Section V.

Before we discuss these special types of descriptions we shall
note some of the aspects of the beginning of a statistical investigation. When confronted with a large mass of unassembled data,
the first important task is that of classification and definition.
Some of the special features involved in this task may be conveniently set forth in terms of the criteria to which a good classification should conform.

1. The terms should be clearly defined.

If we are gathering statistics on unemployment, the term
"unemployed" should be clearly defined. Does it mean wholly
or partially unemployed? Is a worker in a seasonal industry,
such as canning, "unemployed" during the slack season? Does a

temporary lay-off constitute unemployment? Should an individual who does not desire steady work be called unemployed? Are workers on strike unemployed? Our statistics will have little value without such careful definitions.

2. There should be sufficient classes to cover all of the data.

The classification should be exhaustive of all of the classes involved, i.e., all data should be included. To illustrate: A classification of religious denominations in the United States into Protestant, Roman Catholic, and Jewish, would violate this rule, for it omits Greek Catholic, Greek Orthodox, Christian Science, Mormon, etc. When the class of "All others" or "Miscellaneous" is used, this designation should not cover important classes.

3. Only one principle of classification should be used.

A classification of college students into majors in the physical sciences, biological sciences, social sciences, humanities, and summer-school students would violate this rule, for "summer-school" is not a type of major. Controversies may also arise over subtle violations of this rule. A classification of religions into Methodist, Episcopalian, Presbyterian, Baptist, Lutheran, Roman Catholic, etc., would make it appear that the Roman Catholics were the largest religious group. This classification would ignore the common beliefs of all sects within the "Protestant Church."

4. The classes should not overlap.

The classes should be mutually exclusive of each other. Our classification of students above would involve overlapping, since various types of majors who go to summer school would be counted twice. Working students, classified into those who work by day and those who work by night might also involve overlapping for those who work both afternoons and night. Librarians often find it difficult to avoid this error in classifying books. Should a history of politics be classified as history or political science? Henry James, J. M. Whistler, and T. S. Eliot may be classified under the headings of American or English writers, painters, and poets, since they were American by birth and English by adoption.

After our data have been properly classified and grouped, they may be arranged more systematically in a number of ways. We shall not describe the various methods used in presenting material, as by graphs, tables, and so on, except to note that a typical form of classification is found in the "frequency tables," or "frequency distributions," which classify numerical data according to size, i.e., with respect to the number of individuals who have a given characteristic. A simple example is a list of grades in an examination:

Number of students	Grades
5	91–100
12	81– 90
26	71– 80
7	61– 70
3	0– 60

This material may also be exhibited by bars, or pictograms, or other devices.

We shall now discuss the nature of averages, or statistical descriptions which deal with a single characteristic or variable.

Section III: Statistical Averages

A college student is interested in averages other than those of professional baseball players. He is also interested in the average earnings of doctors and lawyers and engineers, and perhaps in what an "average day" in the consular service is like. But just what is meant by "average"? By "average" the statistician means a statement, in summary form, of the "central tendency" in a group of items. By means of such statements of central tendencies, the numerical characteristics of groups may be compared with each other. The statistician uses three types of averages, i.e., three way in which central tendencies are exhibited: the arithmetic mean, the mode, and the median.

Each of these averages states the central tendency in a different way, and we shall find that each has its own peculiar usefulness and limitations. Each is appropriate for some groups and inappropriate for others. We shall discuss each in turn.

1. The arithmetic mean.

The arithmetic mean, which is what most persons have in mind when they speak of "the average," is derived by adding the items and dividing by the number of cases. Thus, if we had a series of items such as 4, 5, 6, 7, 8, 12, the additive total is 42. We then divide by 6 (the number of items) and we have the arithmetic mean: 7. Note that the average does not describe any particular individual in the group, except coincidentally, but gives us only the central tendency in the group as a whole.

In taking the mean, each item should be properly "weighted." Consider the following case. We wish to determine the average grades (the mean) of the students who take accounting courses in a college. We find that in the elementary course the average was 72; in the intermediate course it was 82; and in the advanced course 92. Is the average 246/3, or 82? This would be incorrect, for the items are not properly "weighted." There were 40 students in the elementary class; 20 in the intermediate, and 10 in the advanced class. Each class average should be multiplied, or weighted, by the number of students in the class, and the total divided by the total number of students. We shall then find that our fraction is 5450/70, and that the average is 77.7. The same result, of course, would have been obtained by taking each individual's score, adding all together, and dividing by 70; but it is often more convenient to classify the items before taking the mean.

An average of the kind just described is called a "weighted mean." But all averages are weighted, since the "simple" mean, illustrated by our first example, is one in which each item has a weight of *one*. In each of the accounting classes each student had a weight of one, so that the total for each class would be divided by the number of students. A simple mean is one in which each item is multiplied by 1, in entering into the average.

The use of the weighted mean is particularly important in

averages such as the Consumer's Price Index (or "cost-of-living" index) regularly compiled by the Bureau of Labor Statistics of the U. S. Department of Labor. The Bureau takes a typical expenditure for an average family, in a period chosen as standard, and then computes the changing costs of the same items at regular intervals. But some of these items are more important than others, and so the items are given different "weights." In the following tables we find the weights given to different items in the general Consumer's Price Index (1949) and the weighting of the items which go into the food index:

Consumer's Price Index		*Food Index*	
Food	42%	Cereals and bakery products	13.8
Rent	12	Meats	30.8
Fuel and electricity	4.9	Dairy products	19.1
Household furnishing	4.8	Eggs	6.3
Miscellaneous	19.6	Fresh fruits and vegetables	16.1
Gifts and contribu-		Canned fruits and vegetables	3.1
tions	4.2	Sugar and sweets	3.0
	100%	Fats and oils	3.5
		Dried fruits and vegetables	1.4
		Beverages	2.9
			100%

Thus a rise in the price of one item will not influence the average as much as a rise in the price of another. Each cost is multiplied by its percentage in the whole group, and the total divided by 100, since we multiply by percentages here, and not by a given number of items as in the example of the accounting students.

A warning is required concerning the sometimes illusory appearance of mathematical accuracy in statistics, particularly when we use the arithmetic mean. Let us assume that we wish to know the average number of hours a student devotes to his studies. He tells us that he put in the following hours each day in a given week: 3, 4, 5½, 4, 3, 2. The total is 21½; divided by 6, we find that the mean is 3.5833. The "accuracy" of this mean figured to the fourth decimal point, is misleading, since the

student probably made a rough guess as to the approximate time
he studied each day. The accuracy of the mean would then be
grotesque as compared with the carelessness with which the data
was compiled.

The chief limitation of the mean as an "average" is that the
mean may be misleading as an exhibition of the central tendency in a particular group. This will occur when there is an
extremely wide range between the extremes in a group. There
is then a wide "dispersion," or "deviation," of many items from
the mean. For example, the mean of the following group is 35:
3, 19, 31, 97, 25. Four out of the six items are below the mean
because of the wide range and the extreme dispersion of the
items from the mean. The mean, in this case, is a misleading
"average." The extent of the range is also a very important consideration when we wish to compare two groups with respect to
their central tendencies. To illustrate: In Factory A, nine individuals receive $3000 per year, and one man receives $23,000. In
Factory B, eight individuals receive $5000 each; one receives
$4000, and one receives $6000. The mean is exactly the same for
both ($5000) but the arithmetic mean is a rather meaningless
"average" when applied to the first group. It is because of such
limitations that statisticians use other types of averages.

2. The mode.

The mode is "the average" in the sense that it is the most
typical case, i.e., the item which occurs most frequently. In Factory A the mode was $3000; in B it was $5000. In popular language, when we speak of the "average American girl" we mean
the modal girl, the type who occurs most frequently or is most
frequently encountered. When we use the word "mode" for
"style," we mean what is in fashion, or use.

The mode is more reliable than the mean in one important
respect: it is not influenced by extreme variations, and may thus
be a better indicator when we wish to compare two groups,
such as the two factories. But the mode also suffers from a
serious limitation, as when it is used to describe the central tendency of an array of items such as the following: 9, 8, 7, 6, 3, 2, 2,

2, 1, 1. The mode is 2, but the mean (4.1) is certainly more indicative of the central tendency here. Note also that it is sometimes impossible to state the mode, as when no item occurs more than once.

3. The median.

In a report of the Census Bureau concerning the incomes of the American people for the year 1946, the "median" income for all American families was stated as being $2378. This meant that half the nation's 40,075,000 families received more than that amount and that half received less. The median, in other words, is the value of the middle item in a series of items arranged in the order of magnitude from the lowest number to the highest number. Thus, in the following series of items: 2, 2, 3, 3, 4, 4, 4, 5, 5, 6, 6, 6, 8, 8, 8, 9, 9, 9, 9, 9, 9, the underlined number is the median, since there are 21 items, of which there are 10 below this item and 10 above in the order of the series. When the number of items is an even number, the median is the arithmetic mean of the two middle items. In the series: 2, 5, 6, 8, 15, 29, the median is 7. The number of these items is even (6 items). 6 and 8 are the middle numbers, and 7 is the mean of these numbers.

The median, unlike the mean, is not influenced by wide variations, but may be misleading as a measure of central tendency when we have a peculiar range such as the following: 2, 2, 2, 2, 2, 2, 2, 2, 98, 176. The median here is 2, the same as the mode. The mean would also be misleading here. This points to the need for supplementary information when an average is stated, whether it be the mean, mode, or median.

We shall now sum up our discussion of averages. (1) An adequate understanding of the central tendency of a group requires that we know the mean, the mode, and the median. For some purposes, and depending upon the nature of the array, one of the three averages may give us more useful information than the others. (2) We should always remember that when the range of variations among the items is very large, the three averages may give us quite different results, and each may be

misleading in different ways. When the range of variations
within the group is small, all three averages will give us approximately the same results, as in the following: 3, 4, 5, 6, 6,
7, 8, 9. The mean is approximately 7; the mode and median
are 6 each. But the average alone will not tell us how widely
the items deviate from each other, nor what the range is. In
order to furnish us with this necessary supplementary information, statisticians have devised methods for indicating the
range or dispersion of the items. We shall now turn our attention to these measures of dispersion, which will indicate
the extent of the fluctuations of a given series or array of
items.

Section IV: Measures of Dispersion

By "measure of dispersion" is meant a number which indicates the extent to which the items differ in size from the
average. We have seen that the average may be unreliable as a
picture of the central tendency within a group; thus it becomes
necessary to know how closely most of the items resemble the
average. The devices used here are called dispersion or deviation numbers. We shall examine a few of the important ones.

1. The range.

The range is the numerical difference between the lowest
and the highest number in the group plus 1. If grades in a class
run from 43 to 92, the range is 49 plus 1, or 50. "The mean is
77; the range 50" gives us the average and the extent to which
the items are scattered. It is obvious that the same average may
be found among different ranges, and the same range among
different averages. An example of the latter may be shown by
the following two groups: (A) 1, 7, 8, 9, 10, and (B) 1, 1, 2, 2, 10.
The ranges are the same but the averages quite different. The
range is a satisfactory measure for some purposes, but does not
tell us what the probabilities are that a given individual's score
will fall within a certain part of the range, nor the probable
percentage of cases which will fall within a certain distance

from the mean. Devices for indicating such information will now be considered.

2. The mean deviation.

In the series of grades: 90, 84, 80, 70, 66, the mean is 78. The "mean deviation" states the average (mean) deviation of the items from the mean. To compute it we find the numerical difference between each item and the mean, always subtracting the lower number from the higher, and neglecting plus and minus signs. When the item is higher than the mean, subtract the mean from it; when the mean is higher, do the reverse. Plus and minus signs are·ignored in taking the mean of these items, for otherwise the result would be zero. We then add the deviations, and divide by the number of items. In the series of grades above, the deviations from the mean are 12, 6, 2, 8, 12. The mean of these numbers is 8; so the "mean deviation" is 8. This item is sometimes called the "average deviation" or "average error" (which does *not* mean "mistake"). The mean deviation may also be computed for the mode and the median, when these are used as averages.

The value of the mean deviation is that it informs us that it is probable that most items will fall within the range of 78 ± 8, or between 86 and 70; i.e., most individual's scores will fall within these limits. It is not sufficiently accurate as a guide, however, since the same relative importance is given to large deviations from the mean as is given to small ones. A large deviation, however, makes the mean less representative of the central tendency than would be the case if all of the deviations were small. In order to correct this fault statisticians use the next measure.

3. The standard deviation.

This is the most widely used measure, for it corrects the last-mentioned inadequacy of the mean deviation. It does this by squaring the deviations from the mean before their sum is taken; then it finds the mean of the sum of the squared deviations, and then takes the square root of this mean. We may thus define the standard deviation as the square root of the mean of the sum of the squares of the deviations. In our example above, we would first square each deviation as follows: 144, 36, 4, 64, 144. The sum of these is 392. We then divide by the number of items (5), and we find that the mean of the squares is 78.4. The square root of 78.4 is 8.85, the standard deviation. This is .85 higher than the mean deviation, and tells us that the scattering was greater than was indicated by the mean deviation. The formula for the standard deviation, symbolized by "σ" (sigma) or "S.D." is $\sqrt{\dfrac{\Sigma d^2}{n}}$, in which Σ stands for "summation," or "sum of," "d" for the deviations, and "n" for the number of the items.

Statisticians estimate that there is a probability that approximately two-thirds of the items will fall within the range of the mean, plus or minus the standard deviation. In our previous example, this means that two-thirds of the items will fall within the range of 78 ± 8.85. This probability, however, will hold only when the items are distributed in approximate accordance with the curve of "normal probability." The so-called "normal probability curve" refers to a symmetrical distribution around the mean, as in the following distribution: 95, 90, 85, 80, 75, 70, 65, 60, 55. This is a symmetrical distribution around the mean of 75. Another popular measure used in this connection is the "probable error" (an ambiguous expression used in different senses by statisticians), which usually refers to ".6745 of the standard deviation." Thus, when we know the mean and the "probable error," we know that approximately 50 per cent of the items will fall within the limits of the mean, plus or minus the probable error.

Section V: Correlations

We are now ready to discuss statistical descriptions which show the relationship of two or more characteristics to each other. Our discussion will be limited to the relations of two characteristics or variables. Is there a definite relationship between the extremes in a series of students' I.Q.'s and their grades? If so, then in greater or lesser degree, the two variables (I.Q.'s and grades) are said to be correlated. Note, however, an ambiguity in the use of the word "correlation." In all cases it means the connections of two groups of variables with each other. But the word "correlation" may be restricted in its use to connections which are less than uniform connections. A uniform correlation is what we previously called a "function," illustrated by Galileo's discovery that the speed of a falling body is a function of the time of the fall. We shall call a function a "perfect correlation," but we shall be primarily concerned, in what follows, with connections which are less than uniform, i.e., with groups which show conflicting trends.

Before proceeding to discuss the more technical forms of correlations we shall examine a method, called "statistical associations," for noting the association or connection between two characteristics.

Consider a simple problem: Are red-heads hot-tempered? We require statistical information to answer this question. We must also rephrase the question: Is there a greater tendency for red-heads to be hot-tempered than for non–red-heads? The statement that a certain percentage of red-heads are hot-tempered would be ambiguous with respect to significance unless we knew how the percentage compared with that of other groups. Our problem, then, is to determine whether there is some special connection between red-heads and hot-tempers. Is there a greater tendency for red-heads to be hot-tempered than for non–red-heads? Is the probability greater that a red-head will be hot-tempered than that others will be?

A statistical association should furnish us with the following data: (1) the number of A's which are B's, (2) the number of A's which are −B's, (3) the number of −A's which are B's, and (4) the number of −A's which are −B's. Using the symbols "R" for red-heads, "−R" for non–red-heads, "T" for hot-tempered persons, and "−T" for persons who lack hot tempers, we shall study a sample group of 1000 persons and classify our data as above. (The figures we use will be purely imaginary.) Let us assume that we find that 200 persons in our sample group are R's, that 800 are −R's, that 80 of the R's are T's, and that 200 of the −R's are T's. We then assemble our data in a chart such as that on the following page.

	T's	−T's
200 R's	80	120
800 −R's	200	600

(280 T's)   (720 −T's)

Our table indicates that 280 persons in 1000 are hot-tempered, or 28 per cent. Eighty out of 200 red-heads, or 40 per cent, are hot-tempered, and 200 out of 800 non–red-heads, or 25 per cent, are hot-tempered. This indicates that there is a greater tendency for red-heads than for non–red-heads to be hot-tempered. Similar procedures may be used in many other problems, such as whether there is a greater likelihood for a worker in the silica industry to contract silicosis, etc.

The method of statistical associations, however, is powerless to answer a question such as the following: What is the relationship between the height and weight of individuals? For here we cannot divide our categories into mutually exhaustive pairs, but must deal with indefinitely large series of degrees in our variables. The relationship of the two variables, height and weight, will be found to fluctuate in different degrees, and for such problems we need the more precise mathematical method of correlations.

Correlations are expressed in numbers, running from +1.00 to −1.00. A *positive* invariant correlation is expressed by +1.00, which means that an increase in one variable is invariably accompanied by a corresponding and proportional increase in the other. An *inverse* invariant correlation expressed by −1.00 means that an increase in one variable is invariably accompanied by a decrease in the other. A correlation of 0 (zero) expresses the notion of a complete absence of connection or correlation, and corresponds to the concept of 50 per cent in probabilities. When we toss a coin, there is an even chance that it will fall heads or tails; there is thus no correlation between its falling heads and the fact that it is tossed. But a correlation of +.5 means that there is a definite tendency toward positive correlation, and has no similarity to the concept of .5 in probabilities.

Let us now examine a very simple problem of correlation. Let us imagine that we are seeking to determine the relationship between the height and weight of the warriors in a primitive tribe. Assume that we collect the following data:

Individual	Height	Weight
A	5′ 6″	150
B	5′ 7″	155
C	5′ 8″	160
D	5′ 9″	165
E	5′ 10″	170
F	5′ 11″	175
G	6′	180

This highly unlikely data may be assembled in a "scatter plot." We draw a diagram, marked off as follows: The vertical line, called the "ordinate," indicates the varying heights; the horizontal line, called the "abcissa," indicates the varying weights. We then draw points, representing each individual, on the intersections of the two series, and complete our diagram by connecting the dots by a line:

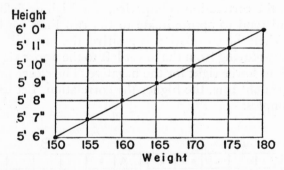

This example represents a case of perfect positive correlation. An increase in one variable is accompanied by an increase in the other. Note the picture which the line represents. A straight line moving from the lower left to the upper right indicates a perfect positive correlation.

If the correlation were a perfect negative one, the line would move from the upper left to the lower right. Example: Let us assume that you are on a Cub plane flying home from a distance of 600 miles at the uniform speed of 100 miles per hour. You decide to keep a record of your distance from your destination in terms of the two variables, "time elapsed" and "miles to go." As the hours increase the distance decreases, so that the higher the point on the ordinate, the lower the point on the abcissa, viz.:

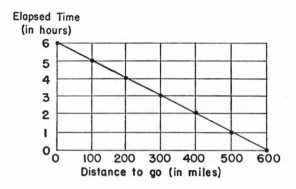

When the correlation is imperfect, but high or definite, the "line" will tend to approximate to the two lines we have described. When the correlation is positive, the line will approximate to one moving from the lower left to the upper right; from upper left to lower right for the negative. The closer the points are to a straight line, the higher the correlation. Let us look at some examples:

The dots in A indicate a higher positive correlation than the negative correlation in B. When there is little or no correlation, the dots will be scattered with no semblance of a line, as in C:

C

The scatter plots, however, give us only a general and imperfect idea as to the correlation when the lines are only fairly well defined. Statisticians accordingly use a mathematical method for computing correlations, expressed in terms of the "coefficient of correlation," symbolized by r. We shall shortly examine the manner in which the precise degree of correlation may be computed, by working out r in a sample problem. We shall employ the formula for r which was worked out by Karl Pearson, the English biometrician, as follows: $r = \dfrac{\Sigma xy}{n\sigma_x\sigma_y}$. This formula will be explained presently.

Our task, let us say, is to determine the correlation between the scores received by students on an imaginary entrance examination, and their subsequent grades in their college work. We shall deal with an oversimplified problem, using a small number of cases for simplicity in exposition, with the warning, however, that a small number of cases is usually an unreliable basis for judgment. We gather our data into two tables, distributing the items in the two variables:

Student	Entrance Grade	College Average
A	94	84
B	88	82
C	86	88
D	84	86
E	78	80
F	74	68
G	70	72
H	66	68

We see at a glance that the correlation is not a perfect one, but nevertheless there does appear to be a real connection. We shall now determine its precise degree by working out r. We assemble our data in a chart such as the following:

1	2	3	4	5	6	7
Entrance Examination	College Average	Deviation of Entrance Exam. from Mean (x)	Deviation of College Averages from Mean (y)	x^2	y^2	xy
94	84	14	5	196	25	70
88	82	8	3	64	9	24
86	88	6	9	36	81	54
84	86	4	7	16	49	28
78	80	−2	1	4	1	−2
74	70	−6	−9	36	81	54
70	72	−10	−7	100	49	70
66	68	−14	−11	196	121	154
Mean: 80	Mean: 79			648 (Σx^2)	416 (Σy^2)	452 (Σxy)

We shall now explain this chart. The first two columns simply give us our tables. The mean of each is shown at the bottom of these columns. The mean of the first is 80 (obtained by dividing the sum of the items by the number of items), and the mean of the second column is 79. The third column tells us how each item in Column 1 deviates from the mean of 80. These are called the x deviations. Column 4 does the same for the deviations in Column 2, and gives us the y deviations. In Column 5, headed by "x^2" we find the x's squared, and at the bottom of the column we find their sum, 648. In Column 6 we find the y's squared, also the sum, and in Column 7 "xy" means "the x deviation times the y deviation." On the top lines of Columns 3 and 4 the x item was 14, the y item 5; their product 70, as shown on the top line of Column 7. Note that one of the items in the last column has a minus sign before it. Minus numbers must always be subtracted from the total of the plus items.

The Pearson formula: $r = \dfrac{\Sigma xy}{n\sigma_x\sigma_y}$ worked out for this problem tells us that the coefficient of correlation is $+.87$. This formula is interpreted as follows:

1. Σxy refers to the number 452 in the last column, or the sum of the xy's.

2. In the denominator we find n, which stands for the number of items found in the two sets of variables, i.e., 8.

3. The symbol σ stands for "Standard Deviation." σ_x stands for the standard deviation in the x column (Column 3) and σ_y for the standard deviation in the y column (Column 4). The formula for the standard deviation, as noted earlier, is $\sqrt{\dfrac{\Sigma d^2}{n}}$. Worked out for the x variable, we proceed as follows: Σd^2 refers to the sum of the squares of all of the deviations found in Column 3, since d stands for deviation. The sum of these deviations is 648 (Column 5). We now divide by n, or 8, and we get 81. We must now find the square root of this number. It is 9. The standard deviation for x, or σ_x is thus 9. The standard deviation for y is worked out in exactly the same manner. We must first find Σd^2 for y. Σy^2 is 416. Divide by 8 and we get 52. The square root of 52 is the standard deviation for y, or 7.21.*

Our standard deviations for x and y are 9 and 7.21 respectively. We are now ready for the final step, or the giving of

---

* The manner in which this square root was derived is shown in this footnote for the benefit of those readers who have *forgotten* the process:

```
        7.21
      _____
    √52.0000...   (Add 0's according to need)
     49   .....   Find the largest number which, when squared, will go into 52. This
                  is 7. (7 × 7 is 49). Place 7 above the top line, and subtract 49 from 52.
     3.00   ...   Bring down two 0's
     2.84   ...   The number 2.84 is derived as follows: Double the first number at
                  the top: 2 × 7 is 14. Now find the number which, when placed at
                  the right of 14, and then multiplied by that number, will come closest
                  to 3.00. We try a 2 after 14: 142, and then multiply by 2, and we get
                  2.84. (141 × 1 would be too small; 143 × 3 too large). Now place a
                  2 after the 7 above the top line.
     ____
     1600
     1441...We now double 72: 144. We place a 1 at the right of 144 and multi-
            ply by 1. Now place the 1 at the right of 7.2, etc.
```

specific values to the symbols in the Pearson formula:

$$r = \frac{\Sigma xy(452)}{n(8)\sigma_x(9)\sigma_y(7.21)} = \frac{452}{519.12} = +.87$$

The interpretation of the "coefficient of correlation," or r requires some comment. Statisticians interpret r as an indicator of the dependence between a variable A and another variable, B. When r, for example, has a value of .5, this is said to indicate a "37 per cent dependence" between the two variables. This means that among all of the factors which determine the amount of B, the variable A will account for 37 per cent of its amount. When the coefficient of correlation is .95 the degree of dependence is 75 per cent; when .99, 88 per cent. Thus, as remarked earlier, a coefficient of correlation of .87 does not mean "a probability of 87 per cent." The higher the coefficient, however, the higher the degree of association between the two variables, and the higher the probability that a change in one variable will be accompanied by a corresponding positive or inverse change in the other.

The degree of association or dependence is often interpreted in accordance with R. E. Chaddock's classification, in his *Principles and Methods of Statistics*. Correlations of less than .3 indicate a low degree of association and are of little significance, especially when the number of related items is small, though this proviso applies in all cases. A correlation of .3 or more, but less than .5, indicates a "moderate" degree of association; .5 and less than .7, "marked" association; .7 and less than .9, "high"; and .9 and over indicates a "very close" association and a high degree of dependence between the variables.

The reader may be interested in a few examples of actual correlations based upon adequate sampling. The following items are from R. S. Woodworth's *Psychology*: The coefficient of correlation between the I.Q.'s of identical twins is +.9, i.e., there is a very close association between them, so that if we find that the I.Q. of one is high, it is very likely that the I.Q. of the other will be high also. In fraternal twins, the coefficient is +.7. The coefficient of correlation between the I.Q.'s and grades in a group of college students is +.6. The correlation between the I.Q.'s of parents and children is +.3. The coefficient of correlation between the height of the forehead and intelligence is .00.